METHODS MATTER

Methods Matter

*Improving Causal Inference
in Educational and
Social Science Research*

Richard J. Murnane
John B. Willett

OXFORD
UNIVERSITY PRESS
2011

KH

OXFORD
UNIVERSITY PRESS

Oxford University Press, Inc., publishes works that further
Oxford University's objective of excellence
in research, scholarship, and education.

Oxford New York
Auckland   Cape Town   Dar es Salaam   Hong Kong   Karachi
Kuala Lumpur   Madrid   Melbourne   Mexico City   Nairobi
New Delhi   Shanghai   Taipei   Toronto

With offices in
Argentina   Austria   Brazil   Chile   Czech Republic   France   Greece
Guatemala   Hungary   Italy   Japan   Poland   Portugal   Singapore
South Korea   Switzerland   Thailand   Turkey   Ukraine   Vietnam

Published by Oxford University Press, Inc.
198 Madison Avenue, New York, New York 10016
www.oup.com

Oxford is a registered trademark of Oxford University Press

Library of Congress Cataloging-in-Publication Data
Murnane, Richard J.
  Methods matter : improving causal inference in educational and social science
research / Richard J. Murnane, John B. Willett.
     p. cm.
  ISBN 978-0-19-975386-4 (hardback)
  1. Education–Research–Methodology.   2. Quantitative research.
I. Willett, John B.   II. Title.
  LB1028.M86 2010
  370.7'2–dc22   2010007441

1 3 5 7 9 8 6 4 2
Printed in the United States of America
on acid-free paper

7/5/11

Contents

Preface

We have collaborated for almost a quarter of a century, meeting every week, usually on Tuesday, for two or three hours during the academic year, in a small, windowless seminar room on the fourth floor of Gutman Library at the Harvard Graduate School of Education. During the summers, we harass each other mercilessly by telephone and e-mail, as we live at opposite ends of Massachusetts. When we meet on Tuesdays, sometimes we are alone; sometimes we invite others to join us. Sometimes we agree, mostly we don't. Sometimes one of us teaches the other, sometimes the reverse. Our arguments do not always conclude in shared understanding, but they usually do. Some topics have taken us many years to resolve. However, two things that have always been present in our meetings, and in our larger collaboration, are a sense of overwhelming personal friendship and an excitement born out of the many "Eureka" moments we have shared. We have really enjoyed taking this journey of discovery together, learning new things at every step.

Our collaboration has not only been immensely satisfying from a personal perspective, it has also been highly productive professionally. You are holding in your hand only the second book that we have written together. But, in the many years between the first book and this one, we have also published more than 30 jointly authored scholarly papers in peer-reviewed journals. The majority of these papers have also been collaborations with generations of enthusiastic and smart doctoral "apprentices," who have worked with us before embarking on their own distinct and successful scholarly paths. There are two great lessons that we have learned. One is that if you challenge yourself constantly with difficult problems that fall outside your comfort zone, you will continue to learn something new. The second is that there is nothing better in one's professional life than sharing such experiences with close friends and future colleagues. We thank a long line of inner-circle apprentices for their hard work and the difficult questions they asked us. Listed in the chronological order with which we worked with them, they include Jim Kemple, Kathryn Boudett, Brian Jacob, Emiliana Vegas, John Tyler, Marie-Andrée Somers, Michal Kurlaender, Kristen Bub, Raegen Miller, Jennifer Steele, Lindsay Page, and John Papay.

We have often wondered out loud to each other: What makes for a successful scholarly collaboration? In our case, it is certainly *not* because we agree. In fact, we have often found that it is our disagreements that spur the most productive and insightful advances of our collaboration. The critical thing, we think, is to not let scholarly and professional disagreements drive you apart personally. There has to be a deep and abiding friendship at the core of any collaboration that feels worth preserving, whatever the nature of the current disagreement over form or function or method.

But, there is more. We have a sense that our collaboration has been successful because we are so different, come from such different places, and have received such different training. Although we were both, at one time in our early careers, teachers of high school math and science, our subsequent experiences diverged. One of us (Murnane) was trained as an economist, the other (Willett) as a statistician. While, to many, these disciplines seem very close both intellectually and methodologically, we ourselves have found that there is sufficient divergence in our backgrounds, skills, and training to surprise us constantly. Sometimes we find that we have learned the same thing in different ways, or that something we think is different is really the same. Clearly, though, it has been a mutual and tireless (perhaps "head-butting" would be a better description) re-examination of all these beliefs and practices—the "stylized" concepts and facts that lie at the center of each of our scholarly domains— that has generated our most productive intellectual activity.

There is another factor as well. We work together at an excellent and supportive professional school, the Harvard Graduate School of Education (HGSE), with wonderful colleagues and students, and we are embedded in a network of superb intellectual and physical resources. More than that, though, neither of us can forget our roots as high school teachers. Most of all, we both want to make education better for the world's children, and believe that improving research on the causal consequences of educational policies and interventions can contribute to improved policymaking. We feel that the development of new research designs and analytic methods would be sterile if it did not address directly the very real and difficult questions that lie at the center of the educational enterprise. Because of this, we have always sought to motivate—and embed—our work in *substance*, in the important questions that educational policymakers ask. We believe that substantive needs are a powerful catalyst to the development of new research designs and data-analytic methods. It is the interplay between substance and method that has always provided us with our most fertile ground and that we seek to preserve in our work together. Once you have a substantive question, then it is clear that *methods matter*!

So, that explains why we work together. But why did we write this book? It is not a decision that we reached either quickly or lightly; in fact, it was more like a decision that evolved, rather than being made. Over the last 15 years, it became clear to us that innovative research designs and analytic practices were being developed constantly, and applied in the social sciences and statistics. We thought that these new methods of *causal inference* had enormous potential for resolving critical problems that plagued education research. After all, don't we want compelling evidence of what works to influence educational policymaking?

Yet, when we examined the scholarly literature that was supposed to inform educational policymaking, we found that most of the quantitative research could not even support credible statements of cause and effect. Consequently, it seemed sensible to facilitate the implementation of the new methods of causal inference in the fields of educational and social science research. We wanted to persuade scholars, policymakers, and practitioners that there were substantial and powerful methods that could improve causal research in education and the social sciences. In our experiences as teachers, the successful migration of innovative ideas across domain boundaries has always demanded that they not only be expressed *understandably*, but *in context*. Those working in education and the social sciences had to be persuaded that there was something worthwhile that would work for them. Consequently, over the last decade and a half, as our own ideas began to crystallize, we tried to draw an adept group of up-and-coming young scholars at our school into an advanced doctoral seminar on causal inference, to worry about the issues with us. From out of that seminar has grown this book.

In our seminar and in this book, our pedagogic approach has been to embed the learning of innovative methods for causal inference in substantive contexts. To do this, we have drawn on exemplary empirical research papers from other fields, mainly economics (because that's a field that at least one of us knows well!), to introduce, explain, and illustrate the application of the new methods. We have asked our students to study these papers with us carefully. At the same time, we have tried to provide them with clear and sensible intellectual frameworks within which the technical bases of the new methods for causal inference made sense. In creating these frameworks, we have opted for conceptual, graphical, and data-based explanations rather than those that are intensively mathematical and statistical. Our objective is to widen the reach and appeal of the methods to scholars who do not possess the same deep technical backgrounds as the developers and early implementers of the methods. We have experienced some success in this effort, and have now brought the same approach to this book. Throughout the book, we have sought to present new methods for causal inference in a way that is sensitive to the practical realities of the educational and social context. We hope not only to make you receptive to incorporating these methods in your own research, but also to see the value of the guidelines provided in the book for judging the quality of the research studies you read.

Many colleagues have helped us as we worked on this book, answering our many questions, providing data from their studies, providing feedback on draft chapters. At the distinct risk of leaving out the names of colleagues to whom we are indebted, we would like to thank Joshua Angrist, David Autor, Felipe Barrera-Osorio, Howard Bloom, Geoffrey Borman, Kathryn Boudett, Sarah Cohodes, Tom Dee, Susan Dynarski, Patricia Graham, Rema Hanna, Caroline Hoxby, Guido Imbens, Brian Jacob, Larry Katz, Jim Kemple, Jeff Kling, Peter Kemper, Daniel Koretz, Victor Lavy, Frank Levy, Leigh Linden, Jens Ludwig, Douglas Miller, Richard Nelson, Edward Pauly, Stephen Raudenbush, Jonah Rockoff, Juan Saavedra, Judy Singer, Miguel Urquiola, Emiliana Vegas, and participants in our causal inference doctoral course. We would especially like to thank Lindsay Page and John Papay, who read the entire manuscript and provided innumerable suggestions for improving it.

The staff members of our Learning Technology Center at HGSE have always gone out of their way to support our computing needs, and have responded to our questions and difficulties with immediate and thoughtful help. We also want to thank our wonderful and extraordinarily efficient assistant at HGSE, Wendy Angus. Wendy has solved numerous logistical problems for us, formatted tables, fixed idiosyncratic problems in our word processing, and been immensely helpful in getting this manuscript out the door. Finally, we very much appreciate the financial support that the Spencer Foundation provided for the research that contributed to this book.

It goes without saying that we are also indebted to the members of our production team at Oxford University Press in New York City. We are particularly grateful to Joan Bossert, Editorial Director, who was receptive to our proposal and directed us to our editor, Abby Gross. We have also enjoyed the constantly responsive support of Jodi Narde, our assistant editor; Mark O'Malley, our production editor; and Viswanath Prasanna, our project manager at Glyph International Production Services, in Bangalore.

Finally, we want to recognize the love we receive constantly from our spouses Mary Jo and Jerri, and from our now grown children, Dan, John, and Kara, who continue to bring much joy to our lives, as well as the occasional challenge.

As co-authors, we have listed our names alphabetically.
Richard J. Murnane
John B. Willett

METHODS MATTER

1

The Challenge for Educational Research

Throughout the world, education is viewed as a mechanism for expanding economic opportunity, enhancing social mobility, developing a skilled workforce, and preparing young people to participate in civic life. Thus, it is no surprise that almost every government wants to improve the quality of its country's educational system. Public resources are scarce, however, and education must compete with demands for improved health care, housing, and nutrition. When resources devoted to educational activities do not improve student achievement, it is difficult for educational policymakers to lay claim to additional resources. For this reason, policymakers need to use available resources wisely and be able to demonstrate that they have done so. To accomplish these objectives, governments need good information about the impacts that particular policy decisions are likely to have on student achievement. Unfortunately, in the past, this kind of information has not been available.

The Long Quest

The call for better empirical evidence upon which to base sound educational policy decisions has a long history, one that is particularly well documented in the United States. In a speech given to the National Education Association (NEA) in 1913, Paul Hanus—a Harvard professor, and later the first dean of the Harvard Graduate School of Education—argued that "the only way to combat successfully mistaken common-sense as applied to educational affairs is to meet it with uncommon-sense in the same field—with technical information the validity of which is indisputable"

(Hanus, 1920, p. 12). For Hanus, this meant that systematic research must be conducted and its findings applied. In his words, "We are no longer disputing whether education has a scientific basis; we are trying to find that basis." In his lengthy speech to the NEA, Hanus identified a number of school policy decisions that he believed should be based on scientific evidence. These included finding an "adequate and appropriate means of determining the qualifications of well-trained and otherwise satisfactory workers for the educational staff . . .," and formulating "courses of study . . . together with suggestions as to methods of teaching." Although educational policymakers today would use somewhat different terms in framing such questions, these same substantive concerns remain pressing in countries around the world: How do we attract and retain skilled teachers? What are the most important skills for students to acquire? What are the most effective pedagogies for teaching these skills?

For educational researchers in Hanus's time, and for many years thereafter, "carrying out scientific research" meant implementing the ideas of scientific management that had been developed by Frederick W. Taylor and laid out in his 1911 book *Principles of Scientific Management.* Taylor's central thesis was that experts could uncover the single "best" way to do a particular job by conducting "time and motion" studies. Then, the task of management was to provide the appropriate tools, and create training, incentives, and monitoring systems to ensure that workers adopted and followed the prescribed methods.

Although Taylor was careful not to apply his methods to any process as complicated as education, many educational researchers were less cautious. One of the most influential proponents of applying Taylor's system of scientific management to education was Frank Spaulding, who earned a doctorate from the University of Leipzig, Germany, in 1894, served as superintendent of several U.S. school districts during the first two decades of the twentieth century, and, in 1920, became head of Yale University's newly formed Department of Education. Speaking at the same meeting of the NEA at which Hanus gave his address, Spaulding described three essentials for applying scientific management to education. He stipulated that we must: (a) measure results, (b) compare the conditions and methods under which results are secured, and (c) adopt consistently the conditions and methods that produce the best results (Callahan, 1962, pp. 65–68).

Most educators today would agree with these essentials, even though many would object to the "Taylorist" ideas that underlie them. However, it was in applying these essentials to education that controversy arose. The "results" that Spaulding used in his research included "the percentage of children of each year of age in the school district that the school enrolls; the average number of day's attendance secured annually from each child; [and] the average length of time required for each child to do a given definite unit of work" (Callahan, 1962, p. 69). The attraction of these indicators for Spaulding was that they could be measured relatively easily and precisely. However, they were not very good indicators of the quality of education that schools provided to children. As a result, despite its popularity among educators anxious to build support in the business community, many thoughtful educators found Spaulding's research to be of dubious value for improving the quality of the education actually provided to children.

In the decades following Spaulding's speech, the creation of standard-ized multiple-choice tests and the development of item-response theory made it possible increasingly to measure students' skills and knowledge in academic domains like reading and mathematics at relatively low cost. Advances in information technology that included the creation and devel-opment of digital computers and user-friendly data-processing software made it possible to manipulate large amounts of quantitative informa-tion. Advances in statistical methods, including the development of multiple-regression techniques, made it possible to better identify and summarize important patterns in data and to test specific hypotheses.

All of these advances contributed to a major milestone in educational research in the United States, the publication of a study entitled *Equality of Educational Opportunity*, in 1966. The study that led to this report was commissioned by the U.S. Congress as part of the Civil Rights Act of 1964. This legislation ordered the U.S. Commissioner of Education to conduct a study of "the lack of availability of equal educational opportunities for individuals by reason of race, color, religion, or natural origin in public educational institutions at all levels" (Coleman et al., 1966, p. iii). The order of the wording in this quotation—race, color, religion, national origin—suggests that the Congress had little doubt that children who were disadvantaged minorities received fewer and lower-quality educational resources than did white children, and that differences in educational resources were the probable cause of differences in academic achievement.

The task of organizing and conducting the congressionally mandated study fell to the eminent sociologist James Coleman. Coleman and his team went well beyond their charge and conducted a quantitative study that sought to account for variation in academic achievement among American children, incorporating information on both their schooling and their family backgrounds. Coleman's research design borrowed heav-ily from research that had been conducted previously in agriculture to estimate the impact of different resource combinations on output levels. Coleman applied this so-called production function methodology to investigate what combinations of educational inputs "produced" particular levels of educational output.

Despite being released on the Friday before the July 4 Independence Day holiday in 1966, the Coleman Report (as it came to be known) did not go unnoticed. As anticipated, it documented that black children had much lower academic achievement, on average, than white children. The surprise was that differences in school resources, such as class size and the educational credentials of their teachers, accounted for almost none of this achievement gap. U.S. Commissioner of Education Harold Howe summarized the main finding of the Report as "family background is more important than schools."[1] Since this interpretation seemed to undercut the initiatives of President Lyndon Johnson's Great Society, which were aimed at reducing race-based economic inequality by improving the schools that served children of color, some policymakers called for an additional, harder look at the data.

This led two prominent Harvard professors, eminent statistician Frederick Mosteller and then political-science professor and later U.S. Senator Daniel Patrick Moynihan, to organize a working group to reanalyze Coleman's data. Their resulting volume, *On Equality of Educational Opportunity*, contained a compendium of papers that revealed a great deal about the academic achievement of American children and the schools they attended (Mosteller & Moynihan, 1972). However, the researchers concluded that the intrinsic limitations of the cross-sectional observational data collected by the investigators in the Equality of Educational Opportunity Survey made it impossible to answer critical questions about whether school resources had *causal* impacts on children's achievement. Consequently, the working group called for better research designs and the collection of representative prospective longitudinal data in order to understand more comprehensively the impacts on children of investments in schooling.

Economist Eric Hanushek was one of the first social scientists to respond to this call. A member of the Moynihan and Mosteller seminar group, Hanushek was well aware of the limitations of the Coleman Report and of the need for the collection of longitudinal data on the achievement of individual children. He collected such data for several hundred children who were attending elementary schools in one California school district. He also collected data describing important attributes of the teacher of each student's class and of the classroom setting, such as the number of students present in the class. Using the same multiple-regression

---

1. As reported in Herbers (1966).

methods that Coleman had employed, Hanushek sought to answer two questions. The first was whether children in some third-grade classrooms ended the school year with higher achievement than children in other third-grade classrooms, on average, after taking into account the achievement levels with which they started the school year. Hanushek (1971) confirmed that this was indeed the case, and that the differences were large enough to be educationally meaningful. This finding was important in the wake of the Coleman Report because it verified what parents and educators already knew, but that the limited nature of the Coleman Report data could not verify—namely, that school quality did indeed matter.

The second question that Hanushek addressed was whether the budgeted resources that school districts used to purchase actually accounted for why children in some classrooms had higher average achievement at the end of the school year than did children in other classrooms. He focused his attention particularly on the roles of teacher experience and teacher qualifications, because these teacher characteristics are rewarded in almost all public-school salary scales in the United States and other countries. Hanushek found that neither the number of years that a teacher had taught nor whether the teacher had earned a master's degree accounted for much of the classroom-to-classroom variation in children's achievement. Neither did class size, the other large source of difference in cost among classrooms. Hanushek's conclusion was that schools were spending money on things such as teaching experience, higher degrees for teachers, and smaller class sizes that did not result in improved student achievement.

Although researchers applauded Hanushek for confirming that school quality did indeed matter, many questioned his conclusions about the inefficiency of schools (Hedges et al., 1994). They pointed out, for example, that in many schools, children with the greatest learning needs were actually being assigned to the smallest classes. Consequently, the low academic achievement of students in small classes may not have meant that class size did not matter. On the contrary, if schools were attempting to equalize student outcomes by providing additional resources to children with the greatest learning needs, then Hanushek's research strategy could not provide unbiased answers to causal questions such as whether there was an academic payoff to reducing class sizes or to paying teachers with greater professional experience more than novices. Progress in answering such questions would await the development of the research designs and analytic methods that are described in this book.

Another impetus to educational research in the 1960s was the increasing involvement of the federal government in American K-12 education.

The passage of the Elementary and Secondary Education Act (ESEA), in 1965, marked the first time that the federal government had provided significant funding for public K-12 education in the United States. Title I of the Act committed federal funds to improving the schooling of economically disadvantaged children. Fearful that the money would not make a difference to poor children, Senator Robert Kennedy insisted that the ESEA require periodic evaluations of whether the program was producing requisite gains in student achievement (McLaughlin, 1975, p. 3). In essence, Senator Kennedy wanted evidence of a causal impact.

Partly in response to the demands for the implementation of more systematic educational research expressed by Daniel Moynihan, who was by now head of President Richard Nixon's Domestic Council, President Nixon announced, in 1970, that the federal government would create the National Institute of Education (NIE). Touted as the vehicle for fostering systematic scholarship that would solve the nation's educational problems, NIE began operation in 1972, with an annual budget of $110 million. Secretary of Health, Education, and Welfare (HEW) Elliott Richardson informed Congress that the administration would request a $400 million budget for NIE within five years (Sproull, Wolf, & Weiner, 1978, p. 65).

By the end of the 1970s, optimism about the ability of empirical research to resolve the important arguments in education that had marked the inauguration of the NIE had turned to pessimism. Soon after the inauguration of Ronald Reagan in 1980, the NIE was dissolved. In part, the demise of the NIE stemmed from a change in the mood of the country. The rapid economic growth of the mid-1960s, which had increased federal tax revenues and fueled the Great Society programs, ended in 1973, and was followed by a decade of very slow growth. Optimism had initially accompanied the sending of U.S. troops to Vietnam in the early 1960s. By the early 1970s, more than 50,000 American deaths and the accompanying failed foreign-policy objectives had changed the country's mood. As Henry Aaron described in his book, *Politics and the Professors* (1978), many citizens stopped believing that government itself could be instrumental in improving the lives of Americans and came to believe that government was a principal cause of the economic malaise in which the country found itself.

The demise of the NIE was not completely the result of the change in the country's mood, however. Another part of the problem had been the unrealistic expectations that had accompanied its birth. Many of the original proponents of the creation of the NIE had invoked comparisons with research conducted by the National Institutes of Health, which had provided radical new medicines such as the Salk vaccine for polio, and the agricultural research that had resulted in the green revolution.

When the NIE's research programs did not produce analogous visible successes for education, it was deemed a failure. Few of its advocates had appreciated how difficult it would be to answer questions posed by policy-makers and parents about the effective use of educational resources.

Yet another part of the explanation for the demise of the NIE, and the low funding levels of its successor, the U.S. Department of Education's Office of Educational Research and Improvement (OERI), was the wide-spread perception that educational research was of relatively low quality. A common indictment was that educational researchers did not take advantage of new methodological advances in the social sciences, particu-larly in the application of innovative strategies for making causal inferences.

In an attempt to respond to the concern about the low quality of educational research, the U.S. Congress established the Institute of Education Sciences (IES) in 2002, with a mandate to pursue rigorous "scientific research" in education. One indication of the energy with which the IES has pursued this mandate is that, in its first six years of operation, it funded more than 100 randomized field trials of the effec-tiveness of educational interventions.[2] As we explain in Chapter 4, the randomized experiment is the "gold-standard" design for research that aims to make unbiased causal inferences.

The Quest Is Worldwide

Although the quest for causal evidence about the consequences of par-ticular educational policies is particularly well documented in the United States, researchers in many countries have conducted important studies that have both broken new ground methodologically and raised new sub-stantive questions. We illustrate with two examples. Ernesto Schiefelbein and Joseph Farrell (1982) conducted a remarkable longitudinal study during the 1970s of the transition of Chilean adolescents through school and into early adulthood. The authors collected data periodically on a cohort of students as they moved from grade 8 (the end of primary school) through their subsequent schooling (which, of course, differed among individuals) and into the labor market or into the university. This study, *Eight Years of Their Lives*, was a remarkable tour de force for its time. It demonstrated that it was possible, even in a developing country that was experiencing extraordinary political turmoil, to collect data on the same

---

2. See Whitehurst (2008a; 2008b). We would like to thank Russ Whitehurst for explaining to us which IES-funded research projects were designed as randomized field trials.

individuals over an extended period of time, and that these data could provide insights not possible from analyses of cross-sectional data. Substantively, the study documented the important role that the formal education system in Chile played in sorting students on the basis of their socioeconomic status. This evidence provided the basis for considerable debate in Chile about the design of publicly funded education in the years after democracy returned to the country in 1989 (McEwan, Urquiola, & Vegas, 2008).

The book *Fifteen Thousand Hours*, by Michael Rutter (1979), describes another pioneering longitudinal study. The research team followed students in 12 secondary schools in inner-city London over a three-year period from 1971 through 1974, and documented that students attending some secondary schools achieved better outcomes, on average, than those attending other schools. One methodological contribution of the study was that it measured several different types of student outcomes, including delinquency, performance on curriculum-based examinations, and employment one year after leaving school. A second was the attention paid to collecting information on variables other than resource levels. In particular, the researchers documented that characteristics of schools as social organizations—including the use of rewards and penalties, the ways teachers taught particular material, and expectations that faculty had of students for active participation—were associated with differences in average student outcomes.

A close reading of the studies by Schiefelbein and Farrell, and by Rutter and his colleagues, shows that both sets of researchers were aware acutely of the difficulty of making causal inferences, even with the rich, longitudinal data they had collected. For example, Schiefelbein and Farrell wrote: "It is important to reemphasize that this study has not been designed as a hypothesis-testing exercise. Our approach has consistently been exploratory and heuristic. And necessarily so" (p. 35). In their concluding chapter, Rutter and his colleagues wrote: "The total pattern of findings indicates the strong probability that the associations between school processes and outcome reflect in part a causal process" (p. 179). Why were these talented researchers, working with such rich data, not able to make definitive causal statements about the answers to critical questions of educational policy? What does it take to make defensible causal inferences? We address these questions in the chapters that follow.

What This Book Is About

In recent decades, tremendous advances have been made in data availability, empirical research design, and statistical methods for making *causal inferences*. This has created new opportunities for investigators to conduct research that addresses policymakers' concerns about the consequences of actions aimed at improving educational outcomes for students. But how can these new methods and data be applied most effectively in educational and social-science research? What kinds of research designs are most appropriate? What kinds of data are needed? What statistical methods are best used to process these data, and how can their results be interpreted so that policymakers are best informed? These are the questions that we address in this book.

The particular designs and methods that we have chosen to describe are sophisticated and innovative, often relatively new, and most have their origins in disciplines other than education. We have sought to present them in a way that is sensitive to the practical realities of the educational context, hoping not only to make you receptive to their incorporation into educational research, but also to persuade you to incorporate them into your own work.

An innovative aspect of our book is that we illustrate all of our technical discussions of new research design and innovative statistical methods with examples from recent, exemplary research studies that address questions that educational policymakers around the world have asked. We explain how these studies were designed and conducted and, where appropriate, we use data from them to illustrate the application of new methods. We also use these same studies to illustrate the challenges of interpreting findings even from exemplary studies and to demonstrate why care in interpretation is critical to informing the policy process.

The studies that we highlight examine a variety of causal questions, examples of which include:

- Does financial aid affect students' and families' educational decisions?
- Does providing students with subsidized access to private schools result in improved educational outcomes?
- Do early childhood programs have long-term benefits?
- Does class size influence students' achievement?
- Are some instructional programs more effective than others?

All of these questions have been the subject of high-quality studies that have implemented cutting-edge designs and applied innovative methods of data analysis. We refer to these high-quality studies throughout our book as we explain a variety of innovative approaches for making causal inferences from empirical data. In fact, by the end of our book, you will find that the phrase "high-quality" itself eventually becomes code for referring to studies that effectively employ the approaches we describe.

Notice that all of the educational policy questions listed here concern the impact of a particular action on one or more outcomes. For example, does the provision of financial aid affect families' decisions to send a child to secondary school? This is a distinctive characteristic of causal questions, and learning to answer such questions is the topic of this book. In our work, we distinguish such causal questions from descriptive questions, such as whether the gap between the average reading achievement of black students and that of white students closed during the 1980s. Although there are often significant challenges to answering descriptive questions well, these challenges are typically less difficult than the challenges you will face when addressing causal questions.

We have written this book not only for those who would like to conduct causal research in education and the social sciences, but also for those who want to interpret the results of such causal research appropriately and understand how the results can inform policy decisions. In presenting these new designs and methods, we assume that you have a solid background in quantitative methods, that you are familiar with the notion of statistical inference, and that you are comfortable with statistical techniques up to, and including, ordinary least-squares (OLS) regression analysis. However, as an interested reader can see by skimming ahead in the text, ours is not a highly technical book. To the contrary, our emphasis is not on mathematics, but on providing *intuitive explanations* of key ideas and procedures. We believe that illustrating our technical explanations with data from exemplary research studies makes the book widely accessible.

We anticipate that you will obtain several immediate benefits from reading our book carefully. First, you will learn how alternative research designs for making causal inferences function, and you will come to understand the strengths and limitations of each innovative approach. In addition, you will learn how to interpret the results of studies that use these research designs and analytic methods, and will come to understand that careful interpretation of their findings, although often not obvious, is critical to making the research useful in the policy process.

What to Read Next

We conclude every chapter with a brief list of additional resources you may want to consult, to learn more about the topics that were discussed in the chapter. In this introductory chapter, the extra readings that we suggest deal primarily with the history of educational research. In subsequent chapters, many of our suggestions are to scholarly papers that provide specialized treatments of the particular technical issues raised in the chapters they accompany.

To learn more about the reasons why the NIE failed to fulfill its much-publicized promise, we suggest reading the 1978 book by Lee Sproull and her colleagues entitled *Organizing an Anarchy*. Jonah Rockoff's (2009) paper "Field Experiments in Class Size from the Early Twentieth Century" provides an interesting and brief history of attempts to estimate the causal impact of class size on student achievement. Grover "Russ" Whitehurst's thoughtful reports (Whitehurst, 2008a, 2008b) on the research agenda that the Institute of Education Sciences developed and supported during the period 2003–2008 describe the challenges of supporting research that is both rigorous and relevant to improving the quality of the education that children receive.

2

The Importance of Theory

A question that governments around the world ask repeatedly is whether using scarce public resources to educate children is a good social investment. Beginning in the late 1950s, and sparked by the pioneering work of Nobel Prize winners Theodore Schultz and Gary Becker, economists developed a theoretical framework within which to address this question. The resulting framework, which became known as *human capital theory*, provided the foundation for a vast amount of quantitative research in the ensuing years. Among the many insights from human capital theory and the empirical work that it generated are the important role education plays in fostering a nation's economic growth, the reason education has its biggest labor market payoffs in economies that are experiencing rapid technological change, and why employers are often willing to pay to train workers to do specific tasks, such as use a new technology, but are typically unwilling to pay for training that improves workers' reasoning skills and writing ability.[1]

Over subsequent decades, social scientists refined the theory of human capital in a variety of ways. These refinements led to new hypotheses and to important new evidence about the payoffs to investments in education, some of which are described in later chapters. The salient point for the

---

1. For many references to the evidence of the role of education in fostering economic growth, see Hanushek and Woessman (2008). For evidence on the especially valuable role of education in increasing productivity in environments experiencing technological change, see Jamison & Lau (1982). The classic reference on the reasons why employers are typically willing to pay for specific training, but not general training, is Becker (1964).

moment is that human capital theory provides a powerful illustration of the role that theory plays in guiding research, especially research into cause and effect. We will return to human capital theory later in this chapter. First, however, we explain what we mean by the term *theory* and the roles that it plays in guiding research in the social sciences and education.

What Is Theory?

According to the *Oxford English Dictionary* (OED, 1989), a theory is "a scheme or system of ideas or statements held as an explanation or account of a group of facts or phenomena; a hypothesis that has been confirmed or established by observation or experiment, and is propounded or accepted as accounting for the known facts; a statement of what are held to be the general laws, principles, or causes of something known or observed."[2] All three parts of this definition contain the notion that, within a theory, a general principle of some kind—the OED calls it a "scheme," a "system," "general laws,"—is intended to "explain" or "account for" particular instances of what we observe on a day-to-day basis.

Theory plays important roles in guiding empirical research in the social sciences and education by providing guidance about the questions to ask, the key constructs to measure, and the hypothesized relationships among these constructs. For example, at the core of human capital theory is the idea that individuals compare benefits and costs in making decisions about whether to undertake additional education. This framework leads researchers to ask what factors should be included among the benefits and costs of acquiring additional education, and how to measure differences among individuals in these benefits and costs or changes in their values over time. Theory also suggests the direction of hypothesized relationships. For example, theory suggests that a decline in the earnings of college graduates relative to those of high school graduates would lead to a decline in the percentage of high school graduates who decide to enroll in college.

Of course, theory is never static. For example, in the first round of an investigation, research questions are often broad and undifferentiated, and any hypothesized intervention is treated simply as a "black box." However, in answering the first-round research question, investigators

---

2. Accessed at the following webpage: http://dictionary.oed.com.ezp-prod1.hul.harvard. edu/cgi/entry/50250688?query_type=word&queryword=theory&first=1&max_to_ show=10&sort_type=alpha&result_place=1&search_id=wpON-NKMyN3-6203- &hilite=50250688

can refine their theory and propose more sophisticated, finer-grained questions that sometimes shed light on the causal machinery within the box.

The development of human capital theory illustrates this. One pattern common across many countries that the theory sought to explain was that, on average, the more formal education that workers had completed, the higher were their labor market earnings. In its initial formulation in the late 1950s, economists treated "formal schooling" as a black box— increases in formal schooling were theorized to improve subsequent wages because they led to increases in the productivity of workers. In a 1966 paper, Richard Nelson and Edmund Phelps unpacked this straight-forward idea, and thereby refined human capital theory, by suggesting that additional education increased productivity because it increased workers' ability to understand and make use of new information. This led them to hypothesize that education would have a greater impact on worker productivity in settings in which technologies were changing than in settings in which technology was static.

Subsequent quantitative research tested this new hypothesis and found support for it. For example, Jamison and Lau (1982) found that education had a larger impact on productivity in agriculture in settings in which green revolution seeds and fertilizers were changing agricultural meth-ods than it did in settings in which techniques were stable and had been passed down orally from one generation to the next. Later contributions to human capital theory developed the idea that if additional education did improve individuals' skills at processing and making use of new infor-mation, it would not only increase their productivity at work, it would also result in improved health and better parenting.[3] These subsequent theo-retical refinements catalyzed a still growing body of quantitative research on the payoffs of education.

Good theory often leads researchers to new ideas that raise questions about the tenets of existing theory. For example, building on the work of Kenneth Arrow and others, Michael Spence (1974) developed a challenge to human capital theory. Spence proposed an alternative theory, which he called *market signaling*. In a simple market-signaling model, high-productivity individuals obtain additional schooling not because it enhances their skills, but because it is a way to signal to potential employ-ers that they possess exceptional qualities, and consequently should be paid higher salaries than other applicants. Thus, a market-signaling model

---

3. In Chapter 10, we describe one important paper in this line of research, written by Janet Currie and Enrico Moretti (2003).

could explain the positive relationship between educational attainments and labor market wages even if education did not enhance students' skills. Market signaling continues to pose an alternative to human capital theory in explaining education–earnings relationships in some settings. Unfortunately, it has proven very difficult to design quantitative research to test the two theories unequivocally, head to head. In fact, many social scientists would argue that both human capital theory and market signaling theory play roles in explaining wage patterns in many societies. For example, the earnings premium that graduates of elite universities enjoy stems in part from the skills they acquired at the university and partly from the signal of high ability that admission to, and graduation from, an elite university conveys.[4]

The French sociologist Pierre Bourdieu posed another alternative to human capital theory to explain the role that education plays in Western societies. In Bourdieu's theoretical framework, education sorts students in ways that contribute to the reproduction of existing social hierarchies. Children in elite families graduate from the best universities and obtain access to prestigious, well-paying careers. Children from lower-class families obtain education that only provides access to low-prestige, lower-paying jobs. In Bourdieu's theory, many sorting mechanisms contribute to this pattern. One is the allocation of educational opportunities by scores on standardized tests that favor the types of knowledge that children from well-to-do families acquire at home. Another is an educational-finance system that favors students from families that already have financial resources. Most objective social scientists recognize that Bourdieu's theory of *social reproduction* sheds light on the role that education plays in many societies.[5] However, as with market signaling, it has proven difficult to compare Bourdieu's theory with human capital theory head to head. In fact, the two theories provide complementary insights into explaining the role that education plays in many settings.

Philosophers of science distinguish between two modes of inquiry, one based on *deductive logic* and the other based on *inductive logic*. Deductive reasoning involves the development of specific hypotheses from general theoretical principles. In the exercise of inductive reasoning, you engage in the reverse of deduction. You begin by observing an unexpected pattern, and you try to explain what you have observed by generalizing it. In other words, with inductive reasoning, you go from particular observations to general principles. The origins of most important theories involve

---

4. For an accessible discussion of human capital and market signaling models, see Weiss (1995).
5. For an introduction to Bourdieu's theory, see Lane (2000).

a mixture of the two types of reasoning. Induction is critical because the theorist is trying to make sense of a pattern he or she has observed or learned about. At the same time, having a rudimentary theory in mind directed the theorist's attention to the pattern. Once theories are formulated, deduction typically becomes preeminent in the formal design and execution of new theory-based research. However, induction often provides the post-hoc insight that is instrumental in refining existing theory.

Both deductive and inductive reasoning have played roles in the development of human capital theory. For example, economists used deductive reasoning to formulate a variety of specific hypotheses based on the general statement of human capital theory. One was that the lower the interest rate high school graduates had to pay on loans for college tuition, the more probable it was that they went to college. Economists also used insights from human capital theory to inform the design of research aimed at estimating the rate of return to a society of investing in education. A consistent result was that the social benefits from universal primary education far exceeded the social costs in most developing countries. Indeed, in most countries, the estimated social rate of return on investments in primary education far exceeded the social rate of return to other possible governmental use of resources, such as investing in physical infrastructure (Psacharopoulos, 2006).

Despite the compelling evidence that primary education was a good social investment in most countries, social scientists observed that many families in developing countries choose not to send their children to school. This observation led researchers to engage in inductive reasoning, in order to formulate possible explanations. One alternative was that families did not have access to primary schools—a supply problem. A second was that families were unaware of the payoffs to education—an information problem. A third was that families could not borrow the money at reasonable interest rates to pay the cost of schooling, costs that might include replacing the labor that the child provided at home—a problem of capital market failure. Yet another hypothesis was that paying for children's schooling was not a good personal investment for parents in cultures in which children did not feel a strong moral obligation to support their parents later in life—a cultural explanation. These hypotheses, all stemming from the observation that the educational investment decisions of many families seemed inconsistent with insights from human capital theory, led to increased attention in human capital theory to the supply of schools, the information available to parents, their ability to borrow at reasonable interest rates, and cultural norms about children's responsibilities to parents. In turn, these hypotheses led to studies that examined the relative importance of these different possible explanations for the educational investment decisions of parents.

Theory in Education

Every educational system involves a large and diverse array of actors whose decisions interact in a great many ways. Governments make decisions about the types of organizations that may offer schooling services and that are eligible to receive partial or full payment for their services from tax revenues. Parents make decisions about the schools their children will attend and the amount of time and energy they will devote to shaping their children's skills and values at home. Children make decisions about how much attention they will pay to school-related work and to the types of interactions in which they will engage with peers. Educators decide where they will work, how they will teach, and how much attention they will pay to individual children. The decisions of these many actors interact in important ways. For example, parents' choices are influenced by their children's efforts in school and by the quality and resources of their local schools. The actions of policymakers regarding licensing requirements and compensation structures influence the career decisions of potential teachers.[6]

The number of different players who contribute to education, and the complexity of their interactions, make it difficult to formulate parsimonious, compelling theories about the consequences of particular educational policies. In contrast, physics is a field with very strong theory—well-developed general principles expressed in mathematical terms from which stem many clearly defined hypotheses that can be tested empirically. In thinking about the role of theory in the social sciences and education, it is important to remember that physics is the exception rather than the rule. In most other fields of scientific endeavor, theory is commonly expressed in words rather than in mathematics, and the general principles are less clearly defined than they are in physics. The reason we mention this is to encourage researchers to define theory broadly, so that it includes a clear description of the policy intervention to be evaluated, the outcomes it may influence, and conjectures about the mechanisms through which the intervention may influence outcomes. (Some writers use the term *theory of action* to refer to these steps.) Rarely will such a description be expressed

---

6. The ideas we describe in this paragraph are taken from Shavelson and Towne (eds., 2002).

in mathematical terms, and it does not need to be. What is important is clear thinking, which is typically informed by a deep knowledge of previous research in the relevant area and a solid grounding in a social science.

One vital part of the work of using theory to inform the design of empirical work investigating causal relationships in education and the social sciences concerns the measurement of key concepts. For example, a hypothesis of great interest in many countries is that reducing class sizes in elementary schools will result in improved student achievement. A little thinking brings the realization that the key conceptual variables relevant to this hypothesis—class size and student achievement—could be measured in many different ways, and the choices could affect the results of the research. For example, in schools in which the student population is mobile, counting the number of students who appear on a class roster would provide a very different measure of class size than would counting the number of students in attendance on any single day. Developing a measure of student achievement raises even more questions. Do scores on standardized reading tests measure literacy skills effectively? Would the research results differ if other measures of student achievement were chosen, such as success at the next level of schooling? We see the process of thinking hard about these measurement issues as part of the task of applying theory to the design of empirical work.

It is often useful to distinguish between two kinds of theories that can inform the design of causal research in education and the social sciences. *Partial equilibrium theories* can shed light on the likely consequences of policy interventions of modest scale undertaken in a particular setting. An example would be the application of human capital theory to predict the consequences of a policy initiative that would offer zero-interest loans for college expenses to high school graduates from low-income families in a particular community. Since only a modest number of students would be affected by the proposed policy, it would be reasonable to assume that the loan program would have no impact on the relative earnings of high school graduates and college graduates.

In contrast, in considering the consequences of a policy initiative that would offer zero-interest college loans to all low-income students in the United States, it would be important to take into consideration that an increase in the supply of college graduates would lower the earnings of this group relative to the earnings of high school graduates. Theories that take into account such indirect effects of policy initiatives are called *general equilibrium theories.*

An important question when choosing a particular theoretical framework to guide the design of causal research in education is whether a partial equilibrium approach will suffice, or whether a general equilibrium approach is necessary. The advantage of a partial equilibrium framework is usually its relative simplicity. However, the simplicity is achieved by the assumption that the intervention is of sufficiently small scale that secondary effects can be ignored. The advantage of a general equilibrium framework is that it provides tools to examine those secondary effects, which are likely to be more important the larger the scale of the policy initiative. One accompanying cost, however, is greater complexity. An even greater cost of adopting a general equilibrium framework as the basis for a social science experiment is that if an intervention has broadly distributed secondary effects, it is very difficult for the investigator to define an appropriate comparison or control group that would not be influenced indirectly by the intervention. For that reason, we share the view of many methodologists that random-assignment experiments and the other analytic techniques that we promote in this book cannot capture the full general equilibrium effects of large-scale policy interventions (Duflo, Glennerster, & Kremer, 2008).

In the next section, we provide an example of how a prominent theory regarding the consequences of *educational vouchers* became more refined over time. We also show the ways that researchers used both partial equilibrium and general equilibrium versions of the theory to shed light on the consequences of particular educational voucher policies.

Voucher Theory

Perhaps the most vigorously contested educational policy issue in the world in recent years has concerned the consequences of using public tax revenues to pay for children's education at private schools. Writing in the early 1960s (Friedman, 1962), the American economist—and later Nobel Prize winner—Milton Friedman argued that the prevailing system of public schools in the United States restricted the freedom of parents to choose the schools that would best serve their children. He advocated the introduction of an "educational voucher" system, which would, in his view, both expand freedom of choice and improve the quality of American education. Friedman's initial statement of voucher theory was elegant. The key policy recommendation was that government should provide educational vouchers of equal value to all parents of school-age children. Parents could then use the vouchers to pay for the education of their children at a public school of their choice or use them to pay part or all of the tuitions at a private school of their choice.

Friedman envisioned several desirable outcomes from a universal voucher system, some easier to measure (increased student achievement and lower schooling costs) than others (enhancement of freedom). The mechanism through which a voucher system would achieve these outcomes was the force of market competition. Part of Friedman's argument was that the introduction of a system of educational vouchers would have its greatest positive impact on the quality of education available to children from low-income families because they have the fewest schooling choices under the prevailing educational system.

Implicit in Friedman's voucher theory were two critical assumptions, both of which came from the application to education of the economic theory of *competitive markets*. The first assumption was that consumers would be free to choose any school for which they could pay the tuition. The second was that the schooling choices that parents made for their children would be independent of the schooling choices that other parents made for their children. These assumptions made sense in competitive markets for consumer goods such as bread. Typically, shoppers can buy any brand of bread that they feel is worth the market price, and their decisions are not directly influenced by the choices made by other consumers. These assumptions simplify enormously the development of theories that predict how competitive markets function.

In the decades following publication of Friedman's voucher theory, however, a growing number of studies documented that the two critical assumptions implicit in Friedman's voucher theory did not hold. One reason is that some children are more expensive to educate than others. For example, children with disabilities, such as dyslexia or hearing problems, require additional resources to help them to master critical skills (Duncombe & Yinger, 1999). If schools are constrained to charge the same tuition to all students, and if the value of the education voucher provided by government is the same for all children, then school administrators have incentives to avoid accepting children who would be expensive to educate.

A second challenge to the assumptions underlying Friedman's voucher theory is that parents recognize that the quality of the education their child receives in a particular school depends on the skills and behaviors of other children attending the same school (Graham, 2008; Hoxby, 2000). These influences, which sociologists call "peer-group effects" and economists call "externalities," complicate the way that educational voucher systems would operate in practice. In particular, schools that attempted to attract students from particular types of families (such as those with well-educated, affluent parents) would seek to refuse admission to children whom their desired clientele would not like to have as classmates.

Taking advantage of advances in computer-based simulation, a number of social scientists developed theoretical models that incorporated cost differentials and peer-group effects. Many of the models also incorporated details of public school finance systems. These are complex general-equilibrium models that treat the school-choice decisions of families as interdependent. Researchers used these theoretical models not only to explore how the introduction of voucher plans with particular designs would affect families' schooling choices, but also how they would influence things like housing prices and families' decisions about where to live.[7] A hypothesis stemming from many of these theoretical models and policy simulations is that a universal educational-voucher system in which the value of the voucher was the same for all children would lead to significant sorting of students from specific backgrounds into particular schools. Subsequent studies of universal voucher systems in Chile (Hsieh & Urquiola, 2006) and in New Zealand (Fiske & Ladd, 2000), in which the vouchers did have the same value for all children, provided evidence supporting this hypothesis. For example, Hsieh and Urquiola (2006) showed that children from the poorest families in Chile tended to be concentrated in low-performing public schools, whereas children from relatively affluent families were concentrated in particular private schools.[8]

Evidence of the importance of cost differentials and peer-group effects has resulted in two subsequent refinements to voucher theory. The first has been the creation of theoretical models predicting the consequences of voucher systems in which the value of the voucher that individual children receive depends on their characteristics.[9] The logic is that a system with appropriately differentiated voucher values might prevent the sorting by socioeconomic status that took place under the single-valued voucher systems in Chile and New Zealand. The second development has been the formulation (and testing) of relatively simple partial-equilibrium models in which only children from low-income families are eligible to receive vouchers. The logic underlying these models is that the family-income limits for participation would reduce the threat of sorting by

---

7. See Hoxby (2003), and Nechyba (2003) for discussions of the importance of general equilibrium models for understanding the consequences of particular voucher plans. For examples of such equilibrium models, see Nechyba (2003, pp. 387–414); Epple and Romano (1998, pp. 33–62); Hoxby (2001); Fernandez and Rogerson (2003, pp. 195–226).
8. Concerned with the sorting by socioeconomic status that took place under its equal-value voucher system, the Chilean government modified its national voucher system in 2008. Under the new system, the vouchers distributed to children from the one-third poorest families in the country (called Priority students) are worth 50% more than those distributed to more affluent families. Private schools that receive higher-valued vouchers are prohibited from charging Priority students any tuition or fees in excess of the value of their voucher.
9. See, for example, Hoxby (2001); Fernandez and Rogerson (2003).

socioeconomic status. We discuss the evaluation of a trial of one such voucher program in Chapter 4.

The consequences of educational vouchers continue to be debated as heatedly today as in the years following Friedman's publication of *Capitalism and Freedom* (1962). However, the debate has become vastly more sophisticated, primarily because of advances in understanding that have stemmed from the interplay of theoretical developments and new evidence. For example, there is widespread recognition today that some children are more expensive to educate than others, that peer-group effects influence student achievement, and that many parents need help in collecting the information that is necessary to make good school choices. These patterns all have implications for the design of future voucher systems and for evaluations of their impacts. The wheel of science continues to turn, and our theories evolve!

What Kind of Theories?

In this chapter, we have chosen our examples primarily from the field of economics because it is the social science discipline we know best. However, theories drawn from other social-science disciplines can also inform the design of causal educational research. Examples include theories of social capital drawn from sociology and theories of child development from psychology. The choice of a theoretical framework within which to embed the design of quantitative research depends on the nature of the causal question being asked and the knowledge base of the investigators.

We do want to emphasize, however, the distinction between social-science theory and statistical theory. In recent decades, important advances have been made in statistical theory that have led to new research designs and analytic methods, many of which are presented in later chapters of this book. New resampling methods for conducting hypothesis tests and methods for estimating statistical power when individuals are clustered in classrooms and/or schools provide two examples. The point we want to emphasize here is that statistical theory, and the methods stemming from advances in statistical theory, are methodological complements to substantive social-science theory, not substitutes.

What to Read Next

For readers interested in learning more about the role of theory in informing causal research in general, and causal research in education in particular, there is much to read. One place to start, which provides an entrée into the relevant literature, is the brief volume *Scientific Research in Education* (Shavelson & Towne, 2002), which is the thoughtful report of a National Research Council Committee in the United States. The 2003 paper by David Cohen, Stephen Raudenbush, and Deborah Loewenberg-Ball entitled "Resources, Instruction, and Research" provides an insightful theory about the conditions under which school resources influence student learning. For a provocative view of the role of theory written by a major figure in 20th-century educational research, see John Dewey's 1929 book, *The Sources of a Science of Education.*

3

Designing Research to Address Causal Questions

One of the first actions that Grover "Russ" Whitehurst, the first director of the Institute of Education Sciences, took after assuming office in 2002 was to commission a survey of educational practitioners and policymakers in order to learn what they wanted from educational research.[1] Not surprisingly, the survey results showed that the priorities of educators depended on their responsibilities. Superintendents and other local education officials were most interested in evidence about particular curricula and instructional techniques that were effective in increasing student achievement. State-level policymakers wanted to learn about the consequences of standards-based educational reforms and the impact of particular school intervention strategies. Congressional staff wanted to know about the effectiveness of different strategies for enhancing teacher quality. Educators at all levels wanted to know about the effect of differences in resource levels, such as class sizes, in determining students' achievement.

Whereas the priorities of educators depended on their responsibilities, the striking commonality in their responses was that practitioners and policymakers—at all levels—wanted to know the answers to *questions about cause and effect*. They wanted to know *if A caused B*, and wanted IES to commission research that would provide them with answers. In this chapter, we discuss the conditions that must be satisfied for such causal questions to be addressed effectively in education, and we introduce some of the major concepts and terms that we use throughout the rest of the book.

---

1. See Huang et al. (2003).

Conditions to Strive for in All Research

Before we begin our discussion of how best to address the causal questions that are so central to educators, we begin with a brief description of the classical elements of good research design in the social sciences and education. We do this because designing *causal* research requires us to pay attention to the central tenets of all good research. Then, within this larger domain, causal research must satisfy an additional set of constraints, and it is these that form the central topic for the rest of our book. We used the expression "strive for" in the title of this section because it is typically difficult to satisfy all of the conditions we describe. We use examples throughout the book to clarify the consequences of not satisfying particular elements of the classical description of effective research design. As you will learn, violation of some of the tenets of appropriate design makes it impossible to make a defensible causal inference about the consequences of an educational policy or intervention. Violation of other tenets does not threaten the ability to make a causal inference, but does limit the ability to determine to whom the results of the study apply. We will return to these issues. However, we begin by stating these elements of good research design.

First, in any high-quality research, whether it be purely descriptive or able to support causal inference, it is critically important that it begin with a clear statement of the research question that will drive the project and the theory that will frame the effort. These two key elements ultimately drive every aspect of the research design, as they provide the motivation and the rationale for every design decision that you ultimately make. They have also been the topics of our first two chapters and, as we have argued, they are completely intertwined. As theories are refined, it becomes possible to pose more complex questions, and these, in their turn, inform refinements of the theory. Light, Singer, and Willett (1990) referred to this as the "wheel of science."

An explicit statement of the research question makes it possible to define the *population of interest* clearly and unambiguously. This is critical in any research. If we do not do it, we cannot build a suitable sampling frame, nor can we know to whom we can generalize the findings of our research. In addition, it pays to be explicit, rather than vague, about the nature of the population of interest. For example, in studying the impact of class size on children's reading skills, it might make sense to define the population of interest to be "all children without special needs in first-grade classrooms in urban public schools in the United States," rather than just "children." Defining the population clearly enables readers who have a particular concern, such as the impact of class size on the learning of autistic children, to judge the relevance of our results to their concern.

Once we have defined the population of interest clearly, we must work hard to sample representatively from that population. Thus, in an investigation of the impact of class size on student achievement in the population defined earlier, we need to decide whether it is feasible to obtain a simple random sample of students from the population of first graders without special needs attending urban public schools in the United States. Alternatively, we might decide that we want to use a more complex sampling plan, such as a multistage cluster sample of school districts, schools, and grades. However we go about sampling, it is critical that the analytic sample that we use in our research be fully representative of the population. This ensures what methodologists call the *external validity* of the research. This refers to the ability to generalize our findings credibly to a known population of interest.

The next important step in any research project is to choose appropriate measures of the key variables that are central to the research, and to ensure their construct validity and reliability for the population under investigation. We should use our knowledge of the research question and its supporting theory to distinguish three important classes of variables: (a) the outcome variable; (b) the principal question predictor, defined as the variable that provides our research question; and (c) the covariates or control predictors. These distinctions will recur consistently throughout our account of causal research, as they do through the account of any high-quality descriptive research project. In our hypothetical investigation of class size and academic achievement, for instance, we might decide to focus on two specific academic outcomes, such as children's reading and mathematics achievement. Our principal question predictor would be a measure of class size. Covariates or control variables might include student demographic characteristics and measures of teacher experience. We would need to exercise care in determining just how we would measure each of these variables. For example, we would need to decide whether we want to measure class size by the number of students enrolled in a class on a particular day, or perhaps by the average of the number of students enrolled on several prespecified dates. We would also want to be sure to measure each student's reading and mathematics achievement using age-appropriate normed and suitably scaled tests. Our decisions should be guided by our research question, our theoretical framework, and the background literature in which they are embedded.

At this point, we want to point out explicitly the one and only distinction between descriptive and causal research. It concerns the principal question predictor that forms the centerpiece of the research design. The critical question for causal research is how the values of the question predictor are determined for each of the participants in the sample.

In our class-size example, if the actions of children, teachers, parents, or school administrators determine the size of the class into which each child is placed, all manner of unobserved forces and choices would undermine our ability to make inferences about the causal impact of class size on children's achievement. On the other hand, if we were to randomly assign children and teachers to classes of different sizes, thereby determining their values on the principal question predictor, we may be able to credibly estimate the causal impact of class size on the achievement of children in the population from which the analytic sample was drawn. The difference is simply in the way that the values of the question predictor, class size, have been determined for each child in the analytic sample and for their teachers. This single issue and its consequences for design, data analysis, and interpretation distinguish credible causal research from all other research. It is the central concern of the rest of our book.

One final step is to ensure that the research is replicated in other samples drawn from the same population. This is important because of the uncertainty that exists in measurement and is built into the probabilistic nature of statistical inference. We will devote considerable attention in this book to describing how different kinds of statistical errors can influence the findings from statistical analysis.

Making Causal Inferences

In their excellent book on the design of social science research, Shadish, Campbell, and Cook (2002, p. 6) cite 19th-century philosopher John Stuart Mill's description of three critical conditions that must be met in order to claim that one thing *causes* another. The first condition is that the hypothesized *cause* must *precede* its anticipated *effect* in time. For example, in investigating whether student achievement depends upon the number of students in the class, it is important to ensure that students had been taught in class settings of a particular size *before* their achievement was measured.

The second of Mill's conditions is that if the levels of the cause differ in some systematic way, then there must be corresponding variation in the effect. For example, if our theory suggests that children taught in classes with fewer students achieved at higher levels, we would anticipate that as the number of students in classes got smaller, the students' achievement would be higher, on average.

The third of Mill's conditions is by far the most important and the most difficult to satisfy in practice. It stipulates that the researcher must be able to discount all other plausible explanations—other than the anticipated causal one—for the link observed between the hypothetical cause and effect.

In the case of an investigation of the impact of class size on student achievement, we must be able to argue compellingly that any observed association between class sizes and subsequent student achievement is not a consequence, for example, of choices that parents may have made about where to send their children to school or decisions by school administrators to assign students with particular characteristics to classes of particular sizes.

The most persuasive way to conduct research that satisfies Mills' three conditions—and thereby successfully address causal questions—is for the researcher to conduct an *experiment*. Following Shadish, Campbell, and Cook (2002, p. 511), we define an experiment as an empirical investigation in which the levels of a potential cause are manipulated by an outside agent functioning independently of the participants in the research, and after which the consequences for an important outcome are measured.

Furthermore, as illustrated in Figure 3.1, we distinguish between two kinds of experiments: randomized experiments and quasi-experiments. The most compelling evidence for making causal attributions typically comes from randomized experiments, defined as experiments in which units are assigned to experimental conditions by a random process, such as the toss of a fair coin (Shadish, Campbell, & Cook, 2002, p. 12). Notice that well-executed *randomized experiments* satisfy Mills's three conditions for making causal inferences: (a) cause precedes effect, (b) different levels of cause can lead to different levels of effect, and (c) random assignment obviates all other plausible explanations for any differences in effect detected. In fact, the random assignment of students and teachers to classes of different sizes by an independent investigator ensures that the children and teachers who were in the different class-size "treatments" are equal on all characteristics—on average—before the experiment begins. Because of randomization, any small and idiosyncratic differences that exist among the groups prior to treatment will fall within the noise that is

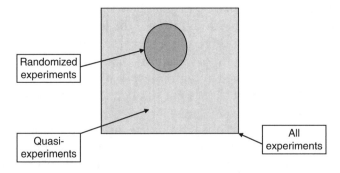

Figure 3.1 Two kinds of experiments.

accounted for naturally by statistical methods used to analyze the resulting outcome data. As we describe more fully in Chapter 4, when individuals are assigned by randomization to different experimental conditions, we say that the groups so-formed are *equal in expectation.*

Quasi-experiments are experiments in which units are not assigned to conditions randomly (Shadish, Campbell, & Cook, 2002, p. 12). It is sometimes possible to make legitimate causal inferences using data from quasi-experiments. Indeed, we devote several chapters of this book to methods for doing so. However, as we illustrate with many examples, researchers need to be prepared to deal with a variety of *threats to the internal validity* of research based on data from quasi-experiments. As we discuss in more detail in Chapter 4, this term refers to threats to the validity of a statement that the relationship between two variables is causal (Shadish, Campbell, & Cook, 2002, pp. 53–61).

Although the interpretation of the evidence from any experiment will depend on the details of the particular case, we want to emphasize one general point. Randomized experiments and quasi-experiments typically provide estimates of the total effect of a policy intervention on one or more outcomes, not the effects of the intervention holding constant the levels of other inputs (Todd & Wolpin, 2003). This matters, because families often respond to a policy intervention in a variety of ways, and the experiment provides evidence about the net impact of all of the responses on measured outcomes. For example, we will describe several experiments in which parents were offered scholarships to help pay for the education of a particular child at a private school. A common outcome in such experiments is a measure of the cognitive skills of children at a later point in time. One response to the policy is to increase the probability that parents send to a private school the child offered a scholarship. However, another response may be that the parents reduce the amount of money that they spend on providing tutoring and enrichment activities for that child in order to free up resources to devote to other children. The experiment provides evidence about the net impact of these two responses (as well as any others). It does not provide an estimate of the impact of the scholarship offer on children's subsequent achievement, holding constant the level of parental resources devoted to tutoring and enrichment.

Past Approaches to Answering Causal Questions in Education

Unfortunately, until fairly recently, most educational researchers did not address their causal questions by conducting randomized experiments or by adopting creative approaches to analyzing data from quasi-experiments. Instead, they typically conducted *observational studies*, defined as analyzing data from settings in which the values of all variables—including those describing participation in different potential "treatments"—are observed rather than assigned by an external agent (Shadish, Campbell & Cook, 2002, p. 510). For instance, hundreds of observational studies have been conducted on the association between class size and academic achievement using achievement data collected from students during the normal operation of a school district. In these settings, the number of students in various classes differs as a result of demographic patterns, the decisions of parents about where to live, and the decisions of school administrators about placement of students into classes.

In observational studies, the skills and motivations of students in small classes may differ from those in larger classes, irrespective of any impact that class size itself may have had ultimately on their achievement. This could be the result of a variety of mechanisms. For example, families with the resources to invest in their children's education may purchase or rent homes in the attendance zones of schools with reputations for having small classes. As a result, the average achievement of students in the schools with relatively small classes may be higher than that in schools with larger classes, even if class size did not have a causal effect on student achievement. The reason could be that those parents who chose to live near schools with small classes used their resources to provide their children with educationally enriched environment at home. This is an example of what methodologists would call an *endogenous* assignment of participants to treatments. By this we mean that assignment to levels of the treatment is a result of actions by participants within the system being investigated—in this case, the decisions of parents with resources to take advantage of the relatively small classes offered in particular schools.

Of course, well-trained quantitative researchers recognized that, as a result of the decisions of parents and school administrators, students placed endogenously in classes of different sizes may differ from each other in respects that are difficult to observe and measure. For many years, researchers responded to this dilemma in one of two ways. One common response was to include increasingly larger and richer sets of covariates describing the students and their families in the statistical models that were used to estimate the effect of treatment on outcome. The hope was that the presence of these control predictors would account for differences in the outcome that were due to all of the unobserved—and endogenously generated—differences among students in classes of different size. Sociologists Stephen Morgan and Christopher Winship (2007, p. 10) refer to the period in which researchers relied on this strategy as "the age of regression." Seminal studies published in the 1980s threw cold water on this "control for everything" strategy by demonstrating that regression analyses that contained a very rich set of covariates did *not* reproduce consistently the results of experiments in which individuals were assigned randomly to different experimental conditions.[2]

A second response, especially common among developmental psychologists, was to accept that analysis of observational data could not support causal inference and to simply avoid using causal language in both the framing of research questions and in the interpretation of research results. For example, researchers would investigate whether children placed in center-based child care had better subsequent performance on cognitive tests than did observationally similar children in family-based child care, and would simply caution that causal attribution was not justified on the basis of their findings. In our view, there are at least two problems with this approach. First, the cautions presented in the "Methods" and "Results" sections of research papers were often forgotten in the "Discussion" section, where researchers would suggest policy implications that depended on an unsupported causal interpretation of their findings. Second, their use of noncausal language meant that these researchers were not accustomed to considering explicitly alternative explanations for the statistical relationships they observed.

Fortunately, in more recent years, social scientists have developed a variety of new research designs and analytic strategies that offer greater promise for addressing causal questions about the impact of educational policies. Many of these new approaches also make use of standard techniques of multiple regression analysis, but apply them in new ways. Explaining these strategies, and illustrating their use, is a central goal of this book.

The Key Challenge of Causal Research

In conducting causal research in education and the social sciences, our central objective is to determine how the outcomes for individuals who receive a treatment differ from what the outcomes would have been in the absence of the treatment. The condition to which the research subjects would have been exposed in the absence of the experimental treatment is called the *counterfactual*. From a theoretical standpoint, the way to obtain an ideal counterfactual would be to use the same participants under both

---

2. See Angrist & Pischke (2009, pp. 86–91) for a discussion of this evidence.

a treatment (e.g., "small" class size) and a "control" (e.g., "normal" class size) condition, resetting all internal and external conditions to their identical initial values before participants experienced either condition. So, you might draw a representative sample of participants from the population, administer the treatment to them, and measure their outcome values afterward. Then, to learn what the outcomes would be under the counterfactual condition, you would need to transport these same participants back to a time before your research was conducted, erase all their experiences of the treatment and the outcome measurement from their memories, and measure their values of the outcome again, after their lives had transpired under the control condition. If this were possible, you could argue convincingly that any difference in each participant's outcome values between the two conditions must be due *only* to their experiences of the treatment.

Then, because you possessed values of the outcome for each individual obtained under both "factual" and 'counterfactual" conditions, you would be able to estimate the effect of the treatment for each participant. We call this the *individual treatment effect* (ITE). You would do this simply by subtracting the value of the outcome obtained under the counterfactual condition from the value obtained under the treated condition. In this imaginary world, you could then average these estimated ITEs across all members of the sample to obtain the estimated *average treatment effect* (ATE) for the entire group. Finally, with a statistical technique like a simple paired *t*-test, you could seek to reject the null hypothesis that the population mean difference in participants' outcomes between the treated and counterfactual conditions was zero. On its rejection, you could use your estimate of the ATE as an *unbiased* estimate of the *causal* effect of the treatment in the population from which you had sampled the participants.

Since time travel and selective memory erasure lie in the realm of imagination rather than research, in practice you always have a "missing data" problem. As we illustrate in Figure 3.2, you never actually know the value of the outcome for any individual under both the treatment and control conditions. Instead, for members of the treatment group, you are missing the value of the outcome under the control condition, and for members of the control group, you are missing the value of the outcome under the treatment condition. Consequently, you can no longer estimate the individual treatment effects and average them up to obtain an estimate of the average treatment effect.

So, you must devise an alternative, practical strategy for estimating the average treatment effect. The reason that this is so difficult to do in practice is that actors in the educational system typically care a lot about which experimental units (whether they be *students* or *teachers* or *schools*) are

	... the value of the outcome in the *Treatment Group* is ...	... the value of the outcome in the *Control Group* is ...
For members of the *Treatment Group* ...	Known	Missing
For members of the *Control Group* ...	Missing	Known

Figure 3.2 The challenge of the counterfactual.

assigned to particular educational treatments, and they take actions to try to influence these assignments. In other words, the assignment of participants to treatments is typically *endogenous* in educational research. A consequence of this is that, in an investigation of the impact of class size on academic achievement, students assigned endogenously to differently sized classes are likely to differ from each other, and not only on dimensions that can be *observed* (such as gender, age, and socioeconomic status), but also on dimensions that remain unobserved (such as intrinsic motivation and parental commitment, both of which are likely to be associated with achievement outcomes).

One positive way to restate this point—and to satisfy Mills's third condition for making compelling causal inferences—is to insist that the assignment of participants to treatments be *exogenous* rather than *endogenous*. According to the *Oxford English Dictionary*, *exogenous* means "relating to *external* causes," and is the natural opposite of *endogenous*, which means "relating to an *internal* cause or origin." In the context of our book, these words have similar, though more refined and specific meanings. When we say that there is "exogenous variation" in the educational treatments that students receive, we mean that the assignment of students to treatments has *not* been determined by participants *within* the educational system— that is, by the students, parents, teachers, or administrators—themselves. Instead, their placement in a particular treatment condition has been determined "externally" by the investigator or some other independent agency.

Of course, you might argue that it is not good enough for assignment to treatment condition to be simply *exogenous*. It is possible, for instance, that even external agents may be biased or corrupt in their assignment of participants to treatment conditions. Typically, though, when we say that assignment to experimental conditions is exogenous, we are assuming that the external agent has exercised his or her opportunity to assign participants in a way that supports causal inference directly. One very simple and useful way that such exogenous variation in experimental conditions can be created is for the investigator to assign participants randomly to treatments. Such an approach was taken in the Tennessee Student/Teacher Achievement Ratio (STAR) experiment (Krueger, 1999).

In the mid-1980s, the Tennessee state legislature appropriated funding for a randomized experiment to evaluate the causal impact of class-size reduction on the reading and mathematics achievement of children in the primary grades. More than 11,000 students and 1,300 teachers in 79 public schools throughout the state participated in the experiment, which became known as Project STAR. In each participating school, children entering kindergarten in the fall of 1985 were assigned randomly by investigators to one of three types of classes: (a) a small class with 13 to 17 children, (b) a class of regular size with 22 to 25 students, or (c) a class of regular size staffed by both a teacher and a full-time teacher's aide. Teachers in each school were also assigned randomly to classrooms. Finally, the research design called for students to remain in their originally designated class type through third grade.

A major theme of our book is that some element of exogeneity in the assignment of units to a treatment is necessary in order to make causal inferences about the effects of that treatment. Expressed in the formal terms used by statisticians and quantitative social scientists, a source of exogenous assignment of units to treatments is necessary to *identify* the causal impact of the treatment. So, when a social scientist asks what *identification strategy* was used in a particular study, the question is about the source of the exogeneity in the assignment of units to treatments. In subsequent chapters, we show that randomization is not the only way of obtaining useful exogenous variation in treatment status and consequently of identifying the causal impact of a treatment. Sometimes, it is possible to do so with data from a quasi-experiment. Sometimes, it is even possible to do so with data from an observational study, using a statistical method known as *instrumental-variables estimation* that we introduce in Chapter 10.

The Tennessee STAR experiment, which the eminent Harvard statistician Frederick Mosteller called "one of the most important educational investigations ever carried out" (Mosteller 1995, p. 113), illustrates the difficulties in satisfying all of the conditions for good research that we described earlier in this chapter. After the Tennessee legislature authorized the experiment in 1985, the State Commissioner of Education invited all public school systems and elementary schools in the state to apply to participate. Approximately 180 schools did so, 100 of which were sufficiently large to satisfy the design criterion of having three classes at each grade level from kindergarten through grade 3. The research team then chose 79 schools to participate.

The process of selecting schools to participate in the STAR experiment illustrates some of the compromises with best research practice that are sometimes necessary in even extremely well-planned experiments. First, the research sample of schools was chosen from the set of schools that volunteered to participate. It is possible that the schools that volunteered differed from those that did not in dimensions such as the quality of leadership. Second, only quite large schools met the design requirements and consequently the STAR experiment provided no evidence about the impact of class size on student achievement in small schools. Third, although the research team was careful to include in the research sample urban, suburban, and rural schools, as the enabling legislation mandated, it did not randomly select 79 schools from the population of 100 schools that volunteered and met the size criteria (Folger, 1989). A consequence of the sample selection process is that the definition of the population of schools to which the results of the experiment could be generalized is not completely clear. The most that can be said is that the results pertain to large elementary schools in Tennessee that volunteered to participate in the class-size experiment. It is important to understand that the lack of clarity about the population from which the sample is taken is a matter of *external validity*. The sampling strategy did not threaten the *internal validity* of the experiment because students and teachers within participating schools were randomized to treatment conditions.

The STAR experiment also encountered challenges to *internal validity*. Even though children in participating schools had originally been randomly and exogenously assigned to classes of different sizes, some parents were successful in switching their children from a regular-size class to a small class at the start of the second school year. This endogenous manipulation had the potential to violate the principal assumption that underpinned the randomized experiment, namely, that the average achievement of the students in regular-size classes provided a compelling estimate of what the average achievement of the students placed in the small classes would have been in the absence of the intervention. The actions of these parents therefore posed a threat to the internal validity of the causal inferences made from data collected in the STAR experiment about the impact of a second year of placement in a small class.

This term, *threat to internal validity*, is important in the annals of causal research and was one of four types of validity threats that Donald Campbell

(1957), a pioneer in developing methods for making causal inferences, described more than a half century ago. As mentioned earlier, it refers to rival explanations for the statistical relationships observed between educational treatments and outcomes. If we can remove all threats to internal validity, we have eliminated all alternative explanations for the link between cause and effect, and satisfied Mills's third condition. Devising strategies to respond to threats to internal validity is a critical part of good social science. Of course, in quasi-experimental and observational research, ruling out *all* potential rival explanations for the hypothesized link between "cause" and "effect" is extraordinarily difficult to do. How do you know when you have enumerated and dismissed all potential rival explanations? The short answer is that you *never* do know with certainty (although, of course, with each rival explanation that you do succeed in ruling out explicitly, the stronger is your case for claiming a causal link between treatment and outcome, even in quasi-experimental and observational research). As we explain in the next chapter, one of the great advantages of the classic randomized experimental design, in which a sample of participants is assigned randomly to different treatments, is that this process eliminates all alternative explanations for any relationship between class size and student achievement. But, even in randomized experiments, things can go wrong, and you may have to provide evidence for the internal validity of your work. In Chapter 5, we describe some of the problems that can crop up in randomized experiments and how skilled researchers have dealt with them.

Perhaps the most important lesson to take away from this chapter is that the active behaviors of the participants in the educational system—teachers, administrators, parents, and students—have enormous impacts on the quality of the education provided in particular schools and classrooms. These active behaviors often make it very difficult to conduct internally valid evaluations of the impacts of educational initiatives, whether they involve the placement of students in smaller classes, the use of new curricula and instructional methods, the installation of new ways to prepare teachers, or the creation of new governance structures. In the chapters that follow, we show how new sources of data, new approaches to research design, and new data-analytic methods have improved our ability to conduct internally valid studies of the causal impact of educational initiatives on student outcomes. We will make use of the terms introduced in this chapter, including *randomized experiment, quasi-experiment, observational study, exogenous, endogenous,* and *threats to internal and external validity.* By the time you have finished reading our book, these terms will be old friends.

What to Read Next

For readers who wish to follow up on the ideas we have raised in this chapter, we recommend Shadish, Campbell, and Cook's comprehensive book (2002) on the design of research, *Experimental and Quasi-Experimental Designs*, and Morgan and Winship's insightful book (2007), *Counterfactuals and Causal Inference*.

4

Investigator-Designed Randomized Experiments

In February 1997, the School Choice Scholarships Foundation (SCSF), a privately funded organization, announced that it would provide scholarships of up to $1,400 to 1,300 children from low-income families who were currently attending public elementary schools in New York City. The scholarships, renewable for at least three years, could be used to pay tuition at either religious or secular private elementary schools. This initiative provided an opportunity for a significant number of low-income parents to do what more affluent parents in a great many countries do—send their children to private school if they are unhappy with their child's neighborhood public school. One indication of the attractiveness of this offer in New York City was that the Foundation received more than 10,000 scholarship applications during a three-month period.

In May 1997, the SCSF held a lottery to determine which applicants were to be offered scholarships. One advantage of using a lottery to allocate offers of the scholarship was that applicants could understand how the opportunity would be allocated and most would perceive the process as fair. A second advantage was that it provided researchers with an opportunity to draw causal conclusions about the consequences for children's academic achievement of receiving an *offer* of a scholarship. In effect, the lottery provided a randomized experiment that researchers could use to investigate the impact on children's subsequent achievement of receiving a tuition "voucher," which parents could then choose to use or not.[1]

---

1. Notice that the treatment in this randomized experiment is "receipt of a private-school tuition voucher," not "attendance at private school," because it was the offer of a voucher that was randomized.

We use data from the SCSF initiative—which we refer to as the New York Scholarship Program (NYSP)—to illustrate ways of working with data from randomized experiments.

In the next section, we present a framework for the design of experimental research, often referred to as the *potential outcomes framework.* Then, in the following section, we describe some simple statistical methods for analyzing the data that are generated in a randomized experiment, and we illustrate these methods using the NYSP example. We draw your attention on two key statistical properties of an estimator of experimental effect—the properties of *bias* and *precision*—that have great relevance for the design of research and subsequent data analysis. Our presentation of basic experimental research in this chapter sets the stage for more complex methodological developments that we describe later in the book.

Conducting Randomized Experiments

The Potential Outcomes Framework

In recent decades, social scientists have based their discussions of research designs for addressing causal questions increasingly on the *potential outcomes framework,* also often referred to as *Rubin's Causal Model* (Holland, 1986). We alluded to this framework in our previous chapter, but we take the opportunity here to formalize our presentation briefly. In the context of the NYSP, Rubin's framework describes the effect of a well-defined treatment—the *receipt* of a tuition voucher representing the offer of a private-school scholarship—on the reading achievement one year later of a sample of children. As described in Chapter 3, what we would really like to do to make a causal inference is not physically possible! This is to observe and compare the subsequent reading achievement of each child under two different yet concurrent experimental conditions: (a) the treatment condition (voucher receipt), and (b) the counterfactual or "control" condition (no voucher receipt). Fortunately, Rubin's Causal Model provides an alternative.

Prior to randomization to experimental condition, there are essentially two "potential" values of each child's subsequent reading achievement outcome. We use $Y_i(1)$ to represent what the value of the ith child's outcome Y would be if the child were assigned to the *treatment* ("1") condition, and $Y_i(0)$ to represent what the value of the outcome would be for the same child if assigned to the *counterfactual* or control ("0") condition. Although *each* of these outcomes is *potentially* observable prior to voucher assignment (which is why Rubin referred to them as "potential" outcomes), ultimately we can only observe one of them, depending on the condition to which the ith child is actually assigned. Nevertheless, if we had access to the values of the two potential outcomes for each child in the population— if we knew both $Y_i(1)$ and $Y_i(0)$ for each child—we could write down the *individual treatment effect* (ITE_i) for each child as the difference between the potential outcomes, as follows:

$$ITE_i = Y_i(1) - Y_i(0)$$

Then, building on this hypothetical situation, the corresponding *average treatment effect* (*ATE*) across all the children in the population would simply be the population average or *expectation* of the individual treatment effects, as follows:

$$ATE = E\left[Y_i(1) - Y_i(0)\right]$$

Of course, once a decision has been made about which children will actually receive a voucher, half of the data required by these statistical models will be missing. For instance, we will not know the value of $Y_i(0)$ for any child receiving a voucher, and we will not know the value of $Y_i(1)$ for any child not receiving a voucher. Nevertheless, Rubin has shown that it is still possible to estimate the ATE from experimental data provided that participants have been randomly assigned to the treatment conditions and that a critical assumption that he refers to as the *stable-unit-treatment-value-assumption,* or SUTVA, holds. When these conditions are met, we can estimate the population ATE (but not the corresponding *individual treatment effects*[ITEs]) by simply differencing the average values of the outcomes in the sample treatment and control groups, as follows:

$$\widehat{ATE} = \left(\frac{\sum_{i=1}^{n_1} Y_i}{n_1}\right) - \left(\frac{\sum_{i=1}^{n_0} Y_i}{n_0}\right)$$

where n_1 and n_0 are the numbers of participants assigned to the treatment and control conditions, respectively, and Y is now the value of the outcome that has actually been observed for each child.[2]

SUTVA is most easily understood by reading through the acronym backward. It is an *assumption* (A), which stipulates that the *treatment-value* (TV)—in other words, the treatment effect—is *stable* (S) for all *units* (U), or participants. One way of thinking about this, in the context of our SCSF initiative, is that the potential outcomes for each child, $Y_i(1)$ and $Y_i(0)$,

---

2. Our brief introduction to Rubin's *Potential Outcomes Framework* is drawn from the excellent review article by Imbens and Wooldridge (2009).

cannot depend on the group to which particular other children have been assigned. Peer-group effects constitute one possible violation of SUTVA in the evaluation of educational interventions. For example, if the impact of voucher receipt on the reading achievement of child i depended on whether the child's next-door neighbor and closest friend also received a voucher (and could then choose to move with him or her from a public to a private school), then this would violate SUTVA. In Chapter 7, we discuss strategies for dealing with the peer-group problem in evaluating the impacts of educational interventions.

We turn now to the practical steps involved in implementing a two-group randomized experiment. Figure 4.1 illustrates these steps. First, a sensible number of participants are *randomly sampled* from a *well-defined population*.[3] Second, the sampled participants are *randomly assigned* to experimental conditions. Here, in the case of a two-group experiment, each is assigned to either the treatment or control condition. Third, a well-defined intervention is implemented faithfully among participants in the treatment group, but not among participants in the control group, and all other conditions remain identical. Fourth, the value of an outcome is measured for every participant, and its sample average estimated separately for participants in the treatment and control groups. Fifth, the sample difference between the outcome averages in the treatment and control groups is computed, providing an estimate of the ATE. Standard statistical methods—for instance, a two-group t-test—are then used to test the null hypothesis of "no treatment/control group differences, in the population." If we reject the null hypothesis, then we can conclude that the treatment has had a causal impact on the outcome. Irrespective of the outcome of the hypothesis test, the ATE is an unbiased estimate of the impact of the treatment in the population from which the sample was drawn.

The reason this process leads to an unbiased estimate of the treatment effect is that, when the assignment of participants to experimental conditions is faithfully random, all factors other than treatment status will tend to be distributed equally between participants in the treatment and control groups. This will be true not only for observed characteristics of individuals in the two groups, such as gender, race, and age, but also for any unobserved characteristics, such as motivation. As a consequence, all rival explanations for any treatment/control differences in the outcome

---

3. As we explain in Chapters 6 and 7, choosing a suitable sample size requires a statistical power analysis.

can be disavowed, and the ATE regarded as a credible estimate of the causal impact of the treatment.

This argument is more complex than it appears on the surface because what is really important is not that the distributions of all characteristics of the individuals in the treatment and control *samples* are identical. In fact, due to the idiosyncrasies of sampling, this may not actually be the case *in the sample*, especially if the experiment includes only a small number of participants. Instead, due to random sampling and random assignment, we anticipate that *potential* members of the treatment and control groups would be identical on all observed and unobserved characteristics *on average, in the population*. A methodologist would say that the treatment and control groups are *equal in expectation*. This means that any differences that may have occurred in observed (and unobserved) characteristics between the treatment and control samples can be regarded as being due to sampling idiosyncrasy. And, of course, such idiosyncratic sampling differences are accommodated automatically by the margin of error that is built into statistical analysis by its probabilistic nature.

Notice that randomization plays two distinct and important roles in the logic of experimental design. Participants are randomly sampled from a defined population and are then randomly assigned to an experimental condition.[4] Each is critical to the success of the experiment. The random selection of participants into the research from the population ensures that participants are truly representative of the population under study, and it is a generic requirement of all good research whether experimental or descriptive. Random selection of participants from a defined population permits you to generalize your findings validly back to that population, and therefore provides *external validity* for the experiment. The second process of randomization, during which participants are assigned to their requisite experimental conditions, provides *internal validity* for your research, meaning that the average difference between the treatment and control groups in the value of the outcome is truly a credible estimate of the causal impact of the treatment.

---

4. From a purely *technical* perspective, it does not matter in which order these two randomizations occur. For instance, for the purposes of this argument, it would be equally effective to label each population member at random as a potential "treatment" or "control" group member and then sample randomly from each of these newly labeled subpopulations into the treatment and control groups. The results would be identical. Of course, this "labeling the population" approach is considerably more impractical. However, conceiving of the process of random selection and assignment in this way does provide a better sense of how members of the treatment and control groups can be equal in expectation—that is, *equal, on average, in the population.*

As explained in Chapter 3, a necessary condition for making a causal inference about the impact of an educational treatment is that assignment of students to their treatment or control status be exogenous. In the experiment depicted in Figure 4.1, we ensure the required exogeneity by the faithful implementation of the random assignment of participants to experimental conditions. Under the random assignment process, each sampled participant is destined with known probability to a particular experimental condition in a process that is completely independent of the participant's personal attributes, backgrounds, choices, and motivations. Participants cannot choose the experimental condition to which they are assigned, nor can they manipulate their assignment once received. Without the *random*—and, therefore, *exogenous*—assignment of participants to experimental conditions, you could not claim that participants in the treatment and control groups were equal in expectation before the start of the experiment. Consequently, your ability to draw unbiased causal conclusions from your findings would be challenged, and the internal validity of your experiment impaired.

An Example of a Two-Group Experiment

To illustrate the design and implementation of a randomized experiment, we turn to the evaluation of the consequences for student achievement of the scholarship offer that the SCSF provided to a random sample of low-income families in New York City. Recognizing that funding constraints would limit participation in the NYSP, a research group led by William Howell and Paul Peterson suggested that a lottery be used to decide which volunteer families would receive the offer of a scholarship to help pay a child's tuition at a private elementary school. Howell and Peterson then commissioned Mathematica Policy Research, an organization with experience in conducting high-quality random-assignment evaluations, to conduct the lottery, follow participating families for three years, and collect the data that would be used to evaluate how voucher receipt impacted children's subsequent academic achievement.[5] Mathematica investigators randomly assigned 1,300 families to a treatment group that received vouchers, and 960 families to a control (or comparison) group that did not.[6,7]

---

5. Using the term made popular by Milton Friedman (and discussed in Chapter 2), the "offer of a scholarship" is often referred to as the "receipt of a voucher."
6. Notice that the sizes of the treatment and control groups do not have to be identical.
7. To reduce attrition of participants from the study, control group families were offered modest payments to induce them to complete the same tests and surveys that voucher recipients completed.

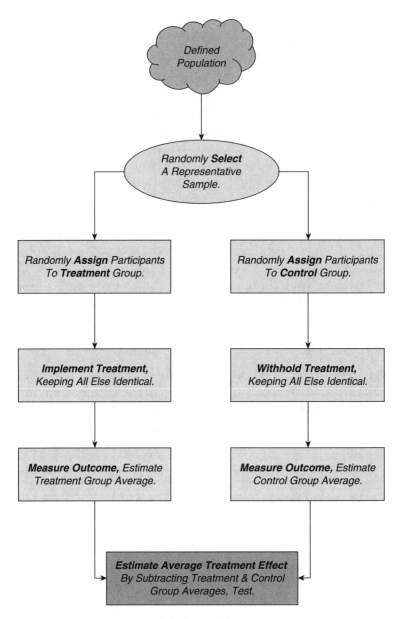

Figure 4.1 Conducting a two-group randomized experiment.

To interpret the results of this experimental evaluation of the NYSP, it is important to understand what it means for a family to be a member of either the treatment or the control group. Assignment to the treatment group meant that the family received a voucher worth as much as $1,400 toward the cost of private-school tuition. It did not mean that the relevant child of every family assigned to the treatment group actually *attended* a private school. Parents who received vouchers had to locate a private school for their child that was to their liking, enroll their child in the school, pay the difference between the value of the voucher and the school's tuition, and deal with any ensuing logistical details, such as arranging transportation to the school for their child. Not surprisingly, about one in five families that received vouchers ended up not sending their child to a private school. Similarly, it is also important to keep in mind that assignment to the control group meant that the family did not receive a tuition voucher. The family still had all of the educational choices available to it that it had before volunteering to participate in the experiment. In particular, families in the control group could still send their children to a private school. In fact, 5% of control group families did so.[8]

On its face, the NYSP evaluation has all the attributes of a "classic" two-group randomized experiment. However, it is important to be clear about the question that the experiment addressed, and the population to which the results apply. The "defined population" from which students who participated in the NYSP experiment were sampled does *not* include all children from low-income families who were enrolled in the relevant grades of the New York City school system in 1997. Instead, it is defined as the population of 11,105 children from low-income families in the New York City public school system whose parents submitted applications for participation in the scholarship program. These *volunteers* constituted the *frame* from which the 2,260 students who actually participated in the experiment were randomly and representatively sampled, and who were subsequently randomly assigned by investigators to the treatment (receipt of voucher) or control (no receipt of voucher) group. Consequently, the external validity of the research findings is limited to generalizations to this defined population and not to the broader population of children from low-income families in the New York City public schools. The reason is that the population of volunteer applicants may differ in critical unobserved ways from eligible families that did not volunteer. For example, applicant families may have hidden reservoirs of entrepreneurship, motivation, and commitment that potentially distinguished them

8. Howell & Peterson (2006), p. 204.

from the eligible families that did not apply for private-school tuition vouchers.

It is also critical to understand that the primary question that the NYSP evaluation addressed concerned the impact of the family's receipt of a tuition voucher on the student's ultimate academic achievement. This is an important topic because, as we discussed in Chapter 2, many governments provide families with vouchers to help pay their children's tuitions at private schools. However, it is important to distinguish the question of whether voucher receipt impacts student achievement from the question of whether attendance at a private school instead of a public school impacts student achievement. In Chapter 11, we explain how instrumental-variables estimation can provide a method of using the lottery-outcome information from random-assignment experiments to address this second research question. However, the analysis described in this chapter addresses the first question, whether the randomized *receipt* of a voucher had a causal impact on children's subsequent educational achievement.

Analyzing Data from Randomized Experiments

The Better Your Research Design, the Simpler Your Data Analysis

One advantage of designing your research as a randomized experiment is that subsequent data analysis can be very straightforward. The reason is that random assignment renders the treatment and control groups equal in expectation on all observed and unobserved dimensions. As a result, you do not need to employ complex data-analytic strategies to adjust your findings for inadvertent unobserved background differences between the treatment and control groups.

For example, in the NYSP evaluation, its causal impact on students' subsequent academic achievement can be estimated easily by contrasting the sample average values of academic achievement between students in the "voucher" and "no voucher" groups. We illustrate this in the upper panel of Table 4.1, for a subsample of African-American children that we have purposefully selected from the NYSP study, using the definitions of race/ethnicity applied by the original authors.[9] For presentational simplicity, we focus on the 521 African-American children who completed

---

9. We thank Don Lara, the director of administration at Mathematica Policy Research, for providing the NYSP data.

Table 4.1 Alternative analyses of the impact of voucher receipt (*VOUCHER*) on the third-grade academic achievement (*POST_ACH*) for a subsample of 521 African-American children randomly assigned to either a "voucher" treatment or a "no voucher" control group (*n* = 521)

Strategy #1: Two-Group t-Test

	Number of Observations	Sample Mean	Sample Standard Deviation	Standard Error
VOUCHER = 1	291	26.029	19.754	1.158
VOUCHER = 0	230	21.130	18.172	1.198
Difference		4.899		1.683
t-statistic		2.911		
df		519		
p-value		0.004		

Strategy #2: Linear Regression Analysis of POST_ACH on VOUCHER

Predictor	Parameter	Parameter Estimate	Standard Error	*t*-Statistic	*p*-value
INTERCEPT	β_0	21.130	1.258	16.80	0.000
VOUCHER	β_1	4.899	1.683	2.911	0.004
R^2 Statistic		0.016			
Residual Variance		19.072			

Strategy #3: Linear Regression Analysis of POST_ACH on VOUCHER, with PRE_ACH as Covariate

Predictor	Parameter	Parameter Estimate	Standard Error	*t*-Statistic	*p*-value
INTERCEPT	β_0	7.719	1.163	6.64	0.000
VOUCHER	β_1	4.098	1.269	3.23	0.001
PRE_ACH	γ	0.687	0.035	19.90	0.000
R^2 Statistic		0.442			
Residual Variance		14.373			

achievement tests prior to entering the NYSP experiment and at the end of their third year of participation. Of these, 291 were participants in the "voucher receipt" group and 230 in the "no voucher" group. Following the procedure adopted by Howell et al. (2002), we have averaged each child's national percentile scores on the reading and mathematics tests to obtain variables measuring composite academic achievement on entry into the study (which we refer to subsequently as covariate *PRE_ACH*) and after the third year of the experiment (which we refer to subsequently as outcome *POST_ACH*).

In the top panel of Table 4.1, we present the results of a two-sample t-test conducted on the third-year academic outcome, by experimental condition.[10] Notice that the sample average achievement of African-American children in the "voucher" and "no voucher" groups at the end of the third year—26.03 and 21.13, respectively—differs by almost 5 points, in favor of the treatment group. This ATE is statistically significant at the 0.05 level ($t = 2.911$, $df = 519$, p-value = 0.004, two-sided test), and we conclude that receipt of a private-school tuition voucher did indeed cause African-American children in this population to achieve at higher levels.

Of course, testing the equality of outcome means between the treatment and control groups can also be completed using ordinary least-squares (OLS) regression analysis, with identical results. In our NYSP subsample of African-American children, for instance, we can regress third-year academic achievement on dichotomous "question" predictor, VOUCHER, which we have defined to indicate whether a participant received a private-school tuition voucher ($= 1$), or not ($= 0$). Our hypothesized regression model is

$$POST\_ACH_i = \beta_0 + \beta_1 VOUCHER_i + \varepsilon_i \qquad (4.1)$$

where $POST\_ACH_i$ is the academic achievement of the ith student, β_0 and β_1 are the regression intercept and slope parameters, respectively, and the ε_i are residuals, subject to the usual OLS distributional assumptions.[11] Because our single question predictor—VOUCHER—is dichotomous (and coded 0/1), the intercept parameter represents the average academic achievement of control group (*no voucher*) participants, in the population. The slope parameter β_1 represents the average treatment effect—the population average difference in academic achievement between children who received a voucher and those who did not—and is therefore the parameter of central interest in the regression analysis.[12] We have fitted

---

10. Note that this is a pooled t-test, in which we assume that the population variance of the outcome is identical in the treatment and control groups.
11. As usual, each person is assumed to draw their residual randomly and independently from an identical normal distribution with mean zero and homoscedastic variance, σ_ε^2.
12. Although we distinguish *two* experimental conditions—"voucher" versus "no voucher"— as usual, we need only a single dichotomous predictor to separate these groups. We could have created two dummy predictors to represent them—for instance, (a) VOUCHER, coded 1 when a participant was in the treatment group, and (b) NOVOUCHER, coded 1 when a participant was in the control group. However, as is well known, it is unnecessary to include both of these question predictors in the regression model, because membership in the treatment and control groups is mutually exclusive, which implies that predictors VOUCHER and NOVOUCHER are perfectly collinear. Therefore, one can be omitted from the model, thereby defining a "reference category." In the model

this model in our subsample of African-American children and present the obtained OLS parameter estimates and goodness-of-fit statistics in the middle panel of Table 4.1.

Notice that the summary statistics generated in the regression and t-test analyses are identical. In the regression analysis, the estimated value of slope parameter β_1 is 4.899, replicating the estimated value of the average treatment effect obtained in the prior t-test analysis. Notice, in addition, that the inferential statistics accompanying the estimated slope parameter, including the standard error of 1.683 associated with the average treatment effect, the t-statistic on β_1 of 2.91, and the p-value of 0.004, are identical to those obtained in the earlier t-test. So, either analysis confirms that the "voucher"/"no voucher" outcome difference is different from 0, in the population ($\alpha = 0.05$).

Of course, you can easily extend the use of such simple statistical techniques for analyzing two-group experimental data to accommodate more complex research designs. For instance, you can extend both the t-test and the regression approaches to handle comparisons among multiple experimental groups, in addition to a control group. Let's suppose, for instance, that investigators in the NYSP experiment had implemented two concurrent voucher treatments, each providing a private-school tuition voucher, but of different monetary value—for example, $1,400 and $4,200 per annum. Families and their children could still have been assigned by lottery to either of these treatment conditions or to the control group. In order to address more complex research questions, subsequent data analyses would have contrasted academic outcomes across the three groups thus defined. For instance, investigators could have used *multiple* regression analysis with the two voucher treatments represented by a pair of dichotomous predictors, *VOUCHER1* and *VOUCHER2*, each coded 0/1 to distinguish each of the voucher conditions from the control group condition. They could then ask the "global" question of whether provision of a voucher (irrespective of its value) affected student outcomes by testing the hypothesis that both the *VOUCHER1* and *VOUCHER2* predictors simultaneously had no impact. It would also be possible to investigate subsequently whether the more valuable voucher had a greater impact on children's academic achievement than did the less valuable one by testing the null hypothesis that the coefficients associated with the two predictors were identical, in the population. Standard data-analytic texts provide detailed guidance for these kinds of statistical analyses.

---

in Equation 4.1, we have omitted the predictor that identifies members of the control group.

Finally, if some children in the treatment or control groups attended the same school subsequently, we would need to modify the analyses to accommodate the more complex error covariance structure that would be present under such clustering. Random effects analyses, multilevel modeling, and generalized least-squares (GLS) regression analysis all provide the required extensions, each appropriate under different restrictions and assumptions. We mention these methods here only in passing, because we return to the issue of participants being clustered in hierarchies—in classrooms, schools, and districts—in Chapter 7, where we grapple more intimately with the idiosyncrasies of the educational setting. For now, we seek only to establish that OLS regression analysis is an acceptable starting point for the analysis of experimental data.

Bias and Precision in the Estimation of Experimental Effects

When we used linear regression analysis to estimate the causal effect of voucher receipt on the academic achievement of our subsample of African-American children (in the middle panel of Table 4.1), the OLS-estimated coefficient on the *VOUCHER* question predictor was our focus of attention. Since the estimated coefficient was positive, statistically significant, and had a magnitude of about 5 points, we concluded that voucher receipt was indeed responsible for increasing the achievement of these students by that amount.

Since we always rely on the estimate of a parameter like this to make a causal inference, it is important that the estimators we employ—like the OLS estimator of regression slope in our NYSP example—have *optimal* statistical properties. Two such properties that are of immense importance in all statistical analyses, including analyses of experimental data, are the *bias* and *precision* of an estimator. In using statistical analyses to support statements about the causal effect of voucher receipt on the academic achievement of African-American children at the end of the third grade, we would like the OLS estimate of the *VOUCHER* impact to be both *unbiased* and as *precise* as possible given the data.

Technical definitions of an estimator's bias and precision are deeply rooted in the central principles of statistical analysis. To understand them conceptually, you must first recall the process of statistical inference itself, which consists of a series of well-defined steps. The process begins when you draw a representative sample of participants from a defined population, assign sample members to different treatments, measure their outcomes, and use these data to estimate the central parameter of interest. Finally, you conduct statistical tests to confirm that your inferences can be generalized validly to the underlying population from which you originally drew the sample.

With this standard inferential machinery in place, let us engage in a "thought experiment." Imagine that we could replicate this entire process of sampling, estimation, and inference many thousands of times, returning sampled members to the population each time with their memories erased and their original condition restored. A process of replication like this would provide many thousands of legitimate estimates of the parameter that is the focus of our research question—in our case, thousands of OLS estimates of the regression slope associated with question predictor *VOUCHER*. For each replication, we would draw a new and different sample randomly from the population and repeat the entire process of experimentation, data collection, and parameter estimation. The many replicate OLS estimates of the impact of voucher receipt would differ, of course, as a result of the natural idiosyncrasies of random sampling. In one replication, for instance, we might obtain an OLS estimate of the *VOUCHER* regression slope of 4.899, as in our current study. In the next replication, the estimate might have a value of 2.7. In a third replication, it might be 6.2.

If you could actually engage in this tedious process of replication, you could also produce a histogram of all the burgeoning pool of replicated estimates. Imagine what this hypothetical histogram would look like. If the estimator had been adequately designed to summarize the data appropriately each time, where would you want the center of the histogram of all these replicated values to lie? What kind of spread would you want it to have? Questions like these are relatively easy to answer. To feel secure that an estimator had been well designed as a credible summary of the population average treatment effect, you would want the hypothetical distribution of all these many replicated values to have two important properties.

First, even though the replicated values would be scattered as a result of the idiosyncrasies of random sampling, you want them to be scattered in some reasonable way around the "correct" answer. That is, you would hope that their replicated values would be centered on the actual value of the population parameter that you were trying to estimate. Suppose, for instance, that the population effect of voucher receipt is actually to add 4.5 points to a student's academic achievement. On average then, the many OLS estimates of this parameter that you obtained in your replications should be scattered around a value of 4.5. In fact, you would probably hope that your many OLS estimates of the *VOUCHER* regression slope—if you had the time and money to obtain them—would ultimately average out to the actual population value of 4.5. If this were the case, then you would be able to say that the OLS estimator was an unbiased estimator of the *VOUCHER* regression slope. This means that although an estimate may not actually equal the underlying population parameter value on any particular occasion of sampling, over many replications the estimates would average to that value. Returning to the world of actual research practice, *unbiasedness* refers to the condition in which, if you were to carry out only a single experiment and analysis, the obtained OLS regression slope would provide an estimated value of the critical parameter that was, on average, "on target."

A second important statistical property that you would like for any estimator is *precision*. In our preceding thought experiment, one estimator would be more precise than another if the scatter that was induced in the estimated values during the hypothetical process of endless replication were smaller. For instance, in our NYSP example, you would undoubtedly find it quite reassuring if the multiple OLS estimates that you obtained over the many replications were grouped very tightly together, rather than being scattered far and wide. The notion of "precision" is a statistical statement about the possible scatter of the many replicated values. Estimators that tend to provide widely scattered estimates on multiple replications are regarded as being *less precise* than those that provide tightly clustered values.

A reasonable summary of an estimator's precision is the *standard deviation* of the many replicated estimates. This is, in fact, the rationale that underlies the *standard error* statistic, which is *the standard deviation of the many estimates* that would be provided in a hypothetical process of replication like the one we have described.[13] If you knew the value of such a standard error statistic for the OLS-estimated *VOUCHER* regression slope, and it were small, then you would anticipate that the many values of the *VOUCHER* regression slope that could be obtained in endless replication would be tightly clustered together. In other words, you could regard the OLS-estimated *VOUCHER* regression slope as being a more precise estimate of the population slope than some other statistic that had a large standard error.

Of course, we are not typically inclined to replicate the entire research process many times simply for the purpose of estimating the standard error of the critical parameter. Fortunately, you do not need to engage in such tedium, providing you are willing to make a set of very particular assumptions. The assumptions, which are described in more detail later, concern a judgment that the scatter of the data in our sample provides a

---

13. Technically, it is the standard deviation of the estimates obtained in infinite re-sampling from a population in which the null hypothesis (that the target parameter is zero) is true.

good estimate of what the data scatter in the underlying population is like. If these assumptions hold, you can obtain not only an estimate of the parameter of interest itself (such as the OLS-estimated *VOUCHER* regression slope) from a single replication of the research, but also an estimate of its standard error.[14]

In the middle panel of Table 4.1, where we display the results of using OLS regression analysis to estimate the average treatment effect in our single subsample of African-American children from the NYSP experiment, we estimate the standard error of the estimated *VOUCHER* regression slope to be 1.683 (about one-third of the size of the slope estimate itself, 4.90). Providing that the assumptions underpinning the OLS estimation process are met in our regression analysis, this estimated standard error gives us great confidence that we likely could not have gotten our particular value of the slope estimate (4.90) accidentally, as a result of the idiosyncrasies of sampling from a population in which there was actually no relationship between voucher receipt and student academic achievement.

Clearly, it makes sense to use estimators that are both *unbiased* and as *precise* as possible. Fortunately, after much technical work in statistical theory, stretching back over a century, methodologists have proven that, *providing its underlying assumptions are met*, an OLS estimator of a regression slope is the best linear unbiased estimator of a linear relationship that can be devised for a given dataset.[15] This means that not only is an OLS estimate an unbiased estimate of the underlying population linear regression slope, it also has the smallest standard error—that is, it is the most precise—among all possible estimators that might be devised from the same data. Consequently, in empirical research that requires the estimation of regression slopes, it makes sense not only to choose OLS

---

14. Today, using high-speed computing, there are ways of estimating standard errors, such as the *jackknife* (Miller, 1974) and the *bootstrap*, (Efron & Tibshirani, 1998), which are "nonparametric" and do not make strong distributional assumptions. Instead, they use a process of "resampling from the sample," which matches our hypothetical "thought experiment," to obtain many estimates of the parameter of interest and then estimate the standard deviation of these multiple estimates to estimate the standard error. When you apply these techniques, you replace the standard OLS parametric assumptions with the raw power of computers and use that power to re-sample, not from the population itself, but from the sample you have already drawn from that population! This idea is founded on the notion that a random sample drawn from a random sample of a population is also a random sample from the population itself.

15. There are other well-known estimators of the regression slope, including those that minimize the *mean absolute deviation* of the data points from the trend line, which has been generalized to provide the methods of quantile regression, and regression based on ranks.

methods as the technique for addressing the research questions but, more importantly, to make sure that all its assumptions are met. It is this last point that is critical for the development in the rest of our book.

But, what are these critical assumptions and how do they impact the bias and precision of the OLS estimator? In specifying a regression model—like the one in Equation 4.1—you make assumptions about both the *structural* and *stochastic* parts of the model. In the structural component of the model (which contains the intercept, the predictors, and the slope parameters), you assume that the hypothesized relationship between outcome and predictor is linear—that unit differences in the predictor correspond to equal differences in the outcome at every level of the predictor. If you suspect that this assumption may not be valid, then you can usually seek transformations of the outcome or the predictor to achieve linearity. In our NYSP example, we are not concerned about the linearity assumption as our principal predictor is a dichotomy that describes voucher receipt. This means that there is only a single unit difference in the predictor with which we are concerned, and that is the difference between assigning a child to the control or the treatment group. In cases in which continuous predictors are included in the regression model, it is more pressing to make sure that the linearity assumption is met.

Notice the presence of the residual in the hypothesized regression model in Equation 4.1. These residuals, by their presence in the model, are also statements about the population, but the statements are about stochastic—not structural—properties. They stipulate that we are willing to believe, in the population, that some unknown part of the value of the outcome for each individual is not directly attributable to the effects of predictors that we have included in the model—in our case, the single predictor, *VOUCHER*. Then, as discussed earlier, to proceed with statistical inference in the context of a single sample of data, we must adopt a set of viable assumptions about the population distribution of the residuals. Under the OLS fitting method, for instance, we assume that residuals are randomly and independently drawn from a distribution that has a zero mean value and an unknown but homoscedastic (that is, constant) variance in the population.[16] Each part of this statement affects a different facet of

---

16. Notice that we have not stipulated that the population residuals are drawn from a *normal* distribution, despite the common practice of assuming that they are normally distributed when standard regression analysis is conducted. We have taken this subtle step because the actual algebraic formulation of the OLS estimate of the regression slope, and its unbiasedness property, derive only from a fitting algorithm that minimizes the sum-of-squared residuals, regardless of their distribution. It is the subsequent provision of ancillary inferential statistics—the critical values and *p*-values of the associated small-sample statistical tests—that depend upon the normal theory assumption.

the OLS estimation process. For instance, that the residuals are "randomly and independently drawn" is the make-or-break assumption for the *unbiasedness* property of the OLS estimator of regression slope. In particular, for this assumption to be true, the regression residuals must be *completely unrelated to any predictors* that are included in the regression model. If you violate this "randomness" assumption—for instance, if the values of the residuals in Equation 4.1 are correlated with the values of predictor, *VOUCHER*, for some reason—then the OLS estimate of regression parameter, β_1, will be a biased estimate of the population average treatment effect.

Let us return to the second property of an OLS estimator that we have deemed important—the property of precision. We have stated earlier that, providing its underlying assumptions are met, an OLS estimate is the most precise estimate of a regression slope that can be devised from a given set of data, and we have introduced the concept of the standard error of the estimated slope to summarize that precision. In our presentation, we have argued that the value of the standard error of the slope estimate depends not only on the data but also on the distributional assumptions made about the population residuals—that they are *homoscedastic* and, ultimately, normally distributed. In fact, adopting these assumptions and provided that the residual homoscedasticity assumption holds, standard regression texts tell us that the estimated standard error of the OLS-estimated *VOUCHER* regression slope in Equation 4.1 is

$$\begin{pmatrix} Standard \\ Error \\ of\ \widehat{\beta}_1 \end{pmatrix} = \sqrt{\frac{\hat{\sigma}_\varepsilon^2}{\sum_{i=1}^{n}\left(VOUCHER_i - \overline{VOUCHER_\bullet}\right)^2}} \tag{4.2}$$

where, on the right-hand side of the equation and within the square root sign, the numerator contains the estimated variance of the residuals, $\hat{\sigma}_\varepsilon^2$, and the denominator contains the sum of squared deviations of the values of predictor *VOUCHER* around their sample mean, $\overline{VOUCHER_\bullet}$. A similar expression for standard error could be crafted if there were multiple predictors present in the model. For our purposes, however, it is sufficient to focus on the single predictor case and the expression in Equation 4.2.

Finally, it is also worth noting that, under the normal theory assumption, an OLS estimate of a regression slope is identical to the maximum-likelihood estimate (MLE). Typically, in standard regression analysis, such hairs are not split and the assumption that population residuals are normally distributed is often bundled immediately into the standard expression of the assumptions.

Inspection of this expression for standard error provides insight into the precision of the OLS estimator of regression slope that has critical implications for data analysis. It is clear from Equation 4.2 that the precision of an OLS slope estimator depends on the variance of the residuals in the particular analysis. Datasets that generate extensive scatter in the residuals lead to OLS estimates of slope that are not very precise. This suggests that if you could design your research so that the residual variance was smaller, then the standard error of your OLS slope estimate would be reduced. Increased precision thus leads to an increase in the magnitude of the t-statistic associated with the regression slope,[17] and a corresponding improvement in your ability to reject the null hypothesis that the regression slope is 0, in the population. As we describe in Chapter 6, we can interpret an improvement in our ability to reject a null hypothesis, all else being equal, as an improvement in the *statistical power* of the analyses. Thus, the lesson we learn here is that, if we use OLS methods and the NYSP data to estimate the average treatment effect of voucher assignment, finding ways to reduce the residual variance present in the regression analysis leads to greater precision for the estimated treatment effect and greater power in determining whether voucher assignment has made a difference to children's subsequent academic achievement.

It is the desire to reduce the magnitude of the residual variation that motivates the inclusion of covariates as predictors in the analysis of experimental data. If you return to Table 4.1 and compare the results of the two regression analyses reported in its middle and bottom panels, you will notice some interesting differences between them. In the middle panel, we have regressed academic achievement on the *VOUCHER* question predictor. The randomization of voucher assignment to participants ensures that the *VOUCHER* predictor is uncorrelated with the residuals in the hypothesized regression model, ensures that our estimate of the treatment effect is unbiased, and permits us to declare that receipt of a private-school tuition voucher *caused* these children's academic achievement to rise by almost 5 points, a statistically significant effect ($p <0.004$; two-sided test). In the bottom panel of the table, we have added a control predictor to the analysis, *PRE_ACH*, the student's academic achievement prior to enrollment in the NYSP experiment. In this second regression analysis, voucher receipt also has a statistically significant and positive causal impact on children's academic achievement ($p <0.001$; two-sided test). Our estimate of its effect, although a little smaller than the estimate obtained in the middle panel, has about the same magnitude, just over 4 points.

---

17. The t-statistic is the ratio of the slope estimate to its standard error.

We are not concerned here with the differences between these two estimates of the causal effect. Because the assignment of vouchers to families and children was random and exogenous, both are unbiased estimates of the average treatment effect in the population.[18] The question we are asking, instead, is: What advantage was there to including the covariate in the regression analysis in the bottom panel, if we could already make an unbiased causal interpretation on the basis of the middle panel? The answer concerns *precision*. Notice that the inclusion of the covariate in the regression analysis in the bottom panel has reduced the magnitude of the residual variance by 25%, from a value of 19.072 in the middle panel to 14.373 in the bottom panel.[19] This has occurred because the prior test score is an important predictor of third-grade academic achievement, and so its inclusion has predicted additional variation in the outcome, with a consequent reduction in the unexplained variation that is represented by the residuals.

This reduction in residual variance is reflected in a substantial reduction in the standard error of the estimated *VOUCHER* regression slope (from 1.683 in the middle panel to 1.269 in the bottom panel). As a consequence, the t-statistic associated with the *VOUCHER* slope rises from 2.911 to 3.23, and we obtain a p-value indicating an even smaller probability that our data derive from a population in which the average treatment effect is 0.[20] Thus, by including the covariate—even though we did not need it to obtain an unbiased estimate of the treatment effect—we enjoy an improvement in statistical power, at the same sample size. This gain in power is reflected in the reduction of the associated p-value from 0.004 to 0.001.

It is important to keep in mind why appropriate covariates are often included in analyses of experimental data. It is certainly not to reduce bias. If you have randomly assigned participants to experimental conditions, then your estimate of the average treatment effect will be unbiased. If your treatment assignment was flawed and not random, then there is little you can do to avoid bias. Regardless of how many covariates you

---

18. Different unbiased estimators of the same population parameter often provide differently valued estimates of the same effect, in the same sample. This is neither unusual, nor problematic, because each estimator is using the data to offer its own "best guess" as to the value of the underlying population parameter. For instance, in a symmetric distribution, the *mean, median,* and *mode* are all unbiased estimators of the "center" of a normally distributed variable in the population. But, each weights the elements of the sample data differently and so the values of the three estimators are unlikely to be identical, even in the same sample of data.

19. Notice that the R^2 statistic has risen correspondingly, from 0.016 to 0.442.

20. Notice that this increase in the t-statistic occurs despite a reduction in the parameter estimate itself from 4.899 to 4.098.

include and whatever stories you tell to motivate their inclusion, you will find it hard to convince your audience that you have removed all the potential bias by "controlling" for these features. Rarely can you fix *by analysis* what you bungled *by design* (Light, Singer, & Willett, 1990). The purpose of incorporating relevant covariates into an analysis of experimental data is to reduce residual variation, decrease standard errors, and increase statistical power.

Covariates appropriate for inclusion in an analysis of experimental data include important exogenous characteristics of individuals that do not vary over time, such as gender and race, and variables whose values are measured *prior* to random assignment. The baseline test scores included in Howell and Peterson's regression model fall into this second category. It is important to keep in mind that it is inappropriate to include as covariates variables whose values are measured after random assignment has been completed because they may be endogenous. An example of the latter would be scores on tests that students took at the *end* of their first year in the NYSP experiment. These latter scores are not candidates for inclusion as covariates in the regression model because their values may have been affected by students' participation in the experiment. Their inclusion would lead to bias in the estimate of the impact of voucher receipt on student achievement measured at the end of three years of participation. We return to these issues throughout the rest of the book, as they are central to our ability to employ a variety of research designs to obtain unbiased estimates of causal effects.

What to Read Next

Larry Orr's 1999 book, *Social Experiments*, describes many challenges in using randomized experiments to evaluate public programs. The book also provides interesting examples from many randomized experiments conducted in the United States. *Learning More from Social Experiments*, edited by Howard Bloom (2005), provides insightful explanations of ways to use data from randomized experiments to explain why the effectiveness of many programs varies from site to site, and the mechanisms through which public programs have their impacts.

5

Challenges in Designing, Implementing, and Learning from Randomized Experiments

In 2002, the U.S. federal government's Institute of Education Sciences created the What Works Clearinghouse (WWC), the mission of which is to evaluate evidence on the effectiveness of education programs, practices, and policies, and to make its conclusions available publicly through its website, http://www.whatworks.ed.gov.[1] As of May 2009, WWC had reviewed more than 2,100 studies to evaluate the effectiveness of interventions in seven topical areas, one of which was elementary-school mathematics. The analysts at WWC examined 301 studies evaluating the effectiveness of 73 different interventions for improving elementary-school students' mathematical skills. They concluded that 97% of the evaluations (292 out of 301) did not meet the WWC's predefined standards for supporting causal inferences, and consequently, did not provide a basis for judging the effectiveness of these interventions.[2] Thus, while the WWC has great promise as a resource for educational decision makers, its value is constrained markedly by the lack of reliable evidence about the effectiveness of education programs and practices.

Random-assignment experiments have enormous potential to fill this void in the evidence. Their strengths include conceptual transparency and the compelling nature of the evidence they can provide. However, carrying

---

1. National Board for Education Sciences (2008, pp. 25–27).
2. http://ies.ed.gov/ncee/wwc/reports/elementary_math/eday_math/, accessed May 29, 2009. We are indebted to Roberto Agodini of Mathematica Policy Research, the principal investigator for What Works Clearinghouse reviews of elementary school math interventions, for providing us with up-to-date information on the number of studies his team had reviewed.

out random-assignment experiments successfully requires great skill and judgment. One reason for this is that there are many critical decisions involved in their design and implementation. A second is that there are many threats to the internal and external validity of randomized experiments, most involving unanticipated actions and responses by participants. A third reason is that implementing random-assignment experiments successfully typically requires an especially high level of cooperation from many groups. Obtaining and retaining the requisite cooperation often require communication skills, negotiating skills, and the ability to respond creatively to unexpected challenges. Fortunately, the body of knowledge about how to design and implement random-assignment experiments successfully in different settings is growing steadily, as is the number of researchers who possess and utilize this knowledge.

In this chapter, we describe some of the decisions involved in designing randomized experiments, some of the threats to the validity of their results, and some promising strategies for obtaining support for randomized experiments from stakeholders. We illustrate these decisions and challenges with examples from several high-quality random-assignment studies. Some of these studies we have already introduced, such as the New York Scholarship Program (NYSP) evaluation and the evaluation of the Tennessee Student/Teacher Achievement Ratio (STAR) experiment. We also introduce and draw on several new randomized experiments. One concerns career academies, an innovative approach to secondary-school education in the United States. Two others concern educational policy initiatives in India. We begin by describing the career academies study.

Critical Decisions in the Design of Experiments

Countries around the world have struggled with the design of secondary-school education programs. In many countries, students are given the option of enrolling in an academic track to prepare for post-secondary education or in a vocational track to prepare for work in a specific occupation. Critics of vocational education argue that it does not prepare students to cope with changing labor markets and that participating in vocational training closes off access to post-secondary education. While conceding these limitations of conventional vocational education programs, advocates argue that the solution lies in improving vocational programs rather than in abandoning the concept and requiring all adolescents to enroll in a traditional academic track.

One response to the call for a different kind of education, especially for students who do not thrive in conventional academic tracks, has been the creation of the *career academy*. The model was developed initially in Philadelphia, in the late 1960s, by Charles Bowser, executive director of the Urban Coalition, in collaboration with two private-sector employers. The first career academy, the Academy of Applied Electrical Science, opened at Edison High School in Philadelphia in 1969, and enrolled 30 tenth-grade students. From there, the concept spread quickly, especially in California. Today, there are more than 2,500 career academies in the United States, more than 750 of which are located in California.[3]

Several common principles motivate the structure and functioning of career academies. First, they are usually small learning communities embedded within larger high schools. Students in career academies take classes together for at least three years, taught by a team of teachers drawn from different disciplines. Second, they offer a college-preparatory curriculum with a career theme that integrates academic and career technical education. Third, generally they include partnerships with local employers who provide work-based learning opportunities, mentoring, and internships to career-academy students.

One reason that the number of career academies has grown so rapidly is that early research using observational designs found that students who enrolled in career academies had better academic outcomes—including higher test scores and grades, and better school-graduation and college-enrollment rates—than observationally similar students who were not enrolled in career academies. In this observational research, the treatment groups consisted of students who chose to enroll in a career academy, and the comparison groups consisted of students who enrolled in more conventional high-school programs and who, on average, had the same observed characteristics as the students in the career academies. Of course, an important criticism of such studies is that students who *chose* to enroll in a career academy may have differed in unobserved ways, such as in their educational motivation, from students in the comparison group. As a result, the results of these observational studies may be biased because differences in outcomes may have stemmed from the unobserved differences between the groups, rather than from differences in the educational treatments that the two groups received.

In 1993, one of the leading contract research firms in the United States, MDRC, undertook an experimental study to assess the educational impact of career academies (Kemple, 2008). Because MDRC conducted a randomized experimental study, the results of its research have received

---

3. The following website, accessed September 10, 2009, provides a description of the history of career academies: http://www.ncacinc.com/index.php?option=com_content&task=view&id=17&Itemid=28.

great attention in education-policy circles and have influenced the design of high-school programs for students who do not thrive in traditional college-track curricula. In designing their study, the MDRC research team made several important decisions that affected what would be learned ultimately from the experiment. All investigators face the same kinds of decisions in planning and executing experimental research. These decisions include: (a) how to define the treatment that is to be evaluated, (b) how to define the population from which study participants will be drawn, (c) what outcomes to measure for each participant, and (d) how long to track those participants over time. Below, we comment on each of these decisions, and their consequences, in the context of our career-academies example.

Defining the Treatment

Clearly, it makes sense to define carefully what the treatment is! Early in their effort to design the career-academies study, MDRC researchers had to face the heterogeneity that existed among the academies that were then in operation in the United States. They had to decide which particular academies would be the research sites in their study and, thereby, become potential exemplars for future academies. At the time, more than 1,000 academies were in operation in public high schools throughout the United States, and they differed in structure, practices, and the length of time they had been in operation. Some had been operating for longer than a decade; others were in their first or second year of operation. Some had embraced all three of the originator's design principles; others had only embraced one or two. Some academies were extremely popular and had many more applicants than their available places; others were still working to attract students.

After visiting many possible sites, the MDRC research team decided to include only academies that had been in operation for at least two years and that embraced all three of the original academy design principles. A consequence of this choice was that their evaluation would then address the impact of a *mature* academy and provide no guidance about the effectiveness of newly created academies. In addition, the randomization requirement of the research design necessitated that participating academies have excess enrollment demand and be willing to use a fair lottery to determine which students would be offered enrollment. In the end, MDRC identified ten career academies distributed across six states that fit the design criteria and were willing to participate in the study. All were located in urban school districts that had above-average school-dropout rates and served substantial percentages of African-American students,

Hispanic students, and students from low-income families. Three of the academies focused on electronics; other areas of focus included health occupations, business and finance, public service, travel and tourism, and video technology. Two of the academies served students in ninth through twelfth grades, and the others enrolled students in grades 10 through 12.

It is important to understand that the "treatment" to be evaluated in the MDRC experiment was actually an *offer* of a place in a career academy, in exactly the same way that the treatment of interest in the NYSP experiment that we described in Chapter 4 was an "offer" of a scholarship to help pay private-school tuition. Students who had good luck in the lottery and were assigned to the treatment group were not required to accept the offer of enrollment. Applicants who had bad luck in the lottery became part of the control group and could choose any other educational program except the career academy offered by their high school. This research design makes sense because career academies are voluntary programs.

However, it is important to understand the implications of the design. If all of the students assigned to the treatment accepted the enrollment offer and none of the students assigned to the control group managed to enroll in a career academy, then a study of the consequences of receiving an enrollment offer would be equivalent to a study of the consequences of actual enrollment in a career academy. However, 16% of the students in the MDRC treatment group decided not to accept the enrollment offer and instead enrolled in other academic programs. Yet, they remain part of the treatment group in MDRC analyses to evaluate the causal impact of the *offer* of treatment. This means that their educational and labor-market outcomes were averaged along with those of students who received an offer and did enroll in career academies, and this average was then compared to the educational outcomes for students in the control group, who did not receive a career-academy enrollment offer. In the language of experimental design, the MDRC experiment was an evaluation of the impact on student outcomes of an *intent* to provide the career-academy treatment, not the impact of the career-academy treatment itself on the student outcomes. This is important to keep in mind when evaluating the results.

To summarize, defining carefully the treatment that will be implemented in an experiment clearly involves tradeoffs, and the decision has great consequences. As a result of the MDRC decision-making process, the research could not answer the broad question: Is it a good investment for an urban school district to initiate career academies? Instead, it could only address the more specific question: Will an offer of enrollment in a mature career academy that embraces the original design principles and has excess demand result in better educational and labor-market outcomes for a particular population of students in urban school districts?

Defining the Population from Which Participants Will Be Sampled

Your choice of the population from which to sample participants for your study will, of course, determine the population to which the results of your experiment can be generalized. In practice, defining the population of potential participants can involve especially difficult tradeoffs when the experimental treatment is the *offer* of enrollment in a particular program, as was the case in the career-academies study. To illustrate these tradeoffs, consider two of the possible options that the MDRC investigators faced. The first option was to define the population of participating students as all ninth graders in a high school that contained a career academy participating in the study. The second option was to define the population of participants as all ninth graders in the school who, after being informed of the opportunities and obligations associated with enrolling in a career academy, expressed an active interest in enrolling.

Under the first option, a random sample of students would be chosen from the population of ninth graders in a school that housed a participating career academy. Then, a fair lottery would be used to assign members of the sample randomly to the treatment and the control group. Members of the treatment group would be offered enrollment in the career academy. If members of the control group asked about admission to the career academy, they would be told that admission was by lottery only and that they had not been chosen. They would be free to choose among the other academic programs offered by their school or any other high school.

Consider the practical consequences of this definition of the population. The assigned treatment group would include many students who actually wanted to enroll in the school's traditional college-preparatory curriculum and who were not interested in the occupational focus of the career academy. Consequently, the percentage of students in the treatment group who accepted the invitation to enroll in the career academy (the so-called take-up rate) would be very low (perhaps as low as 10%). The educational and labor-market outcomes for the other 90% of the students in the treatment group who declined the offer to enroll in a career academy would probably be the same, on average, as the outcomes for members of the control group. In subsequent analyses of the data, since the average outcomes for the treatment group (including those students who did not take up the offer) are to be compared with the average outcomes of those in the control group, one result of the low take-up rate may be an inability to reject the null hypothesis even if participation in a career academy improved outcomes for the 10% of students in the treatment group who accepted the offer. The only way to avoid this conclusion would be to include in the study students from a great many high schools containing career academies. This would make the research extremely expensive to conduct.

Now, consider the second option for defining the population of interest. The school would conduct information sessions in which they describe the career academy option to all ninth graders and explain that the selection of students to receive enrollment offers would be determined by lottery from among those students who demonstrate an active interest in enrolling by participating in an interview and completing an application. Among students randomly assigned to the treatment group from this population, the take-up rate would probably be much higher, perhaps as high as 80%. Again, assuming that participation in a career academy did result in improved outcomes, the higher take-up rate would increase dramatically the probability of rejecting the null hypothesis.

In summary, holding constant the size of the research budget, drawing the research sample from a population of students who express an active interest in career-academy enrollment increases the chances of demonstrating—by statistical analysis—that the offer of enrollment in a career academy improves outcomes. A cost of this choice is that the results provide conclusions that can be generalized only to the population of students who expressed an interest in participating in a career academy, not to the wider population of all students entering the relevant high-school grades. In contrast, drawing the research sample from the population of all students enrolled in the relevant grade in participating schools means that the results can be generalized to this latter population. The disadvantage is that you risk a low take-up rate for the offer, which, in turn, affects the statistical power you have to reject the null hypothesis that the treatment is no more effective than alternatives. Combating this problem would require increasing the sample size massively to improve statistical power and precision. Given the expense of conducting randomized experiments, it is not surprising MDRC investigators chose to draw their research samples from the population of students at each participating school who expressed an active interest in enrolling in their school's career academy.

Deciding Which Outcomes to Measure

From the outset, it was clear that the MDRC study would measure students' test scores, high-school graduation rates, and college-enrollment rates, outcomes that prior observational studies had found to be influenced by career-academy participation. The more difficult question was whether to measure other, nonacademic outcomes. After visiting several career academies and talking with their staffs about the interactive skills that career-academy students acquired during their internships, the MDRC research team decided to measure two quite different sets of additional outcomes. One set consisted of labor-market outcomes, such as employment rates and earnings. The second consisted of family-related outcomes, such as rates of marriage and child support. The logic was that improved labor-market earnings might lead to better marriage prospects for participants and provide more resources for child support.

Of course, as with all aspects of research design, the decision to measure a wide variety of outcomes involves costs. One type of cost is financial—it takes resources to collect, code, and process information on many outcomes. A second type of cost is the possibility that asking participants to provide a great deal of information on follow-up surveys increases the probability that they will drop out of the study, thereby magnifying the problem of attrition from the sample over time. Such attrition poses a significant threat to both the internal and external validity of the study. For these reasons, you must be judicious in deciding which outcomes to measure and how to collect that information in a manner that minimizes the burden on program participants.

Deciding How Long to Track Participants

Learning that a particular intervention has a long-term impact on student outcomes is valuable, and this is the argument for following the participants in an experiment for an extended period of time. From the outset, it was clear that the MDRC study would follow sampled participants for at least four years, the length of time needed for many program participants to graduate from high school and enroll in college. However, this proposed four-year follow-up would provide limited information, at best, on labor-market and family outcomes. For this reason, the research team decided to follow members of the sample for a total of 11 years.

Ultimately, this lengthy follow-up period proved critical to the research findings because results obtained after only four years of sample tracking demonstrated no statistically significant differences between the average academic skills, high-school graduation rates, and college-enrollment rates of students in the treatment and control groups. However, the results after 11 years (eight years after prospective high-school graduation) were quite different. On average, 11 years after the offer of career-academy enrollment, members of the treatment group were earning $2,000 (11%) more per year, on average, than members of the control group (Kemple, 2008). Moreover, the males in the treatment group had higher rates of marriage and of being custodial parents than did those in the control group. Thus, the disparity between the 11-year and the 4-year results provided compelling justification for the expense involved in electing the lengthy follow-up period.

As mentioned earlier, a second type of cost associated with lengthy research studies is the attrition of participants from the research sample. Attrition is a problem in all studies. Students move from one town to another, and do not leave forwarding addresses. Others become annoyed by researchers' questions and refuse further participation, even when they are compensated for completing the interviews. The major problem created by sample attrition is that it undermines the original random assignment of students to the treatment and control groups and, thereby, threatens both the internal and external validity of the experiment. The threat to internal validity is that students who abandon the treatment group may be different in unobserved ways, on average, from those who withdraw from the control group. This destroys the equality in expectation on which causal conclusions rely. The threat to external validity is that selective withdrawal of students from the research sample means that the investigators can no longer be sure to what population the results of the experiment can be generalized.

Of course, attrition from the research sample is more severe the longer the experiment runs. One implication is that it only makes sense to conduct a long-term experiment if the research budget is large enough to locate students who move, and to employ interviewers who are skilled in maintaining the cooperation of participants. The MDRC investigators were able to do this—a remarkably high 81% of the original research sample continued to provide information on their labor-market earnings 11 years after the experiment began! Of course, conducting a high-quality long-term randomized experiment is expensive. The MDRC career academy study cost approximately $12 million. This cost is modest, however, in comparison to the amount of money spent annually on high-school education programs and the importance of providing policymakers with accurate and credible advice on the effectiveness of a popular educational-program design.

Threats to the Validity of Randomized Experiments

In this section, we explain and illustrate some threats to the internal and external validity of randomized experiments. The list of threats to validity that we describe here is by no means exhaustive. We describe others in chapters to come. The purpose of this section is to emphasize that, although randomized experiments are the most effective way to learn about the causal impact of many educational interventions, they are by no means free of threats to their validity. In considering whether to conduct a randomized trial of a particular educational intervention, it is always important to make a list of the significant threats to both internal and external validity and to explore whether it is possible to design the experiment in a way that minimizes these threats.

Contamination of the Treatment–Control Contrast

One threat to the internal validity of a randomized experiment is that the behaviors of participants in the control group may be influenced by interactions with participants in the treatment group, and this can dilute the treatment–control contrast. For example, the ten career academies that were part of the MDRC random-assignment evaluation were all situated within large comprehensive high schools. Consequently, teachers in the career academies undoubtedly interacted with non–academy teachers in their schools. Similarly, students offered places in career academies (the treatment group) interacted with students who applied to their school's academy, but lost out in the lottery (the control group). It is possible that these interactions resulted in changes in the education received by control-group students. For example, non–academy teachers may have introduced some project-based learning activities after hearing from career academy teachers that they worked well. Similarly, students in the control group may have increased their efforts to obtain summer internships in local businesses after hearing about their value from students enrolled in career academies. The MDRC research team conducted surveys of students in the treatment and control groups in order to learn how different the educational experiences of the two groups were. They found that a larger percentage of treatment-group members than control-group members had been exposed to project-based learning and had summer internships. At the same time, some control-group members had participated in these activities. The researchers could not determine the extent to which these activities of the control-group members were influenced by the presence of career academies in their schools (Kemple, 2008).

Cross-overs

One common threat to the internal validity of a two-group randomized experiment occurs when participants "cross over" from the control group to the treatment group, or vice versa, after random assignment has taken place. In Project STAR, for instance, approximately 10% of students switched between the small- and regular-size classes between one grade and the next. These cross-overs jeopardized the internal validity of the experiment because they challenged the original exogeneity of the assignment to experimental conditions, and the consequent equality in expectation between the treatment and control groups that was required for drawing causal inferences. The cross-overs create the possibility that any higher-than-average academic achievement detected among children in small classes may have stemmed at least in part from the uncontrolled sorting of children with unobserved differences between the two experimental conditions. In fact, Krueger (1999) argued that cross-overs did not have a dramatic impact on the results of the Project STAR experiment. The strongest evidence that he cited in support of this conclusion was that the class-size effects that were detected were the largest in the first year of the experiment, before any cross-overs occurred. In Chapter 11, we describe how instrumental-variables estimation can be used to deal with the internal threat to validity created by such cross-overs.

Attrition from the Sample

In a similar fashion, the attrition of participants from the research sample poses an important threat to the validity of a random-assignment experiment. This is because the participants who choose to depart the study may differ from those who remain, in unobserved ways that affect the value of the outcome. Attrition is a particularly serious problem in all experiments that attempt to follow participants for a lengthy period of time. All three of the experiments conducted in the United States that we described earlier fit into this category: the MDRC career-academy experiment followed participants for 11 years, Project STAR for four years,[4] and the NYSP for three years. With such long periods of follow-up, attrition from the research sample was almost inevitable. Half of the students who were present in the Project-STAR kindergarten classes were missing from at least one class over the next three years of the experiment. Thirty-three percent of the students who were part of the initial analytic sample in the NYSP experiment did not take the achievement tests that provided the outcome measures at the end of the third year of the experiment (Howell & Peterson, 2006). Nineteen percent of the students in the MDRC evaluation of career academies did not complete the year 11 survey (Kemple, 2008; Kemple & Willner, 2008).

---

4. After the scheduled completion of the Project STAR experiment, Alan Krueger and Diane Whitmore Schanzenbach raised the funds to follow participants in Project STAR through elementary school and into high school (Krueger & Whitmore, 2000).

In what ways does such attrition affect validity? Attrition from the sample itself, regardless of whether it was from the treatment or control group, may simply make the sample less representative of the underlying population from which it was drawn, thereby undermining *external validity*. Attrition also threatens the *internal validity* of the experiment. The reason is that members who remain in the treatment group may no longer be equal in expectation to members remaining in the control group. Consequently, at least some part of any subsequent between-group differences in outcome could be due to unobserved differences that exist between the members who remain in the treatment and control groups after attrition, instead of being due to a causal effect of the experimental treatment.

One sensible step in evaluating the extent to which sample attrition poses a threat to the internal validity of a study is to examine whether the attrition rate is higher in the control group than in the treatment group, or vice versa. In Project STAR, for instance, 49% of the children assigned initially to small classes in kindergarten had left the experiment by its fourth year. The comparable figure for children assigned initially to regular-size classes was 52% (Krueger, 1999). The percentage of students in the control group of the NYSP who took the relevant achievement tests at the end of the second year of the experiment was 7 points lower than the percentage of students in the treatment group who did so. However, the percentages of the treatment and control groups in the original sample that took the tests at the end of year three of the experiment were similar (Howell & Peterson, 2006). In the career-academy experiment, 82% of the students offered a place in a career academy and 80% of those in the control group did not complete the survey administered in the study's eleventh year (Kemple & Willner, 2008).

Of course, although evidence that the attrition rates in the treatment and control groups of a randomized experiment are approximately equal is comforting, the patterns of attrition in the two groups could still be quite different. One way to examine this possibility is to capitalize on information from a baseline survey administered prior to random assignment to compare the sample distributions of the observed characteristics in the key groups. These include individuals who left the treatment group, those who left the control group, and those who remained in each of these groups. Evidence that the sample distributions of observed baseline characteristics in the four groups are very similar would support the case that attrition from the research sample did not jeopardize the internal validity of the experiment seriously, although such evidence is hardly definitive as it pertains only to the characteristics that were actually measured in the baseline survey. The evaluators of all three of the interventions described in this chapter (STAR, NYSP, and Career Academies) presented this kind of evidence to support the credibility of their causal findings.

Participation in an Experiment Itself Affects Participants' Behavior

We conduct randomized experiments in education and the social sciences in order to learn whether particular interventions have causal impacts on outcomes for well-defined populations, typically consisting of students, but in some cases, consisting of teachers, administrators, or parents. Implicit in the research design of an experiment is the assumption that simple *participation* in the research project does not, by itself, influence participant behaviors and outcomes. *Hawthorne* and *John Henry effects* are terms used to describe violations of this assumption. Hawthorne effects refer to changes in behavior among participants in an experiment that stem from their simply being subjects of study. John Henry effects occur when control-group members work harder to compete with their peers in the treatment group because they are unhappy about having been assigned to the control group.

Some critics of the Project STAR class-size experiment argue that the results of this experiment might have been contaminated by Hawthorne effects.[5] The hypothesis is that teachers who participated in the experiment may have worked extra hard as a result of knowing that they were being observed. Hawthorne effects would have posed an especially serious threat to the internal validity of the experiment if teachers in the treatment groups responded differently to simply being part of a study than did teachers in the control group. A different, but related, problem is that teachers of small classes may have surmised correctly that any evidence from the experiment which showed that smaller classes caused higher student achievement would lead the state government to authorize additional money for further class-size reductions in Tennessee. This potential response to possible use of the experimental results could also have led teachers to work particularly hard to improve their students' test scores during the years of the experiment, in order to improve their own working conditions after the experiment was over.

In his analysis of the data from the STAR experiment, Krueger (1999) argued that Hawthorne effects and responses to the surmised application of experimental findings were not important causes of differences in average student outcomes between treatment and control groups.

---

5. See, for example, Hoxby (2000, p. 1241).

He supported this position by noting that student achievement was inversely related to class size among students in the regular-size classes that made up the control group. Indeed, the magnitude of the estimated effect size for students in these classes was similar to that estimated in the treatment/control comparison. Since teachers and students in these control-group classes would not have been subject to differential Hawthorne effects, and would not have worked harder to make the case for small classes, Krueger sees this pattern in the non-experimental data as bolstering his claim that Hawthorne effects were of no importance in the outcomes of the STAR experiment.

An example of a John Henry effect, on the other hand, would involve students who lost out in the career-academy lottery being so annoyed by their bad luck that they worked harder in school than they would have had they not participated in the lottery. Such a John Henry effect would have resulted in a downward bias in the estimate of the value to students of being offered a place in a career academy. While it is rarely possible to discount totally the possibility that a John Henry effect has occurred, the length of the career-academy program makes it unlikely that this was a significant source of contamination. Annoyance at your bad luck in a lottery seems more likely to elicit a burst of energy for a short period than to result in a sustained increase in effort over a several-year period.

Gaining Support for Conducting Randomized Experiments: Examples from India

Although well-designed randomized experiments provide the most convincing evidence for the causal impact of a variety of educational interventions on student outcomes, they are often not popular among educators. Some are troubled by the practice of inviting families to apply for a particular educational opportunity for their child, such as enroll-ment in a career academy or a scholarship to attend a private school, but then denying access to those families that lose out in the randomization "lottery" and are then assigned to the control group. Many educators would prefer to recruit only as many applicants for an opportunity as there are positions available, or if excess demand exists, to choose only those students whom they see as most likely to benefit from that opportu-nity to participate in the treatment. Some educators are also uncomfortable with the requirement that participants who are assigned randomly to a control group cannot then gain access to an important opportunity, like a career academy or a tuition voucher, even if a space becomes available at a later date. In the next two sections, we describe two random-assignment experiments that researchers from the Abdul Latif Jameel Poverty Action Lab (J-PAL) conducted in order to learn about the benefits of two interventions to improve student achievement in cities in India. The first, which took place in two large cities, examines the consequences of a novel input strategy. The second, which took place in a rural area of India, examines the consequences of a change in incentives for primary-school teachers. The descriptions illustrate some of the practical challenges in conducting random-assignment experiments and some strategies for overcoming these challenges.

Evaluating an Innovative Input Approach

In 2005, 44% of Indian children aged between seven and 12 years could not read a basic paragraph, and 50% of them could not do simple subtraction, although most were enrolled in school.[6] The dominant strategy for improving the quality of education in schools serving low-income children in India and in other developing countries has been to provide more and better resources—such as additional books, blackboards, flip charts; smaller class sizes; and better educated teachers. One obstacle to this school-improvement strategy has been a shortage of funds. A second obstacle has been the difficulty in identifying those inputs that result consistently in greater student achievement. Of course, these two obstacles are related because finance ministers view skeptically requests from education ministers for additional funds to improve school quality when there is no firm evidence that past expenditures have improved student achievement.

In an attempt to improve education for the poor in India, the United Nations Children's Fund (UNICEF), in 1994, provided initial funding for the creation of a nongovernmental organization called *Pratham*, which would work with governmental agencies in India to improve school quality. One of Pratham's first initiatives was a remedial-education program in urban elementary schools, called the Balsakhi Program (the term means "the child's friend"). The program provided urban government schools with an additional teacher, a Balsakhi, who was recruited from the community. Most Balsakhis were young women who had finished secondary school. They received two weeks of training at the beginning of the school year. They also participated in monthly focus groups during the school year, at which they discussed classroom-management issues and new teaching aids designed by Pratham staff. The Balsakhis worked for two

---

6. Banerjee et al. (2007).

hours per day during the regular school day, with groups of 15 to 20 children in the third or fourth grade who had fallen behind academically. They taught a standardized curriculum that focused on the basic literacy and numeracy skills that were part of the regular first- and second-grade school curricula, but that the children in their care had not yet mastered.

The Balsakhi program proved popular in many Indian cities and grew rapidly. Regular teachers liked the program because it removed the least academically able students from their classes for part of the school day. Participating children liked it because the Balsakhi came from their home communities and tended to be more attuned to their problems than were regular teachers. Additional factors contributing to its popularity were the program's low cost and the ease with which it could be maintained and expanded. Indian cities typically have a large supply of young female secondary-school graduates looking for work—all potential Balsakhis. The rate of pay for Balsakhis, between $10 and $15 per month, was about one-tenth the cost of a regular teacher. Moreover, since their training took only two weeks, a high annual turnover rate among Balsakhis did not inhibit program expansion. Nor did a lack of classrooms, because the Balsakhi worked with students wherever space was available, often in corridors or on playgrounds.

The Pratham staff that designed the Balsakhi program had reason to believe that it would enhance children's skills. One reason is that the program concentrated its instruction on fundamental literacy and numeracy skills that lagging students needed in order to comprehend the curricula in the third and fourth grades. A second reason is that the third- and fourth-grade teachers in the regular government schools tended to focus on covering the curriculum by the end of the school year and paid little or no attention to the needs of students whose skills were lagging. Consequently, the Pratham staff reasoned that little would be lost from pulling lagging students out of their regular classroom to work with a Balsakhi. Although this reasoning was persuasive to many school directors and government officials, it did not constitute evidence of program effectiveness.[7]

In the late 1990s, Pratham requested that researchers from J-PAL evaluate how effective the Balsakhi program was in enhancing children's academic achievement. The research team, which included Abhijit Banerjee, Shawn Cole, Esther Duflo, and Leigh Linden, concluded that the best way to answer this question was to conduct a random-assignment experiment. Pratham staff supported the J-PAL researchers' recommendation, and

---

7. We thank Leigh Linden, a member of the J-PAL team that evaluated the Balsakhi program, for providing clarifying comments about the details of the J-PAL team's work on this project.

the research team began the work to design an experiment that would take place during the 2001–2002 and 2002–2003 school years.

Since the program assigned Balsakhis to schools serving low-income children, a logical way to design the experiment would have been to select a sample of schools eligible to participate in the program, and then assign Balsakhis randomly to half of the schools, treating the other half of the schools as a control group. The research team anticipated, however, that school directors in Vadodara and Mumbai, the two cities in western India selected for the evaluation, would have reservations about participating in an experiment with this kind of design. The reason was that schools in the control group would not receive the assistance of a Balsakhi, but would need to subject their students to the extra testing that was to be part of the evaluation.

Recognizing the difficulty in obtaining cooperation for conducting an experiment in which control schools obtained no additional resources, the J-PAL researchers adopted a different design. The alternative that they chose, after consultation with school directors, was to provide one Balsakhi to each school that volunteered to participate in the experiment, and then assign the Balsakhi randomly to either grade 3 or grade 4. Thus, in 2001–2002, the first year of the experiment, half of the government primary schools in Vadodara that participated in the experiment were given a Balsakhi to work with children in grade 3; the other half were given a Balsakhi to work with students in grade 4. In the second year of the experiment, the assignments of Balsakhis to grade levels were switched. Those participating schools that had a Balsakhi in grade 3 in year 1 were given a Balsakhi for grade 4, and vice versa.

In Table 5.1, which is adapted from Banerjee et al. (2007), we illustrate this design. In evaluating the first-year impact on student achievement of having a Balsakhi work with grade 3 children, Group A schools would make up the treatment group and Group B schools the control group. Conversely, in evaluating the first-year impact of having a Balsakhi to work

Table 5.1   Illustration of the research design of the Balsakhi experiment

	Year 1 (2001–2002)		Year 2 (2002–2003)	
Group A	5,264 students in 49 schools		6,344 students in 61 schools	
	Grade 3	Grade 4	Grade 3	Grade 4
	Balsakhi	No Balsakhi	No Balsakhi	Balsakhi
Group B	4,934 students in 49 schools		6,071 students in 61 schools	
	Grade 3	Grade 4	Grade 3	Grade 4
	NoBalsakhi	Balsakhi	Balsakhi	No Balsakhi

with grade 4 children, Group A schools were the control group and Group B schools the treatment group. A similar design was used in assigning Balsakhi to schools in Mumbai that volunteered to participate in the experiment.

An advantage of the research design chosen by the J-PAL researchers was that it allowed them to examine whether the causal impact on student achievement of having access to a Balsakhi for two years was greater than the impact of one year of access. The reason is that children who were in the third grade in Group A schools in the first year of the experiment also received access to a Balsakhi in the second year of the experiment, when the children were in fourth grade. Their achievement at the end of the second year of the experiment (when they had completed grade 4) could be compared to the achievement, at the end of the first year of the experiment, of those children who were in fourth grade in Group B schools in that year.

The results of the evaluation of the Balsakhi experiment were encouraging. In the first year of the evaluation, the Balsakhi program increased student test scores by an average of 0.14 of a standard deviation. In the second year of the evaluation, the average effect of one year's access to a Balsakhi was 0.28 of a standard deviation, and the impacts were quite similar across grades, subject areas, and research sites. The explanation for the larger effect in the second year of the program was that implementation improved.

On the important question of whether access to two years of support from a Balsakhi improved achievement more than one year of access, the results were cautiously optimistic. The evidence from Mumbai indicated that two years of access to a Balsakhi increased student performance on the mathematics examination by 0.60 standard deviations, an impact twice as large as the impact of one year of access.[8]

The research team also examined the persistence of the impact of the Balsakhi program. One year after receiving the support of a Balsakhi, the impact for low-achieving students had declined to approximately 0.10 of a standard deviation. This suggests that the Balsakhi program is better viewed as a vitamin, an intervention that struggling students need continually, than as a vaccination that, once received, protects students from future struggles. However, of greater importance is the message from the evaluation that a remarkably low-cost intervention made an important difference in the achievement of struggling primary school students in

---

8. As explained in Banerjee et al. (2007), riots in Vadodara made it impossible to assess the impact of two years of Balsakhi support in that research site.

Indian cities. This evidence proved important in building support for the Balsakhi program, which now serves hundreds of thousands of children in India.

Evaluating an Innovative Incentive Policy

The second experiment conducted by J-PAL researchers that we describe in this chapter took place in rural India, where high rates of teacher absenteeism are a major problem. For example, teachers in some rural schools in India are absent as many as half of the days that schools are scheduled to be in session. Addressing this teacher-absence problem in government-run schools is difficult politically because public-sector teacher unions in many countries, including India, are powerful. However, in rural India, nongovernmental organizations (NGOs) run many informal education centers that are staffed by adults from local communities. The adults, who typically have only a high-school education, receive training from the NGO and are paid on short-term contracts, at quite low rates of pay. While the teachers' contracts specify that they can be dismissed for excessive absence, their pay does not depend on the number of their absences. Teacher absence from the informal education centers run by NGOs (which we subsequently call schools) has been as great a problem as it is among teachers employed by the government. One difference, however, is that the rural teachers employed by the NGOs lack the political power of the unionized public-sector teachers. Consequently, the options available for administrators to tackle the teacher-absence problem are greater.

In 2001, Seva Mandir, an NGO that runs many one-room informal schools in rural Rajasthan, Western India, approached J-PAL researchers Esther Duflo, Rema Hanna, and Stephen Ryan for help in solving the teacher-absence problem. These economists suggested designing a randomized experiment to assess whether teacher-absence behavior could be modified by restructuring teacher pay. Instead of paying teachers a flat monthly salary, teachers' pay would be based on the number of days that they actually taught. Seva Mandir staff decided to try the approach recommended by the J-PAL researchers, and asked them to design an experiment and evaluate the consequences of the incentive program.

The research team faced two critical challenges in carrying out the experiment. The first was gaining the cooperation of teachers. After consultation with the research team, Seva Mandir explained to teachers that it was trying out a new policy and needed to learn about the consequences. It explained that there were benefits and costs to being in each of the two groups. The control group teachers would be paid 1,000 rupees per month (approximately $23) as in the past, an amount that did not depend on their attendance. Teachers in the experimental group would be paid 50 rupees for every day that they actually taught each month, with a minimum of 500 rupees per month. Consequently, teachers in the treatment group could earn as much as 1,300 rupees per month, but they could also earn only half of their prior pay. Participants were told that a lottery would be used to determine whether they would be placed in the treatment group or the control group.

Once potential participants understood the incentive pay system and how the lottery would work, the process for determining which teachers would be in the treatment group appealed to their sense of fair play. One question that some teachers asked J-PAL researchers during the participant focus-group sessions was why all teachers could not work under the new pay-incentive system. The researchers explained that the Seva Mandir had only sufficient resources to try the new approach with 60 teachers, and that it had concluded that assignment by a fair lottery was the best way to allocate the opportunity.

A second critical challenge was how to measure teacher attendance in far-flung rural schools. The cost of having Seva Mandir staff visit widely dispersed rural schools to monitor teacher attendance frequently would have been prohibitive. In addition, participating teachers would have resented unannounced monitoring visits, and the resentment might have affected their teaching performance. The research team's response to the measurement challenge was to give each teacher a tamper-proof camera that recorded on film the date and time that any picture was taken. Teachers were instructed to have a student take a picture of the teacher accompanied by at least eight students at the beginning of each school day and then, again, at least five hours later, near the end of the school day. The films were collected and developed each month, and the photographic record used to determine each teacher's attendance rate and their pay for the month.[9] Once this data-collection process was explained to teachers, they supported it because it was deemed fair and not subject to the stresses from unannounced visits by Seva Mandir staff.

The results of the 27-month-long experiment showed that basing teachers' pay on the number of days that they actually taught reduced teacher absences markedly, from 42% to 21% of the available working days, on average. Even more important, it resulted in an increase of almost a fifth of a standard deviation in their students' achievement, as measured by

---

9. We thank Rema Hanna for reading a draft of this section and providing clarifying comments about the details of the J-PAL team's work on this project.

tests of mathematics and reading. This impact is only slightly smaller than that of the very expensive small class-size intervention tested in the Tennessee STAR Experiment (Duflo, Hanna, & Ryan, 2008).

What to Read Next

To learn more about the challenges you may face in carrying out randomized field trials, we recommend two additional readings. The first is the insight-filled chapter entitled "Using Randomization in Development Economics Research: A Toolkit," by Esther Duflo, Rachel Glennerster, and Michael Kremer (2008). The second is the NBER working paper by John List, Sally Sadoff, and Mathis Wagner entitled "So You Want to Run an Experiment, Now What? Some Simple Rules of Thumb for Optimal Experimental Design" (2010).

6

Statistical Power and Sample Size

We began the previous chapter by citing statistics from the What Works Clearinghouse (WWC) about the enormous number of completed empirical evaluations of educational interventions that were unable to support causal inference. For example, we noted that among 301 evaluations of the effectiveness of interventions in elementary mathematics, 97% of the studies reviewed could not support a causal conclusion. The most common reason was that the authors of the studies were unable to defend the assumption that participants who had been assigned to the treatment and control conditions were *equal in expectation* before the intervention began.

However, even in studies that meet this condition—for example, because the investigator has assigned members of the analytic sample randomly to treatment and control groups—the effort can be stymied by a sample of inadequate size. If you conduct otherwise well-designed experimental research in a too-small sample of participants, you may estimate a positive impact for your intervention, but be unable to reject the null hypothesis that its effect is zero, in the population. For example, the 3% of studies of elementary-mathematics interventions that met the WWC standards for supporting causal inferences included one evaluation of the causal impact of a curriculum entitled Progress in Mathematics 2006.[1] Had the sample size of this study been larger and all else remained the same, the modest positive results of the evaluation would have been statistically significant.

---

1. http://ies.ed.gov/ncee/wwc/reports/elementary_math/promath_06/, accessed May 29, 2009.

Thus, early in the process of planning research, it makes good sense to decide how many participants you need to include in your sample in order to have a decent chance of detecting any effect that may indeed be present in the population. To make this sample size decision sensibly, you need to conduct what is known as a *statistical power analysis* as part of your research planning process. In this chapter, we explain how to do this. As you will see, an important guiding principle is that you can always manipulate the important facets of your research design, such as sample size, to create a stronger empirical "magnifying glass" for your work. With a more powerful magnifying glass, you can always see finer detail.

We devote this chapter and the next to explaining how to conduct statistical power analyses because we believe that many social-science investigators have been unaware of the true requirements for sample size in effective research design. As a result, much empirical research in education and the social sciences in the past has been underpowered. In this chapter, we describe the link between statistical power and sample size, and establish basic guidelines for figuring out the values that both should take on in high-quality research. We begin by defining the concept of *statistical power*, connecting it to the process of statistical inference with which you are already familiar. Then, we describe the link between power and sample size, and between power and other critical features of the research design. We do this all in the context of the "gold standard" research design for causal research—an experiment in which participants have been randomized individually to either a treatment or a control condition. Then, in the following chapter, we extend our presentation to include the more complex case in which groups of individuals—such as classrooms or schools—are sampled and randomly assigned to experimental conditions.

Statistical Power

Reviewing the Process of Statistical Inference

In introducing the concept of statistical power, we rely again on the example of the New York Scholarship Program (NYSP), which we introduced in Chapter 4. As we described earlier, the NYSP is an example of a two-group experiment in which individual participants were randomly assigned to either a treatment or a control group. Members of the experimental group received a private-school tuition voucher and members of the control groups did not. To facilitate our explanation of the critical statistical concepts in this chapter, we begin by narrowing our focus and addressing the implicit NYSP research question using the simplest appropriate analytic technique available to the empirical researcher. This is a two-group *t*-test of the null hypothesis that there is no difference, in the population, between the average academic achievement of African-American children in the experimental (voucher) and control (no voucher) conditions.

To simplify our explanation of the new statistical concepts in this chapter, we base our presentation on the application of a *one-sided t*-test. This means that—in our introduction of the concept of statistical power—we test the null hypothesis that the average academic achievement of treated children is equal to the average achievement of untreated children versus an *alternative* hypothesis that their achievement is *greater* than that of control children, in the population. This is a strictly *pedagogic* decision on our part and was made to simplify our technical presentation. It contrasts with our earlier *substantive* decision to rely on a two-sided *t*-test in our detailed presentation of the actual analyses and findings from the NYSP project in Chapter 4. There, we assumed that, if the null hypothesis were rejected, the average achievement of children in the population who were offered vouchers could be either greater than, or less than, the average achievement of children not offered vouchers. Generally, in conducting research, a one-sided test should only be used in circumstances in which you can defend a strong prior belief that, if the treatment did have an effect on the outcome of interest, you would know with certainty what the direction of the difference in outcomes would be. This is rarely true in practice, and we do not believe it would be true in the case of empirical analyses of the NYSP data. On the other hand, as we discuss in Chapter 8, an example in which we believe a one-sided test would be appropriate concerns the impact of college scholarship aid on the decisions of high-school seniors to enroll in college. Since scholarship aid reduces the cost of college enrollment, it seems compelling to assume that, if scholarships did have an impact on the percentage of high-school seniors who enrolled in college, that effect would indeed be positive.

Fortunately, whether you choose a directional or a nondirectional alternative for your hypothesis testing, the technical concepts and connections that we introduce in this chapter—and, in particular, the concept of statistical power itself—remain unchanged. Later in the chapter, we describe how critical features of the research design, the measurement of the variables, and the choice of a particular data-analytic approach affect the statistical power in any particular experiment. At that point, we reconsider the decision to adopt a directional versus a nondirectional alternative hypothesis and comment on how it impacts the magnitude of the statistical power.

First, it is useful to recall the steps in the process of statistical inference that we made use of in the top panel of Table 4.1. There, to test the null hypothesis that students who were offered a NYSP voucher had academic achievement three years later that was no different from students who lost out in the voucher lottery, we first adopted a suitable α-level (of 0.05) to fix the Type I error of our test at 5%. Second, we computed the value of an observed t-statistic, obtaining a value of 2.911, using the following formula:

$$t_{observed} = \frac{\left(\overline{POST\_ACH}_V - \overline{POST\_ACH}_{NV}\right)}{\sqrt{s^2\left(\frac{1}{n_V} + \frac{1}{n_{NV}}\right)}} \qquad (6.1)$$

where subscripts V and NV are intended to distinguish the voucher and no-voucher groups, and s^2 and n refer to the pooled variance of post-test academic achievement and the number of African-American children in the respective groups. Third, based on our adopted α-level, we determined a critical value of the t-statistic under the null hypothesis at the appropriate degrees of freedom (here, 519).[2] This critical value, in the case of a one-sided test favoring the experimental voucher group, is 1.648. Fourth, because the magnitude of the observed t-statistic (2.911) exceeded the critical value (1.648), we rejected the null hypothesis that African-American children with, and without, vouchers performed identically in academic achievement, on average, in the population. Hence, we concluded—because our research design was a randomized experiment—that voucher receipt caused the observed difference of about 5 points in academic achievement between members of the treatment and control groups.[3]

---

2. There were a total of 521 children in the sample.
3. You can also proceed by referring to the p-value associated with the statistic of interest. This estimates the probability that you could have obtained your single empirically obtained estimate of the parameter of interest, or something more extreme than it, by an accident of sampling from a population in which the value of the parameter was 0—that is, from a population in which the null hypothesis was true. In the t-test conducted here, for instance, the p-value was 0.004 (Table 4.1, upper panel), meaning it was unlikely that we could have obtained our single empirically obtained average treatment/control difference of 4.899 and its companion t-statistic of 2.911, or something larger, by an accident of sampling from a "null" population. So, we conclude that, in the reality of the actual experiment, we were probably not sampling from a null population, but from an alternative population in which there was indeed a relationship between academic achievement and voucher receipt.

Notice how the construction of the observed t-statistic, which we defined in Equation 6.1, is conceptually appealing. Its numerator is equal to the sample mean difference in academic achievement between the voucher and no-voucher groups. Its denominator is simply the standard error of the difference in means between the groups—that is, the standard error of the quantity that sits in the numerator.[4] So, the observed t-statistic is just the sample mean difference between the voucher and no-voucher groups expressed in appropriate standard error units. More compellingly, provided that the original achievement scores are normally distributed, theoretical work in statistics shows that all such statistics formed in this way have t-distributions. So, we were able to use our existing knowledge of the t-distribution to determine a critical value for comparison with the observed test statistic, in order to carry through on the test.

As you know, through a process of sampling from the underlying population, the observed t-statistic in which we are interested—that is, the "2.911" obtained in our NYSP analyses—derives its value implicitly from an underlying and critically important parameter representing the average difference in academic achievement between African-American children with, and without, vouchers in the population. We write this important population difference in means as $(\mu_V - \mu_{NV})$, where subscripts V and NV refer to the experimental "voucher" and control "no-voucher" groups, respectively and, in what follows, for convenience, we refer to it as $\Delta\mu$. If the mean difference in the population $\Delta\mu$ were large, the corresponding difference in mean academic achievement that we would obtain by drawing samples from that population—and the corresponding value of the accompanying observed t-statistic—would also tend to be large, except that the idiosyncrasies of random sampling might occasionally toss up some radically different value than we had anticipated. Conversely, if the important population mean difference $\Delta\mu$ were actually equal to zero in the population, then any corresponding sample mean difference observed in the sample—and, consequently, the value of the corresponding observed t-statistic—would tend to be close to zero, except for the idiosyncrasies of sampling.

The complete formal logic of hypothesis testing is actually a little more complex than intimated up to this point, and it is from this added complexity that the notion of statistical power derives. When we conduct a hypothesis test, we actually contrast what we have learned from the empirical data with what we might anticipate under a *pair* of hypothetical settings. The first of these settings we have commented upon earlier. It is

---

4. Under the assumption of homoscedasticity for the population residual variance.

described by the null hypothesis H_0, and under it we imagine there exists a hypothetical "null" population in which the important population mean-difference parameter $\Delta\mu$ is actually equal to zero (i.e., we stipulate that H_0: $\Delta\mu = 0$). The second, and equally important, setting is provided by an alternative hypothesis H_A, in which we establish a second hypothetical population where the value of the important population mean-difference parameter is *not 0*, but equal to some non-0 value of magnitude δ (i.e., we will stipulate that $\Delta\mu = \delta$, under the alternative hypothesis H_A). In quantitative research, we are usually interested in rejecting the null hypothesis in favor of the alternative, and then interpreting δ substantively.

Classical hypothesis testing simply contrasts the vicissitudes of the empirical setting, as encapsulated in the single empirically obtained value of the $t_{observed}$ statistic, with the set of values that the test statistic could potentially take on if we were to sample repeatedly and independently from populations in which these null and alternative hypotheses are true, respectively. Of course, we expect that values of $t_{observed}$ obtained in repeated resamplings would be scattered randomly and naturally by the idiosyncrasies of sampling. But, we anticipate that they would be scattered around the value *zero* if we were sampling from the null population, and around some non-zero value that depends on δ if we were sampling from the alternative population.[5] Then, if we found that the actual value of $t_{observed}$ obtained in our actual experiment was close to zero, and fell within a range of values that we might naturally anticipate in the "idiosyncratic scattering from the null" case, we would prefer the "*It came from H_0*" explanation and consequently accept that $\Delta\mu = 0$. If our single empirically obtained value of $t_{observed}$ was large, on the other hand, and looked more like a value that we might have gotten in an "idiosyncratic scattering from the alternative" case, then we will prefer the "*It came from H_A*" explanation and accept that $\Delta\mu = \delta$. Picking a sensible α-level for our test is how we choose between these two potential explanations.

We summarize these aspects of the hypothesis-testing process in Figure 6.1. In the top panel, under the symmetric hill-shaped "envelope," we represent the distribution of the values that a t-statistic could potentially take on, in random resampling from a "null" population in which

---

5. Unfortunately for the pedagogy of our example, the "some non-0 value" to which we refer in this sentence is not δ itself, but a linear function of it. This is because, under the alternative hypothesis, the observed t-statistic has a non-central t-distribution whose population mean is equal to δ *multiplied by a constant whose value is* $\sqrt{\dfrac{v}{2}}\left(\dfrac{\Gamma((v-1)/2)}{\Gamma((v)/2)}\right)$, where v represents the degrees of freedom of the distribution and $\Gamma(\ )$ is the gamma function.

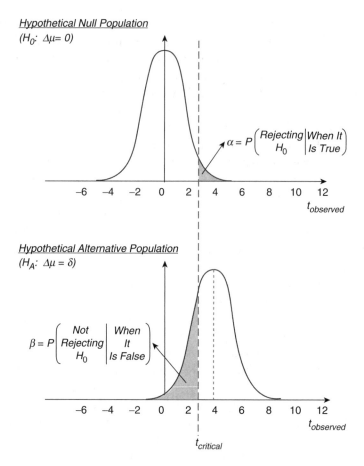

Hypothetical Null Population
$(H_0: \Delta\mu = 0)$

$\alpha = P\left(\begin{array}{c|c} Rejecting & When\ It \\ H_0 & Is\ True \end{array}\right)$

Hypothetical Alternative Population
$(H_A: \Delta\mu = \delta)$

$\beta = P\left(\begin{array}{c|c} Not & When \\ Rejecting & It \\ H_0 & Is\ False \end{array}\right)$

$t_{observed}$

$t_{critical}$

Figure 6.1 Distributions of the observed *t*-statistic ($t_{observed}$) under competing null (H_0) and alternative (H_A) hypotheses, showing the Type I error (α), Type II error (β), and placement of the critical value of the *t*-statistic ($t_{critical}$), for a one-tailed test of population outcome mean differences between a treatment and a control group.

the population mean-difference parameter $\Delta\mu$ was equal to zero. Although *zero* may not be the magnitude that we ultimately hope population outcome mean difference $\Delta\mu$ will have in our actual experiment (in fact, we usually hope that it is not zero), this idea of sampling repeatedly from a "null population" provides us with a useful baseline for subsequent comparison. Conceptually, the curve in the top panel represents something akin to a histogram of all the idiosyncratic values that $t_{observed}$ could possibly take on if we were to resample an infinite number of times from a population in which the population outcome mean difference between treatment and control conditions, $\Delta\mu$, was zero. As in any histogram, the horizontal axis represents the possible values that $t_{observed}$ could attain—actually, these values range from $-\infty$ to $+\infty$. The vertical axis represents the "frequency" with which each value has occurred during the resampling process. However, we are dealing with infinite resampling and a statistic that can take on values ranging continuously between plus and minus infinity. Consequently, we have drawn the exhibit as the envelope of a *probability density function* (or pdf) in which the histogram has been rescaled so that the total area under the envelope is equal to 1. Areas beneath the envelope represent the *probabilities* with which particular *ranges* of values of $t_{observed}$ would occur in infinite resampling from a null population. For instance, the probability that $t_{observed}$ will take on *any* value at all is obviously 1, a value equal to the total area beneath the pdf.[6] Similarly, because the pdf is symmetric and centered on zero, there is a probability of exactly one half—a 50% chance—that a value of $t_{observed}$ sampled at random from the null population will be larger than zero, or smaller than zero.[7]

In the bottom panel in Figure 6.1, we display the situation that would occur under the competing alternative hypothesis, H_A: $\Delta\mu = \delta$. The graphic is essentially identical to that displayed under H_0, but we have shifted the pdf of $t_{observed}$ to the right by an amount that depends on δ—the value we would anticipate for the population outcome mean difference between treatment and control groups if H_A were true.[8] Again, the displaced pdf represents the distribution of all the possible values of $t_{observed}$ that could be obtained if samples were drawn repeatedly and randomly from the alternative population.

To complete our test, we rely on a decision rule that derives from our decision to set the Type I error of our test at 5%. From this decision, we can derive a *critical value* against which to compare the value of the observed test statistic. We do this by determining the value that $t_{observed}$ would have to take on in order to split the null distribution of $t_{observed}$ in the top panel of Figure 6.1 vertically into two parts, with 5% percent of the area beneath its envelope falling to the right of the split and 95% falling to the left.[9] In the figure, we indicate the place at which this split occurs

6. The area beneath the t-distribution is finite, and equal to 1, because its tails asymptote to zero.
7. Not all distributions of test statistics are symmetric and zero at the center. However, the logic of our argument does not depend for its veracity on the particular shape of the pdf we have chosen to display. All that is required is that the pdf of the test statistic, under H_0, be known. Consequently, our argument applies equally well to cases in which distributions are asymmetric (as with the F and $\chi 2$ distributions).
8. Again, under the alternative hypothesis, the pdf of the observed t-statistic is not centered on the value of δ itself, but on a value proportional to it. See footnote 5.
9. Recall that this is a one-sided test.

by drawing a dashed vertical line. The place at which the vertical dashed line intersects the horizontal axis provides the required critical value of the test statistic $t_{critical}$ that we will use in our hypothesis test. Our decision is then straightforward. If $t_{observed}$ is greater than $t_{critical}$, then we conclude that it is probably too extreme to have come legitimately from the null distribution. Consequently, we reject H_0 in favor of H_A, and conclude that parameter $\Delta\mu$ is equal to δ, not zero, in the population from which we have sampled. On the other hand, if $t_{observed}$ is less than $t_{critical}$, we conclude that our single empirical value of $t_{observed}$ was probably sampled from a null population Consequently, we would not reject H_0 in favor of H_A. In other words, by choosing a particular α-level (5%, say) to fix the level of the Type I error, and combining this with our theoretical knowledge of the shape of the pdf of the t-statistic under the null hypothesis, we can carry out the desired test. It is the choice of the Type I error that provides us with the criterion that we need to make the testing decision.

Now focus on the lower second panel in Figure 6.1, which is aligned beneath the first. As we have noted, this lower panel illustrates the "alternative" side of the hypothesis testing situation. In it, we display the pdf of all possible values that an observed t-statistic could take on in repeated resampling from a population in which the alternative hypothesis was true, and parameter $\Delta\mu$ had a non-zero value of δ. Of course, because of sampling variation, it is entirely possible that, in some proportion of resamplings, $t_{observed}$ will take on very small values, perhaps even values less than $t_{critical}$—values that we typically associate with sampling from a null population—even though the alternative hypothesis is actually true. If this were to happen in practice, and we were to base our decision on an artificially small empirically obtained value, we would declare the null hypothesis true. In this case, we would have committed another kind of mistake—called a *Type II error*. Now, we would end up falsely accepting the null hypothesis even though the alternative was, in fact, true. The probability that $t_{observed}$ may be idiosyncratically less than $t_{critical}$, even when the alternative hypothesis is true, is represented by the shaded area under the "alternative" probability density function to the left of $t_{critical}$. Just as symbol α is used to represent the magnitude of Type I error, β is the symbol used to represent the probability of a Type II error.

Finally, notice the horizontal separation of the centers of the pdfs, under the competing null and alternative hypotheses, H_0 and H_A, in Figure 6.1. This separation reflects the difference in the potential values of $\Delta\mu$, under the alternative ($\Delta\mu=\delta$) and null hypotheses ($\Delta\mu=0$).[10]

---

10. Again, the horizontal distance between the centers of the H_0 and H_A pdfs is not equal to δ, but is proportional to it. See footnote 5.

Methodologists refer to the difference between the values of $\Delta\mu$ under H_0 and H_A–that is, δ or a sensible rescaling of it–as the *effect size*. If you conduct a statistical test and reject H_0 in favor of H_A, you can conclude that the important population outcome mean-difference parameter has magnitude δ, rather than zero. In other words, you will be ready to declare that you have detected an effect of the treatment. In analyses for our NYSP experiment, for instance, after rejecting H_0 in favor of H_A, we conclude that $\Delta\mu$ is certainly not zero, and we estimate its value under the alternative hypothesis–that is, δ–by the sample mean difference in the outcome between members of the treatment and control groups.

Under this definition, we could regard the effect size of the voucher treatment as simply equaling our best estimate of δ, and it would be measured in the same units as the outcome–student achievement, in the NYSP experiment. Of course, this scaling is arbitrary, because it is determined by the metric in which the outcome was measured. Two investigators could then end up with different values for the effect size if they chose to measure the same outcome on the same children using one achievement test rather than another. So, for greater uniformity and generality, effect size is usually redefined so that it can be communicated in standard deviation units. Thus, for each different test and test statistic, the mathematical features of the rescaling differ, but the consequences are the same. Once the rescaling is complete, investigators can refer to the effects of their experiments using statements like "a difference of a half standard deviation," "a quarter standard deviation difference," and so on. These kinds of statements can be understood by their colleagues and by remote audiences, regardless of the specific metric of the outcome measurement itself.

Based on these ideas, to facilitate communication, researchers have tended to adopt the set of loose standards that Jacob Cohen (1988) proposed for describing the magnitudes of effect sizes. Cohen proposed that in comparing an average difference in outcome between members of a treatment and a control group, we should regard a difference of eight-tenths (0.8) of a standard deviation a "large" effect, a difference of one-half (0.5) of a standard deviation a "moderate" effect, and two-tenths (0.2) of a standard deviation a "small" effect size.[11] For instance, in the case of the NYSP evaluation, recall that the difference in academic achievement

---

11. Effect size can also be defined in terms of the *correlation* between outcome and predictor. In the NYSP evaluation, an effect size defined in this way would be the sample correlation between the academic achievement outcome and the dichotomous *VOUCHER* predictor, for the sample of African-American children. This correlation has a value of 0.127. When effect sizes are defined as correlations, a coefficient of magnitude 0.10 is regarded as a "small" effect size, 0.25 as a "medium" effect size, and 0.37 as a "large" effect size (Cohen, 1988, Table 2.2.1, p. 22).

between African-American children in the voucher and no-voucher conditions at the end of third grade was 4.899 points (Table 4.1, top panel). The standard deviation of academic achievement for these children was 19.209, and so we would say that effect size in the NYSP evaluation—which is then about a quarter of a standard deviation—was "small."[12] In our experiences, effect sizes of even the most successful interventions in education and the social sciences tend to be "small," when calibrated in Cohen's metric.

Defining Statistical Power

When conducting any hypothesis test, you have only two decisions to make. You can either reject H_0 because your obtained value of $t_{observed}$ is larger than the value of $t_{critical}$, or you can fail to reject it because $t_{observed}$ is smaller than $t_{critical}$. However, whichever of these two decisions you make, you can either be correct or you could have made a mistake. So, there is a "two-by-two" alignment of the testing decision with its consequences that leads to four possible decision scenarios. To two of these, by virtue of our definitions of Type I and Type II error, we can attach probabilities of occurrence. We summarize these four possible decision scenarios, and their associated decision probabilities, in the simplified graphical cross-tabulation in Figure 6.2.

In the figure, we have redisplayed the critical features of the H_0 and H_A pdfs that we displayed in Figure 6.1, along with the probabilities associated with their splitting vertically into parts by the placement of $t_{critical}$ (again represented by the vertical dashed line). The first row of the graphical cross-tabulation summarizes the distribution of $t_{observed}$ when H_0 is true; the second row summarizes its distribution when H_A is true. We comment briefly on each decision scenario below, beginning in the first row.

When H_0 Is True and $\Delta\mu$ Is Equal to Zero (First Row)

- *Right-hand cell.* Even though the null hypothesis is actually true in this row and there are no differences between the treatment and control group outcome means, in the population, you may find that your single empirically obtained value of $t_{observed}$ is idiosyncratically larger than the value of $t_{critical}$ simply by virtue of an accident of sampling. Then, you will reject H_0 by mistake and declare that

---

12. Some argue that effect size is best scaled in terms of the standard deviation of the outcome for participants in the control condition only. In the NYSP evaluation, this would have led to an effect size of (4.899/17.172), or 0.285.

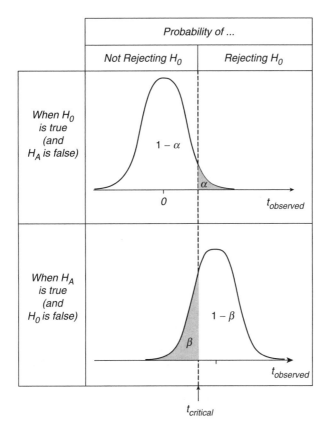

Figure 6.2 Four-way decision scenario, summarizing the probabilities of not rejecting H_0 (1st column) or rejecting H_0 (2nd column) when it is either True (1st row) or False (2nd row), showing the Type I error (α), Type II error (β), and placement of the critical value of the t-statistic ($t_{critical}$), for a one-tailed test of population outcome mean differences between a treatment and a control group.

$\Delta\mu$ is equal to δ incorrectly. In this case, you have made a Type I error, because you have falsely rejected your null hypothesis when it was correct. Such a decision scenario would occur if your actual experiment was one of those unfortunate occurrences in which a sample drawn from a truly null population generated a large value of $t_{observed}$ by an idiosyncratic accident of random sampling. However, because under this scenario H_0 is actually correct, the probability that you will make such a decision is equal to the area under H_0's pdf to the right of $t_{critical}$, which is of course the level of Type I error α that you yourself have picked in advance of the test. Thus, you have direct control over the Type I error probability, and you have an incentive to limit it by choosing a suitably small α-level, such as 0.05, for your test.

- *Left-hand cell.* On the other hand, you may find that your single empirically obtained value of $t_{observed}$ is appropriately smaller than your tabled value of $t_{critical}$, you will correctly fail to reject H_0, and you will be right when you declare that $\Delta\mu$ is equal to zero. In this decision scenario, you have drawn a well-behaved small value of $t_{observed}$ from the null distribution, and it is appropriately less than $t_{critical}$. The probability that this decision scenario will occur is simply the area under H_0's pdf to the left of $t_{critical}$, or the *complement* of your self-selected Type I error, and is therefore equal to $(1 - \alpha)$.

When H_A Is True and $\Delta\mu$ Is Equal to δ (Second Row)

- *Left-hand cell.* In this scenario, even though the alternative hypothesis is true and there are indeed differences between the treatment and control group outcome means, in the population, you may find that your single empirically obtained value of $t_{observed}$ is idiosyncratically smaller than the value of $t_{critical}$, again by an accident of sampling, and you will fail to reject H_0 even though it is false. Thus, you would incorrectly declare that $\Delta\mu$ is equal to zero. This would occur if your experiment was one of those occasions when a random sample from the alternative population happens to toss up an idiosyncratically small value of $t_{observed}$. Consequently, although H_A is actually true, your idiosyncratically small obtained value of $t_{observed}$ leads you to conclude that the sample was drawn from the null population. You have now made a Type II error. The probability that this decision scenario will occur is given by the area under H_A's pdf to the left of the value of $t_{critical}$. It is called the Type II error of the decision-making process, and we represent it by the symbol β. It is again a probability, just like α.

- *Right-hand cell.* Finally, you may find that your single empirically obtained value of $t_{observed}$ is appropriately larger than the tabled value of $t_{critical}$, and you will correctly reject H_0. In this scenario, your alternative hypothesis is true and you will be right when you declare that $\Delta\mu$ is equal to δ. The probability that this decision scenario will occur is equal to the area under H_A's pdf to the right of $t_{critical}$—it is the complement of Type II error, or $(1 - \beta)$.

This two-way cross-tabulation of the decision scenarios illustrates that the magnitudes of the several decision probabilities are interrelated.

To appreciate this fully, recall that, once the pdf of the test statistic has been specified under H_0, the value of $t_{critical}$ depends only on your selection of the α-level. So, if you were willing to entertain a larger Type I error, perhaps as high as 0.10, then your corresponding value of $t_{critical}$ would shrink, so that 10% of the area beneath H_0's pdf can now become entrapped to its right. With your new willingness to entertain this larger Type I error, you would find it easier to reject H_0 because the single empirically obtained value of your observed test statistic would be more likely to exceed the now smaller value of $t_{critical}$. This means that, if you can tolerate increased Type I error, you can more easily reject H_0 and more easily claim detection of a non-zero effect in the population. Of course, in enhancing your chances of claiming such a non-zero effect, you have increased the probability of Type I error—that is, you are now more likely to reject H_0 even when it is true! At the same time, shifting $t_{critical}$ to a smaller value has implicitly moved the vertical splitting of H_A's pdf to the left in Figure 6.2, and thereby reduced the value of the Type II error β. So, you are now more likely to accept H_A when it is true. This intimate—and inverse—connection between the magnitudes of the Type I and II errors is a central fact of statistical life. As you decide to make one type of error *less* likely, you force the other one to become *more* likely, and vice versa. So, you can correctly regard hypothesis testing as a trade-off between the probabilities of two competing types of error.

More importantly, the decision probability featured in the right-hand cell of the lower second row in Figure 6.2, which is of magnitude $(1 - \beta)$, is a central and important commodity in our empirical work. It is the *probability of rejecting H_0 when it is false.* Or, alternatively, it is the probability of accepting the alternative hypothesis when it is true. This is a highly preferred end result for most research—the rejection of the null hypothesis in favor of the alternative, when the alternative is true. For example, in designing the NYSP experiment, investigators were hoping to reject the null hypothesis of no causal connection between voucher receipt and student achievement in favor of an alternative hypothesis that stipulated voucher receipt had a causal effect on student achievement. This important quantity is defined as the *statistical power* of the study and, as you can see from Figure 6.2, it is simply the complement of the Type II error. This means that, knowing the pdfs of our test statistics—such as the t-statistic—under the null and alternative hypotheses, and being willing to set the Type I error level to some sensible value, means that we can actually estimate a value for the statistical power. This can be very useful both during the design of the research and also after the research has been completed. We follow up on these ideas in the section that follows.

Factors Affecting Statistical Power

Given this explanation, statistical power can be estimated prospectively for any research design, provided that you are willing to stipulate four things. First, you must be willing to anticipate the effect size that you hope to detect (e.g., Do you expect to be detecting a small, medium, or large effect?). Second, you must pick the type of statistical analysis you will eventually conduct (e.g., Will you use a t-test of differences in means, or more sophisticated methods of data analysis?). Third, you must pick an α-level for your future statistical inference (Are you happy with the 0.05 level?). Fourth, you must decide on the number of participants you want to include in your sample (Can you afford to recruit 200, 300, 400, or more participants?). The reason that these four decisions determine the statistical power of your prospective analysis is as follows. By choosing the method of statistical analysis, you identify the statistic that will be used to test your hypotheses. Knowing the test statistic and the prospective sample size determines the shape of the test statistic's pdf under H_0. Choice of the effect size then determines the pdf of the test statistic under H_A (typically, by displacing the pdf to the right).[13] Finally, overlaying the α-level on the test statistic's pdf under H_0 then fixes the critical value of the test statistic, which consequently determines the statistical power. We call this a *statistical power analysis*.

Often of greater interest, if you are willing to anticipate the effect size, specify a type of analysis, pick an α-level, and decide on the statistical power you want, you can figure out the sample size that will permit you to reach your analytic objectives. The actual computations underlying such statistical power analyses are complex, and they make use of theoretical knowledge of the mathematical shapes of the pdfs of the different test statistics under the null and alternative hypotheses, and of integral calculus. Consequently, we do not describe them here. But they are available for reference in standard statistical texts, and are most easily carried out by dedicated computer software, much of which is now available free on the Internet.[14] Instead, our purpose here is to give you a ballpark sense of the kinds of sample sizes that are needed for successful experimental research design in education and the social sciences, and the levels of

---

13. Depending on the type of analysis, the test statistic's pdf under H_A may also have a different shape from its pdf under H_0.

14. All the power analyses in this chapter were conducted using the G*Power freeware, v2.0, *GPOWER: A-Priori, Post-Hoc and Compromise Power Analyses for MS-DOS*, Dept. of Psychology, Bonn University, Germany, http://www.psycho.uni-duesseldorf.de/aap/projects/gpower/.

statistical power that they typically provide. In addition, we hope to guide you toward the kinds of design decisions that will enable you to achieve your objectives as an investigator of cause and effect.

To provide you with some intuition about the sizes of sample that are required typically in a successful two-group experiment, we now present estimates of statistical power for an experiment in which we assign a sample of participants randomly and individually to either a treatment or a control condition, so that groups of equal size are formed. We again assume that a one-sided t-test will eventually be used to test a null hypothesis of no group differences in the outcome mean, in the population. For this empirical set-up, in Figure 6.3, we plot the obtained values of statistical power (vertical axis) at different values of the total sample size (the total number of participants in the treatment and control groups combined, on the horizontal axis). We do this for both small effect sizes ($ES = 0.2$, lower pair of curves) and medium effect sizes ($ES = 0.5$, upper pair of curves), at α-levels of 0.05 (solid lines) and 0.10 (dashed lines), respectively. We have not provided plots for the large effect size ($ES = 0.8$) condition because such effect sizes occur rarely in experimental research in education and the social sciences. You can replicate these plots by downloading standard statistical power analysis software from the Internet and inserting these values we have provided for effect size and Type I error (see footnote 14).

Inspecting the figure, you can discern three important relationships between statistical power and the other quantities involved. First, notice that statistical power is always greater when you adopt a more liberal α-level in your statistical testing. In Figure 6.3, at any pairing of effect and sample size, power is always greater when the α-level is 0.10 rather than 0.05. For instance, if you want to detect a small effect size ($ES = 0.2$) with a total sample size of 300, then choosing an α-level of 0.10 rather than 0.05 increases your statistical power from approximately 0.53 to 0.67, an improvement of more than 25%. Our earlier description of the nature of statistical power provides an explanation for why this occurs. Returning to Figure 6.2 and focusing on the first row, you will see that it is the choice of α-level that splits the area beneath the test statistic's pdf under H_0 and determines the test statistic's critical value $t_{critical}$. So, if you deliberately increase the value of α, from 0.05 to 0.10. say, the value of $t_{critical}$ must "shift to the left," so that a larger area (10%) can be entrapped under the H_0 pdf to its right. But, if $t_{critical}$ is shifted, any areas entrapped beneath the alternative probability density function in the second row of the figure must be affected. Specifically, the area to the left of $t_{critical}$ under the H_A pdf will be reduced, decreasing the value of the Type II error β, and increasing its complement, the statistical power.

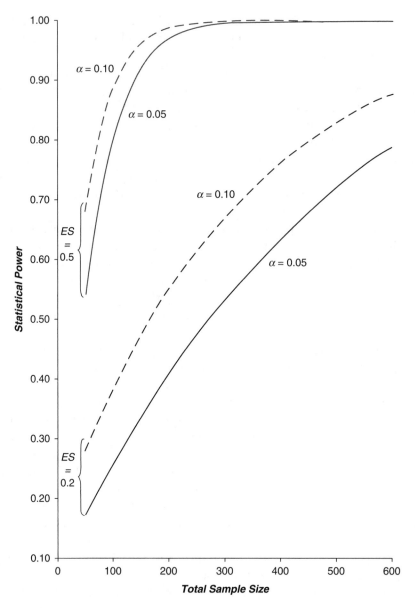

Figure 6.3 Statistical power as a function of total sample size, effect size (0.2 versus 0.5), and α-level (0.05 versus 0.10), for a one-tailed test of population outcome mean differences between a treatment and a control group.

The second important relationship evident in our figure is that, all else remaining equal, you will always have more power to detect a larger effect. In Figure 6.3, with a total sample size of 100 participants randomized to treatment conditions, say, and an α-level of 0.05, you have a power of just over 0.25 to detect a small effect ($ES = 0.2$) and a power of almost 0.80 to detect a medium effect ($ES = 0.5$). Again, the reason for this link between effect size and power can be deduced from our decision-scenario description in Figure 6.2. As we have noted already, the effect size determines the horizontal separation of the test statistic's pdfs under H_0 and H_A. So, if a larger effect size is accommodated, the H_0 and H_A pdfs must be more widely separated along the horizontal axis. But, in the first row of the figure, the center of H_0's pdf is fixed at zero (because it represents the "null" condition). So, as effect size is increased, the pdf of the test statistic under H_A shifts to the right, in the second row of the figure, sliding past the location of $t_{critical}$, the placement of which has been fixed by the earlier choice of α-level under the H_0 pdf. Consequently, the area beneath the alternative distribution to the right of $t_{critical}$ must rise, and statistical power is again increased.

Third, and most important, statistical power is always greater when the total number of participants included in the experiment is larger, all else being equal. This is quite a dramatic effect, as evidenced by the slopes of the power/sample size relationships in Figure 6.3. Notice, for instance, in research to detect a medium effect size ($ES = 0.5$) at an α-level of 0.05, statistical power can be increased from about 0.55 to more than 0.80 by increasing the total sample size from 50 to 100 participants! Although it is more difficult to understand, the reason for this dependency can again be deduced from Figure 6.2. As sample size increases, the pdf associated with any test statistic always becomes slimmer and taller because its values enjoy greater precision—and less scatter on repeated sampling—at larger sample sizes. However, the location of the center of the distribution remains unchanged.[15] So, as the H_0 and H_A pdfs in Figure 6.2 slim down and become more pointy, there are two important consequences, one for each featured pdf. First, in the H_0 pdf in the first row of the figure, the location of $t_{critical}$ must move to the left—that is, the critical value must get smaller—in order to accommodate the fixed choice of α-level adopted for the test. (Recall that choice of α-level splits the pdf under the null distribution vertically, so that an area equal to the Type I error must fall to the right of $t_{critical}$. In a rapidly narrowing distribution, this can only continue

---

15. You can check out this claim using one of the simulations of the distribution of the sample mean as a function of sample size available on the Internet.

to occur if $t_{critical}$ shifts to the left, thereby becoming smaller.) Second, in the second row of the figure, the corresponding narrowing of the H_A pdf causes the area beneath it to be reapportioned on either side of the now fixed value of $t_{critical}$, with less of the area falling to the left and more falling to the right. The shift of the value of $t_{critical}$ to the left in the H_0 pdf in the first row and the reapportioning of the area beneath the H_A pdf in the second row both lead to a reduction in the area beneath the H_A distribution to the left of $t_{critical}$. Consequently, Type II error β is reduced and statistical power $(1 - \beta)$ is increased. We suggest that you download software for computing statistical power from the Internet, and try out some of these computations for yourself, based on experiments that you think you may want to conduct in your own area of substantive interest.

One of our own great concerns as social scientists and methodologists has always been that many empirical investigators do not have a realistic vision of the actual sample sizes that are required to conduct powerful and effective research. It is common that researchers underestimate the numbers of participants required for empirical success. For instance, if you were designing research to estimate the impact of private-school tuition voucher receipt on academic achievement, and you suspected that the effect size you might detect was small (as in the NYSP experiment), you could set your α-level to the "usual" 0.05 level of statistical significance and strive for moderate power in the region of 0.80. From the plot in Figure 6.3, with these values set, you can see that you require a total sample size of about *620 participants*—distributed randomly into equally sized treatment and control groups—to have a reasonable hope of successfully detecting an effect size of 0.20. If you are unhappy with the idea that there is a 20% chance that you would declare the null hypothesis to be true when in fact this is not the case (a Type II error of 0.20), you might want to shoot for a power of 0.90. Then, you would need a total of 860 participants in your sample. This makes even the NYSP experiment a little underpowered for investigating the causal impact of tuition vouchers on African-American children, as there are only 521 of these children in the sample.

If you need more power for your experiment, or if the predicted effect size is smaller than 0.20, or if you want to detect the same treatment effect in multiple subgroups (e.g., among different race/ethnicities), then your sample must be considerably larger than these targets. Do not underestimate the sample size that you will require for your research. In underpowered research, you will never know whether you have failed to reject the null hypothesis because it is true, or because you simply did not have sufficient power to confirm the alternative. This problem plagued many of the studies of elementary-school mathematics interventions that the WWC reviewed.

The Strengths and Limitations of Parametric Tests

Keep in mind that the magnitude of the statistical power available in a particular investigation also depends on the type of statistical technique selected for data analysis. In our earlier examples, to underpin our technical presentation and form a basis of our "ball-park" estimates of power and sample size, we have focused on the simplest possible kind of statistical analysis that you can conduct in data drawn from a two-group experiment—the two-group t-test. In focusing on the use of this simple technique, we intended to provide a "baseline" set of recommendations about sample size and statistical power in research design.

However, many other statistical techniques are available for analyzing data, even for analyzing data from a simple two-group experiment, and some of them are more powerful than others. As a guiding principle, statistical techniques are more powerful when they incorporate more information into the analysis. Other than simply collecting data on more participants, there are two straightforward ways to achieve this—you can either make stronger assumptions about the data and the statistical model upon which the analysis is based, or you can add covariates to the analysis. Generally, analytic techniques that make more stringent assumptions are more powerful than those with weaker assumptions. The reason is that the assumptions themselves constitute a kind of information that is incorporated in the analysis. For example, among techniques for comparing the average outcomes of a treatment and a control group, the t-test is intrinsically more powerful than the nonparametric Wilcoxon rank test. In fact, as a general principle, parametric statistical tests are always more powerful than the corresponding nonparametric tests. This is because the t-test, and other traditional parametric tests like those that automatically accompany ordinary least-squares (OLS) regression analysis and the analysis of variance, make stronger assumptions about the distribution of the outcome in the analyses. The t-test, for instance, assumes that participants' values of the outcome are independently and normally distributed with homoscedastic variance in the treatment and control groups.[16] These stringent assumptions provide additional information that contributes greatly to the power of the analysis. Of course, you don't get anything for nothing. In choosing to use a test like the t-test over the Wilcoxon rank test, you are relying heavily on the validity of these additional parametric assumptions. This means that the added assumptions must be valid in order for the results of your analysis to be correct. If the assumptions are

---

16. Some versions of the t-test relax the population homoscedasticity assumption.

violated, then your answer may be wrong no matter how powerful the technique!

The Benefits of Covariates

A second direct way to bolster the statistical power of your analysis is to add covariates to your statistical models. Techniques like multiple-regression analysis, for instance, are more powerful than simpler techniques like a t-test of differences in means, for this reason. As we described in Chapter 4, a research question about the equality of average academic achievement between a voucher and a no-voucher group can be addressed in data either by a t-test of differences in sample means or by regressing the achievement outcome on a dichotomous "question" predictor that distinguishes participants' membership in the treatment or control group. If no covariates were included in the regression model, both approaches would provide identical answers and have identical power.

However, the regression analysis approach lets you include judiciously selected additional variables—exogenous measures of the children's demographic background, home life, and prior achievement—as covariates or control predictors to the analysis, without increasing the sample size. Providing the new covariates are well behaved—that is, reliably measured, linearly related to the outcome, uncorrelated with the "treatment" predictor,[17] and independent of the existing residuals in the model (exogenous)—their inclusion will tend to increase the proportion of the outcome variation that is predicted when the model is fitted (i.e., increase the value of the R^2 statistic) and thereby reduce residual variance. A reduction in residual variance necessarily implies a shrinking of the standard errors associated with the estimation of regression parameters, and an (inversely proportional) increase in the magnitude of t-statistics associated with the predictors. A larger t-statistic means that you are more likely to reject the null hypothesis and therefore your analysis has greater power at the same sample size. This is evident in the third panel of Table 4.1, where the standard error associated with the VOUCHER predictor has declined from 1.683 to 1.269 on inclusion of student pre-test scores as a covariate, and the t-statistic associated with the impact of the voucher treatment increased correspondingly from 2.911 to 3.23. In general, the impact of covariates on power can be dramatic. For instance, Light, Singer, and Willett (1990) comment that, if you include in your regression analyses

---

17. If treatment status is assigned randomly by the investigator, then the treatment predictor will necessarily be uncorrelated with *all other* exogenous covariates.

a set of covariates that predict about half the variation in the outcome jointly, then you can maintain the same statistical power for your analyses at half the sample size.

The message is clear. There is always an analytic advantage to preferring a more complex statistical analysis over a less complex one because it provides you with an opportunity to increase precision by including covariates. Greater precision brings increased statistical power, and the ability to detect a smaller effect at the same sample size. However, significant knowledge is needed to use complex statistical analyses appropriately. In doing so, you are relying more heavily on the hypothesized structure of the statistical model. You have to ensure that additional assumptions are met. You have to do a good job, analytically speaking, with the new terms in the model. You need to worry about whether the new covariates meet the underlying requirements of the analysis in terms of the quality of their measurement, the functional form of their relationship with the outcome, whether they interact with other predictors in the model, and whether they are truly independent of the existing residuals, as required. Clearly, everything has its price! However, if it is a price that you can pay, the rewards are great.

The Reliability of the Outcome Measure Matters

An additional factor to consider when figuring out how large a sample you will need for your research is the *reliability* of your outcome measure. To this point, we have assumed that the measurement of the outcome variable has been perfectly reliable. Of course, this is rarely the case in practice. All measures of observed quantities suffer from some level of unreliability as a result of the presence of random measurement error. Standardized measures of student achievement, such as those administered in the NYSP experiment, may have reliabilities above 0.90. Measures of many other constructs, particularly those with less precise definitions, or those that seek to document participants' self-reported beliefs and opinions, may have reliabilities that fall as low as 0.60.

Although psychometricians define the reliability parameter formally as a ratio of the population variances of the true and observed scores (Koretz, 2008), you can regard measurement error as being the random "noise" that obscures the true "signal" in an outcome variable. Measures that are less reliable obscure the true signal to a greater extent and therefore make it more difficult to detect treatment effects. This means that one simple approach for assessing the impact of outcome unreliability on statistical power computations is to view it from the context of effect size. Ultimately, we are conducting research so that we can detect the presence of true effects, and so we must account for measurement unreliability in our designation of observed effect size for the purposes of statistical power computation. In other words, because measurement fallibility undermines our ability to detect effects, we must plan our research in anticipation of even smaller effects than we would hope to detect in a world of perfect measurement.

Specifically, if you want to detect a true effect of a particular size, then you must design your research to seek an observed effect size that is equal to the anticipated true effect size, *multiplied by the square root of the reliability of the outcome variable*. The newly attenuated effect size thus obtained can then be incorporated into your power computations in the usual way. To give you some sense of the magnitude of the correction, imagine that you set your α-level at the 0.05 level of statistical significance and are planning to design a two-group randomized experiment that will have a statistical power of 0.80 to detect a small effect ($ES = 0.2$). We noted earlier that you should anticipate requiring a total sample size of 620 participants. If your outcome reliability were less than perfect, but at the level of most published achievement tests—around 0.95, say—then you would need to conduct power analyses in anticipating the detection of a new effect size of 0.195—that is, 0.2 multiplied by the square root of 0.95. To compensate for this small decline in effective effect size, total sample size would have to increase by 32 participants to 652. However, if your outcome reliability fell as low as 0.85, then your sample size would need to rise by 112 participants to 732. Notice that, because we take the square root of the outcome reliability (an estimate that always falls between 0 and 1) before conducting the new power analysis, the impact of measurement reliability—in its typical ranges (0.85 to 0.95)—is mitigated and the impact on sample size is of the order of a few percent. Outcome reliability would have to fall to 0.16, for instance, before measurement unreliability would force you to reclassify a "medium" effect as "small."

Although the impacts on power and sample size are not enormous when the reliability of measurement is reasonably high, it is worth paying attention to the potential impact of measurement reliability on your power analyses. Specifically, we suggest that you incorporate two steps in your research planning in order to deal with reliability of measurement. First, you should always make sure—by pre-research piloting, detailed item analysis, and prior editing and refinement of your instruments—that you administer measures of the highest reliability possible for the construct, audience, and context in your research. Second, you should always anticipate the presence of measurement error in your assessment of effect size and conduct your power analyses at that smaller effect size. Fortunately, with any decently constructed and reasonably reliable measure, this will probably mean that you will only have to increase your anticipated total sample size by a few percent.

The Choice Between One-Tailed and Two-Tailed Tests

Finally, we return to the question of whether it makes sense to adopt a one-tailed (directional) or a two-tailed (nondirectional) test when conducting data analyses. Earlier, in our replication of the original analyses of the NYSP data in Chapter 4, we made use of a two-tailed test. The reason was that we wanted to retain an open mind and proceed as though the jury were still out on the effectiveness of educational vouchers. If we were ultimately to reject a null hypothesis of no group difference in outcome between those randomly assigned vouchers and those not, we did not want to prejudge whether any detected effect favored the voucher recipients or control-group members.

In contrast, when we reviewed the concept of hypothesis testing and introduced the notion of statistical power in this chapter, we made use of a one-tailed test. We did this to make our pedagogic explanations of Type I and Type II error simpler. In particular, this decision allowed us to focus only on the single *upper* tail of the pdf of the test statistic, under H_0, and the area trapped beneath it, in Figures 6.1 and 6.2. Now that these concepts have been established, it makes sense to consider the consequences for statistical power analysis of the choice between a non-directional (two-tailed) and a directional (one-tailed) test. The answer is straightforward.

When you adopt a one-tailed test, essentially you place your entire reservoir of Type I error—typically, 5%—into the area trapped beneath the upper tail of the pdf of the test statistic under H_0 and the critical value. This is what we are illustrating in the first row of Figure 6.2. By adopting an α-level of 5%, say, and insisting on a one-tailed test, we fix the critical value of the t-statistic at the place already displayed in the figure.

If we were to now change our minds and opt for a two-tailed test, we would need to adopt a new critical value for the t-statistic, and this would affect both our Type II error and statistical power. For instance, under the non-directional testing option, we would need to accept that Type I error could potentially occur at either end of the pdf of the test statistic under H_0. We could falsely reject the null hypothesis because the value of $t_{observed}$ was driven to be either too large or too small as a result of the idiosyncrasies of sampling. Either way, we would reject H_0 incorrectly, and commit a Type I error. As a result, we need to split our adopted Type I error level—usually, 5%—into two halves, each of 2.5%. We would then choose a new critical value of the t-statistic, so that 2.5% of the area beneath the pdf of the test statistic (under H_0) was entrapped to the right of its positive value at the upper end and 2.5% of the area was entrapped to the left of its negative value at the lower end.[18] As a consequence, the magnitude of the new $t_{critical}$ must be larger than that currently displayed.

In going from the existing critical value of the t-statistic obtained under the one-tailed test of our initial explanation to the new larger critical value, we have effectively moved the vertical dashed reference line in Figure 6.2—the line that also splits the pdf of the t-statistic under H_A, in the second row of the figure—to the right. Thus, the Type II error (β)—represented by the area entrapped beneath the pdf of the test statistic (under H_A) to the left of the dashed vertical line—will have increased. Concurrently, the statistical power—the complement of that area, to the right of the vertical dashed line—must be reduced. Thus, switching from a one-tailed to a two-tailed test implicitly reduces the power of a statistical test.

We conclude by reminding you then that, in most research, two-tailed tests are the order of the day, even though they are implicitly less powerful than one-tailed tests. Only when you can mount a compelling defense of the argument that a particular policy or intervention can have only a directed impact (positive or negative) on the outcomes of interest, in the population, is the use of one-tailed tests justified.

What to Read Next

If you want to learn more about statistical power, we suggest that you consult the classic text by Jacob Cohen entitled *Statistical Power Analysis for the Behavioral Sciences* (1988, 2nd edition).

---

18. Implicitly, in the two-tailed case, because the pdf of the t-statistic (under H_0) is symmetric, $t_{critical}$ will take on two values of the same magnitude—one positive and the other negative—which are equally spaced on either side of the center of the pdf. During the subsequent test, if the value of the observed t-statistic is positive, it will be compared to the upper positive value of $t_{critical}$; if it is negative, it will be compared to the lower negative value.

7

Experimental Research When Participants Are Clustered Within Intact Groups

A pressing worldwide educational problem is that large numbers of economically disadvantaged children do not learn to read well in elementary school. As a result, they enter secondary school without the ability to comprehend textbooks in the core subjects, and this leads to poor grades, discouragement, and high dropout rates. In response to this widespread problem, Robert Slavin and his colleagues at Johns Hopkins University designed *Success for All* (SFA), a comprehensive school-wide intervention aimed at ensuring that every student in a school performs at grade level in reading by the end of the third grade and subsequently develops the advanced reading skills necessary for academic success.

SFA has many features that differentiate it from most other elementary school reading curricula. It has a highly structured school-wide curriculum that emphasizes "language and comprehension skills, phonics, sound blending, and use of shared stories" in grades K–1 and the use of novels and basal readers in "cooperative learning activities built around partner reading" in grades 2–6 (Borman et al., 2005a, p. 19). In contrast to the typical age cohort-based structure of the traditional elementary school, children participating in SFA are regrouped frequently across age and grade boundaries, so that they can be taught in cooperative learning groups in which all participants share similar reading skills. In addition, students must engage in free-choice reading at home for 20 minutes each evening, and teachers help parents learn how to provide appropriate supervision. When SFA is first introduced into a school, staff from the Success for All Foundation provides training to the school principal, the program facilitator, and the teachers who will implement the program. Finally, the reading achievement of participating children is assessed formally and systematically in every quarter in grades 1 through 6, and the assessments guide children's subsequent placement and remediation.

The SFA program was first introduced into public schools in Baltimore, Maryland, in 1987. During the next two decades, its use spread rapidly. Today more than 1,200 schools, most with economically disadvantaged student bodies, use this school-wide approach to developing students' reading skills. Sparking the rapid early expansion of SFA were the findings of several dozen non-experimental evaluations of the intervention conducted during the 1990s, which showed that the reading skills of children in schools that adopted SFA were better than those of children in "comparison" schools that implemented other reading curricula. However, these were not randomized experiments. Instead, the researchers who conducted the evaluations sought out and selected non-randomly several "comparison" schools that they believed served student populations that were demographically similar to those of the SFA schools and had a history of similarly low reading achievement.

As you know from Chapters 3 and 4, a necessary condition for such evaluations to provide unbiased estimates of the causal impact of SFA is that treatment and comparison groups must be *equal in expectation* on all unobserved dimensions that are correlated with student reading outcomes, prior to treatment. There are two reasons to question whether this condition was satisfied in the early non-experimental evaluations of SFA. First, schools that adopted SFA were required to spend about $75,000 in the first year of program implementation, $35,000 in the second year, and $25,000 in the third year, to pay for the materials and training that the SFA Foundation provided (Borman, 2007, p. 709). Schools that were able to obtain agreement from stakeholders to devote such substantial resources to a single program may have differed from other schools along other important dimensions, such as the quality of their leadership. Second, before a school introduces SFA, the Success for All Foundation requires that four-fifths of the faculty members in the school vote to adopt the school-wide intervention. A result of this requirement may have been that schools that voted to adopt SFA possessed a greater sense of common purpose, on average, than those that adopted more conventional curricular approaches to teaching reading. This difference in commitment to improving children's reading skills could itself have influenced student outcomes positively even if the SFA approach itself was no better than the alternatives.

Given the importance of developing the reading skills of disadvantaged students, the large number of schools using SFA to pursue this goal, and the limitations of available evidence to support its relative effectiveness, in 2000 the U.S. Department of Education provided the funds for a randomized-experimental evaluation of the impact of SFA. As you know from Chapter 4, the strength of this research design is that, *after* random assignment of participants to experimental conditions has taken place but *before* the intervention has begun, treatment and control groups will be equal in expectation on all dimensions, including those that are unobserved. This condition is central to the argument that any subsequent differences in student outcomes between members of the treatment and control groups are due to the differences in the treatments that the groups received.

However, one important respect in which the new randomized-experimental evaluation of SFA differed from that of the New York Scholarship Program (NYSP), which we described in Chapter 4, is that it was *intact* schools—rather than the individual students within them—that were randomized to experimental conditions. There are several reasons why such *cluster-randomized* experimental research designs are more common in education than designs that simply randomize *individuals* to experimental conditions. First, the mix of students enrolled in particular schools is predetermined by social forces that are difficult to change. Second, it is often much easier to overcome parents' and educational leaders' objections to the random assignment of children to treatment conditions if it is done at the school- rather than at the student level. Third, educational interventions themselves—that is, innovative educational treatments—tend to be implemented as policy changes at the classroom, teacher, school, or district level, rather than at the student level. Fourth, recall from Chapter 4 that peer effects are one of the major threats to the internal validity of random-assignment experiments. These are situations in which the impact of a treatment on *one* student may depend on whether particular other students are assigned to the same group. Such interaction effects violate SUTVA. However, as Imbens and Wooldridge (2009) explain, if all of the potential interaction effects are solely among students attending the same school, and if intact schools are randomized to treatment or control groups, the offending interactions are "internalized" into the conception of the treatment itself and no longer pose a problem. Consequently, it remains possible to obtain unbiased estimates of the causal impact of the intervention on the average achievement of students in the school, where our conception of the intervention includes the specific within-school student-to-student interactions it engenders.[1]

In this chapter, we discuss the consequences of randomizing intact groups to experimental conditions in evaluation research. In the next section of the chapter, we describe how the clustering of participants into intact groups affects subsequent analyses of experimental data. Essentially, we argue that if the results of these analyses—particularly the *statistical*

---

1. Imbens and Wooldridge (2009) also explain that it is usually not possible to separate out the direct effects of the intervention on the individual from the indirect effects on that individual that take place via their interactions with other students in their school.

inference—are to be credible, the statistical models on which they are based must sensibly incorporate information on the social hierarchies present naturally in the data. Here, we introduce a *multilevel (random-intercepts) regression model* that includes the *random effects of the intact groups* in its specification, and we explain why it is one appropriate way of dealing with the issues that arise. Then, in the following section, we explain how the presence of intact groups of participants in the evaluation and the accompanying modifications to the statistical models affect the statistical power of the experimental comparisons. In both of these sections, we use data from the random-assignment evaluation of SFA conducted by Geoffrey Borman and his colleagues to illustrate the technical lessons. In the final section of the chapter, we introduce an additional statistical model—the *fixed-effects of groups* multilevel regression model—that is also popular for dealing with the presence of intact groups of participants in experimental research designs. We contrast this model with the random-intercepts specification, briefly describing the pros and cons of each.

Random-Intercepts Multilevel Model to Estimate Effect Size When Intact Groups Are Randomized to Experimental Conditions

Statistical analyses become more complex when participants are grouped naturally into intact groups, and the intact groups are randomized to the treatment and control conditions. This was the case in the evaluation of SFA that Geoffrey Borman and his colleagues conducted (2005a). They began by identifying a set of elementary schools that wanted to adopt SFA. Their initial plan was to randomize these schools to either the SFA treatment or to a control condition (the latter being the continuation of the reading program the school had been using). However, the researchers were only able to locate six schools that would volunteer to take part in the experiment on these terms. Three of these schools were randomly assigned to implement SFA across all their grades, starting at the beginning of the 2001–2002 school year, and the other three retained their existing reading program and served as control schools. We will see later in this chapter that the random assignment of six intact schools to treatment and control conditions provides very little statistical power for subsequent analytic comparisons, regardless of effect size and the number of students present within each school.

So, to induce more schools to participate in the evaluation the following year, the evaluation team altered the incentives. All schools that agreed to join the evaluation at the start of the 2002–2003 school year were permitted to use the SFA program in some of their grades. Randomization was then used to determine whether each of the additional 35 schools that agreed to participate in the evaluation on these terms would implement SFA in grades K through 2 or in grades 3 through 5. Then, the children who attended kindergarten through second grade in the schools that were assigned to the "grades 3 through 5" SFA implementation served as control-group members for the randomly equivalent children who participated in the "K through 2" implementation of SFA in the other schools, and vice versa. In the experimental evaluation of the K through 2 SFA implementation, the "treatment" group included a total of 21 schools (three that implemented the SFA program in all grades, K through 5, and 18 that implemented it in grades K through 2). The "control" group included 20 schools (three of which did not use SFA at any grade level, and 17 that implemented SFA in grades 3 through 5). After the list-wise deletion of 699 children with missing data, the final analytic sample for the K through 2 evaluation consisted of 2,593 children in the SFA treatment group and 2,444 children in the control group, grouped into 41 schools (Borman et al., 2005a). We have included data on children in all of these schools in the analyses that we feature here. However, for pedagogic simplicity, we have limited our attention to children who were in the first grade in the first year in which their school participated in the evaluation.[2] We also focus our attention on a single reading outcome—the child's score on a "Word-Attack" test—that was measured at the end of the first year in which each school participated in the study.[3]

Of course, one cannot get something for nothing. If you adopt a cluster-randomized design for your experiment and thereby benefit from the relative ease with which you can randomize schools rather than students to experimental conditions, you must be prepared to accept increased analytic complexity and, ultimately, a reduction in statistical power. The extent of the penalty depends on the degree to which there is homogeneity among the outcome behaviors of children within the intact groupings. Children in the SFA evaluation shared unobserved experiences with their peers who attended the same school during each school year. These common, unobserved experiences make it difficult to assert that the responses of children within the same school were independent, even discounting the

---

2. We thank Geoffrey Borman for providing the data. Although our findings do not differ substantively from those of the original research, we recommend that readers interested in the evaluation of SFA consult the published papers by Borman and his colleagues. One paper (Borman et al., 2005a), which provides the basis for our presentation, describes the first-year results of the evaluation. A second (Borman, Slavin, & Cheung, 2005b) describes the second-year results, and a third (Borman et al., 2007) describes the results from the third and final year of the evaluation.
3. This was the outcome for which the original authors had the strongest findings in the first year of the evaluation.

common effect of the treatment. Consequently, since schools participated in the design as intact units, it is hard to argue that we have acquired a random sample of participating children within the school or that the corresponding student-level residuals in a standard statistical model are independent within a school. On the contrary, we would anticipate that the residuals of children attending the same school will be correlated, as a result of the common unobserved experiences that they shared over the course of an academic year or longer. The challenge for subsequent statistical analyses—and for any statistical power analyses carried out during the design of the study—is to account sensibly for this potential lack of residual independence among students within each school.

One straightforward and simple analytic approach for estimating the impact of the treatment while dealing with the potential lack of independence among the responses of participants within intact groups is to specify a *random-intercepts multilevel model* to describe the relationship between an outcome and its predictors. This is just a direct and simple extension of the standard ordinary least-squares (OLS) regression approach that we have described earlier in the book. In the case of the SFA evaluation, for instance, we can specify such a multilevel model to represent the causal relationship between a child's word-attack score, represented by continuous variable *WATTACK*, and a dichotomous predictor that distinguishes between children whose schools were assigned randomly to the SFA "treatment" (SFA = 1) or to the control treatment (SFA = 0), as follows:[4]

$$WATTACK_{ij} = \gamma_0 + \gamma_1 SFA_j + \left(\varepsilon_{ij} + u_j\right) \tag{7.1}$$

---

4. Borman et al. (2005a) state their random-intercepts multilevel models using what has become known as a "level-1/level-2" specification of the multilevel model. Under this approach, they specify both a *within-school* ("level-1") and a *between-school* ("level-2") component of the model. For instance, a simplified version of their *within-school* model, without added control predictors, is

$$\text{Level } 1: WATTACK_{ij} = \beta_{0j} + \varepsilon_{ij}$$

And the corresponding between-school model, again without additional covariates, is

$$\text{Level } 2: \beta_{0j} = \gamma_{00} + \gamma_{01} SFA_j + u_{0j}$$

The level-1 intercept parameter β_{0j} represents the *within-school* average of the outcome in the school j and differs from school to school. In the level-2 model, the school-level residuals u_{0j} provide random shocks to the grand intercept γ_{00} and lead to the random intercepts of the schools. The level-1/level-2 specification can be collapsed into a single "composite" model by substituting for parameter β_{0j} from the level-2 into the level-1 model, as follows:

$$WATTACK_{IJ} = \gamma_{00} + \gamma_{01} SFA_j + (u_{0j} + \varepsilon_{ij})$$

Note that the level-1/level-2 specification of the multilevel model is identical algebraically to the random-intercepts regression model in Equation 7.1, with only cosmetic differences in notation. In multilevel modeling, all level-1/level-2 specifications can be collapsed into a single composite model. It is the composite specifications that we choose to present in Equation 7.1.

for the ith child in the jth school. To simplify our presentation, we have omitted from this model a pair of important control predictors that Borman and his colleagues included in their statistical models. One of the omitted covariates represented the child's grade level in school. This is not relevant here because we have limited our analytic sample to children in first grade. The other covariate was the school-level average student pretest score on the Peabody Picture Vocabulary Test (PPVT). We reserve this covariate for inclusion later in our presentation.

Notice that, unlike a standard OLS regression model, our random-intercepts multilevel model in Equation 7.1 contains a *composite* residual that sums two distinct error terms. We have specified the model in this way deliberately to provide a mechanism, within the model, that accounts for the hypothesized lack of independence that may exist among the unpredicted portion of the responses of children within a school. The first term is a *child-level* residual, ε_{ij}, and the second a *school-level* residual u_j. In our hypothesized random-intercepts multilevel model, all children in the same school share the same value of the school-level residual u_j, and this serves to tie together—or correlate—their composite residuals. Consequently, the model does not constrain their composite residuals to be independent of each other, as standard OLS models require. In fitting a random-intercepts multilevel model to data, we assume that each of the constituent error terms, ε_{ij} and u_j, satisfies the usual residual normal-theory assumptions. Thus, we assume that the child- and school-level residuals are distributed independently of each other in the population, that the child-level residuals have a population mean of zero and a variance of σ_ε^2, and that the school-level residuals have a population mean of zero and a variance of σ_u^2.

It is worth pausing at this point to understand why this new multilevel model is referred to as a *random-intercepts* model. The reason becomes evident with a simple reordering of the terms in the model itself, to become:

$$WATTACK_{ij} = (\gamma_0 + u_j) + \gamma_1 SFA_j + \varepsilon_{ij} \qquad (7.2)$$

This tells us that, by including school-level residuals in the model—to capture the hierarchical nature of the data—we have essentially provided each school with its own "random" intercept, represented by $\gamma_0 + u_j$. When we fit this multilevel model to data, we do not estimate each of the school-specific intercepts. Instead, we estimate their mean γ_0 and their variance σ_u^2 (under the assumption that the school-level residuals are drawn randomly from a distribution with mean zero and homoscedastic variance σ_u^2).

We have fitted the random-intercepts multilevel model specified in Equation 7.1 to our subsample of data from the SFA evaluation. It appears

Table 7.1 Parameter estimates, approximate p-values, standard errors, and selected goodness-of-fit statistics for three random-effects multilevel models describing the fitted relationship between the word-attack scores of first-graders, at the end of their first year in the study, and the assignment of their school to either the SFA intervention or the control condition ($n_{schools} = 41$; $n_{students} = 2,334$)

	Fitted Random-Effects Multilevel Models		
	Model #1: The unconditional model	Model #2: Conditional model that contains the main effect of SFA	Model #3: Conditional model that adds the main effect of covariate SCH_PPVT to Model #2
INTERCEPT	477.54*** (1.447)	475.30*** (2.046)	419.82*** (12.558)
SFA		4.363 (2.859)	3.572 (2.340)
SCH_PPVT			0.623*** (0.140)
$\hat{\sigma}^2_\varepsilon$	314.20	314.20	314.20
$\hat{\sigma}^2_u$	78.69	76.61	48.57
R^2_{total}	0.000	0.032	0.091
Intraclass correlation, $\hat{\rho}$	0.200	0.196	0.134

$^\sim p$ <0.10; $^*p$ <0.05; $^{**}p$ <0.01; $^{***}p$ <0.001.

as Model #2 in the third column of Table 7.1.[5] In the table, we include estimates of each of the regression parameters in the model, along with their standard errors and approximate p-values. In addition, at the bottom of the column, we list estimates of the child- and school-level residual variances, the overall R^2 statistic for the fitted model, and an estimate of a new parameter—the intraclass correlation, ρ. Later in this chapter, we define this parameter and explain the important role that it plays in statistical power analyses for this kind of research design. In addition to this

---

5. The random-intercepts multilevel model is easily fitted by standard procedures in widely available statistical software packages, such as PROC MIXED in SAS and XTREG in STATA. It can also be fitted using dedicated software, such as HLM (Raudenbush & Bryk, 2002) and MLWIN (Rasbash, Steele, Browne, & Goldstein, 2009). Although some of these procedures use different estimation algorithms, their results remain essentially identical, within rounding error. Borman and his colleagues (2005a) used the HLM package in their analyses.

fitted model, our table contains two other fitted models: (a) an *unconditional* model that contains no predictors at all, and (b) a second *conditional* model in which we have added the main effect of an interesting school-level covariate, the within-school average value of a prior PPVT student test score, measured before the intervention began.

Before turning to the results of the evaluation itself (as summarized in fitted Models #2 and #3), we focus on the consequences of fitting Model #1–the "unconditional" multilevel model. Parameter estimates from this fitted model are easy to interpret because the model contains no explicit predictors. The estimated intercept in the unconditional model, for instance, tells us that—over all children and schools in our subsample of first-graders—the average word-attack score is 477.54 points ($p < 0.001$). More interesting are the estimates of the child- and school-level residual variances, which are 314.20 and 78.69, respectively. What do we make of these two components of residual variance?

First, it is important to realize—as in a regular OLS-fitted regression model—that when no predictors are present in the model, residual variability and outcome variability are synonymous. If no part of the outcome is being predicted, then outcome variability must equal residual variability. Here, because we have articulated our multilevel residual as a sum of two independent contributions, we have partitioned the outcome variation effectively into its child- and school-level components. In the unconditional multilevel model, the *school-level residual variance* is a summary of the variability in the *school-mean value of the outcome* from school to school. It is often referred to as *between-school* variance. It summarizes the scatter in the outcome among schools. The *child-level residual variance* is what is left over after school-level variance has been removed from the outcome variability. In the unconditional multilevel model, it is the outcome variance among children *within* each school, pooled over the schools. It is often referred to as the *within-school* variance. It describes the scatter in the outcome from student to student within each school.

What we learn from the fitted unconditional model in Table 7.1 is that the *total* sample variance in the word-attack score outcome (392.89) is the sum of a within-school contribution of 314.2 and a between-school contribution of 78.69. Comparing the magnitudes of these two contributions, we notice that the sample outcome variability is made up disproportionately of child-level rather than of school-level variation. We can summarize the proportion of the total sample variance in the outcome at the school level by expressing it as a fraction of the total variance—this fraction is equal to 78.69/392.89, or 0.20. You will find this latter statistic, 0.20, listed under the fitted unconditional model in the bottom row of Table 7.1 and labeled "Intraclass Correlation." It is an important summary statistic that will feature in the analyses that follow, including our subsequent statistical power analyses. It summarizes the fact that, in our current sample of first-graders clustered within schools, 20% of the variation in our outcome can be attributed to differences in the average value of the outcome among schools and that the rest is due to heterogeneity among children within a school. Correspondingly, we define the population intraclass correlation in terms of the *population residual variances* present in our hypothesized random-intercepts multilevel model, as follows[6]

$$\rho = \frac{\sigma^2_{between}}{\sigma^2_{within} + \sigma^2_{between}}$$

$$= \frac{\sigma^2_u}{\sigma^2_\varepsilon + \sigma^2_u}$$

(7.3)

Because it is a proportion, the intraclass-correlation parameter can only take on values that range between 0 and 1. By fitting unconditional Model #1, we have obtained an estimate of it, in our subsample, uncontrolled for any other predictors or covariates, as follows:

$$\hat{\rho} = \frac{\hat{\sigma}^2_{between}}{\hat{\sigma}^2_{within} + \hat{\sigma}^2_{between}}$$

$$= \frac{78.69}{314.20 + 78.69}$$

$$= 0.20$$

You can articulate potential problems that can be caused by the non-independence of participants within intact groups by thinking in terms of the within- and between-group variability in the outcome. First, consider the *clusters* of children—that is, the *schools*—that were enrolled ultimately in the SFA evaluation. Imagine a fictitious scenario in which every child was actually assigned randomly to his or her school at the beginning of the school year. In this scenario, there would be considerable natural variation in reading achievement across all of the children. However, as a result of their initial random assignment to schools, the average reading performance of the children in each school would not differ across schools. In other words, at the beginning of the year, when children were initially

---

6. Another version of this index could just as easily have been defined as the proportion of the sum of the constituent variances that lies within school, or as the ratio of the two constituent variances. By convention, however, Equation 7.3 is the definition that is adopted because of its mapping onto other important parameters defined in traditional analyses of variance and regression analysis.

independent of each other, there would be no variation in average reading performance from school to school—and consequently no "between-school" variation. Instead, all observed variation in reading performance would simply be among children within schools, and the intraclass correlation would be zero.[7]

Of course, things would not remain that way for long, once children began to interact with each other within the school. Over the course of a school year, unobserved, shared school-based experiences would act to homogenize the unobserved responses of children within the school. For example, the influences of strong school directors or constructive peer groups may raise the achievement of all children in some schools, while the influence of weak school directors or destructive peer groups may lower the achievement of all children in other schools. Under this scenario, total variation in reading performance across all of the children in the sample will become partitioned differently by the end of the year. In particular, considerable school-to-school variation in average reading performance may arise, and the intraclass correlation would then no longer be zero. In fact, under the most extreme hypothetical scenario, school-specific influences would become so powerful that all children within a school might end up performing identically on the end-of-year reading achievement test. In this case, all of the variation in reading performance would be "between school" and none "within school," and the intraclass correlation would take on a value of 1.

Thinking through these two extreme scenarios, it becomes clear that the way in which net variation in reading achievement is partitioned—within a school or between schools—is a good indicator of the relative homogeneity of children's responses on the outcome. The reason is that, if all of the outcome variation is situated within school, we can regard children as behaving essentially independently of one another, despite their school affiliations. On the other hand, when all of the outcome

---

7. Of course, this situation never occurs in practice because children are clustered naturally in neighborhoods before they are assigned to schools. And, even then, they are not assigned randomly to neighborhoods. In fact, unobserved forces in the neighborhood act to render children's responses interdependent long before they even get to school, because schools draw from catchment areas within which children share many unobserved opportunities and experiences. Typically, students will arrive in a school already interdependent (that is, with a non-zero intraclass correlation), but it is likely that their interdependence is enhanced by the unobserved common experiences that they share subsequently at the school, over the academic year. In designing effective research, it is critical to take both of these into account and focus on what the intraclass correlation may potentially become, at that point in time at which the final value of the outcome of the evaluation has been measured. In this case, that would be at the end of the school year.

variation is situated between school, then children within a school will have become entirely interdependent and will now be behaving as clones of one another. In the world of real children and real schools, of course, the partition of the variation in the outcome variable usually falls somewhere between these extremes. To estimate the statistical power of research designs that randomize intact clusters of participants to experimental conditions, we must come to understand the relative importance of within-group and between-group contributions to the outcome variation. The magnitude of the intraclass correlation provides us with an important summary of this partition. It features prominently in our subsequent estimation of statistical power for research designs that assign intact groups of participants randomly to experimental conditions.

As we have noted, when between-school variability in the outcome is zero, the magnitude of the intraclass correlation is zero (because its numerator is zero). In this situation, there are no differences among schools, and all variability in the outcome is attributable to differences among children within schools. In this case, we can regard children within a school as behaving completely independently of each other, and there would be no effect of their clustering into intact schools on any of the products of the data analysis, including our estimation of statistical power. In fact, when the intraclass correlation is zero, the total sample of children can be treated as though it were a simple random sample, not a cluster-randomized sample, and the effective sample size in the statistical analysis will equal the total number of children in the sample across all schools.

On the other hand, when between-school variability in the outcome is large (compared to within-school variability), the magnitude of the intraclass correlation will be closer to 1. Under this condition, children within a school will be behaving very similarly, and the clustering of the children within schools will come to dominate any products of the data analysis or statistical power calculation. In fact, as the magnitude of the intraclass correlation approaches 1, the effective sample size in any statistical analysis approaches the total number of schools in the sample, rather than the total number of children. As you can imagine, this has enormous impact on the statistical power of the analysis.

At this point, it seems natural to review the sorts of values of the intraclass correlation obtained typically in empirical settings. It turns out that the specific estimated value that we have obtained here—which was 0.20, in Model #1—is relatively large. In most empirical research in which students are clustered within intact schools, the estimated magnitudes of the intraclass correlations are typically quite small numerically, usually with values of no more than 0.20, and often of less than 0.05. In fact, as a yardstick, methodologists tend to regard values of the intraclass correlation of around 0.01 as "small," those around 0.09 as "medium," and those around 0.25 as "large."[8]

We now turn to the evaluation of the effectiveness of the SFA intervention. In Model #2 of Table 7.1, we present the results of fitting our first "conditional" model, which now includes the critical question predictor, SFA. Notice that the estimated within-child residual variance $\hat{\sigma}_\varepsilon^2$ in this model (which has a value of 314.20) is no smaller than the corresponding value obtained in the fitted unconditional model. This makes sense because the critical SFA question predictor that we have introduced into the model at this juncture is a school-level predictor, as intact schools were randomized to treatment and control conditions in the SFA evaluation. In multilevel modeling, school-level predictors tend to predict school-level variation, and child-level predictors tend to predict child-level variation, although the separation is not always exclusive.[9] Notice that the estimated school-level residual variance $\hat{\sigma}_u^2$ is about two points lower in Model #2 than in the fitted unconditional model. A result of this decline in the fitted between-school residual variance is that the estimated intraclass correlation—now estimated while controlling for the assignment of children to experimental conditions—is 0.196 in Model #2, slightly less than its value in fitted unconditional Model #1. Essentially, the introduction of the school-level SFA predictor has accounted for a small amount of the between-school variability in outcome, reducing the unpredicted school-level variability that remains in the corresponding residual. This, in its turn, has led to a small decline in the magnitude of the estimated intraclass correlation. In other words, the intraclass correlation now describes the within-school interdependence of children that is attributable to all unobserved forces and effects, *except* for the impact of assignment to experimental condition.

Consistent with this prediction of school-level outcome variability, the estimated regression coefficient associated with the SFA question predictor is positive and of magnitude 4.363.[10] As in regular regression analyses of

---

8. Notice that these are approximately the squares of the corresponding standard "small," "medium," and "large" values of the Pearson correlation coefficient.

9. Potentially, the deviation of an individual-level variable from the grand mean can be written as a sum of: (a) the deviation of the individual-level score from the group-level mean, and (b) the deviation of the group-level mean from the grand mean. Unless this latter contribution is zero, any individual-level variable may contain both individual-level and group-level variation, and thus adding an individual-level predictor to a multilevel model could predict both individual-level and group-level variation in the outcome.

10. Notice also that the overall model R^2 statistic has risen from zero to 0.03.

experimental data, this coefficient estimates the treatment effect. It tells us that children who experienced the SFA intervention scored about 4.4 points higher on the word-attack outcome, on average, than did children in the control condition, at the end of the first year of the experiment. This is just over one-fifth of a standard deviation in the outcome, a respectable effect size.[11]

Unfortunately, because of our pedagogic focus on the first-grade subsample of the data, our estimate of the treatment effect does not quite achieve the standard level of statistical significance. Borman and his colleagues (2005a), working in the larger dataset, were able to reject the corresponding null hypothesis and conclude that the SFA intervention was indeed successful in causing children's work-attack scores to be higher, on average, at the end of the first year of the experiment than those of children in the control group, who did not have access to the SFA reading program. We discuss fitted Model #3 later in this chapter, in the context of our statistical power analysis.

Statistical Power When Intact Groups of Participants Are Randomized to Experimental Conditions

As you no doubt suspect from the previous section, the within-cluster homogeneity of participants, as described by the intraclass correlation, has a direct and important impact on the statistical power of any research design that randomizes intact clusters of participants to experimental conditions. Consequently, to determine an appropriate sample size for such designs, in addition to specifying the usual triumvirate of the α-level, anticipated effect size, and required statistical power, you must also specify the magnitude of the intraclass correlation that you anticipate finding across individuals within the intact units you will randomly assign to experimental conditions. Importantly, you need to obtain an estimate of the value of the intraclass correlation *at the point in time in which you measure the value of your outcome*. We investigate and illustrate this dependence in this section, algebraically and graphically, for prototypical experiments similar in all other respects to those that we described in the previous chapter. For instance, imagine that we have been asked to design an evaluation of the first-year impact of SFA. Given that we intend to assign intact schools randomly to the experimental conditions, it would be useful, in

---

11. The outcome standard deviation in our subsample is 19.88.

advance, to figure out how the number of intact clusters (that is, schools), the number of children within each cluster, and the magnitude of the intraclass correlation will affect the statistical power of our design.

You can gain insight into the dependence of statistical power on the clustering of participants within intact groups by examining an expression for the population sampling variance of the estimate of regression parameter γ_1, which in its turn represents the effect of the SFA treatment in Equation 7.1. Under the simplifying assumptions that there are an identical number of n participants (students) present in each of an even number of J intact groups (schools) that have been randomized with an equal number of schools assigned to treatment and control conditions, we can write this population sampling variance as the sum of two parts, as follows:

$$Var\left(\hat{\gamma}_1\right) = \left(\frac{\sigma_\varepsilon^2}{nJ/4}\right) + \left(\frac{4\sigma_\varepsilon^2\left(\rho/1-\rho\right)}{J}\right) \tag{7.4}$$

Examining how the population sampling variance of $\hat{\gamma}_1$ depends on the values of n, J, and ρ is a reasonable approach for gaining insight into the links between these quantities and statistical power because, when the population sampling variance in Equation 7.4 is estimated from sample data and square-rooted, it gives us the standard error of $\hat{\gamma}_1$ for the cluster-randomized evaluation design. And, of course, it is this standard error that serves as the denominator of the t-statistic used for testing the all-important null hypothesis that regression parameter γ_1 is zero, in the population. In other words, it is the standard error that is used in the critical assessment of the causal impact of the SFA treatment on children's reading achievement, at the end of the first year. The larger this standard error, the smaller the magnitude of the corresponding t-statistic, and the harder it will be for us to reject H_0, all else being equal. In other words, when the standard error of the estimated treatment effect is larger, we have less statistical power for detecting an effect of treatment in the cluster-randomized research design. Therefore, although the expression for the population sampling variance in Equation 7.4 does not describe the actual statistical power of the cluster-randomized design, inspection of its functioning does tell us how the statistical power of the cluster-randomized design depends on the magnitude of the intraclass correlation, the number of intact units (schools), and the number of participants (students) per intact unit in the design. We comment on, and illustrate, these important dependencies below.

Statistical Power of the Cluster-Randomized Design and Intraclass Correlation

First, it is worth noting that when the intraclass correlation is zero ($\rho = 0$), for instance, the second term in Equation 7.4 is also zero. In this case, the population sampling variance (and the standard error) of the estimated treatment effect is identical to the corresponding sampling variance (and standard error) that would be obtained under a research design in which the same total number (nJ) of students were randomized individually to the control or treatment groups.[12] In other words, when the intraclass correlation is zero and therefore children are acting independently within schools, the cluster-randomized design converges on the simple individually randomized design and has the same statistical power. However, as the unobserved responses of children within a cluster become more interdependent, the magnitude of the intraclass correlation rises. When this happens, the second term on the right in Equation 7.4 becomes increasingly important in the expression for the population sampling variance in Equation 7.4, and consequently in the determination of the standard error of the estimated treatment effect in the cluster-randomized design. Non-zero values of the intraclass correlation inflate the population sampling variance, and corresponding standard error of the treatment effect, above the value that would be obtained in a simple individually randomized design with the same total number of independent individuals. For instance, when ρ is 0.1, the term $\rho/(1-\rho)$ in the numerator of Equation 7.4 takes on a value of 0.1 divided by 0.9, or 0.1111. Now, the standard error of the estimated treatment effect under the cluster-randomized design is somewhat larger than under an individually randomized design, but the difference is modest. However, if the intraclass correlation were to rise all the way to 0.75, say, implying that the behaviors of children within a school were highly interdependent, then the expression $\rho/(1-\rho)$ would take on a value of 3, and the standard error of the estimated treatment effect in the cluster-randomized design would be substantially larger than that obtained in the simple individually randomized design. Thus, as the magnitude of the intraclass correlation increases, representing increasing interdependence among children within schools, the statistical power of the cluster-randomized design falls dramatically relative to the power of the simple individually randomized design. Fortunately, the

---

12. The requisite OLS population sampling variance is given by the first term to the right of the equals sign in Equation 7.4, or

$$\left(\frac{\sigma_\varepsilon^2}{nJ \, / \, 4} \right)$$

magnitude of the intraclass correlation in educational settings is usually quite small, rarely rising above 0.2, or 0.25 as we noted earlier.

Nevertheless, the impact of the clustering on statistical power is consequential. To illustrate the dependency more concretely, we present "ballpark estimates" of the statistical power for a cluster-randomized research design similar to that used in the SFA evaluation. In Figure 7.1, we display the anticipated relationship between the statistical power of a cluster-randomized research design (on the vertical axis) versus the number of clusters (intact schools) in the study (on the horizontal axis), for detecting a small effect size (0.2) at three typical values of the intraclass correlation (0, 0.05, and 0.1) with an α-level of 0.05, on a one-sided test. We repeat the display for cluster-randomized designs in which each of the hypothetical schools contains: (a) 50 children (*top panel*) and (b) 100 children (*bottom panel*).[13] We have included the case in which the magnitude of the intraclass correlation is zero in order to establish a point of reference with the power analyses that we presented in the preceding chapter (where we offered similar ballpark estimates of statistical power and sample size for a simple individually randomized design).

Inspection of the top panel of the figure confirms our algebraic analysis of the impact of intraclass correlation on statistical power, at a fixed number of clusters and a fixed cluster size. For instance, when the intraclass correlation is zero, we need around 13 schools—with a total of approximately 650 students—to reach a moderate statistical power of 0.80. A zero intraclass correlation implies that participants are behaving independently, even though they are grouped within intact clusters, and these sample sizes are consistent with our power analyses in the previous chapter, in which we concluded that about 620 children were required for an experiment in which participants were randomly and individually assigned.[14]

However, notice what happens when we raise the hypothetical value of the intraclass correlation to 0.05. Now, we need approximately 45 schools, each containing 50 students—for a grand total of almost *four times as many participants*—to achieve the same statistical power of 0.80! When the value

---

13. The power computations were carried out using Optimal Design for Multi-Level and Longitudinal Research, Version 0.35 (Liu et al., 2005). The accompanying manual is a good source for further details of statistical power computation in the cluster-randomized design.

14. Two factors contribute to the small difference between the estimated requisite sample size, 650, reported here and the estimate of 620 described in the previous chapter. The first is the impact of rounding error in the power computation algorithms of the different software we have used. The second is that that you cannot make up a sample of exactly 620 out of intact groups of 50.

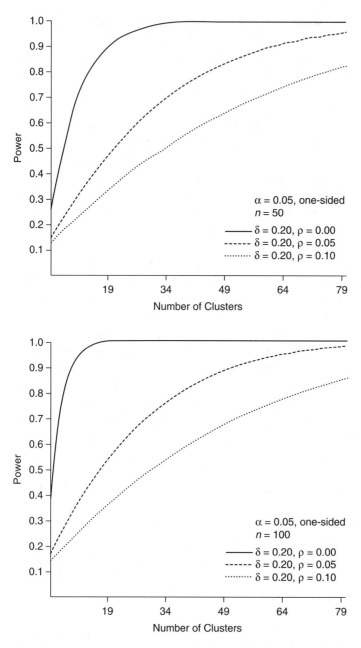

Figure 7.1 Anticipated relationship between statistical power of a cluster-randomized research design versus number of clusters (schools), for a small effect size (0.2), at three values of intraclass correlation (0, 0.05, and 0.1), α-level of 0.05, on a one-sided test. *Top panel*: 50 children/school. *Bottom panel*: 100 children/school.

of the intraclass correlation rises to 0.1, the impact is even more dramatic. Moderate power is not achieved until around 75 schools have been included in the sampling plan, for a total sample size of 3,750 students. The patterns displayed in Figure 7.1 illustrate that the statistical power of a cluster-randomized design is indeed very sensitive to the value of the intraclass correlation.

Consider now the impact on the statistical power of a cluster-randomized design of the number of participants within a cluster (in the SFA evaluation, the total number of children in grades K-2 within a school). In the expression for the population sampling variance in Equation 7.4 (and the corresponding standard error of the treatment effect), the number of participants within a cluster n appears only in conjunction with the number of clusters J as a product, to represent total sample size nJ. In addition, it is present only in the denominator of the first term that follows the equal sign. Thus, it plays the same role in the determination of the statistical power of the cluster-randomized design as it does in an individually randomized design in which the same total number of "unclustered" participants were randomized to experimental conditions. Thus, as the number of participants within a cluster is increased (for a fixed number of clusters), the total sample size must increase, the population sampling variance (and the corresponding standard error of the treatment effect) must decrease, and the statistical power improve, as we expect from our arguments in the previous chapter. However, in Equation 7.4, we note that it is only the magnitude of the first term to the right of the equal sign that is diminished by this increase in the total sample size, regardless of the contribution of the second term. Thus, we anticipate that any control over statistical power that is provided in the cluster-randomized design by manipulating the number of participants within a cluster must offer benefits no different than we would expect for the same sample size increase in the simpler individually randomized design. But, in a cluster-randomized design, its contribution is rapidly dominated by the impact of any increase in the magnitude of the intraclass correlation and in the number of clusters, both of which appear in the second term to the right of the equal sign in Equation 7.4.

You can see the dependence of the statistical power of a cluster-randomized design on the number of participants within a cluster in Figure 7.1 by comparing the corresponding prototypical power values in the top and bottom panels, at the same number of clusters and the same intraclass correlation. Notice, for instance, that increasing the number of participants present at each school from 50 to 100 students has only a marginal impact on the power of the prospective analysis. With 50 students at each school and an intraclass correlation of 0.05, about 45 schools are required to achieve a power of 0.80, for a total of 2,250 students. With 100 participants at each school and 45 schools, the statistical power provided by the design rises only to around 0.85—an increase of just over 6%, obtained by doubling the total number of students in the sample!

The most important mechanism for increasing the statistical power of a cluster-randomized design is the investigator's ability to manipulate the number of intact clusters that are randomized. This is evident in the expression for population sampling variance in Equation 7.4. Here, the number of clusters in the design appears in the denominator of the second term to the right of the equal sign. As the number of clusters in the design is increased, the contribution of the second term to the inflation of the standard error is rapidly diminished, and the standard error will approach that of a corresponding simple and individually randomized design. These effects occur in addition to the impact of the intraclass correlation, but are mediated by its magnitude. In Figure 7.1, we see these dependencies in the shapes of the trend lines that represent the relationships between statistical power and the number of clusters that appear in both panels. In all cases (except when the intraclass correlation is zero), regardless of the intraclass correlation and the number of participants within a cluster, statistical power increases rapidly when clusters of participants are added to the design. In fact, although the relationships are curvilinear, it is clear that—if you have 50 students per school and an intraclass correlation of 0.05—you can easily double your power from around 0.40 to 0.80, say, by increasing the number of schools you sample from 15 to 45. Statistical power in a cluster-randomized design lies much more in the number of clusters than in the number of participants per cluster.

Our final comment in this section returns us to a topic that we have discussed in the previous chapter. It concerns the benefit of including covariates in analyses of experimental data. Our previous message has been that, once participants have been randomized to experimental conditions, the inclusion of covariates in an analysis is always a good idea because it tends to reduce residual variance and thereby reduces the standard errors of the parameter estimates. This, in turn, tends to enlarge the associated t-statistic and diminish the corresponding p-values, leading to improved statistical power.

The key theme, then, is *reduction of residual variance*. If the inclusion of a covariate acts to reduce residual variance in an analysis of any kind, statistical power will increase. Of course, when participants are clustered into intact groups, we have learned that it is appropriate to model their behavior in a random-intercepts multilevel model that contains a *pair* of residuals. Fortunately, reductions in residual variance at either the individual or group level will reduce the standard errors of parameter estimates and improve statistical power. More often than not, however, in settings in which the intraclass correlation is non-zero—that is, when the intact grouping of participants has indeed influenced their unobserved behaviors—one approach will be superior. It will typically be more effective, from the perspective of increasing statistical power, to reduce group-level residual variance by including group-level covariates than to reduce individual-level residual variance. This conclusion echoes a similar conclusion that we reported in the previous section, where we noted that the statistical power of a cluster-randomized design tends to be more sensitive to the number of intact groups than to the number of participants within those groups.

Essentially, the magnitude of the intraclass correlation is more sensitive to changes in between-group residual variance than to changes in within-group residual variance. This matters because statistical power is very sensitive to the magnitude of the intraclass correlation. In fact, a reduction in between-group residual variance will always lead to a greater increase in statistical power than a corresponding reduction in the within-group residual variance. This means, of course, that when you seek covariates to include in analyses of clustered data, you would be well advised to first seek out effective group-level covariates.

Following Borman and his colleagues (2005a), the only difference between our fitted Models #2 and #3, in Table 7.1, is that the latter includes the covariate, *SCH_PPVT*, which is the school-specific average value of children's scores on the PPVT prior to the start of the evaluation.[15] Notice that the addition of this school-level covariate to the model results in a dramatic reduction in the estimated between-school residual variance, from 76.61 to 48.57, while the within-school residual variance remains unchanged. As a result, the estimated intraclass correlation falls from its "large" value of 0.196 in Model #2 to an almost "medium" value of 0.134 in Model #3. There is a concomitant reduction in the standard error of the estimated effect of the SFA treatment from 2.859 to 2.340. Unfortunately, in this particular example, these changes were offset by a reduction in the size of the parameter estimate itself, from 4.353 to 3.572. Consequently, the value of the t-statistic does not differ very much. This example is atypical, and the take-away remains that the addition of

---

15. Rather than estimate the average score of children in our subsample on this pretest and use it as the covariate, we took advantage of the school-average pretest PPVT score that was provided by Borman et al. (2005a), in their larger dataset. Repeating our analyses with this latter average replaced by a within-school average obtained in our subsample provided similar, if slightly weaker, results.

cluster-level covariates is often an extremely effective way to increase the statistical power of a cluster-randomized design.

Fixed-Effects Multilevel Models to Estimate Effect Size When Intact Groups of Participants Are Randomized to Experimental Conditions

The random-intercepts multilevel model specified in Equation 7.1 is a common, effective way of estimating treatment effects while accounting for the clustering of participants within intact groups. However, the field of multilevel modeling itself is large and complex, and there are other ways of specifying a statistical model in order to account for the impact of participant clustering. In this section, we describe one common alternative to the random-intercepts multilevel model.

Specifying a Fixed-Effects Multilevel Model

Before leaving the topic of multilevel models, we describe one simple alternative strategy for taking into account the impact of intact clusters of participants in the statistical analysis. This flexible and robust strategy, called the method of *fixed-effects*, has great utility in a wide variety of analytic settings. Its origins are easy to grasp through further inspection of the alternative specification of our random-intercepts model in Equation 7.2, which we repeat here:

$$WATTACK_{ij} = \left(\gamma_0 + u_j\right) + \gamma_1 SFA_j + \varepsilon_{ij} \qquad (7.5)$$

Recall that we used this alternative specification to motivate our argument that this multilevel model could be referred to appropriately as a "random-intercepts" model. The reason was that introducing a school-specific residual u_j into the model was tantamount to providing each school in our SFA universe with its own intercept, $(\gamma_0 + u_j)$. And, of course, because the school-level residuals u_j were assumed to be drawn from an underlying random distribution, we had then effectively specified a multilevel model with a set of school-specific "random intercepts." Hence, the name we adopted for the model.

We can press this argument even further, however, and rewrite Equation 7.5, so that each school is presented as having its own actual intercept α_j as follows:

$$WATTACK_{ij} = \alpha_j + \gamma_1 SFA_j + \varepsilon_{ij} \qquad (7.6)$$

where $\alpha_j = \gamma_0 + u_j$. There is no difference between the two specifications. However, the latter specification leads one to ask the obvious question: Why do these school-specific intercepts, which are needed to resolve the problem of intact groups, need to be random? Why can't they be fixed? That is, why can't we specify a multilevel model that contains an intercept parameter for each school? In fitting the model to the data from the SFA evaluation, there would be 41 such intercepts, one for each of the 41 schools in the sample.

In practice, you can easily introduce such a set of intercepts into any regression model by creating a set of dichotomous predictors to distinguish the school membership of each child, and then including these dichotomous variables as predictors in the statistical model. For instance, we could create new dichotomous variables S_1 through S_{41} to represent the 41 schools in our SFA subsample, setting each of these dummies equal to 1 when the child was a member of that school, 0 otherwise. Thus, all of the students in the first school would have a value of 1 for dichotomous predictor S_1, and a value of 0 for all the other school dummies. Children in the second school would have a value of 1 for dichotomous predictor S_2, and a value of 0 on all the others, and so on. Then, to resolve the problem of the clustering of participants within schools, instead of fitting the model in Equation 7.1 to the SFA data by the method of random effects, we could fit the following model:

$$WATTACK_{ij} = \left(\alpha_0 + \alpha_2 S_{2j} + \alpha_3 S_{3j} + \ldots + \alpha_{41} S_{41j}\right) + \gamma_1 SFA_j + \varepsilon_{ij} \quad (7.7)$$

Notice, as usual, when a vector of dummy predictors represents a global effect like that of "school," we have dropped one of the dummy predictors from the model and nominated its associated school—here, the first school—arbitrarily as our "reference" category. Then, the included overall intercept, here α_0, represents the population average value of word-attack score in the reference school, and the remaining α-coefficients represent the difference between the population means of each school and the omitted school.[16] Finally, notice that the only residual now remaining in the model is the child-level residual ε_{ij}. Because this latter residual satisfies regular OLS assumptions implicitly, we can use OLS regression methods to fit the model.

---

16. We could have achieved the same ends by eliminating the standard intercept α_0 and retaining all of the school dummy predictors and their corresponding slope parameters. Then, each parameter would represent the population average word-attack score in its associated school, without the necessity to declare one as a "reference" school. The results from the two alternative methods would be substantively identical.

A model such as Equation 7.7, in which each intact school has its own intercept, is referred to as a *fixed-effects of schools* model, and the coefficients associated with the dummy predictors represent those fixed effects. Unfortunately, there is a problem in using this model to examine the relative effectiveness of SFA, which you will recall was a school-wide approach to teaching reading. If you try to fit the fixed-effects of schools model in Equation 7.7 in our SFA data, the statistical software will typically balk. Depending on how the software is written, the program will either cease to function or will respond by dropping one term—probably the predictor SFA, and its associated slope parameter—from the model. In either case, the analysis may fail, and the effect of the SFA intervention on the outcome will certainly not be estimated. The reason is that perfect collinearity exists between the SFA predictor and the full collection of school dummies. Recall that the SFA treatment was randomized to intact schools, and so predictor SFA is a dichotomous school-level predictor that possesses no variation within school. In other words, all the children in grades K-2 in any school have the same value as the SFA predictor. So, SFA is a predictor that essentially distinguishes between two types of school. Of course, the dichotomous school predictors already in the model are also doing the same job. For instance, let's suppose that schools 21 through 41 were the control schools. Then, if we knew that a schoolgirl had a value of 1 for any of the corresponding dummy predictors, S_{21} through S_{41}, we would know that she attended a control school, and we would not need to know her value on variable SFA. Alternatively, if she had a value of zero on this same set of school indicators, we would know for sure that she had been assigned to the treatment condition.[17] In fact, once the vectors of school dummies are included as predictors in the model, they absorb all of the school-level variation in the outcome, and you can no longer add any other school-level predictors to the model. Consequently, you cannot include the critical school-level question predictor SFA, whose associated regression parameter addresses the all-important research question at the heart of the evaluation!

Given that you cannot include a school-level question predictor, such as SFA, in a model that contains the fixed effects for schools, you may be tempted to ask: What use then are such fixed-effects models? The answer

17. This explanation suggests a strategy that could be used effectively to estimate the impact of the SFA treatment even in a fixed-effects-of-schools model from which the SFA predictor had been omitted because of its complete redundancy. After fitting the model containing all the school dummies and no SFA predictor, you can then compare the average of the population intercepts of all the SFA-designated schools with the average of the population intercepts of all non-SFA-designated schools using a post-hoc general linear hypothesis (GLH) test, or linear-contrast analysis.

is that they are very useful if you want to control all variation in the outcome *at one level* and pose an important research question *at another*. This is a situation that occurs frequently in educational research, where children are not just nested within a two-level hierarchy, but within hierarchies that are many levels deep. Thus, children may be nested within intact classes, which are then nested within schools, which are nested within districts, and so on. For instance, although we cannot retain the SFA predictor in a multilevel model that contains the fixed effects of schools, we could include the fixed effects of a school district, thereby controlling all variation in the outcome at this higher level of clustering. In addition, we could continue to account for the nesting of children within school by using the standard random-effects strategy of including a school-level residual. Such combining of the methods of fixed and random effects proves to be a flexible analytic strategy for handling the grouping of participants at multiple levels.

For instance, in the Tennessee Student/Teacher Achievement Ratio (STAR) experiment, kindergarten students in each of 79 large elementary schools were assigned randomly to either a small class (13–17 students), a regular-size class (22–25) students, or to a regular-size class with a full-time teacher's aide. Kindergarten teachers in participating schools were then randomly assigned to classes. Over the year, of course, even though students were originally assigned randomly to classes, their shared unobserved experiences over the academic year could "build up" an intraclass correlation of substantial magnitude. In evaluating the impact of the experimental treatments on children's academic achievement, it then becomes important to take into account that kindergarten students and teachers were randomized to experimental conditions in intact classes within each participating school, so that they were nested within both classrooms and schools. The corresponding analyses can accommodate this complexity by estimating the treatment effects in a statistical model that contains the random effects of a classroom and the fixed effects of schools. In other words, you can fit a random-intercepts model with a class-level residual, but include a set of dichotomous control predictors to distinguish among the schools.

Choosing Between Random- and Fixed-Effects Specifications

As we have described, if you are in a situation in which the level at which you want to assign participants to experimental conditions is not completely collinear with the nesting of the participants in their intact groups, you have deliberate choices that you can make about your multilevel-model specifications. In analyzing data from the STAR experiment, for instance, one option is simply to include random effects for children (ε), classes (u), and schools (v), as follows:

$$Y_{ics} = \beta_0 + \beta_1 SMALL_{cs} + \beta_2 REGULAR_{cs} + \beta_3 X_{ics} + (\varepsilon_{ics} + u_{cs} + v_s) \quad (7.8)$$

where Y_{ics} represents the end-of-the-school-year academic achievement of the ith child in the cth class in school s, question predictor $SMALL_{cs}$ is set equal to 1 for all children in the cth class in school s if it is a "small" class (and 0, otherwise), and question predictor $REGULAR_{cs}$ is set equal to 1 for all children in the cth class in school s if it is a regular-size class with a teacher's aide (and 0, otherwise). Children in the control group of "regular" classes, without a teacher's aide, would have zero values on both question predictors. Variables X_{ics} represent a vector of control predictors. Such models can be fitted by most multilevel modeling software, and the population variances of the random effects at the student, class, and school levels estimated. Alternatively, you could do as Krueger (1999) did, and capture the clustering of classes within schools by including the fixed effects of school, as follows:

$$Y_{ics} = \beta_{0s} + \beta_1 SMALL_{cs} + \beta_2 REGULAR_{cs} + \beta_3 X_{ics} + (\varepsilon_{ics} + u_{cs}) \quad (7.9)$$

where we have eliminated the school-level residual and, instead, permitted each school to have its own intercept, β_{0s}. The model is then fitted with a vector of school dichotomies included as predictors to permit the separate school-level intercepts to be estimated.

Of course, faced with the decision of whether to analyze the STAR data with a multilevel model that includes the fixed effects of schools or a multilevel model that includes the random effects of schools, how should you decide which to adopt? The decision is not trivial, as each approach has its own advantages and disadvantages.

One disadvantage of the fixed-effects approach is that the inclusion in the statistical model of a dichotomous predictor to distinguish each intact group of participants in the design may increase the number of regression parameters that must be estimated vastly, with a corresponding sacrifice of degrees of freedom. For example, Krueger (1999) needed to include 78 school-specific parameters in addition to the overall intercept to account for the 79 schools included in the STAR study. The random-effects approach, on the other hand, handles the clustering of participants within groups, and in the process only adds a single extra residual-variance parameter to the model (at each additional level of clustering).

In our SFA example, it is the population between-school residual variance, σ_u^2, that must then be estimated. Thus, an advantage of the random-effects approach over the fixed-effects approach is the smaller number of parameters to be estimated.

On the other hand, the fixed-effects approach is clearly superior to the random-effects approach in one important way. By including a vector of unique dummy predictors to distinguish the intact groups present in the analysis, the fixed-effects approach accounts for the main effects of all possible observed *and* unobserved time-invariant differences among the groups. It does not matter if the fixed effects that represent the intact grouping are correlated with other predictors in the model at any level, because regression analysis is designed to permit predictors to be correlated. In contrast, if you choose to represent the impact of the intact groupings as random effects, you assume implicitly that the group-level residuals are uncorrelated with other predictors that may be present in the model. If this assumption fails, then the results of your analysis may be biased. The reason is that when residuals and predictors are correlated in any regression model, bias accrues.

Borman and his colleagues were justified in choosing a random-effects of schools specification for their evaluation of the SFA intervention because the random assignment of schools to experimental conditions assured that the school-specific component of the residuals could not be correlated with the critical question predictor that distinguished members of the treatment and control groups. Krueger, on the other hand, chose a model specification that included the fixed effects of schools in his evaluation of the STAR experiment because randomization of participants to experimental conditions was carried out at the class level (that is, within schools). Consequently, unmeasured differences among schools (for example, in the quality of the school directors) could have been correlated with other control predictors included in the multilevel model, such as the number of years each teacher had taught. In that situation, the random-effects specification may have produced biased estimates of parameters of the model.

The key question to answer in deciding whether to adopt a random-effects or a fixed-effects specification of the statistical model in those cases in which you have a choice has to do with whether you can defend the assumption that unobserved differences among the intact groups are uncorrelated with other predictors present in the model. If so, you should prefer the random-effects specification because it preserves your degrees of freedom. However, this is a strong assumption. Typically, it is only in situations in which intact groups have been assigned randomly to treatment or control group status that this assumption is justified.

Fortunately, a test developed by Hausman (1978) can provide guidance in making the decision of whether to adopt a random-effects or fixed-effects specification in situations in which it is possible to fit both types of models. This test is based on the logic that, if unobserved differences among groups are uncorrelated with other predictors in the model, then estimates of the model parameters obtained under the random-effects specification will be very similar to those obtained under the fixed-effects specification (although, of course, the standard errors will differ because of the difference in degrees of freedom). Many statistical software packages (including Stata) provide this test.

What to Read Next

If you want to follow up on the topics of multilevel data analysis and statistical power estimation in cluster-randomized designs, a good place to start is with the insight-filled paper by Stephen Raudenbush and his colleagues entitled "Strategies for Improving Precision in Group-Randomized Experiments" (2007). You might then turn to Raudenbush and Anthony Bryk's 2002 book, *Hierarchical Linear Models: Applications and Data Analysis Methods*. Finally, Larry Orr's 1999 book, *Social Experiments*, provides a thoughtful exposition of a variety of issues that researchers face in designing field experiments with randomization at different levels.

8

Using Natural Experiments to Provide "Arguably Exogenous" Treatment Variability

The cost to families of investing in their children's education is of concern the world over. In some developing countries, the question is whether charging fees for enrollment in secondary school reduces access to education markedly for low-income families. Recently, some countries, beginning with Brazil and Mexico, have turned this question on its head and examined whether charging negative prices (that is, making cash payments to low-income families that enroll their children in secondary school) will increase enrollment (Fiszbein, Schady, & Ferreira, 2009). In the United States and other industrialized countries, the focus is on the impact of college cost on decisions to enroll in post-secondary education. In every country, knowledge of the sensitivity of families' educational decisions to the cost of education is critical to sound educational policy-making. A challenge, then, is to provide compelling evidence about the causal impact of a change in cost on families' educational decisions.

As we have argued in Chapter 4, a randomized experiment provides the most persuasive strategy for answering educational policy questions about the causal impact of school fees or scholarships on families' educational enrollment decisions. Indeed, as we explain in Chapter 14, a number of recent randomized experiments have shed new light on the impact of costs on school-enrollment decisions. Researcher-designed randomized experiments on this topic are often difficult to carry out, however, due to cost and difficulty in obtaining the requisite cooperation of participants and educational institutions. As a result, researchers often try to learn from experiments that occur naturally.

These "natural" experiments are situations in which some external agency, perhaps a natural disaster, or an idiosyncrasy of geography or birth date, or a sudden unexpected change in a longstanding educational policy "assigns" participants randomly to potential "treatment" and "control" groups. The challenge for the researcher is to recognize such natural experiments when they occur and to be prepared to deal with the opportunities and challenges they present.

In the next section of this chapter, we explain the respects in which investigator-designed experiments and natural experiments are similar and the respects in which they are different. We then use data from two excellent studies to illustrate how researchers have taken advantage of natural experiments to address important policy questions about cause and effect. In the subsequent section, we point out sources of natural experiments that have proven productive in the past, and we summarize their common features. Then, we describe two important threats to internal validity that are an integral part of working with data from a special kind of natural experiment that has what we will refer to as a *discontinuity design*. We then explain how a novel analytic approach known as *difference-in-differences estimation* responds sensibly to one of these validity threats.

Natural- and Investigator-Designed Experiments: Similarities and Differences

Central to the internal validity of an experiment is the assignment of participants to the experimental conditions. When we say that experimental assignment is exogenous, we mean that it is beyond any possible manipulation by the participants themselves, so that membership in either a treatment or a control group is totally independent of the participants' own motivations and decisions. So, when investigators assign participants in an experiment randomly to experimental conditions, the assignment is exogenous because, by definition, participants in a fair lottery cannot influence the outcome. Randomized assignment, in turn, renders members of the treatment and control groups equal in expectation prior to the intervention. Consequently, any between-group difference detected in the average value of the outcome, post-treatment, must be a causal consequence of the intervention itself.

Participants are sometimes randomized to different program options, to innovative practices, or to different incentives by exogenous mechanisms that are not under the direct control of an investigator, but still provide the equality in expectation prior to treatment that supports causal inference. Provided that we can argue persuasively that those participants who are then subject to the contrasting and naturally occurring "experimental" conditions are indeed equal in expectation prior to treatment, we have a logical basis for making unbiased inferences about the causal impact of the treatment. However, although data from natural experiments can sometimes be analyzed in the same way as data from investigator-designed experiments, you may need to modify your analytic strategy to respond to additional threats to internal validity that may occur when an experiment arises naturally.

Two Examples of Natural Experiments

We begin by describing examples of two prototypical natural experiments. The first occurred when the U.S. Department of Defense introduced military draft lotteries during the Vietnam War era. Each lottery created two experimental groups of young males who were arguably equal in expectation and differed only in that one group was offered—that is, could be drafted into—military service, whereas the second could not. Our second example occurred when the federal government ended, in 1982, a program that had previously provided college financial aid to children who were the survivors of Social Security beneficiaries. This abrupt policy shift meant that high-school seniors in and before 1981, whose fathers were deceased Social Security recipients, were "assigned" effectively to a treatment group that received an offer of college financial aid. High-school seniors immediately after 1981, whose fathers were deceased Social Security recipients, were not made this aid offer. So long as these groups of high-school seniors were otherwise equal in expectation, we are presented with naturally formed experimental groups that differed only in the offer of aid.

The Vietnam-Era Draft Lottery

The question of whether military service affects long-term labor-market outcomes for participants is a question many governments ask in the process of designing manpower policies. As Joshua Angrist (1990) pointed out, this question cannot be answered by using census data to compare the long-term earnings of men who served in the military and those who did not serve. The reason is that men are not usually assigned randomly to military service. Instead, men who have relatively unattractive employment opportunities in the civilian sphere may tend to enter the military. Unobserved differences between those who volunteer to serve and those who do not may therefore create bias in the estimation of the long-term labor market consequences of military service.

A natural experiment that took place during the Vietnam War era provided Angrist with an opportunity to obtain unbiased estimates of the impact of military draft eligibility on long-term labor market outcomes. Between 1970 and 1975, the U.S. Department of Defense conducted five draft lotteries that determined which American males in a particular age group were eligible to be drafted into military service. The 1970 lottery included men aged 19 through 26, and the lotteries in the four subsequent years included men aged 19 to 20. In each lottery, a *random-sequence number* (RSN), ranging from 1 through 365, was assigned to each birth date. Then, only men in the relevant age cohorts whose birthdays had RSNs less than an exogenously determined ceiling, which was specified by the Department of Defense each year, were subject to induction. Angrist called such men "draft-eligible." A simple comparison of the annual earnings in the early 1980s for the group of men in a particular cohort who were draft-eligible with those who were not provides an unbiased estimate of the impact on earnings of being draft-eligible.

Note that the treatment being administered in this natural experiment is "eligibility for the draft," not the actual experience of military service. This is because it is only the assignment of young men to draft eligibility that was randomized, not military service itself. Indeed, some of those in the draft-eligible "treatment group" avoided military service by enrolling in college, by being declared unfit for military service due to physical limitations, or by having been arrested prior to the draft. Among white males born in 1950, 35% of those declared draft-eligible as a result of having a low draft number actually served in the military, compared to 19% of those declared draft-ineligible (Angrist, 1990; Table 2, p. 321). Of course, the fact that many draft-eligible men did not serve in the military, and some men who were not draft-eligible did serve, does not threaten the unbiased estimation of the impact of being "draft-eligible" on later labor-market outcomes. In fact, this natural experiment resembles the New York Scholarship Program (NYSP), the investigator-designed experiment in which the treatment was the randomized offer of a scholarship to help pay private-school tuition. As explained in Chapter 4, not all families that received the scholarship offer sent their child to a private school. As we will see in Chapter 11, it is possible to use a more sophisticated technique, called *instrumental-variables estimation*, to tease out the causal impact of actual military service (or actual private-school attendance), using the original randomly assigned offer as an "instrument." In this chapter, however, we focus only on estimating the impact of draft eligibility on later labor-market earnings.

Combining information from the draft lotteries with information on subsequent earnings from the Social Security Administration, Angrist estimated the impact of draft-eligibility status on future annual earnings, separately for white and non-white men, in the several birth cohorts in which the draft lotteries were conducted. He found, for instance, that white men in the 1950 birth cohort who were draft-eligible in the 1970 lottery earned approximately $1,100 less in 1984 (when they were 34 years of age) than did men in the same birth cohort who were not draft-eligible (Angrist, 1990; Table 1, p. 318).[1]

As with an investigator-designed experiment, statistical analyses of these data are straightforward. The hypothesis that there is no difference in population-average annual earnings at age 34 between the two groups can be tested in several ways. For instance, we could apply standard ordinary least-squares (OLS) methods, regressing annual earnings at age 34 (*EARN34*) on a dummy predictor that represents whether the man was draft-eligible. Alternatively, we could carry out a two-group *t*-test to compare the average annual earnings at age 34 of men who were draft-eligible with those who were not. In fact, this test can be carried out directly using statistics provided in Angrist's paper (1990; Table 1), which lists sample estimates of the difference in average annual earnings and also the standard error of the difference, as follows:

$$1950\,\text{Birth}\,\text{Cohort}:$$

$$
\begin{aligned}
t &= \frac{\overline{EARN34_{1\bullet}} - \overline{EARN34_{0\bullet}}}{s.e.\left(\overline{EARN34_{1\bullet}} - \overline{EARN34_{0\bullet}}\right)} \\
&= \frac{-1143.30}{492.2} \\
&= -2.323
\end{aligned}
\tag{8.1}
$$

where $\overline{EARN34_{1\bullet}}$ represents the average annual earnings at age 34 of white males who were draft-eligible (the treatment group) and $\overline{EARN34_{0\bullet}}$ represents the comparable average annual earnings of white males who were not draft-eligible (the control group).[2] Although Angrist did not report explicit sample sizes for this particular comparison, the difference in annual earnings is clearly statistically significant ($p < 0.03$, using a normal

---

1. Angrist reports all dollar amounts in 1978 dollar values.
2. In Equation 8.1, we employ the standard statistical practice of indicating that an average has been formed from the values of a variable over members of a group by using a "dot" to replace the *index*—or subscript—that distinguishes the members of the group.

approximation, two-tailed test), suggesting a considerable negative impact of draft eligibility on future earnings, on average.[3]

Notice that this natural experiment possesses almost all of the attributes of an investigator-designed experiment. Participants were members of a defined population—all the young males in particular age ranges, in specific birth cohorts. There were explicit and well-defined experimental conditions—in our version of Angrist's example, these are framed in terms of draft eligibility. Young men assigned to the "draft-eligible" and "not draft-eligible" conditions were arguably equal in expectation initially because a lottery was used to pick the RSNs. An appropriate outcome—annual earnings later in life—that was hypothesized to be sensitive to the impact of the treatment was measured. It seems like the key difference between an investigator-designed experiment and Angrist's draft lottery research is that the assignment of participants to experimental conditions in the latter was carried out by an external agency, in this case, officials in the U.S. Department of Defense.

Of course, it makes good sense to capitalize on any experiment, natural or investigator-designed, that permits us to address our research questions. If we can find appropriate data from a viable natural experiment, then we should capitalize on it. However, using data from a natural experiment often adds an element of complexity to the research. First and foremost, we must be able to argue convincingly that the "natural" assignment of individuals was indeed exogenous—in other words, that being declared draft-eligible by virtue of one's birth date and the lottery outcome was utterly beyond the influence of the participants themselves. This is an easy case to make, given that the RSNs were assigned to birth dates by fair lotteries under the control of government agents who were remote from participants. We must also be able to argue persuasively that participants assigned to the different experimental conditions were initially equal in expectation. This condition was also satisfied in the draft-lottery case. The reason is that even though men with particular birth dates (those born in the winter, say) may differ in unobserved ways from those born on other dates (in the summer), these unobserved differences were distributed randomly across the experimental conditions by the lottery that assigned RSNs to birth dates.

In recent years, lotteries have been often used to allocate places in public schools in the United States for which demand exceeds supply.

---

3. We argue that a two-sided test makes sense for this example because it represents the theoretical position that the treatment group could have either better or worse average labor-market outcomes than the control group. We discuss the choice between one- and two-tailed hypothesis testing in Chapter 6.

These lotteries have provided many additional natural experiments with designs similar to those of the military service lotteries we describe above. In their turn, researchers have used these lotteries to evaluate the causal impacts on subsequent student outcomes of the offer of a place in a variety of different types of schools. These include charter schools (Abdulkadiroglu et al., 2009; Angrist et al., 2010; Dobbie & Fryer, 2009; Hoxby & Murarka, 2009), small secondary schools (Bloom et al., 2010), and selected "effective" public schools in comparison to regular neighborhood schools (Deming, 2009; Deming et al., 2009). We describe the evidence from some of these studies in Chapter 14.

The Impact of an Offer of Financial Aid for College

Although school-choice lotteries expand the list of potential natural experiments with random-assignment designs, the number of experiments with this kind of design that occur naturally is modest. Natural experiments occur more frequently when a natural disaster or an exogenous change in a policy or practice leaves temporally contiguous groups of individuals exposed to different treatments. Susan Dynarski (2003) makes use of an interesting natural experiment with this kind of "discontinuity" design. She used a sudden change in federal policy to estimate the causal impact of an offer of financial aid for post-secondary education on the decisions of high-school seniors about whether to go to college, and their subsequent success if they did attend.

Between 1965 and 1982, the Social Security Survivor Benefits (SSSB) Program in the United States offered $6,700 (expressed in year 2000 dollars) in college financial aid to the 18- to 22-year-old children of deceased, disabled, or retired Social Security recipients. In 1981, the U.S. Congress eliminated the SSSB program, mandating that otherwise eligible children who were not enrolled in college as of May 1982 would not receive the SSSB college-aid offer. Using the National Longitudinal Survey of Youth, Dynarski identified students in cohorts of high-school seniors, just before and just after the policy change, who would have been eligible for the aid offer because their fathers were Social Security recipients who had died. She argued that, other than differing in receipt of the offer of college aid, these two groups of students were equal in expectation initially. However, the 137 high-school seniors who satisfied SSSB eligibility requirements immediately before the policy change (in the years 1979 through 1981) received the college financial-aid offer and therefore constituted the treatment group. The 54 high-school seniors who satisfied SSSB eligibility requirements immediately after the policy change (1982 and 1983) received no SSSB-related financial-aid offer and made up the control group.

All else being equal, subtracting the average value of the outcome for the control group from the average value of the outcome for the treatment group provides an unbiased estimate of the causal impact of the financial-aid offer on the subsequent college-going behavior of students whose fathers were deceased. This is often called a "first-difference" estimate of the treatment effect. Notice that the action by the Congress to eliminate the SSSB program allowed Dynarski to study the causal impact of financial aid on the college-enrollment decisions of students without facing the ethical questions that an investigator-designed randomized experiment might have elicited.

We focus here on the first of several outcomes that Dynarski studied—whether the student attended college by age 23. We define $COLL_i$ as a dichotomous outcome variable that we code 1 if the ith high-school senior attended college by age 23 and 0 otherwise. We present summary statistics on outcome $COLL$ in the upper panel of Table 8.1, in rows that distinguish the treatment and control groups of students whose fathers were deceased.[4] The first row in the upper panel contains summary information on the 137 high-school seniors who received the SSSB aid offer in the years 1979 through 1981 (our "treatment" group). The second row contains parallel information on the 54 high-school seniors who would have been eligible for SSSB aid in 1982 through 1983, but did not receive an SSSB aid offer because the program was cancelled (our "control" group). The sample averages of $COLL$ in the treatment and control groups are 0.560 and 0.352, respectively, which means that 56% of students who received an offer of tuition aid attended college by age 23, whereas only 35% of those who did not receive the offer did so.

Provided that this "natural" assignment of high-school seniors whose fathers were deceased to the treatment and control conditions rendered the two groups equal in expectation initially, we can obtain an unbiased estimate of the population impact of a financial-aid offer on college attendance by age 23 among students with deceased fathers. One method is to simply estimate the sample between-group difference in outcome means D_1:

$$D_1 = \left\{ \overline{COLL}_\bullet^{(Father\ Deceased,\ 79 \to 81)} - \overline{COLL}_\bullet^{(Father\ Deceased,\ 82 \to 83)} \right\}$$
$$= 0.560 - 0.352 \tag{8.2}$$
$$= 0.208$$

---

4. We thank Susan Dynarski for providing her dataset. All our analyses of these data account for the cluster sampling and weighting in the complex survey design of the NLSY.

Table 8.1 "First difference" estimate of the causal impact of an offer of $6,700 in financial aid (in 2000 dollars) on whether high-school seniors whose fathers were deceased attended college by age 23 in the United States

(a) *Direct Estimate*

H.S. Senior Cohort	Number of Students	Was Student's Father Deceased	Did H.S. Seniors Receive an Offer of SSSB Aid?	Avg Value of COLL (standard error)	Between-Group Difference in Avg Value of COLL	H_0: μ_{OFFER} = $\mu_{NO\ OFFER}$	
						t-statistic	*p*-value
1979–81	137	Yes	Yes (*Treatment Group*)	0.560 (0.053)	**0.208***	2.14	0.017†
1982–83	54	Yes	No (*Control Group*)	0.352 (0.081)			

ˉ*p* <0.10; * *p* <0.05; ** *p* <0.01; *** *p* <0.001.
†One-tailed test.

(b) *Linear-Probability Model (OLS) Estimate*

Predictor	Estimate	Standard Error	H_0: $\beta = 0$;	
			t-statistic	*p*-value
Intercept	0.352***	0.081	4.32	0.000
OFFER	0.208*	0.094	2.23	0.013†
R^2	0.036			

ˉ*p* <0.10; * *p* <0.05; ** *p* <0.01; *** *p* <0.001.
†One-tailed test.

In Equation 8.2, we have used superscripts to distinguish students in the 1979, 1980, and 1981 cohorts whose fathers were deceased (and who received the aid offer) from those in the 1982 and 1983 cohorts whose fathers were deceased (and who did not receive an offer of financial aid). We learn that the percentage of the first group that enrolled in college by age 23 was almost 21 percentage points larger than the percentage of the second group that did so. From the standard errors listed in Table 8.1, we can also estimate a *t*-statistic for testing the null hypothesis that an offer of financial aid did not affect college attendance among students whose fathers were deceased by age 23, in the population, as follows:[5]

$$t = \frac{\overline{COLL.}^{(Father\ Deceased,79\rightarrow81)} - \overline{COLL.}^{(Father\ Deceased,82\rightarrow83)}}{s.e.\left(\overline{COLL.}^{(Father\ Deceased,79\rightarrow81)} - \overline{COLL.}^{(Father\ Deceased,82\rightarrow83)}\right)}$$

$$= \frac{\overline{COLL.}^{(Father\ Deceased,79\rightarrow81)} - \overline{COLL.}^{(Father\ Deceased,82\rightarrow83)}}{\sqrt{s.e.\left(\overline{COLL.}^{(Father\ Deceased,79\rightarrow81)}\right)^2 + s.e.\left(\overline{COLL.}^{(Father\ Deceased,82\rightarrow83)}\right)^2}} \quad (8.3)$$

$$= \frac{(0.560 - 0.352)}{\sqrt{(0.053)^2 + (0.081)^2}}$$

$$= \frac{0.208}{0.097}$$

$$= 2.14$$

We could also have summarized and tested the impact of the receipt of the higher-education financial-aid offer in the same dataset by using OLS methods to fit a linear-probability model or we could have used logistic regression analysis to regress our outcome *COLL* on a dichotomous question predictor *OFFER*, defined to distinguish students in the treatment and control groups (coded 1 if relevant students became high-school seniors in 1979, 1980, or 1981, and therefore received an offer of post-secondary tuition support; 0 otherwise), as in the case of an investigator-designed experiment. We present the corresponding fitted linear-probability model in the lower panel of Table 8.1. Notice that the parameter estimate associated with the treatment predictor has a magnitude identical to our "difference estimate" in Equation 8.2.[6] Using either of these strategies, we can reject the standard null hypothesis associated with the treatment effect, and conclude that the offer of financial aid did

---

5. The results of this *t*-test are approximate, as the outcome *COLL* is a dichotomous, not continuous, variable.
6. Notice that the standard error associated with the main effect of *OFFER*, at 0.094, is slightly different from the estimate provided in Equation 8.3, which had a value of 0.097. This occurs because, although both statistics are estimates of the standard error of the same treatment effect, they are based on different assumptions. The OLS-based estimate makes the more stringent assumption that residuals are *homoscedastic* at each value of predictor *OFFER*—that is, essentially, that the within-group variances of the outcome are the same in both the treatment and control groups, although the hand-computed estimate permits these within-group variances to differ.

indeed induce a substantial percentage of students whose fathers were deceased to enter college before age 23 (p <0.02).[7]

Notice that the abrupt change in federal SSSB policy in 1981 is a key characteristic of this natural experiment, and is responsible for defining who was in the treatment and who was in the control group. It is as though students whose fathers had died were arrayed along an underlying dimension defined by the year in which they became a high-school senior and an arbitrary cut-off year was picked independently by an external agency at the end of 1981. Because of this, high-school seniors immediately to the left of the discontinuity were arbitrarily assigned to the treatment group, although those immediately to the right became the control group. In interpreting the implications of our findings causally, not only do we rely on the assumption that the timing of the policy disruption was determined exogenously, we must also make sure that we generalize our findings only to the subpopulation of high-school seniors from whom we sampled implicitly —that is, those whose fathers were deceased and who graduated from high school immediately before, or immediately after, the policy change. Such highly specific limits on interpretation are an important facet of any causal research that makes use of a discontinuity design.

Sources of Natural Experiments

Since natural experiments with discontinuity designs provide frequent opportunities for estimating the causal impacts of educational interventions or policies, it is valuable to learn to spot them when they occur. Understanding the common components of a standard discontinuity design can help you to do so. All natural experiments with discontinuity designs incorporate:

- an underlying continuum along which participants are arrayed. We refer to this continuum as the "assignment" or "forcing" variable,
- an exogenously determined cut-point on the forcing variable that divides participants explicitly into groups that experience different treatments or conditions, and
- a clearly defined and well-measured outcome of interest.

As should be clear from our description of Dynarski's (2003) work on the impact of an offer of financial aid on the college-going behavior of

---

7. Note that we used a one-tailed test because we had a strong prior belief that the offer of scholarship aid would increase the probability of college attendance, not decrease it.

high-school seniors whose fathers had died, abrupt changes in policy provide one important source of potential natural experiments. In such cases, the forcing variable represents the passage of time, and the exogenous cut-off point is provided by the date on which the policy change took hold.

Disasters that change unexpectedly the circumstances under which education and labor markets operate provide another useful source of natural experiments. For example, in 2005, the devastation caused by Hurricanes Katrina and Rita led Louisiana public-school officials to reassign a large number of students from lower-quality schools in Orleans Parish, Louisiana, to higher-quality suburban schools. Bruce Sacerdote (2008) showed that this exogenous shift in the quality of the schools these children attended led to improvements in the average long-term achievement of affected students, even though they and their families experienced the disruptions associated with unanticipated residential moves. In 1986, the Chernobyl nuclear accident resulted in the in utero exposure to radiation of large numbers of children living in a particular part of Sweden. Douglas Almond, Lena Edlund, and Marten Palme used data from before and after this tragic accident to show that in utero exposure to radiation reduced the average educational attainment of the affected children (Almond, Edlund, & Palme, 2007).

It is not only the passage of time that can provide a credible forcing variable. Differences in policies, practices, or incentives that occur naturally across adjacent geographical jurisdictions (for example, across school attendance zones, school districts, or provinces) provide another useful source of natural experiments. In such cases, the forcing variable—the continuum along which participants are arrayed in the discontinuity design—is spatial. Sandra Black (1999) used a natural experiment of this type to study the causal impact of school quality on housing prices. She did this by comparing the average prices of houses located just on either side of elementary school attendance boundaries in particular school districts in Massachusetts. Her basic assumption was that, after controlling for the physical characteristics of houses and the attributes of neighborhoods, the only reason that houses close to, but on opposite sides of, school-attendance boundaries would differ in selling price is that they were located in the attendance zones of different elementary schools. Black found that parents were willing to pay 2.5% more for a house that allowed their children to attend an elementary school whose average test scores were 5% higher. Ian Davidoff and Andrew Leigh (2008) conducted a similar analysis using data from Australia and reached a similar conclusion.

Research by John Tyler, Richard Murnane, and John Willett (2000) provides another example of a study that took advantage of a natural experiment involving spatial differences to study an important educational-policy question. These researchers wanted to know whether receipt of the General Educational Development (GED) credential improved subsequent average earnings for high-school dropouts with low academic skills. Their critical natural experiment stemmed from exogenous differences among adjacent states in the United States in the minimum passing score that individuals must attain on the seven-hour battery of examinations to obtain the GED credential. Tyler and his colleagues compared the subsequent earnings of GED test takers who scored just high enough to earn the credential in a state with a low passing score with the earnings of GED test takers who achieved the same score, but did not receive the credential because they lived in a state with a relatively high minimum passing score. These comparisons led the researchers to conclude that receipt of the GED credential increased the earnings of white school dropouts with weak academic skills by 14%.

A third source of natural experiments arises when policies that, having arrayed individuals along an academic or social dimension such as a score on a standardized test, then administer different educational treatments to students who fall on different sides of an exogenously specified cut-point on this forcing variable. A policy implemented by Chicago public schools provides an interesting example of this type of natural experiment. As part of a district-wide accountability initiative, the district mandated that, beginning in the 1996–1997 school year, third-graders who did not achieve scores of at least 2.8 grade equivalents on the Iowa Test of Basic Skills (ITBS) reading and mathematics examinations taken at the end of the school year must participate in a six-week summer-school program. At the end of the mandatory program, participating children would retake the ITBS tests. Those who failed to achieve scores of at least 2.8 grade equivalents were compelled to spend another school year in the third grade.

Brian Jacob and Lars Lefgren (2004) recognized that the Chicago initiative provided a natural experiment that they could use to study the causal impact of the mandatory summer school and its associated school promotion policy on students' subsequent achievement. Third-grade students were arrayed on a forcing variable defined by their end-of-school-year score on the ITBS mathematics test. There was a clearly defined exogenous cut-point on this forcing variable: a minimum score of 2.8 grade equivalents. Students whose scores fell below the cut-point received an educational treatment—mandatory summer school—which students with scores at, or above, the cut-point did not receive. There was a clearly defined outcome, the students' scores on the ITBS mathematics test at the end of the subsequent school year. Jacob and Lefgren found that there were a great many Chicago students who scored just below, or just above, the 2.8 cut-off point on the end-of-third-grade mathematics examination. By comparing the average mathematics scores of these two groups one year and two years later, they estimated the causal impact of the mandatory summer school and associated promotion policy. They found that the treatments increased average student achievement by an amount equal to 20% of the average amount of mathematics learning that typical Chicago public school third-graders exhibited during the school year, an effect that faded by 25%–40% over a second year.[8]

John Papay, Richard Murnane, and John Willett (2010) took advantage of a structurally similar natural experiment in Massachusetts. Beginning with the high-school class of 2003, Massachusetts public school students have had to pass state-wide examinations in mathematics and English language arts in order to obtain a high-school diploma. Students take the examinations at the end of the tenth grade, and those who fail to score above the exogenously defined minimum passing score may retake the examinations in subsequent years. The research team found that being classified as just failing on the mandatory mathematics test (when compared to those students who just passed) lowered by 8 percentage points the probability that low-income students attending urban high schools graduated on time. Since the research had a discontinuity design, the comparison was between low-income urban students whose scores fell just below the minimum passing score on the forcing variable and those whose scores fell just above the minimum passing score.

Other examples of natural experiments of this type originate in the rules that schools and school districts adopt to set maximum class size. In settings with maximum class-size rules, students are arrayed on a forcing variable defined by the number of students enrolled in a school at their grade level. If the number of enrolled students is less than the maximum class size, say, 40 students, then the students' class size will be equal to the number of students enrolled in that grade level. However, if the number of enrolled students is slightly greater than the maximum class size, say, 42 students, then the expected class size would be 21 students because a second class must be added to the grade in order to comply with the maximum class-size policy. As with other natural experiments, students in schools with class-size maximums have then been arrayed implicitly on a forcing variable (enrollment at that grade level), an exogenous cut-point

---

8. Jacob and Lefgren (2004, p. 235). The policy also applied to sixth-graders, and the results of the intervention were different for this group than for third-graders.

(the class-size maximum) has been defined, and students who fall just to one side of the cut-point experience different educational treatments (class sizes) than do students who fall just to the other side of the cut-point. Discontinuity studies of the impact of class size on average student achievement that were based on maximum class-size rules have been conducted using data from many countries, including Bolivia, Denmark, France, Israel, the Netherlands, Norway, South Africa, and the United States.[9]

In summary, natural experiments occur most frequently with discontinuity designs, and are derived usually from three common sources of discontinuity. First, a natural disaster or an abrupt change in a policy can assign individuals or organizations that are in the same geographical jurisdiction randomly to different educational treatments at temporally adjacent points in time. Dynarski (2003) analyzed data from a natural experiment of this type. Second, exogenous differences in policies across geographical jurisdictions at the same point in time can assign individuals or organizations randomly to different policies based on their location. Tyler and his colleagues (2000) made use of a natural experiment of this type. Third, policies in a particular jurisdiction at a particular point in time can assign individuals randomly to different educational treatments based on their values on a forcing variable such as a test score, a measure of socioeconomic status, or the number of students enrolled in a grade in a particular school. As we explain in the next chapter, Angrist and Lavy (1999) studied a natural experiment of this type.

Some natural experiments fall into more than one category. For example, the natural experiment created by the Chicago mandatory summer-school policy that Jacob and Lefgren (2004) studied falls into both our first and third categories. We have already described how that study fell into the third category—with end-of-school-year scores on the third-grade ITBS mathematics achievement test as the forcing variable. However, it also falls into the first category—with a temporal forcing variable—because Chicago students who were in the third grade in the 1996–1997 school year were subject to the policy, whereas those who were in the third grade in the 1995–1996 school year were not. In fact, Jacob and Lefgren took advantage of both of these attributes of the natural experiment cleverly in their analytic strategy.

9. Relevant studies include: Browning and Heinesen (2003); Leuven, Oosterbeek, and Rønning (2008); Case and Deaton (1999); Dobbelsteen, Levin, and Oosterbeek (2002); Boozer and Rouse (2001); Angrist and Lavy (1999); Urquiola (2006), and Hoxby (2000).

Choosing the Width of the Analytic Window

In the investigator-designed NYSP randomized experiment and in the natural randomized experiment created by the Vietnam era military lotteries, participants were simply assigned randomly to treatment or control status in a given year or at a given point in time. As a result, the groups assigned to the different experimental conditions were unequivocally equal in expectation prior to treatment.[10] More serious concerns can be raised about the equality of expectation assumption, however, when we rely on experiments with a discontinuity design to make our causal comparisons. In making use of this latter design and using a simple *t*-test to compare groups, we find ourselves having to argue that the analytic samples of participants who fall within a narrow analytic window or "bandwidth" on either side of the cut-off on the forcing variable constitute treatment and control groups that are also equal in expectation prior to treatment.

This raises the question of how narrow the analytic window must be in order for this assumption to be credible? Certainly, the narrower the analytic window around the cut-point, the more confident we can be in the "equality in expectation" assumption for the groups thus defined, and therefore in the *internal validity* of the experimental comparison. By narrowing the bandwidth on either side of the cut-off score, we can make it more likely that the equality in expectation assumption will be met. But as we do this, the sample sizes in the "treatment" and "control" groups thus defined must necessarily decline, along with the statistical power of the experimental comparison. So, to capitalize effectively on a natural experiment with a discontinuity design, we must strike a sensible balance between internal validity and power by manipulating the bandwidth on either side of the cut-point. We return to the Dynarski (2003) study to illustrate the tradeoff.

Recall that Dynarski pooled high-school seniors whose fathers had been deceased from both 1979 and 1980 into her discontinuity-defined treatment group, along with those from 1981 (the last group to enjoy SSSB benefits before the policy change). She included in her control group not only students with deceased fathers who were high-school seniors in 1982, the first year in which SSSB college benefits were not available, but also those who were high-school seniors in 1983. Alternatively, Dynarski could have defined her treatment group as containing

---

10. An exception would be the case in which participants succeed in subverting their assignment and "cross-over" to the condition to which they were not assigned. In Chapter 11, we describe a solution to this problem.

only 1981 high-school seniors with deceased fathers and her control group as including only 1982 high-school seniors with deceased fathers. Tightening her focus on the students with deceased fathers who were most immediately adjacent to the cut-off year would have strengthened Dynarski's claim that the treatment and control groups were likely to be equal in expectation, prior to treatment. The reason is that this decision would have provided little time for anything else to have occurred that could have affected college enrollment decisions for the relevant high-school seniors. However, this would also have reduced the sample sizes of her treatment and control groups dramatically, thereby reducing the statistical power of her research. Even with the slightly broader criteria that Dynarski did use, there were only 137 high-school seniors in the treatment group and 54 in the control group—a comparison that provides very limited statistical power.

On the other hand, Dynarski could have expanded her definitions of the treatment and control groups. For example, she might have included in her treatment group all students with deceased fathers who graduated from high school in any year from 1972 through 1981. Similarly, she could have included in her control group students with deceased fathers who graduated from high school in any year from 1982 through 1991. Using such a ten-year window on either side of the discontinuity certainly would have increased her sample size and statistical power dramatically. However, had Dynarski widened the analytic window around the cut-point, she would have found it more difficult to argue that seniors in the treatment and control groups were equal in expectation initially. The reason is that unanticipated events and longer-term trends might have had a substantial influence on high-school seniors' college-enrollment decisions. For example, the differential between the average earnings of college graduates and high-school graduates fell dramatically during the 1970s and then rose rapidly during the 1980s.[11] As a result, the incentives for high-school seniors to attend college in the early 1970s were quite different from the incentives facing high-school seniors in the late 1980s. Thus, widening the analytic window would have cast into doubt the claim that any observed difference between the treatment and control groups in college-going by age 23 was solely a causal consequence of the elimination of the SSSB financial-aid offer.

Taking these limiting cases into account, it may seem reasonable to assume that high-school seniors with deceased fathers in the years within

---

11. For a discussion of the causes and consequences of trends in the college/high-school wage differential, see Freeman (1976), Goldin and Katz (2008), and Murnane and Levy (1996).

a very narrow band immediately on either side of the policy disruption—for example, within the bandwidths chosen by Dynarski—were indeed equal in expectation on all observed and unobserved dimensions (other than their exposure to the offer of financial aid). If this is true, then we can regard those with deceased fathers who became high-school seniors in 1979 through 1981 as having been randomized to the treatment group and those with deceased fathers who became seniors in 1982 and 1983 as having been randomized to the control group. Coupling this assumption with plausibly exogenous treatment variation in a suitable outcome, we can obtain an unbiased estimate of the causal impact of an offer of financial aid on the college-enrollment decisions of the subpopulation of high-school seniors with deceased fathers who graduated just before and just after the policy change that occurred at the end of 1981.

This tension between internal validity and statistical power in the application of discontinuity research designs is a difficult and important problem. Typically, there is no single correct answer to the question of how narrow the analytic window needs to be in order to analyze credibly data from experiments with a discontinuity design. In fact, rather than picking a single fixed width for this analytic window, investigators often conduct a sequence of analyses with ever-widening bandwidths, and assess whether their substantive findings are sensitive to the bandwidth. We return to this issue in the next chapter, where we discuss an extension of the discontinuity approach called the *regression-discontinuity* design.

Threats to Validity in Natural Experiments with a Discontinuity Design

As stated earlier, a critical assumption underlying causal research with a discontinuity design is that the group of participants just to the "left" of any cut-off are equal in expectation on all dimensions, other than their exposure to the treatment, to those just to the "right" of the cut-off. There are two critical threats to the validity of this assumption. The first concerns the impact of any underlying "secular" relationship between the outcome and the forcing variable on estimated treatment effects. If such a relationship exists, then there may be a difference between the treatment and control groups in the mean value of the outcome that stems from their (small) separation on the forcing variable rather than from the impact of the treatment that was available on one side of the cut-off and not on the other. The second threat concerns actions by participants themselves. If participants are aware of the nature of the forcing variable and the location of the cut-off, they may be able to act to transfer themselves knowingly from one side of the cut-off to the other. This jeopardizes the exogeneity of the assignment process and undermines the assumption of equality of expectation for those in the treatment and control groups. We discuss each of these threats in turn.

Accounting for the Relationship Between the Outcome and the Forcing Variable in a Discontinuity Design

In a previous section, we estimated the impact of the offer of financial aid on college-enrollment rates by comparing the enrollment rates of eligible high-school seniors with deceased fathers in the 1979–1981 (treatment) and 1982–1983 (control) cohorts of such students. A critical assumption underlying this approach was that the only respect in which the treatment and control group differed was that the former received an offer of SSSB financial aid for college and the latter did not. If this assumption is defensible, then any difference between the treatment and control groups in the rate of college enrollment can be attributed causally to the aid offer.

There are reasons to question the critical assumption, however, because events other than the termination of the SSSB financial-aid program that took place during the years 1979–1983 may have also affected college-enrollment rates. For example, in 1978, President Jimmy Carter signed the *Middle-Income Student-Assistance Act* (MISAA). This legislation made almost all students eligible for a subsidized federal loan under the Guaranteed Student Loan (GSL) program. In 1981, the same year in which the Reagan administration eliminated the SSSB program, it also repealed MISAA. Thus, the attractiveness of enrolling in college for students with deceased fathers (those students who make up our treatment and control populations) may not only have been influenced by the termination of the SSSB program, but by other factors as well.[12]

Notice that it is the very use of the discontinuity design itself that has led to this problem, because individuals have been assigned to a treatment or control group depending on whether their value on the forcing variable (in this case, chronological year) fell above or below an arguably exogenous cut-off point. We do not face this problem in standard investigator-designed randomized experiments nor in natural experiments with simple random-assignment designs, such as the Vietnam era military draft lotteries. The reason is that random assignment of young

---

12. See Dynarski (2003, p. 283, fn. 14). As our colleague Bridget Long pointed out, another factor that influenced college-enrollment rates during the period 1978–1983 was an increase in college tuition prices.

men within each yearly cohort to either the treatment or control group allayed the problem. With a random-assignment design, chronological year would simply function as a stratifier, and the equality of expectation assumption would be met by the randomization of participants to the different experimental conditions within each yearly stratum, and, hence, overall. In a discontinuity design, on the other hand, participants in the treatment and control conditions are, by definition, drawn from groups at immediately adjacent values of the forcing variable (adjacent by year, by geography, by test score, or by whatever defines the forcing variable on which the exogenous cut-off has been imposed). Then, if an underlying relationship exists between outcome and forcing variable (as it often does!), the resulting small differences between participants in the treatment and control groups on their values of the forcing variable may also result in differences in the outcome between the groups.[13]

When faced with this kind of threat to the internal validity of a natural experiment with a discontinuity design, investigators often respond by correcting their estimate of the treatment effect using what is known as a *difference-in-differences* strategy. Recall that we construed our estimate of the impact of a financial-aid offer in the Dynarski example as simply the difference in the sample average value of the binary outcome *COLL* between seniors with deceased fathers assigned to the financial–aid-offer treatment group and those assigned to the no financial-aid-offer control group. As shown earlier, we can estimate and test this difference easily, once we have chosen an appropriate bandwidth on either side of the cut-off score within which to estimate the respective average values of the outcome. In what follows, we refer to this as the *first difference*, D_1, and we presented it earlier in Equation 8.2 and Table 8.1.

Now let's correct our first difference for the anticipated threat to validity due to the small chronological difference in years of assignment between the treatment and control groups. We can do this by subtracting, from the first difference, a *second difference* that estimates the consequences of any "secular" trend in college-going by age 23 that might have affected all high-school seniors over the same period, including those eligible for SSSB benefits. To do this, we need to estimate this latter secular trend over time, so that it can be "subtracted out." In the case of Dynarski's

---

13. One can also argue that this "secular trend" problem is exacerbated when the forcing variable is not continuous, but is coarsely discrete (as were the "years" in the Dynarski example). If the assignment variable were continuous and the cut-off selected exogenously, then—in the limit—participants in the vanishingly small regions to either side of the cut-off would be mathematically equal in expectation, by definition. However, the number of participants—and hence the sample size in the ensuing natural experiment—in these infinitesimal regions would also be disappearingly small.

financial-aid example, the data themselves provided an appropriate second difference. If there was a secular trend in college-going by age 23 over these years, it might be reasonable to assume that it would affect in the same way high-school seniors whose fathers had died and those whose fathers had not died. If this assumption is true, then we can estimate the secular trend over the relevant years in the college-going behavior of seniors whose fathers had not died, and subtract this second difference from our earlier estimated first difference to obtain a corrected estimate of the treatment effect.

We present the relevant statistics in Table 8.2, and illustrate them in Figure 8.1. In the first two rows of the table, we replicate the estimation of the original first difference from Table 8.1, and display it graphically in the left-hand panel of Figure 8.1. Notice that the line segment joining the sample average values of outcome *COLL*, before and after the cancellation of the SSSB program, has a decidedly negative slope, and declines from 0.560 to 0.352 between the before and after periods, an almost 21 point decline in the percentage of high-school seniors with deceased fathers who attended college by age 23. In the third and fourth rows of Table 8.2, we present parallel information on the trend in college-going among those high-school seniors whose fathers had not died. For these students, notice that there is also a decline in the sample average values of

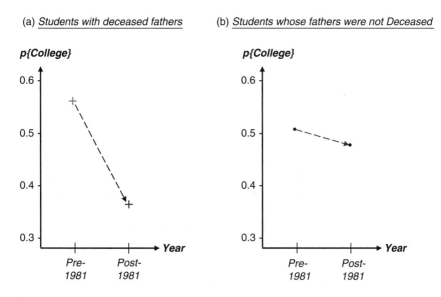

Figure 8.1 Sample probability of attending college by age 23 among high-school seniors, in the United States, immediately before and after the elimination of the SSSB program, by whether their fathers were deceased or not.

COLL, but that its magnitude (0.026) is considerably smaller than that of the first difference. We display this second difference in the right-hand panel of Figure 8.1, where the line segment joining the sample average values of *COLL*, before and after the cancellation of the SSSB program, has a smaller negative slope.

Now, we have two estimated differences. We could argue that our first difference D_1 estimates the *population* impact (call this Δ_1) on college-going by age 23 of *both* the elimination of financial aid *and* any impact of a secular decline in college-going over the same period. Our second difference D_2 provides an estimate of just the population secular decline in college-going over this same period (call this Δ_2). We can now remove the impact of the secular time trend from our estimate of the causal effect of financial aid by subtracting the second difference from the first, as follows:

$$D = D_1 - D_2$$

$$= \left\{ \overline{COLL.}^{\left(\substack{Father \\ Deceased \\ 79 \to 81}\right)} - \overline{COLL.}^{\left(\substack{Father \\ Deceased \\ 82 \to 83}\right)} \right\}$$

$$- \left\{ \overline{COLL.}^{\left(\substack{Father\ Not \\ Deceased \\ 79 \to 81}\right)} - \overline{COLL.}^{\left(\substack{Father\ Not \\ Deceased \\ 82 \to 83}\right)} \right\} \tag{8.4}$$

$$= (0.560 - 0.352) - (0.502 - 0.476)$$

$$= 0.208 - 0.026$$

$$= 0.182$$

This provides a difference-in-differences estimate of 0.182 for the effect of the financial-aid offer on college-going by age 23 for high-school seniors with deceased fathers in the years around 1981. This is the first difference of 0.208 minus the second difference of 0.026. Thus, the difference-in-differences estimate of the causal impact of financial aid is a little smaller in magnitude than the first-difference estimate obtained earlier, but its sign is the same and it continues to support the notion that the elimination of SSSB financial aid made it less probable that high-school seniors would go to college by age 23. We have more confidence in the difference-in-differences estimate than in the first-difference estimate because it

Table 8.2 Direct "difference-in-differences" estimate of the impact of an offer of $6,700 in financial aid (in 2000 dollars) on whether high-school seniors whose fathers were deceased attended college by age 23, in the United States

H.S. Senior Cohort	Number of Students	Was Student's Father Deceased?	Did H.S. Seniors Receive an Offer of SSSB Aid?	Avg Value of COLL (standard error)	Between-Group Difference in Avg Value of COLL	"Difference in Differences"	
						Estimate (standard error)	p-value
1979–81	137	Yes	Yes (Treatment Group)	0.560 (0.053)	0.208 (First Diff)		
1982–83	54	Yes	No (Control Group)	0.352 (0.081)		0.182* (0.099)	0.033†
1979–81	2,745	No	No	0.502 (0.012)	0.026 (Second Diff)		
1982–83	1,050	No	No	0.476 (0.019)			

$^{~}p$ <0.10; $^{*}p$ <0.05; $^{**}p$ <0.01; $^{***}p$ <0.001.
†One-tailed test.

contains a (linear) adjustment for any potential underlying secular relationship between college-going by age 23 and chronological year.

Now that we have constructed an estimate of the treatment effect by differencing these two differences, we can no longer use a standard two-group t-test to evaluate the null hypothesis of no difference in the population-average college-going between students who received an offer of financial aid and those who did not. Instead, we need to test a new null hypothesis, as follows:

$$H_0 : \Delta = \Delta_1 - \Delta_2 = 0 \tag{8.5}$$

This hypothesis can be tested by comparing the sample difference-in-differences estimate to its own standard error, to provide a t-statistic of the following form:[14]

---

14. This test is approximate because outcome, COLL, is dichotomous.

$$t = \frac{\left\{\left[\overline{COLL.}^{\binom{Father\ Deceased}{79\to81}} - \overline{COLL.}^{\binom{Father\ Deceased}{82\to83}}\right] - \left[\overline{COLL.}^{\binom{Father\ Not\ Deceased}{79\to81}} - \overline{COLL.}^{\binom{Father\ Not\ Deceased}{82\to83}}\right]\right\}}{s.e.\left[\left\{\left[\overline{COLL.}^{\binom{Father\ Deceased}{79\to81}} - \overline{COLL.}^{\binom{Father\ Deceased}{82\to83}}\right] - \left\{\overline{COLL.}^{\binom{Father\ Not\ Deceased}{79\to81}} - \overline{COLL.}^{\binom{Father\ Not\ Deceased}{82\to83}}\right\}\right\}\right]}$$

$$= \frac{\left\{\left[\overline{COLL.}^{\binom{Father\ Deceased}{79\to81}} - \overline{COLL.}^{\binom{Father\ Deceased}{82\to83}}\right] - \left\{\overline{COLL.}^{\binom{Father\ Not\ Deceased}{79\to81}} - \overline{COLL.}^{\binom{Father\ Not\ Deceased}{82\to83}}\right\}\right\}}{\sqrt{\begin{array}{l}\left[s.e.\left(\overline{COLL.}^{\binom{Father\ Deceased}{79\to81}}\right)\right]^2 + \left[s.e.\left(\overline{COLL.}^{\binom{Father\ Deceased}{82\to83}}\right)\right]^2 \\ + \left[s.e.\left(\overline{COLL.}^{\binom{Father\ Not\ Deceased}{79\to81}}\right)\right]^2 + \left[s.e.\left(\overline{COLL.}^{\binom{Father\ Not\ Deceased}{82\to83}}\right)\right]^2\end{array}}} \quad (8.6)$$

$$= \frac{(0.560 - 0.352) - (0.502 - 0.476)}{\sqrt{(0.053)^2 + (0.081)^2 + (0.012)^2 + (0.019)^2}}$$

$$= \frac{0.182}{0.099} = 1.84$$

This t-statistic is large enough to reject the null hypothesis using a one-tailed test with Type I error = 0.05 ($p < 0.03$).[15] Consequently, we again conclude that financial aid matters in the decision to go to college by age 23 in the population of high-school seniors whose fathers were deceased in 1981.

We noted earlier that we did not necessarily need to use a t-test to test the size of the population first difference. Instead, we could regress

---

15. This is based on a normal approximation because of the large total sample size ($n = 3,986$) across the four groups.

outcome *COLL* on the dichotomous question predictor, *OFFER*, which distinguished between the treatment group (cohorts 1979, 1980, and 1981) and the control group (cohorts 1982 and 1983). We can use a similar regression approach to obtain the difference-in-differences estimate (Equation 8.4), along with its associated standard error and ancillary test statistics. It is a direct extension of the method we introduced in Chapter 4 for using regression analysis to estimate a treatment effect in a regular random-assignment experiment. In that case, we regressed the outcome variable on the main effect of a single dichotomous question predictor, which had been defined to distinguish participants in the treatment and control groups. The coefficient associated with this predictor provided the required estimate of the treatment effect, essentially an estimate of the first difference we have described above. Here, our modeling must be a little more subtle in order to incorporate the impact of the hypothesized second difference appropriately into the regression model and thereby remove it from the estimate of the treatment effect.

We proceed by defining one additional predictor and forming its statistical interaction with the "old" question predictor. We illustrate the structure of the ensuing dataset in Table 8.3, where we present a handful of cases from the Dynarski dataset. Columns one through three of the table list the student *ID*, the high-school senior cohort to which the student belongs, and his or her value of *COLL* (our outcome). Then, we list the value of the original question predictor *OFFER*, which denotes whether the high-school senior is a member of one of the three cohorts prior to the cancellation of the SSSB policy (its value is set to 1 for the 1979, 1980, and 1981 cohorts; and to 0 for the 1982 and 1983 cohorts). Finally, we add a new predictor, *FATHERDEC*, to distinguish high-school seniors whose fathers were deceased (and will therefore contribute to the estimation of the first difference) or not (and will therefore contribute to the estimation of the second difference). *FATHERDEC* is set equal to 1 for students whose father was deceased, 0 otherwise.

To obtain the difference-in-differences estimate of the impact of offer of SSSB financial aid to students with deceased fathers, and its associated test statistics, as shown in Equations 8.4 through 8.6, we simply regress outcome *COLL* on the main effects of predictors *OFFER* and *FATHERDEC*, and on their two-way interaction, in the new dataset. The hypothesized regression model is

$$
\begin{aligned}
COLL_i = \beta_0 &+ \beta_1 OFFER_i + \beta_2 FATHERDEC_i \\
&+ \beta_3 \left(OFFER_i \times FATHERDEC_i \right) + \varepsilon_i
\end{aligned}
\tag{8.7}
$$

Table 8.3 Information on cohort membership and college attendance by age 23 in the
United States for selected high-school seniors in the 1979, 1980, 1981, 1982, and 1983
cohorts, with accompanying information on whether they were offered financial aid
(those in cohorts 1979–1981) and whether their father was deceased

ID	High-school Senior Cohort	Attended College by Age 23, (COLL)	Offered Financial Aid? (OFFER)	Father Deceased? (FATHERDEC)
7901	1979	1	1	1
7902	1979	0	1	1
7903	1979	1	1	0
7904	1979	1	1	1
...				
8001	1980	1	1	0
8002	1980	1	1	1
8003	1980	0	1	1
8004	1980	0	1	0
...				
8101	1981	0	1	1
8102	1981	1	1	0
8103	1981	1	1	0
8104	1981	1	1	0
...				
8201	1982	1	0	1
8202	1982	0	0	0
8203	1982	0	0	0
8204	1982	0	0	1
...				
8301	1983	0	0	1
8302	1983	1	0	1
8303	1983	0	0	1
8304	1983	1	0	0
...				

where regression parameters β and residual ε have their usual meanings,
and subscript i distinguishes among high-school seniors in the dataset. The
estimated value of parameter β_3—the coefficient associated with the two-
way interaction of predictors OFFER and FATHERDEC—turns out to be
identical to the difference-in-differences estimate of the treatment effect.[16]

---

16. The reason why the regression model in Equation 8.7 embodies the difference-in-
differences approach is easily understood by taking conditional expectations
throughout, at all possible pairs of values of predictors OFFER and FATHERDEC.
This provides population expressions for the average value of the outcome in each of
the four groups present in the difference-in-differences estimate, which can then be
subtracted to provide the required proof.

Table 8.4 Regression-based (linear-probability model) "difference-in-differences" estimate of the impact, on high-school seniors, of an offer of SSSB financial aid on the college attendance by age 23 in the United States ($n = 3,986$)

Predictor	Estimate	Standard Error	H_0: $\beta = 0$	
			t-statistic	p-value
Intercept	0.476***	0.019	25.22	0.000
OFFER	0.026	0.021	1.22	0.111
FATHERDEC	−0.123	0.083	−1.48	0.070
OFFER × FATHERDEC	0.182*	0.096	1.90	0.029†
R^2	0.002			

¯p <0.10; * p <0.05; ** p <0.01; *** p <0.001.
†One-tailed test.

In Table 8.4, we present parameter estimates, standard errors, and associated test statistics from the fitted model. Notice that $\hat{\beta}_3$ has a value of 0.182, identical to our earlier hand-computed difference-in-differences estimate in Equation 8.3. As expected, we can reject the single-parameter null hypothesis test associated with it (p <0.03).[17] Although it provides the same answer, the regression-based approach to difference-in-differences estimation is clearly superior to the direct computation approach illustrated earlier. This is because, once you have laid out the difference-in-differences analysis in its regression-analysis format, you can easily increase your statistical power by adding further exogenous covariates such as gender, race, and family size to the fitted model to reduce the residual variance, as Dynarski did.

Notice that, in this presentation, we have used a linear-probability model and OLS regression analysis to estimate the treatment effect, even though our outcome, *COLL*, was dichotomous. We did this to illustrate the conceptual basis of the difference-in-differences regression strategy

---

17. Notice that the standard error associated with the two-way interaction of *OFFER* and *FATHERDEC*, at 0.096, is marginally different from the estimate provided in Equation 8.6, which had a value of 0.099. This small difference occurs because, although both are estimates of the standard error of the corresponding statistic, they are based on slightly different assumptions. As usual, the OLS-based estimate makes the more stringent assumption that residuals are *homoscedastic* at each level of predictors *OFFER* and *FATHERDEC*—that is, that the within-group variances of the outcome are the same in all four groups, although the hand-computed estimate permits the within-group variances to differ, in the population. If the more stringent assumption of homoscedasticity had been applied in both cases, then the standard-error estimates would have been identical and equal to the regression-based estimate.

more readily and also to match the findings in Dynarski's paper. However, even if we had specified a more appropriate nonlinear logit (or probit) model, the predictor specification would have been identical and the results congruent.

Finally, note that we have made two additional assumptions in obtaining our difference-in-differences estimate of the treatment effect. Both these assumptions concern whether it is reasonable to use this particular "second" difference in average outcome to adjust for any secular trend in the college-going decisions of high-school seniors whose fathers were deceased. One of the assumptions is mathematical, the other conceptual.

First, in computing both the first and second differences, we are making the "mathematical" assumption that it is reasonable to use a simple difference in average values to summarize trends in the outcome as a function of the forcing variable, and that the mere subtraction of these differences from one another does indeed adjust the experimental effect-size estimate for the secular trend adequately. For instance, in our current example, we obtained the first difference by subtracting the average value of *COLL* in a pair of groups formed immediately before and after the 1981 cut-point, for both the high-school seniors whose fathers had died and for those whose fathers had not died. Both these differences are therefore rudimentary estimates of the slope of a hypothesized linear trend that links average college-going and chronological year (grouped as stipulated in our estimation), in the presence and absence of any experimental treatment, respectively. Our confidence in the appropriateness of these differences—and the value of the difference-in-differences estimate derived from them—rests heavily on an assumption that the underlying trends are indeed linear and can be estimated adequately by differencing average outcome values at pairs of adjacent points on the horizontal axis. These assumptions will not be correct if the true trend linking average college-going to year is nonlinear. We have no way of checking this assumption without introducing more data into the analysis and without conducting explicit analyses to test the assumption. However, as we will see in the following chapter, in which we describe what is known as the regression-discontinuity design, if more data are available, there are not only ways of testing the implicit linearity assumption, but also of obtaining better estimates of the conceptual "second difference."

Our second assumption is substantive, rather than mathematical, and concerns the credibility of using the sample of students whose fathers had not died to estimate an appropriate second difference. In our presentation, we followed Dynarski in making the hopefully credible argument that the trend in the average college-going rate for students whose fathers were *not* deceased provided a valid estimate of the trend in the college-going rate for students whose fathers *were* deceased. Of course, this may not be true. Regardless, our point is that you must be cautious in applying the difference-in-differences strategy. As the Dynarski (2003) paper illustrates, it can be an effective strategy for analyzing data from a natural experiment with a discontinuity design and for addressing an important educational policy question. However, as we have explained, there are additional assumptions underlying its use, and the researcher's obligation is to defend the validity of these assumptions, as Dynarski did so successfully in her paper.

Actions by Participants Can Undermine Exogenous Assignment to Experimental Conditions in a Natural Experiment with a Discontinuity Design

A second, quite different threat to the internal validity of causal inference in discontinuity designs stems from the potential voluntary choices and actions of individual research subjects. It is often the case that individuals would prefer to be in the treatment group than in either the control group or outside the research sample entirely.[18] For example, most high-school seniors would like to have an offer of SSSB financial aid for college. When individuals can influence whether they are assigned to the research sample or can influence the probability that they are assigned to the treatment or the control group, our causal inference is challenged. The reason is that allocation to experimental conditions then only *appears* to be exogenous but, in fact, is not. As a result, the critical assumption that members of the treatment and control groups are equal in expectation prior to treatment is violated.

Consider the case of the natural experiment that Dynarski utilized. Her treatment and control groups both consisted of students whose fathers had died, but constituted before and after the cut-point on the forcing variable, chronological year. To justify this, she needed to make the potentially credible assumption that during the treatment group years (1979–1981), no father ended his life in order to provide SSSB eligibility for his child. Recall, however, that during the years from 1965 to 1981, it was not only high-school seniors with deceased fathers who were eligible for SSSB benefits, but also those whose fathers were disabled or retired Social Security beneficiaries. Thus, Dynarski could have increased her sample size by including students with retired or disabled fathers in her

---

18. Of course, there are also circumstances in which individuals would prefer *not* to be in the treatment group. For example, most third-graders in the Chicago public schools hoped not to be assigned to mandatory summer school.

research sample. She chose not to do this for good reason. During the years in which the SSSB program was in effect, some fathers of college-bound high-school seniors could have chosen to retire or to press a disability claim in order to acquire SSSB benefits for their child. Demographically similar parents of students who were high-school seniors in 1982–1983 would not have had this incentive. Such actions could have led to unobserved differences between participants in the treatment and control groups thus defined, including perhaps differences in their interest in enrolling in college. Thus, including students with disabled or retired fathers in the research sample would probably have introduced bias into the estimation of the treatment effect, and undermined the internal validity of the research. In subsequent chapters, we return to these threats to the exogeneity of the assignment of individuals to treatment and control groups in natural experiments with a discontinuity design.

What to Read Next

Joshua Angrist and Jorn-Steffen Pischke provide an accessible explanation of the difference-in-differences approach on pages 227–243 of their book *Mostly Harmless Econometrics* (2009). In a paper entitled "Semiparametric Difference-in-Differences Estimators," Alberto Abadie (2005) describes a strategy for dealing with situations in which the researcher may want to question the appropriateness of available estimates of the second difference. In a paper entitled "Natural 'Natural Experiments' in Economics," Mark Rosenzweig and Kenneth Wolpin (2000) use illustrations from several studies to point out additional threats to the validity of research based on data from natural experiments.

9

Estimating Causal Effects Using a Regression-Discontinuity Approach

Reducing class size has become a popular educational policy initiative in many countries. One reason is that it is popular among both teachers and parents. A second is that it is an easy policy to implement. On the other side of the ledger, reducing class sizes is extremely expensive. First, there is the cost of additional classrooms. Then, there is the cost of additional teachers. For example, in a school with 480 students, 12 teachers are needed to staff classes containing 40 students each. However, 16 teachers—one-third more—are required to staff classes of 30 students. In most countries, teacher salaries absorb more than half of the national education budget. As a result, reducing class sizes from 40 to 30 students increases total educational expenditures by at least one-sixth.

The popularity of class-size reductions and their cost make important the question of whether they result in improved student outcomes. Hundreds of studies have attempted to address this question. Unfortunately, almost all were fundamentally flawed because they were based on observational data from research designs in which the variation in class size was the result of the endogenous actions of school administrators and parents. As we explained in Chapter 3, when the levels of the question predictor—such as class size—are set endogenously, it is not possible to obtain unbiased estimates of the causal impact of class size on student outcomes.

Of course, one approach to solving this problem is to conduct a randomized experiment in which both students and teachers are assigned randomly to classes of different sizes by the researcher. The Tennessee Student/Teacher Achievement Ratio (STAR) experiment provides a compelling illustration of this approach. As we described in Chapter 3, research based on the STAR experiment showed that children placed in kindergarten and first-grade classes of 13–17 students exhibited greater reading and mathematics skills at the end of the school year than did children placed in classes of 21–25 students.

Unfortunately, researcher-designed randomized experiments of class size are extremely rare. So, researchers who want to estimate the causal impact of class size on student achievement often seek out natural experiments in which class sizes have been determined exogenously by educational policies that are beyond the control of the participating teachers and students. Educational policies that dictate the maximum number of students that may be taught in a single class sometimes provide such natural experiments. In this chapter, we describe how Joshua Angrist and Victor Lavy estimated the causal impact of class size on the reading achievement of elementary-school children in Israel by taking advantage of a maximum class-size policy called Maimonides' rule. In the process, we extend the difference-in-differences strategy of the previous chapter to what has become known as the *regression-discontinuity* design.

Maimonides' Rule and the Impact of Class Size on Student Achievement

Joshua Angrist and Victor Lavy (1999) used data from an interesting natural experiment in Israel to examine whether class size had a causal impact on the achievement of third-, fourth-, and fifth-grade students. The source of their natural experiment was an interpretation by a 12th-century rabbinic scholar, Maimonides, of a discussion in the 6th century Babylonian Talmud about the most appropriate class size for bible study. Maimonides ruled that class size should be limited to 40 students. If enrollment exceeded that number, he stipulated that another teacher must be appointed and the class split, generating two classes of smaller size.[1] Of critical importance to the work of Angrist and Lavy is that, since 1969, the Education Ministry in Israel has used Maimonides' rule to determine the number of classes each elementary school in Israel would need, each year, at each grade-level. Children entering a grade in a school with an enrollment cohort of 40 students or fewer, for instance, would be assigned to a single class containing that number of students. In another school with an enrollment cohort of size 41 at the same grade level, an extra teacher would be hired and two classes established, each containing 20 or

---

1. As reported in Angrist and Lavy (1999, p. 534).

21 students. If the size of the enrollment cohort was 44 students, each would be assigned to a class of 22 students, and so on.

Thus, Maimonides' rule is a mechanism for assigning class size. To use it, children are arrayed by their values on a forcing variable that describes the total enrollment in the grade-level cohort in their school. Children are then assigned to "treatment" and "control" groups with "small" and "large" class sizes, depending on whether their grade-level cohort size falls just above, or just below, the exogenously (in this case, biblically) determined cut-off of 40. In fact, under rabbinical rules, similar disjunctions also occur at cohort enrollments that are subsequent multiples of 40. For example, at grade-level cohort sizes of 80 and 120, cohorts are split into three and four classes, respectively. Angrist and Lavy argued that the operation of Maimonides' rule provided a natural experiment for estimating the causal impact of class size on students' academic achievement.

Before presenting our re-analyses of a subset of Angrist and Lavy's (1999) data, we need to clarify one critical attribute of their dataset. Most of their data were collected at the class-aggregate level, so their unit of analysis is the classroom, not the individual student within the class. From the perspective of statistical power, this is not a major concern because, as we explained in Chapter 7, when data on intact groups are analyzed, the statistical power of the analyses depends more strongly on the *number of classrooms* present than on the *number of students* within each classroom, even when the magnitude of the intraclass correlation is quite small. Because Angrist and Lavy analyzed data on more than 2,000 classrooms at each grade level, their statistical power remained high even in analyses of subgroups of classrooms formed from those grade-specific cohorts whose enrollments fell close to the Maimonides-inspired cut-off.

In Table 9.1, we present summary statistics and related information on the average fifth-grade reading achievement in schools in which the values of the forcing variable—the size of the grade-level enrollment cohort—ranged from 36 to 46 students.[2] In the fifth and sixth rows, for instance, which are shaded, we present the cohort means of the class-average reading achievement (column 6) in schools in which the fifth-grade enrollments (column 1) were either 40 or 41 students. We restrict our attention to these two specific enrollment cohorts initially because you will notice that they fall immediately on either side of the first Maimonides cut-off at 40.

---

2. We thank Joshua Angrist for providing these data. The complete dataset contains grade-level, school-specific enrollment cohorts that range in size from 8 through 226, all of which are used in the research described in Angrist and Lavy (1999). For pedagogical simplicity, we focus on a subset of the data in which grade-level cohort enrollment sizes fall close to the first Maimonides-inspired class-size cut-off of 40 students.

Table 9.1 Fifth-grade average reading achievement and average class size (*intended* and *observed*) in Israeli Jewish public schools, by fifth-grade enrollment-cohort size, around the Maimonides-inspired cut-off of 40 students

Fifth-Grade Cohort Size	Number of Classrooms in Cohort	Class Size in Cohort		Nominal Class Size "Treatment"	Average Reading Achievement in Cohort	
		Intended Size	Observed Average Size		Mean	Std. Dev.
36	9	36	27.4	Large	67.30	12.36
37	9	37	26.2	Large	68.94	8.50
38	10	38	33.1	Large	67.85	14.04
39	10	39	31.2	Large	68.87	12.07
40	**9**	**40**	**29.9**	**Large**	**67.93**	**7.87**
41	**28**	**20.5**	**22.7**	**Small**	**73.68**	**8.77**
42	25	21	23.4	Small	67.60	9.30
43	24	21.5	22.1	Small	77.18	7.47
44	17	22	24.4	Small	72.16	7.71
45	19	22.5	22.7	Small	76.92	8.71
46	20	23	22.7	Small	70.31	9.78

In each row in the table, we also list the number of classrooms of that cohort size in the sample (column 2), the intended and observed average class sizes in those classrooms (columns 3 and 4), and the standard deviations of the class-average reading achievement across the classes in the cohort (column 7). We also label the cohort by whether it provides a nominally "large" or "small" class-size treatment to the students it contains (column 5). Notice that average reading achievement does indeed appear to differ by class size. Children entering fifth grade in enrollment cohorts of size 36 through 40, who would be assigned to "large" classes by Maimonides' rule, tend to have average achievement in the high 60s. On the other hand (except in cohorts containing 42 children), children entering the fifth grade in enrollment cohorts of sizes 41 through 46, and who are therefore assigned to smaller classes by Maimonides' rule, tend to have average achievement in the mid-70s.

If the schools contributing the 37 classrooms that are listed in the fifth and sixth rows of Table 9.1 had obeyed Maimonides' rule to the letter, we would anticipate a "large" average class size of 40 in the nine schools that had an entering cohort with an enrollment of 40 and a small average class size of 20.5 (that is, half of 41) in the 28 classrooms in schools in which 41 students started the school year in the fifth-grade cohort. However, for reasons not yet apparent, among those large classes that were intended to contain 40 students, the observed average class size is actually less than 30. In the small classes that were intended to have an average size of 20.5, the observed average class size is closer to the intended class size. However, at 22.7, it is still two students larger than the Maimonides' rule-intended class size. Inspecting the data on these classrooms, on a school-by-school basis, provides a clue as to why these anomalies are observed "on the ground." Among the schools with 40 children in their fifth-grade entering cohort, only four of the nine classrooms actually have class sizes of exactly 40. One of the remaining classrooms contains 29 students, and the other four have class sizes around 20.[3] Thus, actual class sizes were smaller than the class sizes intended by application of Maimonides' rule. One possible explanation for this difference hinges on the timing of the enrollment measure. Cohort enrollments in this dataset were measured in September, at the beginning of the academic year. It is possible for a student to be added after the start of a school year to a fifth-grade cohort with an initial size of 40 students, and then for the class to be divided subsequently into two.

Is the discordance between actual class sizes and those anticipated by application of Maimonides' rule problematic for our evaluation? The answer is "not necessarily," providing we keep the specific wording of our research question in mind. Recall the important distinction that we made between "intent-to-treat" and "treated" in our discussion of the New York Scholarship Program (NYSP) in Chapter 4. In the NYSP, it was receipt of a private-school tuition voucher—which we regarded as an expression of intent to send a child to private school—that was assigned randomly to participating families. It was the causal impact of this offer of a private-school education that could then be estimated without bias. Of course, subsequently, some of the families that received vouchers chose not to use them, and so the act of actually going to private school involved considerable personal choice. This means that variation in a private-school treatment, across children, was potentially endogenous. Consequently, a comparison of the average achievement of children attending private schools and those attending public schools could not provide an unbiased estimate of the causal impact of a private-school treatment. Nonetheless, it remained valuable to obtain an unbiased estimate of the causal impact of the expressed intent to treat—that is, of the offer of a subsidy for private-school tuition through the randomized receipt of a voucher—because it is such offers that public policies typically provide.

---

3. The actual sizes of these four classes were 18, 20, 20, and 22.

The natural experiment linking class size and aggregate student reading achievement among Israeli fifth-graders provides an analogous situation. The Maimonides' rule-inspired class sizes are the intended treatment, and we can estimate the causal effect on student achievement of this intent to place each student into either a large or small class. It is certainly useful to know the impact of such an offer, because it provides information about the consequences of a policy decision to use Maimonides' rule to determine class sizes. However, it does not tell us how an actual reduction in observed class size would affect student achievement.[4]

A Simple First-Difference Analysis

Providing the application of Maimonides' rule led to exogenous offers of large and small classes to groups of students who were equal in expectation at the start of the fifth grade, we can compare their average reading achievement at the end of the academic year and obtain an unbiased estimate of the causal effect of the difference in intended class sizes. As we explained in Chapter 8, one simple way to proceed with such an analysis is to estimate and test a first difference in student achievement between classes that were intended to be large and those intended to be small. In Angrist and Lavy's data, there are nine schools with fifth-grade age-enrollment cohorts of 40 students, and 28 schools with age-enrollment cohorts of 41 students. So, according to Maimonides, fifth-grade classes in the former schools were intended to be large and those in the latter schools small, at the beginning of the academic year. At the end of the year, the overall average achievement score was 73.68 in the classes intended to be small and 67.93 in the classes intended to be large—a first difference of 5.75 points in favor of the classes that were intended to be small. We can reject the corresponding two-group null hypothesis ($t = 1.75$, $p = 0.044$; one-sided test), and conclude that, in the population of fifth-grade classes in age cohorts of size 40 and 41, in Israel, being offered enrollment in smaller classes caused higher achievement.[5]

On its surface, this difference of almost 6 points seems very large—after all, the standard deviation of average achievement across all 37 classrooms

---

4. In Chapter 11, we explain how exogenous variation in the *offer* of a treatment can be used to tease out the causal impact of the actual treatment, using *instrumental-variables estimation*.
5. This test treats classroom as the unit of analysis, and the degrees of freedom reflect a count of those classes.

in this comparison appears to be 8.81, and so the almost 6-point differ-ence is about three-quarters of a standard deviation. However, remember that our unit of analysis is the classroom, and so the standard deviation of 8.81 summarizes the scatter of average reading achievement from class-room to classroom, not from student to student within class. We know from other research that there is usually much greater variation in achieve-ment among students within classrooms than between, and the former has been ignored in these aggregate analyses. In fact, when students are nested within classes, an intraclass correlation of around 0.10 is typical. Given this, we can guess that the total standard deviation of reading achievement across both classrooms and students would be approximately 28 points.[6] This means that the 5.75-point difference we have estimated here is actually less than a quarter of a standard deviation, an effect size similar in magnitude to the effect of class size on achievement that Krueger (1999) reported among kindergarten and first-grade students in the Tennessee STAR experiment.[7]

A Difference-in-Differences Analysis

Recall the logic underlying the assumption of equality in expectation across the cut-off on the forcing variable in a natural experiment with a discontinuity design. We argued that, if the cut-off were determined exog-enously, then only idiosyncratic events—such as the haphazard timing of birth—will determine whether a particular student fell to the left or right of the cut-off on the forcing variable, at least within a reasonably narrow "window" on either side of the cut-off. If this argument is defensible, then any unobserved differences between the students who were offered large classes and those offered small classrooms at the beginning of the aca-demic year will be inconsequential. On the other hand, we cannot ignore the possible presence of a sizeable "second difference." Even though stu-dents who received large-class offers and those who received small-class offers are separated nominally by only one child on the underlying forc-ing variable (the enrollment-size continuum), it is possible that there may

---

6. A between-class standard deviation of 8.81 in reading achievement corresponds to a variance of 77.62, which is 10% of the total variation, if the intraclass correlation coef-ficient is 0.1. Thus, the total variation in reading achievement is ten times this, or 776.2, and the standard deviation 27.9.
7. Remember that the intended difference between "large-offer" and "small-offer" classes in the Israeli setting was slightly less than 20 students, whereas the corresponding differ-ence in the STAR experiment was eight students.

be a non-trivial "secular" trend that links aggregate student achievement and overall enrollment-cohort size, independent of any impact of the class-size offer. This would bias our first-difference estimate of the effect of the class-size offer on achievement.

Angrist and Lavy (1999) report a link between family socioeconomic status and school size in Israel. They comment that schools with larger grade-level enrollments tend to be located in big cities and to serve relatively prosperous families, whereas schools with smaller enrollments tend to be located in rural areas and serve relatively poor families. This means that we can anticipate a positive relationship between neighborhood socioeconomic status and grade-level enrollment that poses a threat to the internal validity of our natural experiment. The reason is that the achievement of students in the class-size control and treatment groups defined discontinuously on either side of the cut-off will differ not only in terms of the offer of class size, but perhaps also because of a small underlying difference in their socioeconomic status. And, since academic achievement and socioeconomic status are usually linked, even a small difference in the latter may lead to a consequential impact on the former.

When faced with such threats to the internal validity of a natural experiment with a discontinuity design, we can respond by adopting a *difference-in-differences* strategy, as we described in the last chapter. In the current example, for instance, we could choose to correct the estimated first difference of 5.75 points by subtracting a second difference D_2, formed from the difference in average academic achievement between a pair of adjacent grade-enrollment cohorts, such as those of size 38 and 39, that also differ in enrollment by one child but do not differ in experimental condition (i.e., in both cohorts, children were offered large classes). From rows three and four of Table 9.1, for example, this estimated second difference would be 68.87 minus 67.85, or 1.02 scale points. Then, providing we are confident that this second difference captures the natural impact on achievement of a cohort-enrollment difference of one child (whether falling between cohorts 38 and 39, or between cohorts 40 and 41), we can adjust the first difference for the impact of the secular trend in achievement by cohort-enrollment size by subtracting the second difference from the first. This provides a difference-in-differences estimate of 4.73 (= 5.75 − 1.02) for the average increase in achievement among fifth-graders who received the offer of a smaller class. Unfortunately, although this estimate is only about 20% smaller than our first-difference estimate (5.75), we can no longer reject the associated null hypothesis

($t = 0.71$; $df = 53$; $p = 0.24$).[8] Nevertheless, the direction of the effect of class size remains positive and is of only slightly smaller magnitude.

Of course, the modest power of this comparison stems predominantly from our decision to restrict ourselves to analyzing data on only the 57 (= 10 + 10 + 9 + 28) schools in the enrollment cohorts of size 38, 39, 40, and 41 that formed the sub samples for the difference-in-differences estimate. We could easily increase the number of classrooms that participate in the test by widening our window around the cut-off—that is, by redefining the groups that we choose to participate in the estimation of the first and second differences. For instance, we could increase the number of cohorts to be included in the first difference by pooling enrollment cohorts of size 39 and 40 (into a new "control" group) and by pooling enrollment cohorts of size 41 and 42 (into a new "treatment" group). The second difference could then be formed by contrasting the average outcome of pooled cohorts of sizes 37 and 38 with the average outcome of pooled cohorts of sizes 35 and 36. Under this redefinition of window width, a total of 111 schools would contribute to the difference-in-differences estimate, with a concomitant increase in statistical power. Of course, as we explained in Chapter 8, widening the bandwidth within which we form sample averages and differences not only alters the magnitude of the difference-in-differences estimate, it also puts greater pressure on the equality- in-expectation assumption and the experiment's internal validity.

---

8. One-sided test, with t-statistic computed from the summary statistics presented in Table 9.1, as follows:

$$t = \frac{\left\{\overline{Y}_{\bullet}^{[41]} - \overline{Y}_{\bullet}^{[40]}\right\} - \left\{\overline{Y}_{\bullet}^{[39]} - \overline{Y}_{\bullet}^{[38]}\right\}}{\sqrt{\left(\dfrac{s_{[41]}^2}{n_{[41]}}\right) + \left(\dfrac{s_{[40]}^2}{n_{[40]}}\right) + \left(\dfrac{s_{[39]}^2}{n_{[39]}}\right) + \left(\dfrac{s_{[38]}^2}{n_{[38]}}\right)}}$$

$$= \frac{\{73.68 - 67.93\} - \{68.87 - 67.85\}}{\sqrt{\left(\dfrac{8.77^2}{28}\right) + \left(\dfrac{7.87^2}{9}\right) + \left(\dfrac{12.07^2}{10}\right) + \left(\dfrac{14.04^2}{10}\right)}}$$

$$= \frac{4.73}{6.63} = 0.71$$

where superscripts and subscripts listed in brackets, in the numerator and denominator, distinguish enrollment cohorts of sizes 38, 39, 40, and 41, respectively.

We return to this issue next, where we illustrate how you can use the regression-discontinuity approach to be more systematic about these choices and can examine the sensitivity of findings to alternative bandwidths.

A Basic Regression-Discontinuity Analysis

Initially, we estimated our first difference from the average reading achievements of classes in enrollment cohorts of size 40 and 41 and our second difference from the average reading achievements of classes in the enrollment cohorts of size 38 and 39. This leads to overall average differences in reading achievement of 5.75 and 1.02, respectively. We argued that the first difference was attributable to the sum of two effects: a difference of one child in the size of the enrollment cohort plus a difference in the class-size offer. We also argued that the second difference was due only to the former (a difference of one child in cohort-enrollment size). Consequently, differencing these differences leads to an unbiased estimate of the treatment effect—that is, the impact on achievement of students being offered, by Maimonides' rule, either a small class or a large class.

Notice that, conceptually, the second difference is simply a rudimentary estimate of the slope of a *linear* trend in average reading achievement as a function of cohort-enrollment size for cohorts containing fewer than 41 students. Our confidence that subtracting this second difference from the first difference will produce an unbiased estimate of the treatment effect rests on three assumptions. The first is that the trend which relates student achievement to the enrollment-cohort size to the left of the discontinuity is linear. The second is that this linear slope can be estimated well by differencing the average reading achievement values (67.85 and 68.87) at two adjacent points (in this case, in cohorts with enrollments of 38 and 39 students) along the enrollment continuum to the left of the discontinuity imposed by Maimonides' rule. The third assumption is that the linear trend established to the left of the discontinuity would simply extend through the discontinuity if there were no exogenous disruption in class size. In other words, we assume that the second difference provides an unbiased estimate of what the difference in average student achievement would have been between classes of size 40 and 41, in the absence of an offer of an exogenous reduction in class size, from large to small, in the two adjacent enrollment cohorts.

These are not trivial assumptions. The first and third may not be correct if any underlying trend linking average achievement to the forcing variable is nonlinear. The second may not be correct if there is large stochastic variation (scatter) in the average achievement of the students in adjacent cohorts. If that is the case, then a slope estimate based on only two data points could be very imprecise. Clearly, the difference-in-differences method of estimating the magnitude of the treatment effect relies heavily on sample average achievement values at just four values of cohort-enrollment size. Fortunately, in situations where more data are available, as is the case here, a regression-discontinuity (RD) approach allows us to test and relax these assumptions.

It is clear from Table 9.1 that we know a lot more about the potential relationship between average student achievement and cohort-enrollment size than we have exploited so far. For example, based on these data, we could obtain estimates of the crucial second difference in several different ways. For instance, we could use the average achievement information for the students in cohorts with enrollments of size 37 and 38 to estimate a second difference of −1.09 (= 67.85 − 68.94). Similarly, the achievement information for enrollment cohorts of size 36 and 37 provides another second difference estimate of +1.64 (= 68.94 − 67.30). Recall though, that the original estimate of the second difference, based on cohorts of size 38 and 39, was +1.02 points. Averaging these multiple estimates of the second difference together leads to an overall average second difference of 0.52, which is perhaps a more precise estimate of the underlying achievement versus the cohort-enrollment linear trend than any estimate derived from a particular pair of adjacent data points to the left of the cut-off. When we can estimate many second differences like this, how do we figure out what to do and where to stop? In fact, we are not even limited to estimating second differences that are only "one child apart" on the cohort-enrollment size forcing variable. For example, we could use the average achievement information for enrollment cohorts of sizes 36 and 39 to provide a second-difference estimate of +0.52 (= [(68.87 − 67.30)/3]. Finally, although averaging together multiple second-difference estimates does draw additional relevant information into the estimation process, it does so in a completely ad hoc fashion. The RD approach that we describe next provides a more systematic strategy for incorporating all the additional information into the estimation process.

To facilitate understanding of the RD approach, examine Figure 9.1. This figure displays selected sample information from Table 9.1 describing the overall class-average reading achievement of Israeli fifth-grade children plotted against the sizes of grade-level enrollment cohorts of size 36 through 41. Notice that there is moderate vertical scatter—of about one scale point, up or down—in the class-average reading achievement of children in enrollment cohorts of size 36 through 40 (all of whom were offered large classes by Maimonides' rule). Notice also that this vertical scatter is quite small in contrast to the approximately 6-point difference

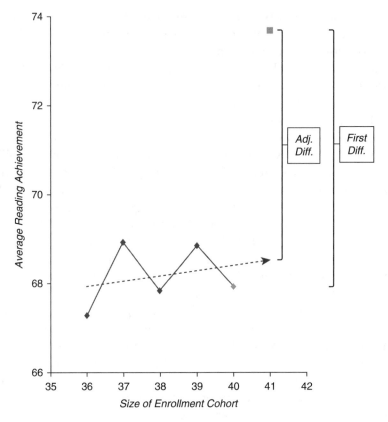

Figure 9.1 Fifth-grade class-average reading achievement in Jewish public schools in Israel, averaged across classes within cohort versus the size of the enrollment cohort, with an exploratory pre–cut-off trend line superimposed (*dashed arrow*).

between the class-average achievement of children in grade-level cohorts of size 40 and 41 (the latter being offered small classes by Maimonides' rule).

Inspection of the figure also provides visual support for the notion that class-average reading achievement depends on the value of the cohort-enrollment-size forcing variable. Indeed, despite the intrinsic scatter of the averages around the trend, the figure suggests that this underlying relationship may be linear, over this narrow range of enrollment cohorts. Seizing on this, we have superimposed an arrow-tipped linear trend line on the plot to summarize the "pre-Maimonides" relationship between class-average reading achievement and the forcing variable, cohort-enrollment size, over these pre–cut-off cohorts.[9] We have then projected this line forward until it intersects the vertical dotted line drawn above the point on the x-axis that corresponds to a cohort enrollment size of 41 students. The vertical elevation of the tip of this arrow at this dotted line indicates our "best projection" for what class-average reading achievement would be in a cohort with an enrollment of 41, if Maimonides' rule had not intervened. If the projection is credible, then the "adjusted vertical difference" between the tip of the arrow and the "observed" class-average achievement in this cohort will be a better estimate of the causal impact of the exogenous offer of a class-size reduction than any of the separate piecewise difference-in-differences estimates. This is because the new adjusted difference incorporates evidence on the achievement/enrollment trend from all the enrollment cohorts from size 36 through 40 systematically, and then uses it to adjust the estimated first-difference estimate for this trend. We label the "first-difference" and "adjusted" estimates of treatment impact on the plot in Figure 9.1. These are the basic ideas that underpin RD analysis.

Of course, projections like that which we imposed on Figure 9.1 can be constructed less arbitrarily by specifying and fitting an appropriate regression model to the original data, rather than by working with within-cohort size averages and sketching plots, as we have done in our illustration. For instance, we can extract from Angrist and Lavy's original dataset all the information on the 75 classrooms pertaining to fifth-grade enrollment cohorts of sizes 36 through 41. We can then specify a regression model to summarize the pre–cut-off achievement/enrollment trend credibly and project it forward to the cohort of enrollment size 41, while including in the model a dedicated regression parameter to capture the vertical "jig" that we hypothesize occurs between the projected and observed class-average reading achievement for classes offered to members of the enrollment cohort of size 41. Estimation of this latter "jig" parameter, obtained by standard regression methods, would provide an adjusted RD estimate of the differential effect on student class-average reading achievement of an offer of "small" versus "large" classes generated by the exogenous application of Maimonides' rule.

To complete these analyses, we create two additional predictors in the Angrist and Lavy dataset. We illustrate their creation in Table 9.2, where we list selected cases (classrooms) from enrollment cohorts of size 36 through 41 students (we have omitted data on some cohorts in Table 9.2

---

9. We obtained this exploratory trend line by regressing cohort-average reading achievement on cohort enrollment size in cohorts of size 36 through 40, using ordinary least-squares (OLS) regression analysis.

Table 9.2 Class-average reading achievement and intended class size for the first three fifth-grade classes in enrollment cohorts of size 36 to 41 (enrollment cohorts of size 37 and 38 omitted to save space) in Israeli Jewish public schools

Class *ID*	*READ* Class-Average Reading Achievement	*SIZE* Cohort Enrollment Size	*CSIZE* Centered Cohort Enrollment Size (= *SIZE*–41)	*SMALL* (0 = large class; 1 = small class)
3601	51.00	36	−5	0
3602	83.32	36	−5	0
3603	64.57	36	−5	0
...				
...				
3901	46.67	39	−2	0
3902	68.94	39	−2	0
3903	74.08	39	−2	0
...				
4001	73.15	40	−1	0
4002	60.18	40	−1	0
4003	52.77	40	−1	0
...				
4101	69.41	41	0	1
4102	80.53	41	0	1
4103	55.32	41	0	1
...				

to save space, but these data were included in our computations). In the second and third columns, we list values of class-average reading achievement, *READ*, and the corresponding enrollment-cohort size, *SIZE*, for the first three classrooms in each cohort. We also list two new variables to act as predictors in our RD analyses. First, we have created the new dichotomous predictor *SMALL* to indicate classrooms in those cohorts in which, as a result of Maimonides' rule, the offered class size is small. In this reduced dataset, this is only for classrooms formed from enrollment cohorts that contain 41 students. Second, we have "recentered" the forcing variable—that is, the original enrollment-cohort *SIZE* predictor—by subtracting a constant value of 41 from all values to form a new predictor labeled *CSIZE*. This new predictor takes on a value of zero for classes in the cohort of enrollment 41, and its non-zero values measure the horizontal distance in the size of each cohort from the cohort of 41 students. Thus, for instance, *CSIZE* has a value of "−1" for classrooms in enrollment cohorts of 40 students.

To conduct an RD analysis in these data, using cohorts of enrollment 36 through 41, we regress outcome *READ* on the main effects of new predictors *CSIZE* and *SMALL*, as follows:

$$READ_i = \beta_0 + \beta_1 CSIZE_i + \beta_2 SMALL_i + \varepsilon_i \qquad (9.1)$$

In this regression model, parameters β_1 and β_2 represent the main effects of predictors *CSIZE* and *SMALL*. However, β_2 addresses our research question directly by providing an RD estimate of the treatment effect. You can gain insight into how parameters in this model function by rewriting Equation 9.1 with predictor *CSIZE* replaced by the original cohort *SIZE* predictor, minus 41, and by taking expectations throughout to eliminate the residuals and obtain an expression in population means, as follows:

$$E\{READ_i\} = \beta_0 + \beta_1 (SIZE_i - 41) + \beta_2 SMALL_i \qquad (9.2)$$

Then, by substituting predictor values for prototypical children, we can see that the hypothesized population-average value of *READ* among the children who were offered a small class (*SMALL* = 1) because their cohort size was 41 is

$$E\{READ_i | SIZE = 41; SMALL = 1\} = \beta_0 + \beta_1 (41 - 41) + \beta_2 (1)$$
$$E\{READ_i | SIZE = 41; SMALL = 1\} = \beta_0 + \beta_2 \qquad (9.3)$$

We can also obtain an expression for the hypothesized population-average value of *READ* among children who were offered a large class (*SMALL* = 0), but then project their achievement to the 41st cohort (*SIZE* = 41), as follows:

$$E\{READ_i | SIZE = 41; SMALL = 0\} = \beta_0 + \beta_1 (41 - 41) + \beta_2 (0)$$
$$E\{READ_i | SIZE = 41; SMALL = 0\} = \beta_0 \qquad (9.4)$$

Then, subtracting Equation 9.4 from Equation 9.3, you can see that regression parameter β_2—the parameter associated with the predictor *SMALL* in Equation 9.1—represents the population difference in average reading achievement that we hypothesize to occur between children offered prototypical small-class sizes and large-class sizes, at an enrollment cohort size of 41. This is exactly the parameter that we wanted to estimate.

Notice the critical role played by the recentering of the original forcing variable—enrollment-cohort size—to provide new predictor *CSIZE*.

This recentering relocates the origin of the enrollment-cohort size axis to the cohort of size 41, and thereby redefines the role of the intercept parameter β_0. The intercept now represents the population class-average reading score that we would expect "untreated" children (i.e., those offered large classes) to achieve if they had been members of an enrollment cohort of 41 students, but were offered education in a large class rather than a small class. This projection forward from the pre-Maimonides secular trend provides an appropriate counterfactual in our comparison. Parameter β_2—representing the "vertical jig" in population class-average achievement that we hypothesize will occur at the enrollment-cohort size of 41—captures the size of the treatment effect, and is the focus of our data analyses.

In summary, these features that we have described apply to all RD models. In RD models, we regress the outcome on two important predictors. One is a continuous predictor—the forcing variable—that arrays observations (here, classrooms) along a continuum that includes an exogenously defined cut-point. The forcing predictor is usually recentered so it has a value of zero at, or just beyond, the cut-point. The second is a dichotomous predictor that specifies on which side of the exogenously defined cut-off a particular observation lies, and consequently to which experimental condition it has been assigned implicitly. In Table 9.3, we provide ordinary least-squares (OLS) estimates and ancillary statistics obtained by fitting the regression model specified in Equation 9.1 in the subsample of 75 classrooms that make up the enrollment cohorts of size 36 to 41 in the Angrist and Lavy dataset. The estimated coefficient, +5.12, on the dichotomous regressor, *SMALL*, is an RD estimate of β_2, the impact on average reading achievement of an offer of a class-size reduction from large to small, at a cohort size of 41, the cut-off determined exogenously by Maimonides' rule. Unfortunately, in our analyses, this

Table 9.3 Regression-discontinuity estimate of the impact of an offer of small versus large classes on class-average reading achievement, using data from classes in the fifth-grade enrollment cohorts of size 36 through 41 in Israeli Jewish public schools

Predictor	Estimate	Standard Error	t-statistic	p-value
INTERCEPT	68.6**	3.51	19.5	0.00
CSIZE	0.124	1.07	0.116	0.91
SMALL	5.12~	4.00	1.28	0.10†
R^2	0.066			

~p <0.10; *p <0.05; **p <0.01
†One-sided test.

RD-estimated causal impact of offered class size is not statistically significant ($p = 0.10$; one-sided test), even though there are now 75 classrooms in the analytic sample. Finally, note that the regression coefficient associated with the forcing predictor *CSIZE* has a positive value (0.124), indicating the positive relationship between classroom-average reading achievement and cohort enrollment size. However, we cannot reject the null hypothesis that it is actually zero in the population. We turn next to ways to extend the basic RD methodology in order to refine these estimates and increase statistical power.

Choosing an Appropriate Bandwidth

Now that we have established the basic principles of the RD approach, many sensible extensions are possible. For instance, why should we restrict our analytic sample only to enrollment cohorts to the left of the exogenously imposed class-size maximum and to the single enrollment cohort of size 41 to the right of the cut-off? Why not widen the analytic window on the right to include information on enrollment cohorts of size 42 through 46 to supplement the analysis? We could easily model the secular achievement/enrollment trend to the right of the cut-off too, and project it back to obtain an improved estimate of class-average achievement in small-offer classes, for comparison with the projection from the pre-cut-off trend from large-offer classes. After all, once the exogenous disruption to the enrollment/class-size offer relationship has occurred at the Maimonides-inspired maximum class size of 40, shouldn't the underlying trend linking class-average achievement and enrollment-cohort size "pick up" again, as before? In fact, with this expanded mandate, the statistical model in Equation 9.1 would not even have to change. Parameter β_2 would continue to represent the hypothesized population difference in class-average reading achievement between children offered their education in small and large classrooms, at an enrollment cohort size of 41. We would simply be strengthening our estimation of this same parameter, by widening the analytic window on the right and thereby increasing our sample size. In the same spirit, why include only enrollment cohorts that contain 36 students and more on the left, and the cohorts containing only up to and including 46 students on the right? Why not include information from enrollment cohorts of size 30 through 50, or size 20 through 60? We consider these issues in more detail in what remains of this section, as we illustrate some of the consequences of increasing bandwidth.

Of course, increasing the bandwidth will usually draw more classes into the analysis. This will tend to increase the statistical power and precision of our estimation of the all-important vertical "jig"—the coefficient on question predictor *SMALL*—that addresses our research question at the Maimonides-inspired cut-off. However, increasing the bandwidth on either side of the cut-off also raises important questions about the potential functional form of the secular achievement/enrollment trend that we are modeling by including "forcing" predictor *CSIZE* in the RD model. We return to these questions in the next section, which we illustrate with evidence from an important paper by Ludwig and Miller (2007). However, for the moment, we continue with our Angrist and Lavy example in order to gain more insight into how we might choose an appropriate analytic bandwidth in an RD analysis.

First, let's consider expanding the analytic sample to include all classrooms in the Angrist and Lavy dataset that pertain to grade-level enrollment cohorts of size 36 through 46. The addition of classes from enrollment cohorts of size 42 through 46 increases the number of cases with positive values of the recentered forcing predictor *CSIZE*. Even though we have expanded our analytic sample by adding 105 classrooms in enrollment cohorts of size 42 through 46, we can continue to address our research question by fitting the same "standard" RD model that we specified in Equation 9.1. In addition, we can continue to interpret its parameters in almost the same way. Predictor *CSIZE* continues to account for the hypothesized linear trend linking cohort-enrollment size and class-average achievement. Note that the model now stipulates that—apart from the impact of the exogenous disruption in the offer of class size—the linear trend continues on both sides of the cut-off with the same slope, as represented by parameter β_1. Predictor *SMALL* continues to provide for a vertical "jig" in class-level achievement at the 41st cohort, a result of the Maimonides-inspired exogenous disruption in the offer of class size at that point. Its associated parameter β_2 continues to summarize the impact of that disruption on class-average reading achievement there. Notice that information from enrollment cohorts of size 36 through 40 is used to project the secular trend forward to the cohort of size 41, as before. However, now information from the cohorts of size 41 through 46 is also used to predict the trend backward, again to the 41st cohort. As a result, we no longer need to rely solely on the observed values at the single 41st cohort to provide the upper end of our estimate of average achievement (as in our initial RD analysis). Then, provided we are modeling the achievement/enrollment trend appropriately on both sides of the cut-off (by the hypothesized linear relationship between achievement and *CSIZE*), we obtain both an improved estimate of the slope of that relationship and of the average treatment effect itself, now articulated as the vertical separation between a pair of population-average achievement values at the cut-off. Finally, we benefit from the increased statistical power that comes with the anticipated increase in the sample size.

We present estimates of all parameters and ancillary statistics from this analysis in Table 9.4. The results support and strengthen our earlier conclusions. Although our estimate of the average treatment effect of +3.85 is almost 25% smaller than the comparable estimate of 5.12 in Table 9.3, its standard error is much smaller (at 2.81 instead of 4.00), a result of the addition of 105 classrooms to the sample. Consequently, the p-value associated with the corresponding one-sided test of average treatment impact has fallen from .10 to .09.

Now it becomes tempting to widen the analytic window even more, in the hope of further increasing statistical power. We present a summary of the results of doing so in Table 9.5, where we have incorporated additional enrollment cohorts into the analysis. In the first and second row, we repeat the findings from the two RD analyses that we have already completed: (a) the first analysis with all classrooms in schools with September enrollments of 36 through 41, and (b) the second analysis that added the enrollment cohorts of size 42 to 46. Recall that, in the process, our sample of classes has more than doubled to 180 and, while the estimate of the average treatment effect shrank in magnitude from 5.12 to 3.85, it remained positive and its precision increased. As we increase the bandwidth still further, these trends continue. Consider the last row of the table, where the comparison now includes 423 classrooms. Here, the fundamental finding remains that there is a benefit to being offered education in a smaller class, and the estimated effect size—which measures the "vertical jig" in average achievement between students offered education in "Large" and "Small" classes—has remained stable. Note that the addition of more classrooms has also increased statistical power dramatically

Table 9.4 Regression-discontinuity estimate of the impact of an offer of *Small* versus *Large* classes on class-average reading achievement, using data from classes in the fifth-grade enrollment cohorts of size 36 through 46 in Israeli Jewish public schools

Predictor	Estimate	Standard Error	t-statistic	p-value
INTERCEPT	68.7**	1.92	35.82	0.00
CSIZE	0.171	0.436	0.39	0.70
SMALL	3.85~	2.81	1.37	0.09†
R^2	0.046			

~p <0.10; *p <0.05; **p <0.01
†One-sided test

Table 9.5 Regression-discontinuity estimates of the causal impact of an offer of *small* versus *large* classes on the class-average reading achievement of fifth-grade students in Israeli Jewish public schools, for several analytic window widths around the Maimonides-inspired cut-off in class size of 40 students.

Window Width	Number of Classrooms in Each Comparison	Predictor: *SMALL*			Predictor: *CSIZE*		R^2 Statistic
		Estimate	Standard Error	*p*-value	Estimate	*p*-value	
{36,41}	75	5.12~	4.00	0.10†	0.12	0.46	0.066
{36,46}	180	3.85~	2.81	0.09†	0.17	0.35	0.046
{35,47}	221	4.12*	2.50	0.05†	0.02	0.48	0.038
{34,48}	259	4.01*	2.31	0.04†	0.00	0.50	0.036
{33,49}	288	3.67*	2.16	0.05†	-0.01	0.48	0.030
{32,50}	315	2.97~	2.04	0.08†	0.03	0.44	0.026
{31,51}	352	2.93~	1.94	0.07†	0.04	0.41	0.026
{30,52}	385	3.36*	1.84	0.04†	-0.04	0.37	0.020
{29,53}	423	3.95**	1.80	0.02†	-0.14	0.12	0.015

~p <0.10; *p <0.05; **p <0.01
†One-sided test.

and reduced the size of the *p*-values associated with the effect of question-predictor *SMALL*. In fact, when the RD regression model is fitted to the data from the 423 classrooms that make up the enrollment cohorts between 29 and 53 students in size, we can readily reject the associated null hypothesis of no treatment effect (p = .02, one-sided test).

But, how wide can we increase the bandwidth and continue to believe in the credibility of our results? Certainly, when we were using a first-difference or a difference-in-differences approach, it is clear that the narrower our focus around the Maimonides' cut-off, the more confident we could be in the equality-in-expectation assumption for children thus pooled into large-offer and small-offer classrooms, and therefore in the internal validity of any comparison between these groups. But, as we narrowed the window of analytic attention to those cohorts with enrollments successively closer to, and on either side of, the cut-off, the number of classes included in the comparison decreased and the statistical power for detecting an effect declined. Increasing the bandwidth, on the other hand, certainly increased sample size and statistical power, but may have also increased the challenge to the internal validity of the comparison. In particular, when we make use of either a first-difference or a difference-in-differences approach in our Angrist and Lavy example, the further we expand our bandwidth to include enrollment cohorts far from those with grade-level enrollment of 40 or 41 students, the less plausible is our assumption that students in the groups being compared are equal in expectation on all unobserved dimensions. Indeed, as Angrist and Lavy point out, socioeconomic status and population density are positively related in Israel. As a result, children in enrollment cohorts of vastly different sizes are likely to differ dramatically in family socioeconomic status and in other unobserved respects that may be related to academic achievement. This would be an especially serious problem if we were relying only on a first difference as our estimate of the treatment effect, as we would be successively pooling into our treatment and control groups cohorts that were progressively less equal in expectation prior to treatment.

However, the situation with regression-discontinuity analyses is thankfully less stark. The reason is that we are not pooling the more remote cohorts into our nominal treatment and control groups. Instead, we are using the more remote cohorts in conjunction with the nearer ones—and their relationship with the forcing variable—to *project* the estimated treatment effect *at the cut-off*, where the assumption of equality in expectation is indeed met. In other words, because our estimate of the treatment effect pertains only at the cut-off, it may remain internally valid there, regardless of how many additional data points are added into the analyses, and from how far afield they are drawn. It does not matter if cohorts remote from the cut-off are not equal in expectation with other cohorts as remote on the other side, provided we can be confident that we are using the information they offer to better project our expectations for any difference in average outcome at the cut-off. Of course, doing so requires the correct modeling of the relationship between the outcome and the forcing variable.

To capitalize effectively on natural experiments with an RD design, we must therefore strike a sensible balance between adequate statistical power and defensible modeling of the trend that links the outcome to the forcing variable along which the exogenous cut-off is specified. From a mathematical perspective, over a sufficiently short range, all such trends are locally linear. In the Angrist and Lavy dataset, the requirements of local linearity may support inclusion of enrollment cohorts of size 36 through 41, or even the cohorts of size 29 through 35. However, if there is evidence of curvilinearity in the underlying outcome/forcing-variable trend, then we must either limit our bandwidth, so that the local linearity assumption is met, or we must model the trend with a functional form that has more credibility than the linear. We illustrate this point with evidence from another important study.

Generalizing the Relationship Between the Outcome and the Forcing Variable

In 1965, the federal government in the United States established *Head Start*, a program designed to improve the life chances of young children from low-income families. The program had several components, including the provision of preschool education, nutritious meals, and health-care services such as immunizations, screening for physical and mental ailments, and referrals to community health services. Since its inception, Head Start has grown enormously and currently serves more than 900,000 children at an annual cost of more than $7 billion. The size and cost of Head Start have led to concern about the program's benefits. Of particular interest is the question of whether participation in Head Start provides children with *long-term* benefits. In 2007, Jens Ludwig and Douglas Miller published a paper that sheds important light on the answer to this question.

Ludwig and Miller's identification strategy capitalized on a particular aspect of the way that Head Start was administered in its first year. The basic method of implementation was that community-based organizations that wanted Head Start programs had to submit applications to the Office of Economic Opportunity (OEO), the federal agency that administered the program. OEO officials feared that this application process would leave the poorest communities in the nation underserved because these communities tended to lack the organizational capacity to develop strong applications. So, the OEO used data from the 1960 Census to locate the 300 counties in the nation with the highest poverty rates (those with poverty rates of 59.2% and above). The OEO then sent young staffers into these 300 counties with a mandate to help local community-based organizations develop strong applications for Head Start funding. Counties with poverty rates just below the 59.2% cut-off did not receive any special aid in applying for these grants.

Ludwig and Miller recognized that the OEO decision to supply grant-writing assistance to the poorest 300 counties in the United States provided a natural experiment with an RD design that they could exploit to explore the impacts of an offer of Head Start on children's long-term outcomes. In essence, the OEO had arrayed counties along a forcing variable that displayed the county-level poverty rate. It then specified a cut-off (at a poverty rate of 59.2%) to divide counties exogenously into two groups. Counties with poverty rates at or above (to the "right" of) the cut-off received grant-writing assistance. Counties just to the "left" of the cut-off—with poverty rates of less than 59.2%—did not receive grant-writing assistance. We use evidence from Ludwig and Miller's innovative study to illustrate extensions of the basic RD approach, especially ways of modeling the all-important relationship between the outcome and the forcing variable.

Ludwig and Miller actually carried out two sets of analyses using the same RD approach. Although the two sets of analyses differ only in the definitions of the outcome, their conceptual underpinnings are subtly different, and the distinction has pedagogic value here. In the first set of analyses, Ludwig and Miller use their RD approach to examine differences in counties' funding for, and participation in, the Head Start program as a consequence of receipt of grant-writing assistance, or the lack of it. In these analyses, poverty rate is the forcing variable, exogenous assignment to grant-writing assistance is the treatment, and Head Start funding and participation are the outcomes. The results of these analyses showed that grant-writing assistance did indeed lead to differences in Head Start funding and participation immediately following receipt of the assistance.

Ludwig and Miller's second set of analyses focused on a more remote set of outcomes, the longer-term child health and schooling outcomes that had motivated the research initially. Here, poverty rate was again the forcing variable and exogenous assignment to grant-writing assistance again defined the experimental conditions. However, now, the impact of *participating* in Head Start on future child outcomes is the substantive focus, and so grant-writing assistance—which remains the principal question predictor—has become an exogenously assigned expression of *intent to treat* by Head Start. We will refer to this as an offer to participate in Head Start. So, essentially, the authors have addressed two different sets of causal questions. The first is: Did receipt of grant-writing assistance lead to increases in a county's participation in, and funding for, Head Start? The second is: Did grant-writing assistance (which constitutes an intent to treat with Head Start) lead to improvement in future child outcomes? In both cases, because receipt of grant-writing assistance was exogenously assigned around the RD cut-off, causal inferences could be made. All that differed between the two analyses is the set of outcomes. We now turn to an overview of Ludwig and Miller's innovative RD strategy, and offer a brief summary of their findings.

The researchers used data from two sources. The first consisted of aggregate data from the National Archives and Records Administration (NARA) on county-level poverty rates and Head Start funding and participation in the 1960s. The second consisted of individual-level data from the National Educational Longitudinal Study (NELS), which provided information on a nationally representative sample of children who were first interviewed as eighth-graders in 1988, and who completed follow-up interviews through 2000. Ludwig and Miller found that the NELS sample contained 649 children who had lived in counties with 1960 poverty rates among the 300 poorest, and 674 who had lived in the one of the next 300 poorest counties. In all of their analyses, they treated the county as their unit of analysis.[10]

In their first set of analyses, Ludwig and Miller examined whether the exogenously defined poverty-rate cut-off for grant-writing assistance did indeed result in a discontinuous jump in the availability of Head Start programs in poor counties, as measured by funding levels per child in the appropriate age group. They did this by comparing Head Start spending per four-year-old in 1968 for two groups of counties, just on either side of the exogenously defined cut-off. The treatment group consisted of countries with poverty rates between 59.2% (the minimum for receiving the OEO application aid) and 69.2% (10 percentage points above the cut-off), and the control group consisted of those with poverty rates from just below 59.2% (the 301st poorest counties in the U.S.) to 49.2% (10 percentage points below the cut-off). They found that Head Start spending per student in the first group (which contained 228 counties) was $288 per four-year-old, whereas the comparable figure for the second group was $134. They found similar results when they compared the spending levels for groups defined within different bandwidths (for example, in analytic windows that contained only those counties that fell within 5 percentage points of the poverty cut-off). This gave the researchers confidence that the OEO intervention did influence the availability of Head Start in these counties markedly. Ludwig and Miller also verified that the difference in Head Start participation rates between counties with poverty rates just above the OEO poverty cut-off for support and those with poverty rates just below this cut-off continued through the 1970s. This proved important in locating data that would permit them to examine the long-term effects of Head Start availability on children's outcomes.

As Ludwig and Miller explain, the principal statistical model that they fitted in their study is a generalization of the simple linear RD model that we specified in Equation 9.1. They wrote it as

$$Y_c = m(P_c) + \alpha G_c + v_c \qquad (9.5)$$

Although the similarity between this model and our standard RD model in Equation 9.1 is not immediately apparent, due to differences in notation, the two are essentially the same. In Equation 9.5, Y_c is the value of an

---

10. Thus, they aggregated child-level outcome measures from the NELS to the county level.

outcome for the cth county, and could represent the average value of the Head Start participation rate, say, in that county in a chosen year. The forcing variable P_c is the poverty rate in the cth county 1960, recentered so that it has a value of zero at the poverty rate cut-off of 59.2%. Dichotomous question predictor G_c is the principal question predictor and indicates whether the cth county received grant-writing assistance from the OEO (1 = received assistance; 0 = otherwise). Thus, its associated regression parameter α (which corresponds to regression parameter β_2 in Equation 9.1), represents the causal impact of the grant-writing assistance on the outcome, estimated at the poverty-rate cut-off of 59.2%. The stochastic element in the model, v_c, is a county-level residual.

The principal difference in appearance between the hypothesized models in Equations 9.1 and 9.5 revolves around the term $m(P_c)$, which is intended as a generic representation of the functional form of the hypothesized relationship between the outcome and the forcing variable, P. Ludwig and Miller first modeled the outcome as a linear function of the forcing variable, as we did in our earlier example, but they allowed the population slopes of the relationship to differ on opposite sides of the discontinuity. They achieved this by replacing function $m(P_c)$ by a standard linear function of P and then adding the two-way interaction between it and question predictor G as follows:

$$Y_c = \beta_0 + \beta_1 P_c + \alpha G_c + \beta_2 \left(P_c \times G_c \right) + v_c \tag{9.6}$$

With this specification, the fitted linear relationship between centered poverty rate P and the county-level Head Start participation rate for counties to the left of the cut-off (for which $G = 0$) is

$$\widehat{Y}_c = \widehat{\beta}_0 + \widehat{\beta}_1 P_c \tag{9.7}$$

and the fitted relationship for counties to the right of the cut-off is:

$$\widehat{Y}_c = \left(\widehat{\beta}_0 + \widehat{\alpha} \right) + \left(\widehat{\beta}_1 + \widehat{\beta}_2 \right) P_c \tag{9.8}$$

But, since forcing variable P is centered at the cut-off, and despite the permitted difference in its hypothesized slope on the two sides of the cut-off, you can demonstrate by subtraction that parameter α continues to capture the average causal impact of grant-writing assistance on the Head Start participation rate (don't forget to set the value of P_c to zero before you subtract!).

Ludwig and Miller initially fit Equation 9.6 with a bandwidth of 8 percentage points in the poverty index on either side of the cut-off.

This resulted in a sample size of only 43 counties. Their estimate of the impact of the grant-writing assistance on the Head Start participation rate was 0.238, with a standard error of 0.156. Thus, although the point estimate indicated that grant-writing assistance increased by 23.8 percentage points the probability that a child participated in Head Start, across the cut-off, the associated null hypothesis of no effect could not be rejected.

This led Ludwig and Miller to expand their analytic window to include counties with poverty rates that fell within a bandwidth of 16 percentage points on either side of the discontinuity. Doing so increased their sample size to 82 counties. However, inspection of their data led them to suspect that, within this wider range of data, the relationship between the Head Start participation rate and the poverty-rate forcing variable was curvilinear. It also appeared to differ on either side of the cut-off. They recognized that one solution to this problem was to specify a polynomial relationship between outcome and forcing variable. So, they fitted RD models with flexible quadratic specifications, allowing the curvilinearity to differ on either side of the cut-off. In Equation 9.9, we present their flexible quadratic specification:

$$Y_c = \beta_0 + \beta_1 P_c + \beta_3 P_c^2 + \alpha\, G_c + \beta_2\left(P_c \times G_c\right) + \beta_4\left(P_c^2 \times G_c\right) + \upsilon_c \qquad (9.9)$$

With this specification, they estimated that treatment effect α was 0.316, with a standard error of 0.151. Thus, with this specification and bandwidth, they could reject the null hypothesis that grant-writing assistance had no impact on the rate of children's participation in Head Start.

In Figure 9.2,[11] with smooth dashed curves on either side of the cut-off, we display the fitted quadratic relationships between Head-Start participation rate and the county poverty-rate forcing variable that were obtained in Ludwig and Miller's analyses. Notice, first, that the shape of the fitted relationship is very different to the left of the cut-off point than to the right. In addition, one dramatic limitation of the quadratic specifications on either side of the cut-off is that the shapes of the fitted curves are constrained to be symmetric around their maximum or minimum. Given that these curves are fitted to a modest number of cases, it seems quite plausible that the fitted curvilinear relationships between outcome and forcing variable could be highly sensitive to atypical outcome values and the leverage exercised by a very small number of atypical data points. Moreover, since the estimate of the average treatment effect $\hat{\alpha}$ comes

---

11. Figure 9.2 is a reproduction of Figure I, Panel B, from page 175 of Ludwig and Miller's 2007 paper.

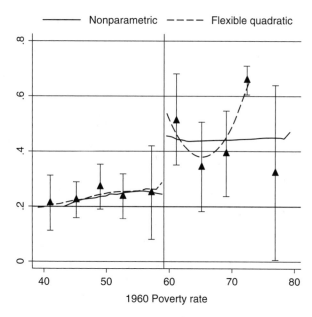

Figure 9.2 Estimated discontinuity in Head Start participation at the Office of Economic Opportunity cut-off for grant-writing support, using data from the National Educational Longitudinal Study (NELS) first follow-up sample. Reproduced with permission from Ludwig and Miller (2007), Figure I, Panel B, p. 175.

from a comparison of the projections of the quadratic relationships onto a vertical line through the cut-off, from the respective sides, small differences in the fitted quadratic relationship on either side of the cut-off could have a large impact on the magnitude of the estimated average treatment effect. This realization led Ludwig and Miller to revise their analytic strategy in two ways. First, they explored the sensitivity of their results to the choice of outcome/forcing-variable functional form and of bandwidth, an approach that we suggest should always be used with RD designs. Second, they re-estimated their treatment effects using a non-parametric smoothing approach, known as *local linear-regression analysis*, to obtain the fitted relationships on either side of the cut-off. The fitted curves from this latter approach can also be seen as the solid and slightly more jagged trend lines in Figure 9.2.[12]

---

12. To learn more about local linear regression analysis, see Imbens and Lemieux (2008) or Bloom (forthcoming).

In their second set of analyses, Ludwig and Miller used an identical RD strategy to estimate the impact of an *offer* of Head Start support—again represented by the cut-off–assigned receipt of grant-writing assistance—on longer-term child health- and school-related outcomes. One question concerned whether an offer of Head Start participation reduced the incidence of mortality among children. To examine this, Ludwig and Miller turned to county-level data from the Vital Statistics Compressed Mortality Files (CMF). They constructed an outcome measure that summarized the one-year mortality rate in each county for children aged five to nine, due to causes that participation in Head Start might have prevented, given the health-care components included in the program. They formed this outcome measure for each year from 1973 through 1983, these being the years through which they expected that the gaps in Head Start participation that were caused by the receipt of grant-writing assistance persisted. Relevant causes of death included tuberculosis, diabetes, anemias, meningitis, and respiratory causes. The outcome measure excluded deaths due to injuries and cancer among the children because the authors reasoned that these causes of death would not have been affected by Head Start participation between the ages of three and four.

The results of adopting the flexible-quadratic and local linear specifications in their RD regression model, and of using a bandwidth of 16 percentage points on either side of the cut-off on the poverty-rate forcing variable, are displayed in Figure 9.3.[13] The estimated causal effect of the offer of Head Start services is −2.201 from the local linear specification, with a standard error of 1.004. As Ludwig and Miller explain (p. 179), this estimate implies that any increased participation in Head Start that stemmed from receipt of the grant-writing assistance reduced the annual mortality rate among children aged five to nine by more than one-third. This result and those from similar RD models fitted with other health and educational outcomes show that an offer of Head Start, as initially implemented in poor counties with poverty rates close to 59%, had dramatic long-term benefits for participating children.

Specification Checks Using Pseudo-Outcomes and Pseudo–Cut-offs

Ludwig and Miller reasoned that one way to strengthen the claim that their RD methodology provided an unbiased estimate of the causal impact

---

13. Figure 9.3 is a reproduction of Figure IV, Panel A, from page 182 of Ludwig and Miller's 2007 paper.

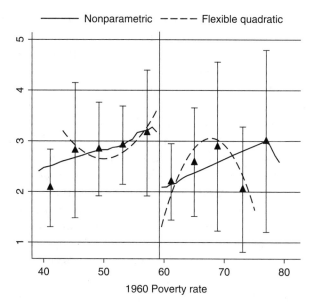

Figure 9.3 Estimated discontinuity in county-level mortality rate for children aged five to nine, 1973 through 1983, from causes that could be affected by Head Start, at the Office of Economic Opportunity cut-off for grant-writing support. Reproduced with permission from Ludwig and Miller (2007), Figure IV, Panel A, p. 182.

of an offer of Head Start on subsequent outcomes was to show that their approach revealed no effects for outcomes that they hypothesized should *not* have been influenced by the OEO grant-writing assistance program. One such outcome was county-level per capita spending in 1972 on social programs other than Head Start. This check was important to perform because, if a discontinuity in per capita social spending for programs other than Head Start were detected, it would jeopardize their claim that Head Start participation was the cause of the improved health and education outcomes for children in the treatment-group counties. Ludwig and Miller were able to demonstrate that when they fitted their hypothesized RD regression models that incorporated this new "pseudo-outcome," their estimate of any treatment effect was so small that they could not reject the null hypothesis that it was zero.

Ludwig and Miller used similar reasoning in estimating the impact on health-related pseudo-outcomes that they hypothesized should not have been influenced by Head Start participation. One such outcome consisted of county-specific death rates among five- to nine-year-olds in the years 1959 through 1964, from deaths due to causes that participation in Head Start might have prevented. Since these years were prior to the introduction of Head Start, a positive treatment effect would have undercut the causal interpretation of their main results. By refitting their main RD models with this new "prior" outcome measure, they were again able to demonstrate that there was no effect.

Finally, another useful specification check that Ludwig and Miller employed was to examine whether there were differences in the outcome at points along the poverty-rate forcing variable other than at the legitimate 59.2% cut-off. The logic underlying this check is that a key assumption underlying the RD approach is that the relationship between the outcome and the forcing variable should be *smooth* at points other than the cut-off. Before examining their data in detail, Ludwig and Miller arbitrarily chose a pseudo–cut-off at the 40% poverty rate, and refitted their RD models, this time with the forcing variable centered at the new pseudo–cut-off. They did not find any statistically significant differences in outcomes at this pseudo–cut-off.[14] Their visual inspection of a bivariate plot of outcome versus forcing variable also did not reveal the presence of discontinuities at poverty rates other than at the value of 59.2% that had been exogenously determined.

In summary, Ludwig and Miller's detailed knowledge of the Head Start program and their collection of a wide variety of outcome measures enabled them to conduct additional tests and sensitivity analyses that lent credibility to their results. For example, their knowledge of the details of the process that the OEO used to encourage Head Start applications from low-income counties enabled them to define a sharp cut-off on their forcing variable, county-level poverty rate. Their knowledge of the timing of the introduction of Head Start and the timing of the grant-writing assistance allowed them to demonstrate that this assistance affected counties' participation in Head Start, but not their participation in other federally funded social programs. Their knowledge of the types of health-care screening and immunizations provided by Head Start allowed them to distinguish between subsequent causes of death that could have been influenced plausibly by Head Start participation and those that could not have been. This is another example of a theme we emphasized as early as Chapter 3: detailed knowledge of the operation of programs and a thoughtful theory of action about how they might influence the outcomes are central to conducting high-quality impact evaluations.

---

14. Ludwig and Miller's examination of pseudo–cut-points is described in their 2005 NBER Working Paper, but not in their 2007 published paper.

Regression-Discontinuity Designs and Statistical Power

The RD approach can be used not only to analyze data from many natural experiments, but also as the basis for researcher-designed experiments. Ludwig and Miller's description of the OEO initiative illustrates this point. Since OEO—not the investigators—ranked all counties in the United States in terms of their 1960 poverty rate and provided the treatment of grant-writing support to the 300 poorest counties, we regard this as a natural experiment. However, if researchers had been asked in 1965 to design a strategy for evaluating the consequences of an offer of Head Start on children's long-term outcomes, they could have implemented the same research design themselves. One reason that an investigator might be tempted to adopt an RD design in this example, rather than a randomized-assignment design, is that providing assistance to the 300 poorest counties, with the slightly less needy serving as controls, would be easier to defend ethically to members of Congress who were concerned about equity than would the assignment of poor counties randomly to treatment and control groups.

A recent evaluation of the federal government's Reading First initiative provides another example. Reading First was the $1 billion per year centerpiece of the No Child Left Behind Act of 2001, the U.S. federal government's main legislative program aimed at improving the education of low-achieving students from low-income families. The Reading First initiative provided substantial grants to local school districts (through their states) for use in implementing a set of instructional practices that research had shown to be effective in teaching children to read. The goal of the program was to assure that all children read at, or above, grade level by the end of third grade. The legislation also mandated that the U.S. Department of Education's Institute of Education Sciences (IES) commission a study of the impact of Reading First on teachers' instructional practices and on children's reading achievement.

The original intent of the IES was that the mandated impact evaluation would be designed as an experiment with the random assignment of eligible schools to the treatment and control conditions. However, this proved impossible because, by the time the IES had awarded a contract for the design and conduct of the impact evaluation to two contract research organizations, Abt Associates and MDRC, local school districts had already received their Reading First grants and had implemented their own processes for assigning schools to participate in the grant program.

Fortunately, many school districts had made use of assignment processes that facilitated the estimation of causal impacts via an RD design.

Each district had done so by creating a needs-based index across all elementary schools in the district and then had provided Reading First grants to the schools with the highest needs-based rank. Such an index could then serve as the forcing variable in an RD evaluation. In some districts, the index was formed from only a single variable, such as the percentage of third-graders reading below grade level. Other districts had formed a composite index based on multiple measures, such as the average reading score at each grade level, and the percentage of children in each school eligible for free or reduced-price lunches. The number of variables that contributed to the needs-based ranking did not matter. What was important was that districts created a quantitative rating of all elementary schools, their district-specific forcing variable, then chose a cut-point on that ranking exogenously to separate schools that received Reading First grants from those that did not, and did not deviate from its decision rule. If these conditions were met, and if the research team could model the relationship between Reading First outcomes and the schools' rankings credibly, then data from these sites could be used to obtain an unbiased estimate of the impact of Reading First at the cut-off.

Careful investigation of the school-assignment processes in different school districts and states convinced the research team that 16 districts had indeed used quantitative needs-based ranking systems to determine which elementary schools had received Reading First grants. In addition, one state had employed this approach to allocate Reading First funds to schools. Each of these 16 districts and the one state provided natural experiments that the research team could use to evaluate the impacts of the intervention. In total, 238 elementary schools from the 16 districts and one state were included in the evaluation. Half of the 238 schools had received grants because the value of their needs-based ranking fell just above the exogenously determined cut-off in their districts. The other half did not receive grants because their needs-based ranking fell just below the respective cut-off value.[15]

The decision to base the research design on the assignment processes that the districts themselves had devised was advantageous in terms of obtaining participant cooperation. It is likely that cooperation would have been less forthcoming at many sites if the research team had insisted that the districts choose a sample of schools that could benefit from Reading First, and then had required that schools in this sample be assigned

---

15. As explained in the final report of the evaluation (Gamse et al., 2008), the evaluation of Reading First included one group of schools in addition to those in the 16 school districts and one state that employed an RD design in allocating funds. This one district assigned ten schools randomly to treatment or control status.

randomly to treatment or control groups. This is an important lesson in designing research. Creating quantitative indices of need to serve as a forcing variable, and then specifying an exogenous cut-off to determine which individuals or schools receive the treatment, can both satisfy ethical concerns about providing resources to the most needy and provide a basis for a sound impact evaluation using an RD design.

Of course, there are tradeoffs. In particular, there are two substantial and related costs in specifying treatment and control groups according to which side of an exogenous cut-point on a forcing variable that individuals or schools fall, instead of using random assignment to specify the groups. The first is that the evaluation results pertain only to schools that fall close to the cut-point. The second cost concerns statistical power. When you employ an RD design, you are essentially projecting to the right and left extremes of two point-clouds, one on either side of the cut-off. In such predictions, at the end or just beyond the end of the respective point-cloud, statistical precision is always disproportionately low and the standard error of the difference in projections—that is, of the estimated average treatment effect—will be large. Consequently, the sample size required in an impact evaluation with an RD design typically must be almost three times the size of the sample that would be required in an equivalent random-assignment experiment of the same statistical power (Bloom, forthcoming).

Additional Threats to Validity in a Regression-Discontinuity Design

As we mentioned in Chapter 8, many countries, states, provinces, and local school systems operate under stringent rules about maximum class sizes. The publication of Angrist and Lavy's (1999) Maimonides' rule paper catalyzed widespread interest in using the implementation of these rules to estimate the causal impact of class size on student achievement. Since the publication of their seminal paper, researchers have used RD approaches to analyze data from many settings where maximum class size rules have been enacted, including Bangladesh, Bolivia, Denmark, France, the Netherlands, Norway, and the United States. However, just because a maximum class-size rule is in existence in an educational system does not mean that it necessarily provides a sound basis for estimating the causal impact of class size on student academic outcomes. This is even the case when the maximum class-size rule is enforced quite rigidly, and the actual class sizes experienced by students in grade-level enrollment cohorts that lie just on either side of the class-size maximum are thereby intentionally different.

One threat to the validity of studies that use an RD approach to estimate the impact of a treatment such as the rule-based assignment of students to a small class is that participants in the educational process may be able to manipulate their placement on the forcing variable, so that their allocation to experimental conditions only appears to be exogenous but, in fact, is not. This occurs when participants have both an incentive to alter their position on the forcing variable so they are on one side of the treatment cut-off, or the other, and an opportunity to do so. Such actions by individuals, school heads, or other actors in the educational system may jeopardize the assumption of equality in expectation across the experimental conditions prior to treatment and result in bias in the estimation of the causal impact of interest.

Miguel Urquiola and Eric Verhoogen (2009) provide a description of how such a situation occurred in Chile, a country with a particularly interesting educational system. Since 1981, Chile has had an educational tuition-voucher system in place. Almost half of the elementary- and secondary-school students in urban areas of the country attend private schools, most of which participate in the tuition-voucher program. The majority of the private schools are for-profit institutions. Private schools that participate in the voucher system receive a per student payment (the value of the voucher) from the government. Unlike public schools, private schools are free to charge tuition and to select students as they see fit, including basing admission decisions on student test scores.

One requirement on all public and private schools that participate in the voucher system in Chile is that their class size may not exceed 45 students. If more than 45 students are enrolled in a school at a particular grade level, the school must create two classes at that grade level. Urquiola and Verhoogen (2009) show that the operation of the rule creates a relationship between class size and fourth-grade enrollment in Chile that is strikingly similar to the pattern that Angrist and Lavy detected in Israel. As illustrated in Figure 9.4,[16] class sizes rise linearly with fourth-grade enrollments up to 45 students. Then, a sharp discontinuity occurs. In schools with fourth-grade enrollments of 46 students, classes tend to have 22 or 23 students. This pattern suggests that the operation of the class-size rule provides a natural experiment that could be used to estimate the causal impact of class size on student achievement in Chile.

However, Urquiola's discussions with educators in Chile revealed that principals of private schools who participated in the voucher system

---

16. Figure 9.4 is a reproduction of Figure 5 from page 198 of Urquiola and Verhoogen's (2009) paper.

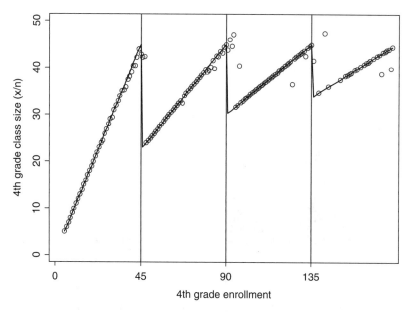

Figure 9.4 Fourth-grade enrollment versus class size in urban private-voucher schools in Chile, 2002. Based on administrative data for 2002. The solid line describes the relationship between enrollment and class size that would exist if the class-size rule were applied mechanically. The circles plot actual enrollment cell means of fourth- grade class size. Only data for schools with fourth-grade enrollments below 180 are plotted; this excludes less than 2% of all schools. Reproduced with permission from Urquiola and Verhoogen (2009), Figure 5, p. 198.

typically had strong incentives to manipulate their admissions policies in order to control their grade-level enrollments (and possibly student background characteristics). If one of these schools admitted a 46th student into a particular grade, its revenue would increase by the amount of the per student government payment plus any additional tuition charged. However, its costs would increase disproportionally by the salary and benefits that the school must then pay to obtain an additional teacher and the cost of providing an additional classroom. Thus, most private schools had strong incentives to keep grade-level enrollments at, or just below, 45 students, or multiples of it like 90 or 135 students. Exceptions were schools that sought to attract children whose parents wanted small classes and were willing to pay high tuition to get them. In this case, the socioeconomic status of families in private schools with grade-level enrollments of 46 or 47 students (and respective class sizes of 23 or 24 students) would be higher than that of children in private schools with grade-level enrollments of 44 or 45 students. This would violate the assumption that students in a narrow window of enrollment sizes around the class-size

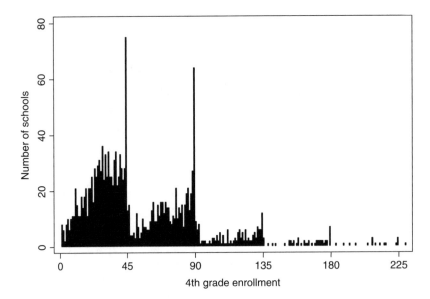

Figure 9.5 Sample histogram of fourth-grade student enrollment in urban private subsidized schools in Chile, 2002. Enrollment data are drawn from administrative records for 2002. For visual clarity, only schools with fourth-grade enrollment below 225 are displayed. This excludes less than 1% of all schools. Reproduced with permission from Urquiola and Verhoogen (2009), Figure 7, Panel A, p. 203.

maximum were equal in expectation, prior to treatment, especially on socioeconomic status.

Urquiola and Verhoogen investigated whether the responses of private-school principals and parents to the maximum class-size rules may have resulted in such a violation of the exogeneity assumption. They first examined the distribution of fourth-grade enrollments among private schools in the urban areas that participated in the voucher system. As illustrated in Figure 9.5,[17] they found sharp grade-level enrollment peaks at exactly 45, 90, and 135 students. In fact, more than five times as many schools reported fourth-grade enrollments of 45 students as reported fourth-grade enrollments of 46 students. The number of schools that reported fourth-grade enrollments of 90 was more than seven times the number that reported fourth-grade enrollments of 91 students. As the authors noted, the explanation is that school leaders simply controlled their

---

17. Figure 9.5 is a reproduction of Figure 7, Panel A, from page 203 of Urquiola and Verhoogen's (2009) paper.

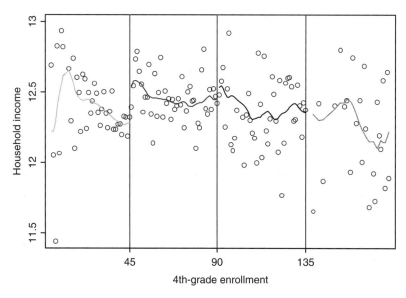

Figure 9.6   Household log-income versus fourth-grade student enrollment in urban private voucher schools in Chile, 2002. Income comes from 2002 individual-level SIMCE data aggregated at the school level. Enrollment is drawn from administrative data for the same year. The figure presents "raw" enrollment-cell means, along with the predicted values from a locally weighted regression model fitted within each enrollment segment. Only data for schools with fourth-grade enrollment below 180 are plotted; this excludes less than 2% of all schools. Reproduced with permission from Urquiola and Verhoogen (2009), Figure 8, Panel A, p. 204.

student admissions so as to avoid the burdens associated with providing additional classes.

The researchers next examined the sample distributions of student characteristics close to the enrollment cut-offs. They found evidence that students in enrollment cohorts of size just above the class-size maximum of 45 were considerably different, on average, from those immediately below. As illustrated in Figure 9.6,[18] students in schools with fourth-grade enrollments just above the cut-off of 45 students tended to come from families with higher household incomes than did those in schools with fourth-grade enrollments of 45 students. A result of this difference is that a simple comparison of the average achievement of students in a narrow window of fourth-grade enrollments around the class-size maximum of 45 would result in an overestimate of the impact of class size on achievement.

18. Figure 9.6 is a reproduction of Figure 8, Panel A, from page 204 of Urquiola and Verhoogen's 2009 paper.

The reason is that the students assigned to the smaller classes came from families with more resources than those assigned to larger classes.

The Urquiola and Verhoogen study of class-size determination in Chile illustrates two lessons about a critical threat to the internal validity of studies that attempt to make causal inferences using data drawn from natural experiments, especially those with discontinuity designs. The first is the importance of learning a great deal about the context from which the data derive, including the nature of the educational system, the incentives that the natural experiment creates for educators and parents to alter their behavior, and the opportunities that are present for responding to these incentives. The second lesson is the importance of examining the data closely to see if there is any evidence that actions by educators, parents, or others resulted in a violation of the critical "equal in expectation immediately on either side of the cut-off, prior to treatment" assumption underlying this research approach to making causal inferences. As Urquiola and Verhoogen's paper illustrates, exploratory graphical analyses often prove highly effective in detecting violations of the assumptions that underlie the RD identification strategy.

What to Read Next

To learn about the history of the RD strategy for making causal inferences, read Thomas Cook's erudite paper, "Waiting for Life to Arrive: A History of the Regression-Discontinuity Design in Psychology, Statistics and Economics," which appeared in a 2008 special issue of *The Journal of Econometrics* dedicated to RD methodology. Other papers in this volume provide a rich set of ideas for determining appropriate bandwidths, for estimating the relationship between the outcome and the forcing variable, and for examining threats to the internal validity of particular applications. For an especially clear exposition of recent research on the RD approach, read Howard Bloom's forthcoming chapter entitled "Regression-Discontinuity Analysis of Treatment Effects."

10

Introducing Instrumental-Variables Estimation

There is little question that formal education provides a variety of benefits to recipients. But are there also benefits that accrue not just to the individual student? Economists use the term *externalities* to refer to benefits from education that do not accrue to the individual student. The U.S. educational reformer, Horace Mann, writing in 1846, expressed the value of such externalities to countries with democratic forms of government: "The universal and ever-repeated argument in favor of free schools has been, that the general intelligence which they are capable of diffusing, is indispensable to the continuance of a republican form of government."[1] The importance of externalities to society writ large has provided a rationale for using governmental resources to pay for at least part of the cost of education.

Social scientists have looked for empirical evidence that externalities to educational investments do indeed exist. However, compelling evidence has been difficult to find. Many studies have documented strong positive associations between educational attainments and adult civic participation. For example, observational data confirm repeatedly that it is more probable that citizens who have attended college will vote than will those who have not. Of course, the existence of strong positive links between the educational attainments of individuals and their subsequent voting behavior does not necessarily mean that increasing educational attainments would *cause* increases in civic engagement. The positive associations that we find in observational data could easily be the result of unobserved

---

1. Mann (1891, vol. IV, p. 113).

self-selection. In other words, individuals who are particularly intelligent or highly motivated may be especially likely to enroll in, and graduate from, college. It also may be more probable that these same particularly intelligent or highly motivated individuals will vote than other citizens. You will recognize this as yet another example of a theme that we have emphasized throughout this book: *statistical patterns detected in observational data do not, on their own, provide evidence of causal relationships.*

Up to this point in our book, we have relied on investigator-designed experiments or natural experiments to provide the required exogenous variation in treatment that is necessary for making causal inferences. However, it is often difficult to gain support for a random-assignment experiment or to find a suitable natural experiment. So, it is useful to ask whether there are other ways to proceed. For instance, might it be possible to locate and carve out somehow an "exogenous part" of the variability in a potentially endogenous predictor and use only it to estimate the impact on a subsequent outcome, claiming for it an interpretation of causality? In this chapter, we show how, under certain conditions, this can be achieved, using an innovative and flexible statistical technique called *instrumental-variables estimation* (IVE). The data example that we use to illustrate our application of IVE comes from an observational study by Thomas Dee, in which he tested Horace Mann's hypothesis.

Introducing Instrumental-Variables Estimation

Dee (2004) used data from a nationally representative longitudinal survey to investigate the causal impact of educational attainment on individuals' civic participation. As with earlier observational studies, Dee reports a strong positive bivariate correlation between educational attainment and subsequent civic engagement. Adults with high levels of schooling are more likely to register to vote, to vote more regularly, and to volunteer their time to public causes than are adults who have completed relatively few years of schooling. However, as Dee notes, this does not necessarily mean that schooling *causes* increases in civic awareness and participation. The reason is that, in observational data, participants have chosen their own levels of educational attainment, rather than those levels being assigned exogenously. Consequently, differences among participants in both educational attainment and civic participation may be a consequence of differences in unobserved traits, such as motivation, or a result of unobserved differences among families and communities in which participants were raised. In fact, the arrow of causality may not even point *from* attainment *to* engagement at all. For instance, Dee (2004, p. 1698) suggests that "individuals who grew up in cohesive families and communities that stressed civic responsibility may also be more likely to remain in school."

As Dee's study illustrates, instrumental-variables estimation sometimes provides a method of obtaining an asymptotically unbiased estimate of the causal impact of an endogenous variable, such as educational attainment, on an outcome of interest. However, before turning to a description of this useful technique, it is important to understand the meaning of the term *asymptotic unbiasedness*. It means that the bias contained in IV estimates obtained from small samples may be substantial, but that this bias disappears as sample sizes grow very large.[2] Statisticians also use the term *consistent* when referring to estimators with this property.[3] So, although IVE provides a valuable tool for estimating causal effects in particular circumstances, we pay for this extended reach. To keep the record straight, throughout this chapter and the next, we will be careful to stipulate that IV estimates are either asymptotically unbiased or consistent, rather than simply being "unbiased."

Although the application of IVE to real data can be complex, the key idea is straightforward. First, note that observed differences among participants in the values of the question predictor (such as educational attainment) may conceal an unknown mixture of endogenous and exogenous variation. Sometimes it is possible to carve out a part of this variation that is *arguably exogenous* and use only it in your estimation of causal impacts on an outcome. Success at this task—as you might expect—requires information beyond a simple knowledge of the values of the outcome and question predictor. In addition to these two variables, you must also have data—for each participant—on a special kind of background variable that we later call an *instrument* and whose critical properties we describe below. By integrating this instrument in a particular way into the analysis, you can identify exogenous variation that is present in the question predictor and use only it to obtain an asymptotically unbiased estimate of the causal impact of the question predictor on an outcome

---

2. There is no agreement among methodologists on the definition of a "very large" sample. In reality, sample size would have to go to infinity to satisfy a purist. In addition, what is "very large" for one estimator may not be "very large" for another.

3. Are the properties of asymptotic unbiasedness and consistency the same? Greene (1993, p. 107) actually offers three formal definitions of asymptotic unbiasedness, one of which is also the formal definition of the statistical property of consistency. He states that an estimator is asymptotically unbiased when its expected value tends to the parameter value as sample size approaches infinity. An estimator will be consistent if, in the limit, it converges in probability on the parameter value. He comments that both properties go hand in hand, and that they are usually used interchangeably.

like civic engagement. Dee used IVE to analyze data from the *High School and Beyond* (HS&B) dataset, which contains rich information on large samples of American students who were first surveyed in 1980. Dee focused his research on students who were members of the HS&B "sophomore cohort," meaning that they were tenth-graders in American high schools in 1980. This sophomore cohort was resurveyed in 1984 (when respondents were around 20 years old) and again in 1992 (when they were around 28 years old).[4] Here, we focus on a subsample drawn from Dee's data, consisting of 9,227 of the original HS&B respondents.[5]

In panel (a) of Table 10.1, we present univariate descriptive statistics on the two key variables in our analyses. Our outcome variable *REGISTER* measures active adult civic participation and this information was obtained when respondents were about 28 years old. It is dichotomous and indicates whether the respondent was registered to vote in 1992 (1 = registered; 0 = not registered); about two-thirds (67.1%) of the respondents were registered to vote in that year. Our principal question predictor *COLLEGE* is also dichotomous and coarsely summarizes respondents' educational attainment as of the 1984 administration of the HS&B, when respondents were about 20 years old (1 = had entered a two- or four-year college by 1984; 0 = had not entered). Slightly more than half of the respondents (54.7%) had entered college by this time.

Bias in the OLS Estimate of the Causal Effect of Education on Civic Engagement

In panel (b) of Table 10.1, we present a sample correlation matrix that summarizes the bivariate relationship between later civic engagement (our outcome *REGISTER*) and earlier educational attainment (our question predictor *COLLEGE*) in the sample. Although the magnitude of the sample bivariate correlation between these variables is quite small, it is both statistically significant and positive (0.187, p <0.001, one-sided),

---

4. We thank Thomas Dee for providing the data on which he based his 2004 paper.
5. Because dichotomous outcomes were involved, Dee (2004) relied on a more sophisticated approach based on the simultaneous-equations estimation of a bivariate probit model. Here, for pedagogic clarity, we begin by adopting a simpler analytic approach that specifies a linear-probability model (LPM). To better meet the demands of our LPM model, we have limited our sample to respondents for whom a two-year college in their county was located within 35 miles of their base-year high school when they attended tenth grade, and for whom there were ten or fewer such two-year colleges within the county. We have also eliminated 329 cases that had missing values on the critical variables. Consequently, our estimates differ marginally from Dee's (2004) published estimates, although the thrust of our findings and his remain the same. Readers interested in the substantive findings should consult his paper.

Table 10.1 Civic engagement (in 1992) and educational attainment (in 1984) for 9,227 participants in the sophomore cohort of the HS&B survey. (a) Univariate statistics on the outcome *REGISTER* and question predictor *COLLEGE;* (b) sample bivariate statistics for the same variables; and (c) OLS regression analysis of *REGISTER* on *COLLEGE*

(a) Univariate Statistics:

Variable	Mean	Standard Deviation
REGISTER	0.6709	0.4699
COLLEGE	0.5471	0.4978

(b) Sample Bivariate Correlations and Covariances:

Variable	Sample Relationship with:	
	REGISTER	*COLLEGE*
Correlation:		
REGISTER	1.0000	
COLLEGE	**0.1874*****,†	1.0000
Covariance:		
REGISTER	0.2208	
COLLEGE	0.0438	0.2478

(c) OLS Regression Analysis: Outcome=REGISTER

	Parameter	Estimate	Standard Error
INTERCEPT	β_0	0.5741***	0.0071
COLLEGE	β_1	**0.1769*****,†	0.0097
R^2		0.0351	

~p <0.10; * p <0.05; ** p <0.01; *** p <0.001
†One-sided test.

indicating that respondents who had higher educational attainment in 1984 tended to be more engaged civically in 1992, as Dee hypothesized.

Below the sample correlation matrix in the middle panel of Table 10.1, we provide the corresponding sample covariance matrix. Covariance is a useful summary of the bivariate (linear) relationship between two variables that will feature prominently in the explanations that follow in this chapter. It is useful to think of it as an *unstandardized correlation coefficient,* and its value in this case is 0.044.[6] Because covariance is an unstandardized

---

6. Like the correlation coefficient, the covariance statistic summarizes the linear association between two variables. The sample covariance of Y and X—represented by

index, its value is not proscribed to fall between −1 and +1 (which are the limiting values of the correlation coefficient), and so its absolute magnitude can be more difficult to interpret. However, as we will see later, there are advantages to having an index of association that contains the scales of the component variables. Also, because the covariance of a variable with itself is simply its variance, the elements that fall on the diagonal of a covariance matrix contain those variances. You can recover the companion correlation coefficient by direct computation from the elements of the corresponding covariance matrix. For instance, in panel (b) of Table 10.1, the sample variances of variables *REGISTER* and *COLLEGE* are 0.221 and 0.248, respectively, meaning that their corresponding standard deviations are the square roots of these quantities, 0.470 and 0.498. The estimated correlation between these two variables is then simply their sample covariance divided by the product of their sample standard

---

symbol s_{YX}—is

$$s_{YX} = \frac{\sum_{i=1}^{n}(Y_i - \bar{Y}_{\bullet})(X_i - \bar{X}_{\bullet})}{n-1}$$

So, by definition, the *variance* of a variable is the *covariance of the variable with itself*:

$$s_{YY} = \frac{\sum_{i=1}^{n}(Y_i - \bar{Y}_{\bullet})(Y_i - \bar{Y}_{\bullet})}{n-1} = \frac{\sum_{i=1}^{n}(Y_i - \bar{Y}_{\bullet})^2}{n-1} = s_Y^2$$

$$s_{XX} = \frac{\sum_{i=1}^{n}(X_i - \bar{X}_{\bullet})(X_i - \bar{X}_{\bullet})}{n-1} = \frac{\sum_{i=1}^{n}(X_i - \bar{X}_{\bullet})^2}{n-1} = s_X^2$$

The definition of the sample correlation, r_{YX}:

$$r_{YX} = \frac{\sum_{i=1}^{n}(Y_i - \bar{Y}_{\bullet})(X_i - \bar{X}_{\bullet})}{\sqrt{\left\{\sum_{i=1}^{n}(Y_i - \bar{Y}_{\bullet})^2\right\}\left\{\sum_{i=1}^{n}(X_i - \bar{X}_{\bullet})^2\right\}}}$$

$$r_{YX} = \frac{\sum_{i=1}^{n}(Y_i - \bar{Y}_{\bullet})(X_i - \bar{X}_{\bullet})}{\sqrt{\left\{\sum_{i=1}^{n}(Y_i - \bar{Y}_{\bullet})^2\right\}\left\{\sum_{i=1}^{n}(X_i - \bar{X}_{\bullet})^2\right\}}}$$

This can be rewritten as:

$$r_{YX} = \frac{s_{YX}}{s_Y s_X} \text{ or } \frac{\sum_{i=1}^{n}\left(\frac{Y_i - \bar{Y}_{\bullet}}{s_Y}\right)\left(\frac{X_i - \bar{X}_{\bullet}}{s_X}\right)}{n-1}$$

and so, *correlation* is the *covariance between two variables*, each standardized to mean zero and unit standard deviation.

deviations, $0.044/(0.470 \times 0.498)$ or 0.187, as recorded in the top half of panel (b).

Finally, in panel (c) of Table 10.1, we present the companion ordinary least-squares (OLS) regression fit, for the same outcome/predictor relationship. As you would expect from the statistical test on the corresponding bivariate correlation coefficient, question predictor *COLLEGE* has a positive and statistically significant impact on outcome *REGISTER* ($p < 0.001$, one-sided).[7] This tells us that, on average, the fitted probability that a respondent will be registered to vote in 1992 is 17.7 percentage points higher for those who were college entrants by 1984 than for those who were not.[8] Of course, as Dee explained, there is no reason to believe that this regression coefficient is an unbiased estimate of the causal effect of educational attainment on civic engagement because levels of educational attainment were not assigned randomly and exogenously to participants. Because the students who went to college may have differed in unobserved ways from those who did not, the relationship between *COLLEGE* and *REGISTER* detected in these data could easily have been due to unobserved influences on civic engagement that are omitted currently as predictors and hence reside in the stochastic part of the statistical model, the residuals. As we show below, this means that the question predictor and residuals may be correlated, and the resulting OLS estimate of regression slope may be biased. Nevertheless, having this "naïve" OLS-estimated summary of the observed relationship is a good place for us to begin.

Actually, we do not need to conduct a full-blown regression analysis to obtain the OLS estimate of the *REGISTER* on *COLLEGE* slope in panel (c). With a single predictor in the regression model, an OLS-estimate of slope can be obtained directly from the elements of the sample covariance matrix in panel (b) by dividing the sample covariance of the outcome

---

7. This hypothesis test is identical to the test on the correlation coefficient in panel (b).
8. Our naïve OLS regression analysis includes no individual-, county- and state-level covariates and takes no account of the natural clustering of National Longitudinal Survey of Youth (NLSY) respondents within their base-year high schools, as does Dee (2004) in his more complete analysis. We omitted these features at this point for pedagogic clarity. In the following section, "Incorporating Multiple Instruments into the First-Stage Model," we illustrate the inclusion of additional covariates into our analyses. Finally, in sensitivity analyses not presented here, we have repeated all analyses presented in this chapter using robust standard errors estimated to account for the clustering of participants within their base-year high schools. Although this increases the standard errors associated with our central regression parameters by around 15%, our basic results do not differ.

and question predictor by the sample variance of the question predictor, as follows:

$$\hat{\beta}_1^{OLS} = \left(\frac{s_{YX}}{s_X^2} \right)$$

$$= \left(\frac{s_{(REGISTER,COLLEGE)}}{s_{COLLEGE}^2} \right) \tag{10.1}$$

$$= \frac{0.0438}{0.2478}$$

$$= 0.177$$

Notice that this estimate is identical to that obtained in the OLS regression analysis in panel (c). The intimate link among the sample covariance of outcome and predictor, the sample variance of the predictor, and the OLS-estimated slope, in a simple linear regression analysis, emphasizes the utility of the sample covariance matrix as a summary of variation and covariation in the data. More importantly, we will soon see that it provides insight into the functioning of the OLS slope estimator itself and lights the way for us to instrumental-variables estimation.

But first, let's examine how the presence of endogeneity in the question predictor results in bias in the OLS estimator of the causal impact of education on civic engagement. We begin by specifying a statistical model that describes how we believe educational attainment affects civic engagement. To keep notation simple in what follows, we do this in generic form:

$$Y_i = \beta_0 + \beta_1 X_i + \varepsilon_i \tag{10.2}$$

for the ith member of the population, with conventional notation and assumptions.[9] In our civic-engagement example, generic outcome Y would be replaced by *REGISTER*, generic predictor X would be replaced by

---

9. As usual, in specifying this simple model, we hypothesize that a linear relationship exists between Y and X in the population and that the unpredicted part of Y—residual ε—is distributed independently and identically across population members with zero mean and homoscedastic variance σ_ε^2. In our current example, the outcome—*REGISTER*—is actually dichotomous and so a more appropriate specification of its relationship with predictors would use a nonlinear logit or probit function. However, our linear-probability model in Equation 10.1 is a useful first approximation and has considerable pedagogic advantage. When predictor values are distributed over a similar range at both levels of the dichotomous outcome, as is the case in the restricted subsample with which we have chosen to work here, the linear slope of the fitted linear-probability model is usually close in value—if not identical—to the slope of the tangent to the fitted logit and probit functions at the average value of the predictor. Thus, under these conditions, fitting a linear-probability, logit, or probit model usually leads to the same substantive conclusion.

COLLEGE, and slope parameter β_1 would describe the causal effect of education on civic engagement.

We can manipulate this statistical model directly using covariance algebra, which leads us to interesting conclusions about slope parameter, β_1. For instance, if we take covariances with predictor X throughout the equation in the population, we have:

$$Cov(Y, X) = Cov(\beta_0 + \beta_1 X_i + \varepsilon_i, X_i)$$
$$= \beta_1 Cov(X, X) + Cov(\varepsilon, X) \qquad (10.3)$$
$$= \beta_1 Var(X) + Cov(\varepsilon, X)$$

Or, in a more parsimonious notation:

$$\sigma_{YX} = \beta_1 \sigma_X^2 + \sigma_{\varepsilon X} \qquad (10.4)$$

Now, dividing throughout by the population variance of question predictor X, we have:

$$\left(\frac{\sigma_{YX}}{\sigma_X^2}\right) = \beta_1 + \left(\frac{\sigma_{\varepsilon X}}{\sigma_X^2}\right) \qquad (10.5)$$

In Equation 10.5, notice that the population covariance of Y with X, σ_{YX}, divided by the population variance of X, σ_X^2, can only be equal to the impact of education on civic engagement, β_1, when the second term on the right-hand side of the equation is zero. This, in its turn, can only happen if the population covariance of the predictor and the residual ($\sigma_{\varepsilon X}$) is zero. In other words,

$$\left(\frac{\sigma_{YX}}{\sigma_X^2}\right) = \beta_1, only\, when\, \sigma_{\varepsilon X} = 0 \qquad (10.6)$$

Consequently, because we are accustomed to forming (implicitly, in our OLS regression analyses) the sample ratio of these same covariance and variance terms on the left-hand side of this equation to obtain an estimate of the population regression slope, we learn from Equation 10.6 that an OLS estimator of slope will only be an unbiased estimator of the population causal relationship β_1 when predictor X and residual ε are uncorrelated in the population.[10] It is for this reason that the assumption of residual independence, which stipulates that predictors and residuals must be uncorrelated in the population, is so critical in OLS regression analysis, and it is the reason that we have worried repeatedly about the presence of any such potential correlations throughout this book.

---

10. The covariance algebra that we present here only illustrates the *asymptotic unbiasedness* of the OLS estimator of slope. Using a more detailed application of statistical theory, we can also show that it is also unbiased in small samples.

We know from statistical theory that if predictor and residuals are uncorrelated, then an OLS estimate of the slope coefficient—formed by replacing the featured population covariance/variance ratio by its sample equivalent, s_{YX}/s_X^2—will be an unbiased estimate of the population relationship. On the other hand, if the predictors and residuals are correlated, than an OLS estimate of slope will be biased.[11] So, to accept a value of 0.177 as an unbiased estimate of the impact of college enrollment on civic engagement in our data example, we must be convinced that educational attainment is truly independent of the residuals in the statistical model. This would certainly be the case if levels of educational attainment had been assigned randomly to participants. However, it may not be the case when participants have chosen their own educational attainment, and the question predictor will be arguably endogenous. In summary, when a question predictor like educational attainment is potentially endogenous, we cannot rely on standard OLS methods of estimation to provide an unbiased estimate of its causal impact on an outcome. Instead, we need to use a different approach.

In the top panel of Figure 10.1, we present a standard graphical analogy or *Venn diagram* that is useful for thinking about variation in, and covariation between, variables in *either* the sample *or* the population. In what follows, we use it to marshal arguments about the variation and covariation of outcome Y and question predictor X in the population. In the top panel, for instance, we display a pair of intersecting ellipses, each shaded a different grey. The total area of the upper *light-grey* ellipse represents the population variability in the outcome σ_Y^2 (as labeled in both panels of the figure). Similarly, the total area of the lower *medium-grey* ellipse represents the population variability in the question predictor σ_X^2 (again as labeled in both panels of the figure). The overlap between the two ellipses—their intersection—symbolizes the population covariance of outcome variable and question predictor, σ_{YX}. In the analogy, when the outcome and predictor are strongly related, their covariance σ_{YX} is large, as is the area of intersection of the two ellipses. When the outcome and predictor are weakly related or not related at all, their covariance σ_{YX} will be small or zero, and the area of overlap of the two ellipses will be correspondingly small or zero. Conceptually, the ratio of the area of intersection to the total area of the upper light-grey ellipse then represents the proportion of the total variability in outcome Y that has been successfully predicted by question predictor X. It is estimated, in the sample, by the familiar R^2 statistic. The area of the upper light-grey ellipse that falls

---

11. The magnitude and direction of the bias are given by the second term on the right in Equation 10.5, and so the larger the covariance of predictor and residual, the greater the magnitude of the bias.

(a) _OLS Approach_

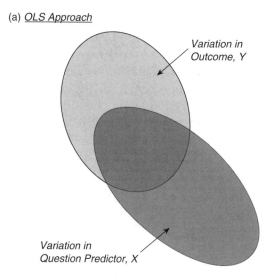

Variation in
Outcome, Y

Variation in
Question Predictor, X

(b) _IV Approach_

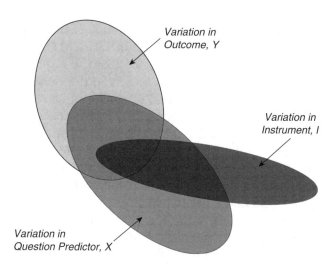

Variation in
Outcome, Y

Variation in
Instrument, I

Variation in
Question Predictor, X

Figure 10.1 Graphical analog for the population variation and covariation among outcome Y, potentially endogenous question predictor X, and instrument, I, used for distinguishing the OLS and IV approaches (a) OLS Approach: bivariate relationship between Y and X, (b) IV Approach: trivariate relationship among Y, X, and I.

beyond the intersection of the two ellipses represents the population variation in outcome Y that is therefore unpredicted by question predictor X. In other words, it represents the population residual variation.

Next, remaining in the top panel of the figure, examine the area of intersection of the outcome and question predictor ellipses in comparison to the total area of the lower medium-grey ellipse (which represents σ_X^2).

From Equation 10.6, we know that population regression slope β_1 equals the population covariance of Y and X divided by the population variance of X (provided that predictor and residuals are uncorrelated, in the population). Consequently, on the Venn diagram in the upper panel, the population regression slope, β_1, is represented by the area of intersection of the two ellipses (representing σ_{YX}) divided by the total area of the lower medium-grey ellipse (representing σ_X^2). So, when the area of the intersection is small compared to the total area of the lower medium-grey ellipse—that is, when σ_{YX} is small compared to σ_X^2—the population regression slope is small, in magnitude. On the other hand, when the population covariance of outcome and predictor is large compared to the variability in the predictor, the area of overlap will be large compared to the total area of the lower medium-grey ellipse, and the population regression slope has a larger magnitude. Working with this visual analogy for variation and covariation between outcome and predictor provides a useful explanatory tool here, and in what follows throughout the chapter.

There is an obvious yet important condition embedded in our algebraic statements that underpin the OLS estimator that must also hold if OLS estimation is to succeed. We mention it here because it is the precursor to an analogous condition that must be satisfied for the IVE technique to be effective. In Equation 10.5, notice that the population variance of the question predictor, σ_X^2, which appears in the denominators of both quotients on either side of the equal sign, cannot be zero. If it were zero, and we had divided throughout the equation by it (as we did!), the resulting quotients would be infinite and the value of the population regression slope β_1 indeterminate and inestimable. From a logical perspective, this makes sense. Why? Because it is just another way of stating that you can't detect a relationship between an outcome and a question predictor if there is no variation in the predictor—in other words, if all observations in the sample have the same value for question predictor X. In our visual analogy, of course, a "no variation in X" condition would correspond to the area of the lower medium-grey ellipse in the top panel shriveling up to nothing, rendering meaningless its intersection with the upper *light-grey* ellipse that represents the population variability in the outcome σ_Y^2.

In addition to needing variability in X (so that the outcome can be predicted by it), the presence of the population variance of the question predictor σ_X^2 in the denominator of the second term to the right of the equal sign in Equation 10.5 is also important. What does this second term represent? As we have implied earlier, this quotient represents the bias that will be introduced into an OLS estimate of the population slope if the question predictor and the residuals are correlated, in the population. Notice that the bias term is again a quotient: the covariance of predictor and residual, divided by the population variance of the predictor. This suggests that the magnitude of the bias that could be obtained in an OLS estimate of slope is sensitive not only to any covariation that may be present between question predictor and residual but also to the amount of variation present in the predictor itself. There will be a perfect storm when predictor and residuals are correlated (so that the sample estimate of numerator $\sigma_{\epsilon X}$ is non-zero) *and* there is little variation in the predictor (so that the sample estimate of σ_X^2 also approaches zero). In this case, the impact of any bias present due to the covariation of predictor and residuals in the numerator will be inflated, in the quotient, by the presence of the very small quantity that is present in the denominator. Clearly, this is another good reason to design research to ensure that you have substantial variability in the question predictor.

Instrumental-Variables Estimation

In the current example, we possess observational data on an interesting outcome—*REGISTER*, a measure of civic engagement—and an important question predictor—*COLLEGE*, a measure of educational attainment. Our theory suggests that there should be a causal relationship between the latter and the former. Consequently, we would like to use our observational data to obtain a credible estimate of the causal impact of educational attainment on civic engagement. However, we suspect that question predictor *COLLEGE* is potentially endogenous because participants have been able to choose their own levels of educational attainment. As a result, an OLS estimate of the relationship between *REGISTER* and *COLLEGE* may provide a biased view of the hypothesized underlying population relationship between civic engagement and educational attainment. What can we do to resolve this? How can we use the available observational data to estimate the population relationship between these two constructs, while avoiding the bias introduced into the results of the standard OLS process by the potential endogeneity in *COLLEGE*?

In statistics, as in life, it is usually the case that we can always do better if we have some way to incorporate additional useful information into our decisions. Setting all skepticism aside, let's imagine for a moment that we had information available on an additional and very special kind of variable—mysteriously named *I*, for "instrument"—that has also been measured for all the participants in the sample. Let's ask ourselves: What properties would such an instrument need to have, to be helpful to us? How could we incorporate it into our analysis, if we wanted to end up with an unbiased estimate of the critical relationship between civic engagement and educational attainments, in which we are interested?

Although this seems to be a completely inhospitable analytic situation, we can gain insight by again applying covariance algebra to the hypothesized population regression model featured in Equation 10.2. This time, though, instead of taking covariances throughout with predictor X, let's take them with our new instrument I. This leads to the following result:

$$Cov(Y, I) = Cov(\beta_0 + \beta_1 X_i + \varepsilon_i, I_i)$$
$$= \beta_1 Cov(X, I) + Cov(\varepsilon, I) \tag{10.7}$$

Or, again, more parsimoniously:

$$\sigma_{YI} = \beta_1 \sigma_{XI} + \sigma_{\varepsilon I} \tag{10.8}$$

Dividing through by the population covariance of X and I, we have:

$$\left(\frac{\sigma_{YI}}{\sigma_{XI}}\right) = \beta_1 + \left(\frac{\sigma_{\varepsilon I}}{\sigma_{XI}}\right) \tag{10.9}$$

Here, surprisingly, notice a second interesting consequence of the specification of the population linear regression model. From Equation 10.9, we see that the population covariance of Y with I (σ_{YI}) divided by the population covariance of X with I (σ_{XI}) is again equal to our critical parameter representing the key population relationship of interest (β_1), provided that the second term on the right-hand side of the equation is zero. And it is zero when our new instrument is uncorrelated with the residuals in the population regression model. That is,

$$\left(\frac{\sigma_{YI}}{\sigma_{XI}}\right) = \beta_1, \text{ when } \sigma_{\varepsilon I} = 0 \tag{10.10}$$

In other words, if there were some way to locate an instrument I that is *incontrovertibly uncorrelated with the population residuals in the "question" model*, we would be home free. Then, the slope of the causal relationship between civic engagement and education in the population would simply be equal to the ratio of two important population covariances: (a) the covariance of the outcome and instrument, σ_{YI}, and (b) the covariance of question predictor and instrument, σ_{XI}. So, if I were known and its values are measured in the sample, we could simply estimate each of these respective covariances by their corresponding sample statistics, and replace them in the quotient by their sample equivalents. This would provide us with an (asymptotically) unbiased estimate of the causal impact of education on civic engagement in the population. We call this alternative estimator the instrumental-variables estimator of β_1:

$$\hat{\beta}_1^{IVE} = \left(\frac{s_{YI}}{s_{XI}} \right) \tag{10.11}$$

Because statisticians refer to covariance as one of the "second moments" of a bivariate distribution, we refer to the expression on the right-hand side of Equation 10.11 as the *method-of-moments* IVE of β_1, to distinguish it from other instrumental-variables estimates of the same parameter that we describe later in this chapter (such as the *two-stage least-squares* and *simultaneous equations modeling* IV estimates). It is also sometimes referred to as the *Wald estimate*, especially when both the question predictor and the instrument are dichotomous, to celebrate the intellectual contributions of the well-known statistician, Abraham Wald.

Let's briefly summarize what has happened here during our introduction of this new method-of-moments IV estimate. First, while conducting an OLS regression analysis of a theorized causal relationship between an outcome Y and a question predictor X, we have developed a concern about the potential endogeneity of the question predictor. We have become worried that there is perhaps a non-zero correlation between question predictor and residuals, in the population, because of choices that participants were able to make about their values of the question predictor. This has led us to abandon the regular OLS estimator of the hypothesized causal relationship of interest. In its place, we have imagined that we can locate another variable—which we have called the *instrument I*—that we are absolutely convinced is uncorrelated with those same residuals, in the population. If this is the case, then we now know that we can use sample information on the new instrument, along with information on the original outcome and question predictor, to form an alternative and (asymptotically) unbiased estimator of the population relationship of interest. All our problems appear to be solved!

Although this is a perfectly fine argument from a statistical perspective and provides us with an interesting alternative estimator of an important relationship, you might readily respond that we have simply swapped one strong assumption (that the residuals are uncorrelated with the question predictor) for another (that the same residuals are uncorrelated with the instrument). In addition, you might reasonably question whether it is possible to locate such "instruments" in practice, or whether they are simply mythical beasts, like unicorns. However, it turns out, in practice, that it is indeed sometimes possible to locate such an instrument and to defend the critical assumption that it is uncorrelated with the residuals in the regression model that represents the research question being asked. When this can be done, we have a perfectly reasonable alternative way of obtaining an asymptotically unbiased estimate of the hypothesized causal relationship between the outcome and question predictor, even when the values of the question predictor itself may have been assigned endogenously. We take up these practical issues in detail later, when we analyze our data example further and when we survey different types of instruments that have been used successfully in social science research, having withstood the careful scrutiny of experts.

For the moment, let's set aside these difficulties and focus on the simplicity and conceptual clarity of the notion of IVE itself. In Table 10.2, we have reproduced our previous naïve findings and also introduced the variable that we claim works well as an instrument in our investigation of the causal impact of educational attainment on civic engagement. This variable is *DISTANCE*. It is a continuous variable that describes, in miles, the distance between the high school that each respondent attended as a tenth-grader (in 1980) and the nearest two-year (community or junior) college in the respondent's home county at that time. Notice that, on average, high schools were just less than 10 miles from the nearest two-year college, but that the sample standard deviation of this distance is almost as large as the mean, indicating that there is considerable variability in the values of the potential instrument.

In what follows, following Dee, let's regard instrument *DISTANCE* as a measure of respondents' *potential educational access to higher education* immediately after high school. We will also argue, with somewhat more difficulty, that this variable is unlikely to be correlated with the residuals in the regression of outcome *REGISTER* on the potentially endogenous question predictor *COLLEGE*. One way to think about this is to imagine that the locations of local two-year colleges had been distributed randomly around participants' high schools (and, implicitly, randomly around the locations of participants' homes). Then, we could argue that those whose homes were closer to the nearest two-year college would naturally be more likely to enter into some kind of higher education. In other words, by virtue of their arguably random geographic placement with respect to a local two-year college, participants had in some sense received an exogenous "offer" of educational attainment, over and above the impact of any personal factors, such as motivation, that may affect the college enrollment decision endogenously. If this is true, then the residuals in the regression of civic engagement on educational attainment (the latter variable being one in which the omitted endogenous causes of the relationship naturally reside) will not be correlated with the instrument *DISTANCE*, and our key assumption is satisfied. Thus, although some part of the variation in

Table 10.2 Civic engagement (in 1992) and educational attainment (in 1984) for 9,227 participants in the sophomore cohort of the HS&B survey. (a) Univariate statistics on the outcome *REGISTER*, question predictor *COLLEGE*, and instrument, *DISTANCE*; (b) sample bivariate statistics among the same three variables; and (c) a method-of-moments instrumental-variables estimate of the *REGISTER* on *COLLEGE* regression slope

(a) Univariate Statistics

	Mean	St. Dev.
REGISTER	0.6709	0.4699
COLLEGE	0.5471	0.4978
DISTANCE	9.7360	8.7022

(b) Sample Bivariate Correlations and Covariances:

	Sample Relationship with:		
	REGISTER	*COLLEGE*	*DISTANCE*
Correlation:			
REGISTER	1.0000		
COLLEGE	**0.1874*****,†	1.0000	
DISTANCE	−0.0335***	−0.1114***	1.0000
Covariance:			
REGISTER	0.2208		
COLLEGE	0.0438	0.2478	
DISTANCE	−0.1369	−0.4825	75.730

(c) Method-of-Moments IVE Estimate

	Parameter	Estimate
Cov(REGISTER, DISTANCE)	$\sigma_{(REGISTER,\ DISTANCE)}$	−0.1369
Cov(COLLEGE, DISTANCE)	$\sigma_{(COLLEGE,\ DISTANCE)}$	−0.4825
IVE *Estimate*	β_1	**0.2837**

~p <0.10; * p <0.05; ** p <0.01; *** p <0.001
†One-sided test.

educational attainment may have been determined endogenously through participants' personal choices and attributes, some other part of it may be exogenous and related to *DISTANCE*. If this is truly the case, then we can employ *DISTANCE* as an instrument to obtain an asymptotically unbiased estimate of the causal relationship between civic engagement and educational attainment using the new methods we have just described.[12]

---

12. Of course, there may be reasons why the proximity of participants to their local institutions of higher education is not determined randomly and exogenously. We discuss

First, and perhaps most importantly, notice that the endogenous question predictor *COLLEGE* and instrument *DISTANCE* are indeed related. The greater the distance between a tenth-grader's high school and the nearest community college (when they were in high school), the lower the probability that the student will enroll in college subsequently ($r = -0.111$, $p < 0.001$, Table 10.2, panel (b)). In addition, our outcome *REGISTER* has a negative and even smaller, but again statistically significant, correlation with the instrument *DISTANCE* ($r = -0.033$; $p < .001$, Table 10.2, panel (b)). Thus, the greater the distance between a tenth-grader's former high school and the nearest two-year college, the less probable it is that the student registered to vote as an adult. Substituting the corresponding sample covariances into Equation 10.11, we obtain an asymptotically unbiased method-of-moments IVE of the impact of college enrollment on the probability of registering to vote, as follows:

$$\widehat{\beta}_1^{IVE} = \left(\frac{s_{YI}}{s_{XI}} \right)$$
$$= \frac{s_{(REGISTER,\ DISTANCE)}}{s_{(COLLEGE,DISTANCE)}} \quad (10.12)$$
$$= \frac{-0.1369}{-0.4825}$$
$$= 0.284$$

Notice that this coefficient is positive and almost double the magnitude of the corresponding OLS estimate (0.177, Table 10.1). This suggests that the probability that an individual will register to vote, as an adult, is about 28 percentage points higher among college entrants than among those who did not enroll in college. Provided that our instrument—the distance of the respondent's high school from the nearest two-year college in the same county—satisfies the critical assumption we have described earlier, then this new value of 0.284 is an asymptotically unbiased estimate of the impact of educational attainment on civic engagement.

It is useful to explore the logic upon which this new method of estimation is based. Conceptually, during the IVE process, we use our instrument—which we regard as exogenous *by assumption* (and therefore uncorrelated with the residuals in the main regression model)—to carve out part of the variation in the question predictor that is also exogenous

---

three common objections—and the strategies that can be used for dealing with them—later in this chapter, in the section "Proximity of Educational Institutions," where we describe research conducted by Janet Currie and Enrico Moretti (2003) in which they used proximity as an instrument.

and then we use only that latter part in the estimation of the regression slope. We can illustrate this statement by extending our earlier graphical analogy to the lower panel of Figure 10.1. In the new panel, we have replicated the original Venn diagram in the upper panel, with the same pair of overlapping light- and medium-grey ellipses representing the variances and covariance of the outcome and question predictor, as before. Then, across these two intersecting ellipses, we have carefully overlaid a third dark-grey, almost black, ellipse to represent variation in our instrument I. Notice that this latter ellipse has been drawn to overlap both the first two ellipses, thereby co-varying uniquely with both. However, it does *not* overlap any of the original *residual* variation in Y, which as we have explained is represented by that part of the upper light-grey ellipse that falls beyond the reach of variation in the question predictor X. We have drawn the new figure like this because, by definition, a successful instrument must not be correlated with those residuals, and therefore there can be no overlap of instrument and residual variation. Finally, in the lower panel, we also suggest that there may be some substantial part of the instrument's variation that is independent of variation in the question predictor; this is why we have drawn the dark-grey "instrumental" ellipse sticking out to the right of the lower medium-grey "question predictor" ellipse.

When we carry out successful IVE, it is as though we have allowed the dark-grey ellipse that represents variation in the instrument to *carve out* the corresponding parts of the original medium-grey "X" ellipse and the medium-on-light-grey "Y on X" overlap, for further analytic attention. And, because variation in the instrument is exogenous (by an assumption that we still need to defend), the parts that we have carved out must also be exogenous. Then, in forming our IV estimator, we restrict ourselves implicitly to working with only the variation in outcome and question predictor that is shared (i.e., that intersects or covaries) with the new instrument within the lower dark-grey ellipse. Within this shared region, we again form a quotient that is a ratio of a "part" to a "whole" to provide our new instrumental-variables estimate of the Y on X slope. This quotient is the ratio of the covariation shared between outcome and instrument to the covariation shared by question predictor and instrument, respectively. Identify the corresponding regions for yourself on the plot. They are the regions where the light-, medium-, and dark-grey ellipses overlap, and where the medium- and dark-grey ellipses overlap, respectively. In a sense, we have used the instrument to carve up the old dubious variation and covariation in both outcome and question predictor into identifiable parts, and have picked out and incorporated into our new estimate only those parts that we know are—by assumption, at least—unequivocally exogenous.

Careful inspection of the critical regions on the Venn diagram confirms that things are even more subtle and logical than this! From the figure, we see that, during IV estimation—exactly as was the case during OLS estimation—we are again forming a ratio of the covariation between outcome Y and predictor X and variation in predictor X. However, now we are doing it *within a new region that has been defined by the variation in the instrument.* You can see, for instance, that our new IV estimate still contrasts the areas of an overlapping light- and medium-grey (Y and X) region and a medium-grey region (X) but now the entire shebang falls within a new and restricted dark-grey region. In other words, *our new IV estimator enacts exactly the same principles as the old OLS estimator, but within the region defined by the exogenous variation of the instrument.*

In addition to understanding the useful parallels between OLS and IVE, it is also important to understand the respect in which interpretations of the IV estimator are limited by the localization of our analytic attention to only the light- and medium-grey variation that *falls within* the newly defined dark-grey ellipse. This is a region in which variation in the question predictor is entirely *contained* or *localized* within the variation in the instrument itself.[13] In terms of our example, for instance, by using IVE to estimate the relationship between civic engagement and educational attainment, we are relying on only that part of the original person-to-person variation in educational attainment that covaries with— you might say "is sensitive to"—differences in the distance of the participants' high schools from their nearest two-year college. All other variation in educational attainment, from person to person, is no longer used in forming our estimate.

For this reason, IV methods provide an asymptotically unbiased estimate, not of the overall *average treatment effect* (ATE), but of what is often referred to as the *"local" average treatment effect* (LATE). In our example, for instance, this means that it is only the variation in college enrollment that is affected by the distance to the nearest two-year college upon which we have capitalized in estimating the effect of educational attainment on civic engagement. The estimate does not provide any information about the impact of education on civic engagement for individuals whose college-enrollment decision was not influenced by the distance between their high school and the nearest two-year college. Of course, if the effect

---

13. The IV estimator also capitalizes on that part of the variation in outcome Y that is localized within the region of instrumental variation. However, in the lower panel of Figure 10.2, you can see that this part of the variation in Y—as defined by the overlap of the Y and I regions—is also a subset of the variation in X that falls within the variation in I, and so our statement about the latter encompasses the former.

of the educational attainment treatment on voter registration is homogeneous across all sectors of the population, then the average and the local average treatment effects will be identical and both represented by the same population slope β_1. On the other hand, it is possible that the treatment effect may be heterogeneous across different sectors of the population. We return to these issues in the next chapter, when we clarify further the substantive interpretation of the LATE estimate.

Finally, notice that, when we use IVE, we restrict our analytic focus in one other important way. By working only within the dark-grey ellipse that describes variation in the instrument, we have restricted ourselves to a region of variation in both outcome and question predictor that is smaller than the original region of variation with which our initial OLS regression analysis was conducted. Of course, artificially limiting the variation in outcome and predictor that is being incorporated into any analysis means that the obtained estimate will usually have lower precision—that is, its standard error will be larger than the corresponding (but biased) OLS estimate. Thus, in using IV methods to provide an asymptotically unbiased estimate of the causal relationship of interest, we have traded away some of our original precision and statistical power, making it harder to reject the corresponding null hypothesis, for the benefit of knowing that we now have an asymptotically unbiased estimate. Unfortunately, if we choose an instrument that has very limited variation (and whose associated dark-grey ellipse consequently covers a very small area), we exacerbate this problem enormously. An instrument of limited variation can only "carve out" a small part of the variation in outcome and question predictor for incorporation into the IV estimate. So, the standard error of the IV estimate will be large, and the statistical power of the analysis will be low. We expand on these problems below when we discuss the issues of working with "weak" instruments.

Two Critical Assumptions That Underpin Instrumental-Variables Estimation

IVE is an approach that offers important advantages to empirical researchers who seek to draw unbiased causal conclusions from quasi-experimental or observational research settings. However, it is critical to keep in mind that any application of IVE depends strongly on additional assumptions not required of OLS methods. Aside from the usual functional form assumptions that underpin the utility of covariance as a measure of linear association and the standard normal-theory assumptions on which any associated statistical inference will depend, the algebra that leads to

Equations 10.9 and 10.10 shows that there are *two additional assumptions* that a variable must satisfy if it is to serve as a viable instrument. In practice, the veracity of one of these assumptions proves relatively easy to confirm. Unfortunately, this is not the case for the second assumption.

The "easy-to-prove" condition for successful IVE is that *the instrument must be related to the potentially endogenous question predictor* (in other words, the population covariance of question predictor and instrument, σ_{XI}, cannot be zero). This condition seems obvious, from both a logical and a statistical perspective. If the question predictor and instrument were not related, then no corresponding regions of outcome and question predictor variation would be carved out by the dark-grey ellipse in the lower panel of Figure 10.1, and σ_{XI} would be zero, thus rendering the quotients in Equations 10.9 and 10.10 indeterminate (infinite). In simpler terms, if the question predictor and instrument are unrelated, then we cannot use the instrument successfully to carve out *any part* of the variation in X, let alone any exogenous variation, and so our IVE will inevitably fail. Fortunately, in the case of our civic-engagement example, this is not the case. We have confirmed that the instrument and question predictor are indeed related, using the hypothesis test that we conducted on their bivariate correlation in panel (b) of Table 10.2. We can reject the null hypothesis that *COLLEGE* and *DISTANCE* are unrelated, in the population, at a reassuring $p < 0.001$.[14]

The second important condition that must be satisfied for successful IVE is that *the instrument cannot be related to the unobserved effects (i.e., the original residuals) that rendered the question predictor endogenous in the first place*. In other words, the covariance of instrument and residuals, $\sigma_{\varepsilon I}$, must be zero. We see this throughout the algebraic development that led to the IV estimator in Equations 10.9 and 10.10. The condition is also appealing logically. If the instrument were correlated with the residuals in the original "question" equation, it would suffer from the same problem as the question predictor itself. Thus, it could hardly provide a solution to our endogeneity problem.

---

14. The *t*-statistic associated with the rejection of the null hypothesis that the instrument and question predictor are uncorrelated, in the population, is equal to 10.76. This *t*-statistic—because only a single degree of freedom is involved in the test—corresponds to an *F*-statistic of magnitude 115.9 (the square of 10.76). Such *F* statistics are often used to gauge the strength of particular sets of instruments. Some methodologists have suggested that sets of instruments should be considered "weak" if the associated *F*-statistic has a magnitude *less than 10* (Stock, Wright, & Yogo, 2002). Although this cut-off is arbitrary, it is easily applied in more complex analyses in which multiple instruments are incorporated and the required *F*-statistic is obtained in a *global* (GLH) test of the hypothesis that all the instruments had no *joint* effect on the question predictor.

Although the population covariance of the instrument and the question predictor σ_{XI} cannot be zero if IVE is to succeed, there are even problems if the instrument is only weakly related to the question predictor. By this, we mean that it is still a problem *data-analytically* if the population covariance of instrument and question predictor σ_{XI} is small. You can understand this by inspecting Equation 10.9. Notice that the population covariance of question predictor and instrument σ_{XI} appears in the denominator of both quotients in this expression for the population regression slope β_1. It is present in the quotient that ultimately becomes the basis for the IV estimator itself $(\sigma_{YI} / \sigma_{XI})$ and also in the quotient that describes the bias $(\sigma_{\varepsilon I} / \sigma_{XI})$. Both of these quotients will be impacted dramatically if the instrument is weak and the value of σ_{XI} is small. This creates two problems. First, with a weak instrument, the estimate of the population regression slope itself will become increasingly sensitive to the presence of any aberrant data points in the point cloud that are influential in determining the sample covariance of the outcome and the instrument s_{YI}. Second, suppose that the population covariance of instrument and residuals from the question equation $\sigma_{\varepsilon I}$ is not *exactly* zero (as is required for successful IVE), but close to it. This will not matter if the instrument is strong, and its covariance with the question predictor σ_{XI} is large because the ratio of the two will then be very small, as required. But, if the instrument is weak, and its covariance with the question predictor close to zero, then the impact of any covariance between residuals and instrument—no matter how small—may still result in a large bias in the IV estimate.

Unfortunately, the way that we have stated our second condition for successful IVE—there must be a zero correlation between instrument and the residuals in the question equation—does not provide any practical guidance for checking that the condition is true. This is because we have framed the condition in terms of *unobserved* quantities—the residuals—whose existence we hypothesize in the population, but that we do not observe directly. Does this mean that, when using IVE, we must simply rely on our personal belief in the credibility of the instrument? Or, is it possible to translate the framing of the second condition into something that is at least amenable to validation by logical argument, if not observation? Fortunately, the answer is "Yes!" and a clue to the reframing is offered by again inspecting the lower panel of Figure 10.1, where we display our visual analogy for IVE. We have drawn this figure to ensure that the dark-grey ellipse that describes variation in the instrument does not overlap with the light-grey ellipse that describes variation in the outcome *except within the medium-grey ellipse that describes variation in the question predictor.* This illustrates that the only path from the instrument to the ultimate outcome goes through the question predictor. If there had been a direct path from the instrument to the outcome, we would have seen an overlap between the dark and light-grey ellipses that was *not* contained within the medium-grey ellipse.

Thus, the second critical assumption of IVE, which we have stated formerly above as "instrument and residuals must be uncorrelated," can be reframed as *"there is no direct path from instrument to outcome, except through the question predictor."* This means that, in seeking a successful instrument, we need to find a variable that is related to the potentially endogenous question predictor (we call this "the first path"), and which in turn is related to the outcome ("the second path"), but there is *no path linking the instrument directly to the outcome* (i.e., there is "no third path"). So, you can think of the IVE process as one in which instrument I ultimately and indirectly predicts outcome Y, but its influence passes only through question predictor X, rather than passing directly to the outcome from the instrument itself. If you find yourself able to argue successfully that there is no third path in your particular empirical setting, then you have a viable instrument! This is often the most difficult challenge you face as an empirical researcher who wants to employ IVE.

Thomas Dee argued that this condition held in the data that he used in his civic-engagement study. In fact, he invoked economic theory to argue that his distance instrument would be negatively related to college attendance because the longer a student's commute, the greater the cost of college attendance. Dee argued that, after conditioning on observed covariates, students' high schools (and implicitly, their homes) were distributed randomly around their local two-year college. Consequently, *DISTANCE* becomes a credible instrument because it predicts some part of the variation in educational attainment, and it only affects future civic engagement *through its relationship with attainment.* So, using IV estimation, he could tease out an asymptotically unbiased estimate of the causal impact of educational attainment on civic engagement. As we will see below, there is a long tradition in empirical research in economics and the social sciences of using such measures of access as instruments for otherwise endogenous question predictors like educational attainment.

Alternative Ways of Obtaining the Instrumental-Variables Estimate

The method-of-moments approach to IVE that we have described works well when you have a single outcome, a single question predictor, and a single instrument. Usually, however, the IV approach is applied in more complex data-analytic settings. For instance, you may want to obtain an IV estimate after controlling for background characteristics of the participants. This can be useful for either improving the precision of your estimate, or for strengthening the argument that your instrument satisfies the "no third path" assumption. Alternatively, you may want to include multiple instruments in a single analysis. Or, perhaps your research question requires the presence of several potentially endogenous question predictors in the principal regression model. Or, you may want to set aside the assumption of linear relationships implicit in the covariances of Equation 10.10 and entertain nonlinear relationships among instrument, question predictor, and outcome.[15] In these settings, it is useful to have alternative ways of implementing the IV approach, without directly dividing a pair of sample covariances into each other. Two very useful approaches for doing this are the methods of *two-stage least squares* (2SLS) and *simultaneous equations modeling* (SEM). These are both alternative ways of implementing the same IV strategy that we have described above.

Obtaining an Instrumental-Variables Estimate by the Two-Stage Least-Squares Method

One useful analytic strategy for obtaining an IV estimate is to split up the process of IVE into two consecutive steps, or stages, and make use of OLS regression analysis at each step. This is referred to as the *Two stage least Squares* (2SLS) approach to IV estimation. Historically, 2SLS has been a popular and flexible way of conducting IVE, largely because it applies a trusty statistical method (OLS regression analysis) in a novel and accessible way to obtain an improved estimate.

Conceptually, the 2SLS approach takes the rationale that we have already described for IVE and applies it in a *stepwise* fashion. In the previous section, we argued that the role of the instrument in IVE was to be responsible for carving out an exogenous part of the variation in a question predictor, so that we could use *only this part*—rather than the remaining potentially endogenous variation—in our estimation of the population regression slope that provided the research focus. When you implement a 2SLS approach, you actually carry out this process explicitly, one step at a time. You first "carve out" exogenous variation in the potentially endogenous question predictor X by actually regressing it on your designated

---

15. This is what Thomas Dee (2004) does in his analysis of the civic engagement data. He uses a probit, rather than a linear, functional form in modeling the hypothesized relationships between the outcome *REGISTER* and the question predictor *COLLEGE*, and between the latter variable and the instrument *DISTANCE*.

instrument, I, and then estimating and outputting the predicted values, $\widehat{X}$, for each person. These predicted values then contain only the exogenous part of the question predictor variation because the instrument used to predict those values was itself exogenous.

This means that, at the first stage of the 2SLS process, we fit an OLS regression model to the hypothesized relationship between the endogenous question predictor and instrument, as follows:

$$1^{st}\ Stage: X_i = \alpha_0 + \alpha_1 I_i + \delta_i \qquad (10.13)$$

where the first-stage parameters α_0 and α_1 represent the requisite intercept and slope, and δ_i is the first-stage residual that contains that part of question predictor X that remains unpredicted at the first stage (and, hopefully, contains all of the potentially endogenous variation) for the ith student. You can, of course, fit this first-stage model by OLS methods. Since the instrument is exogenous, it is implicitly uncorrelated with residuals δ in the first-stage model.

In the upper panel of Table 10.3, we present the results of fitting this first-stage model in our civic-engagement dataset, where we have regressed the potentially endogenous question predictor *COLLEGE* on the instrument *DISTANCE*. The first-stage *COLLEGE* on *DISTANCE* regression slope is non-zero ($p < 0.001$) in the population, and consequently

Table 10.3 Civic engagement (in 1992) and educational attainment (in 1984) for 9,227 participants in the sophomore cohort of the HS&B survey. IV estimation of the *REGISTER* on *COLLEGE* relationship using 2SLS, with *DISTANCE* as the instrument

(a) 1st Stage: Outcome = COLLEGE

	Parameter	Estimate	St. Error
INTERCEPT	α_0	0.6091***	0.0077
DISTANCE	α_1	−0.0064***	0.0006
R^2		0.0124	

(b) 2nd Stage: Outcome = REGISTER

	Parameter	Estimate	Corrected St. Error
INTERCEPT	β_0	0.5157***	0.0480
$\widehat{COLLEGE}$	β_1	**0.2837***,†**	0.0873
R^2		0.0223	

~$p < 0.10$; * $p < 0.05$; ** $p < 0.01$; *** $p < 0.001$
†One-sided test.

instrument and question predictor are indeed related.[16] Although the estimated size of the first-stage slope is small, -0.0064, the potential distances between high school and local two-year college are large. So, for instance, if the distances between a high school and the nearest two-year college for a pair of prototypical students differed by the sample mean distance of 9.74 miles (from panel (a) of Table 10.1), we would predict that their probabilities of later entry into higher education would differ by just over 6 percentage points (with the predicted probability of enrollment lower for the student who attended the high school that was more remote from a two-year college).[17]

Predicted values are easily estimated for participants by substituting their values on the instrument I into the first-stage fitted model. All statistical software packages can compute and store such predicted values automatically, but they can also be computed by hand. For instance, from the fitted first-stage model in Table 10.3, the predicted value of *COLLEGE* for the first participant in the dataset—whose high school was situated four miles from the nearest college—is $[0.609 - 0.0064(4)]$ or 0.583.

Once you have obtained the required predicted values from the first-stage fit, you complete the second stage of the 2SLS process by simply regressing the ultimate outcome Y on the newly computed "exogenous" part of the question predictor, now represented by $\widehat{X}_i$ (and *not* on the original and potentially endogenous question predictor X_i). So, the statistical model for your second-stage OLS regression analysis becomes:

$$2^{nd}\ Stage:\ Y_i = \beta_0 + \beta_1 \widehat{X}_i + \varepsilon_i \qquad (10.14)$$

with the usual notation. Fortuitously, this second-stage estimate of parameter β_1 is identical to the estimate we obtained earlier by the method-of-moments IVE approach. In the lower half of Table 10.3, we provide the results of the 2SLS analysis for the civic-engagement example. Notice that our estimate of 0.284 ($p < .001$) for the *REGISTER* on *COLLEGE* regression slope is indeed identical to the method-of-moments IV estimate that we presented in Table 10.2.[18]

---

16. As noted earlier, the *F*-statistic associated with the prediction of *COLLEGE* by *DISTANCE* in the first-stage analysis is 115.9, exceeding the cited "weak" instrument cut-off of 10 by a considerable margin (see footnote 14).

17. This computation is $-.0064 \times 9.74$, which equals $-.0623$.

18. We can use covariance algebra to confirm this claim. In the population, predicted values of question predictor X are represented by $\alpha_0 + \alpha_1 I_i$, and can replace $\widehat{X}_i$ in Equation 10.14, leading to the "reduced" model:

$$Y_i = \beta_0 + \beta_1 \widehat{X}_i + \varepsilon_i = \beta_0 + \beta_1 (\alpha_0 + \alpha_1 I_i) + \varepsilon_i$$

We can also use our earlier graphical analogy for IV methods to illustrate the process of 2SLS estimation. In Figure 10.2, we replicate the original light-, medium-, and dark-grey ellipses that represent the variation and covariation among our outcome, Y, potentially endogenous question predictor, X, and instrument, I, from the lower-panel in Figure 10.1. To reflect the stepwise nature of the 2SLS approach, we have replicated the original Venn diagram and presented it twice, illustrating the first-stage and second-stage facets of the 2SLS process by "dimming out" the unneeded portions of the figure at each stage. We present these new figures, with their respective dimmed-out portions, in the two panels of Figure 10.2 . The Venn diagram for the first stage of the 2SLS process is at the top; the diagram for the second stage is at the bottom.

Recall that, in the first stage of the 2SLS process, question predictor X is regressed on instrument I. We illustrate this in the upper panel of Figure 10.2 by featuring the medium-grey ellipse that represents variation in X overlapping the dark-grey ellipse that represents variation in I. Their overlap represents not only their covariation and success of the first-stage regression analysis, but also the part of the variation in question predictor X that has been "carved out" as exogenous, and captured in the respective predicted values $\widehat{X}_i$. It is this part of the variation in the question predictor that is then carried through to the second stage of the 2SLS process, by the data analyst, as fitted values. So, we have redrawn this part of the variation in X in the lower panel as an identical truncated partial ellipse, relabeled as "Predicted Variation in Question Predictor X ." This partial ellipse is darkened to acknowledge that it represents a portion of the question-predictor variation. Finally, it is the overlap between the complete light-grey ellipse that describes variation in the outcome Y and the

---

Reorganizing and taking covariances with I, throughout the reduced model, we have

$$Cov(Y_i, I_i) = Cov\big((\beta_0 + \beta_1\alpha_0) + \beta_1\alpha_1 I_i + \varepsilon_i, I_i\big)$$

Because the covariance of a constant with I, and that of the residuals with I, are both zero, this reduces to:

$$\sigma_{YI} = Cov(\beta_1\alpha_1 I_i, I_i) = \beta_1\alpha_1\sigma_I^2$$

Reorganizing and making β_1 the subject of the formula, we have:

$$\beta_1 = \frac{\sigma_{YI}}{\sigma_I^2} \times \frac{1}{\alpha_1}$$

We can re-express the first-stage slope parameter, α_1, by $(\sigma_{XI} / \sigma_I^2)$, from taking covariances with I throughout the first-stage model, to obtain

$$\beta_1 = \frac{\sigma_{YI}}{\sigma_I^2} \times \frac{1}{\sigma_{XI} / \sigma_I^2} = \frac{\sigma_{YI}}{\sigma_{XI}}$$

This is identical to the expression in Equation 10.10.

(a) *First Stage*

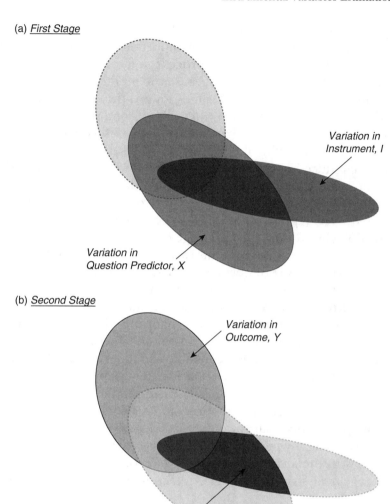

*Variation in
Instrument, I*

*Variation in
Question Predictor, X*

(b) *Second Stage*

*Variation in
Outcome, Y*

*Predicted Variation in
Question Predictor, X*

Figure 10.2 Graphical analog for the population variation and covariation among outcome Y, potentially endogenous question predictor X, and instrument, I, used for presenting the 2SLS approachs: (a) *First stage*: Relationship between X and I, distinguishing predicted values, $\widehat{X}$, (b) *Second stage*: Relationship between Y and $\widehat{X}$.

newly darkened partial ellipse that denotes now exogenous variation in the question predictor that defines the second-stage relationship. Notice that the eventual areas of variation and covariation defined by this process are identical to those defined in our original presentation of the IV approach in Figure 10.1. Consequently, IV estimates resulting from the two estimation methods are identical.

The 2SLS approach provides concrete insight into one of the problems with IVE. When you estimate the all-important "exogenous" predicted values of X in the first stage of the process, you sacrifice variation in the question predictor automatically because the predicted values of X inevitably shrink from their observed values toward the sample mean, unless prediction is perfect. Then, when you fit the second-stage model, regressing the outcome on the newly predicted values of the question predictor, the precision of the estimated regression slope β_1 is impacted deleteriously by the reduced variation present in the newly diminished version of the question predictor. Consequently, the standard error of the new slope will be larger than the corresponding standard error obtained in a naïve (and biased) OLS regression analysis of the outcome/question predictor relationship. The weaker the first-stage relationship, the less successful you will be in carving out exogenous variability to load into the predicted values of X. This means that when the first-stage relationship is weak, it will be difficult to detect a relationship at the second stage unless your sample is extremely large. This is the inevitable trade-off involved in implementing IVE—you must forfeit variation in the question predictor (hopefully forfeiting the *endogenous* portion of the variation, and retaining as much of the exogenous as possible), so that you can eliminate bias in the estimated value of β_1! But, as a consequence, you sacrifice precision in that estimate.[19] It seems like a pretty decent trade, to us.

This trade-off between bias and precision is evident in our civic engagement example. Notice that the R^2 statistic in the first stage of the 2SLS process is only slightly more than 0.01. Consequently, the standard error associated with the all-important *REGISTER* on *COLLEGE* slope in the second-stage analysis is quite large. In fact, if you compare the standard

---

19. In presenting this conceptual introduction to 2SLS, we have overlooked deliberately a small adjustment to the standard errors of the parameter estimates that must be applied in the second-stage fit. Notice that in panel (b) of Table 10.3, we have indicated in the column heading that the standard errors have been "corrected." The correction involves re-computing the second-stage sum-of-squared residuals (SSE) and inserting the corrected value into the standard error computation in the second-stage model fit. The "corrected" raw residuals—which are then squared and summed to provide the corrected SSE—are obtained by subtracting from the observed value of the outcome a corresponding predicted value, for each participant. However, in the corrected case, the required predicted value is obtained by substituting the participant's *original* value of the question predictor into the second-stage fitted model (rather than his or her *predicted* value). Fortunately, the correction need not be carried out by hand, as it is implemented automatically in all standard 2SLS computer algorithms. For a single predictor, the corrected standard error of the 2SLS estimate of β_1 equals the standard error obtained in the OLS fit of the second-stage model multiplied by the square root of the ratio of the corrected SSE and the nominal SSE (Wooldridge, 2002, pp. 97–99).

errors of the regression coefficients associated with the question predictor, *COLLEGE*, in the earlier naïve OLS analysis (Table 10.1) and the more sophisticated 2SLS analyses (Table 10.3), you will find that they differ almost by a factor of 10! Fortunately, we possess quite a large sample of participants, and this offsets the loss of precision. As a result, we retain sufficient statistical power to reject the null hypothesis.

Obtaining an Instrumental-Variables Estimate by Simultaneous-Equations Estimation

Throughout our introduction to the 2SLS approach, you have seen that the IV strategy involves the statistical modeling of two hypothesized relationships: (a) the first-stage relationship between a potentially endogenous question predictor and an instrument, and (b) the second-stage relationship between an outcome and an endogenous question predictor. We can represent these hypothesized relationships together, by the following pair of statistical models:

$$X_i = \alpha_0 + \alpha_1 I_i + \delta_i$$
$$Y_i = \beta_0 + \beta_1 X_i + \varepsilon_i \tag{10.15}$$

Under the 2SLS approach, you fit these two models in a stepwise fashion, with a predicted value replacing the measured value of the endogenous predictor in the second-stage fit. However, you can also fit the two hypothesized models simultaneously, using the methods of *simultaneous-equations modeling*, or SEM, and again you will obtain identical results.[20]

As is the usual practice with the SEM approach, we first present our hypotheses in Figure 10.3 as a *path model* that specifies the hypothesized first- and second-stage relationships among the several variables simultaneously. In the figure, outcome Y, question predictor X, and instrument I are symbolized by rectangles, and the connections among them are represented by single-headed arrows, each pointing in the hypothesized direction of prediction.[21] The path model contains all our hypotheses and assumptions about the IV approach. For instance, the solid single-headed arrow linking instrument I to question predictor X embodies our first important assumption that the instrument I is related directly to question predictor X, with slope parameter α_1 (the first path). Then, a second

---

20. This technique is also often called *structural-equations modeling* or *covariance structure analysis*. It is typically carried out using software such as LISREL and EQS.

21. In path models, a single-headed arrow indicates a connection that possesses a hypothesized causal direction, such as that between predictor and outcome, and a double-headed arrow indicates simple covariation between a pair of variables with no explicit causal direction implied.

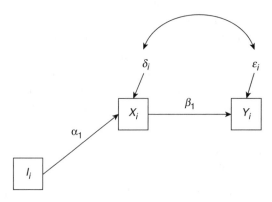

Figure 10.3 Path model presenting hypothesized population relationships among an outcome Y, a potentially endogenous question predictor X, and an instrument, I.

hypothesized path links question predictor X directly to ultimate outcome Y, with slope parameter β_1 (the second path). Together, these paths embody the notion that instrument I is related to question predictor X, and indirectly through it, to ultimate outcome Y. But, the lack of an arrow representing a direct path between instrument I and outcome Y makes explicit our critically important "no third path" assumption.

Notice that our hypothesized path model also contains two shorter solid arrows, each pointing slightly backward into question predictor X and outcome Y, respectively. These shorter solid arrows represent the residuals, δ and ε, featured in the first- and second-stage models in Equation 10.15. As usual, the first residual δ is that part of question predictor X that is unpredicted in the first stage; the second residual, ε, is that part of outcome Y that goes unpredicted in the second stage. We have also made one subtle addition to the path model that is unannounced in the algebraic specification of the first- and second-stage statistical models in Equation 10.15. Namely, in our path model, we have permitted the first- and second-stage residuals to covary, and have represented their covariation by the curved double-headed arrow that links them, at the top of the figure.

Including in the hypothesized path model this connection between the first- and second-stage residuals is critical if we want to use SEM to provide an identical IV estimate of slope parameter β_1. It is the presence of this link between the two residuals in the hypothesized path model that ensures that only variation in X that has been predicted by instrument I acts to determine the magnitude and direction of the estimated "question" slope parameter β_1. Essentially, by having instrument I predict potentially endogenous predictor X, we partition the question predictor's variation into two parts: (a) the valuable "predicted" part (which is related to I, and is therefore exogenous), and (b) the problematic "unpredicted" part or residual, which contains any endogenously determined component that was originally part of X. Both of these parts of the original variation in X may be correlated with the ultimate outcome, Y, but it is only the exogenous first part that we want to determine our estimate of β_1. We make sure that this happens by providing a "back door" route—via the covariation of the first- and second-stage residuals—by which any potentially endogenous component of X can take whatever relationship it wants with outcome Y. Then, our estimate of regression slope β_1 depends only on the components of variation that our IV estimation process requires.

In Table 10.4, we present IV estimates for our civic engagement example obtained by SEM. As expected, the estimates, their standard errors, and the associated statistical inference match those provided by our earlier approaches to IVE, and the associated R^2 statistics match those that we obtained in the first and second stages of the 2SLS analysis. Consequently, we offer no further interpretation of them here. One small advantage of using SEM estimation to fit the first- and second-stage models simultaneously, however, is that the estimation process yields an estimate of the correlation between the residuals in the first- and second-stage models. In our example, for instance, the estimated correlation between the errors in the two models is −0.1151, which is negative and statistically significant. This provides evidence that IVE was indeed required and that

Table 10.4 Civic engagement (in 1992) and educational attainment (in 1984) for 9,227 participants in the sophomore cohort of HS&B survey. IV estimation of the *REGISTER* on *COLLEGE* relationship, using SEM, with *DISTANCE* as the instrument

	Parameter	Estimate	St. Error
1st Stage: Outcome = COLLEGE			
INTERCEPT	α_0	0.6091***	0.0077
DISTANCE	α_1	−0.0064***	0.0006
R^2		0.0124	
2nd Stage: Outcome = REGISTER			
INTERCEPT	β_0	0.5157***	0.0480
COLLEGE	β_1	**0.2837***,†**	0.0873
R^2 statistic		0.0223	
Error Correlation	ρ	−0.1151	

~p <0.10; * p <0.05; ** p <0.01; *** p <0.001
†One-sided test.

a path needed to be found by which the endogenous variation in the *COLLEGE* question predictor could be linked to the final outcome, *REGISTER*.

The conceptual underpinnings of the SEM approach to IV estimation can again be illustrated using our graphical analog for variation and covariation among outcome Y, potentially endogenous question predictor, X, and instrument I. Not without some explanatory difficulty, however, so pay attention. In Figure 10.4, we have again reproduced the trivariate

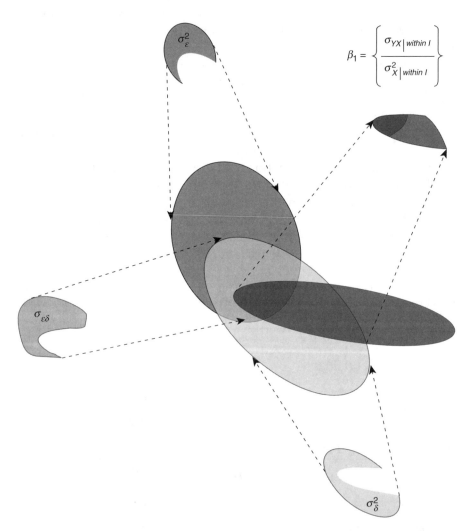

$$\beta_1 = \left\{ \frac{\sigma_{YX \mid within\ I}}{\sigma^2_{X \mid within\ I}} \right\}$$

Figure 10.4 Graphical analog for the population variation and covariation among outcome Y, potentially endogenous question predictor X, and instrument, I, used for distinguishing the different variance components identified under the SEM approach.

distribution of these three variables from the lower panel of Figure 10.1. Although we have left the size and shape of all three original ellipses unchanged between figures, we have modified the construction and labeling of the Venn diagram to reflect the components of variation that are identified by the way that the statistical models have been specified under the SEM approach. Recall that this consists of two things: (a) the two model specifications in Equation 10.15, along with (b) the additional assumption that the residuals in the first- and second-stage models can covary. In this new version of the graphical analog, we show how the SEM model specification maps the two residual variances σ_δ^2 and σ_ε^2 and the residual covariance $\sigma_{\varepsilon\delta}$ onto existing parts of the Venn diagram. First, the population variance of the residuals in the first-stage model σ_δ^2 consists of all variation in question predictor X that is *not related* to variation in the instrument; thus, it corresponds to the area of the medium-grey ellipse that does *not* intersect with the dark-grey ellipse. Second, the population variance of the residuals in the second-stage model σ_ε^2 consists of all variation in outcome Y that falls *beyond* the reach of that part of the variation in the question predictor that covaries with the instrument; thus, it corresponds to the area of the light-grey ellipse that does *not* overlap with the intersection of the medium- and dark-grey ellipses. Finally, the population covariation of the first- and second-stage residuals $\sigma_{\varepsilon\delta}$ is represented by the overlap of these latter two regions, in the center of the figure, and labeled off to the left. By specifying the SEM model as in Equation 10.15, *and* permitting their residuals to covary, the areas of variation and covariation among the residuals are partitioned effectively from among the joint ellipses, leaving behind the same ratio of smaller areas to contribute to the estimation of the population regression slope, as before. We provide a final conceptual expression for this parameter in the upper right of the figure, to emphasize the point.

Finally, you might reasonably ask, if several methods are available for obtaining an identical IV estimate, is one preferable to another? If you are in the simplest analytic setting with which we opened this chapter—a single outcome, a single potentially endogenous predictor, and a single instrument—it doesn't matter. Whichever analytic approach you use, you will get the same answer. However, generally, we recommend using either 2SLS or SEM because these approaches can be extended more readily to more complex analytic settings. (We introduced the simple method-of-moments IV estimator at the beginning of this chapter solely for its pedagogic value in establishing the basic principles and assumptions of the IV approach.) We ourselves find the 2SLS approach especially amenable to thoughtful data analysis, as it is simply a doubled-up application of traditional OLS methods. So, all of the usual practices of good regression analysis—graphical exploration of the data, standard methods of testing and ease of interpretation, the use of residual diagnostics and influence statistics—can be brought to bear at either stage of the analysis. Moreover, both can be extended to incorporate a nonlinear functional specification in either the first- or second-stage model or both. We now turn to an illustration of these extensions.

Extensions of the Basic Instrumental-Variable Estimation Approach

Now that we have explained how the standard IVE strategy involves the fitting of a pair of linked statistical models, either sequentially by 2SLS or simultaneously by SEM, the way is open to extend the basic approach to the more complex analytic situations that we often face in practice. The extensions include adding covariates as control predictors to the first- and second-stage models, using multiple instruments in the first-stage model, estimating models with multiple endogenous predictors in the second-stage model, and using nonlinear model specifications. We consider each of these extensions in turn.

Incorporating Exogenous Covariates into Instrumental-Variable Estimation

Just as it was not necessary—but could be beneficial—to include control predictors in the analysis of experimental data, you can also include selected covariates into an IV analysis. For example, in the models described in his 2004 paper, Dee included many control predictors at the individual, family, community, and county levels. At the individual level, he controlled for important demographic characteristics of participants such as their age, gender, race, and religious affiliation, as well as prior academic achievement. At the family level, he included covariates that described parental levels of education and family income when the participant was a teenager (i.e., at the HS&B baseline survey administration). At the community and county level, he included fixed effects representing the census division of participants' base-year high school, and he controlled for the average civic attitudes and parental educational attainment in the participants' communities when they were teenagers.

Fundamentally, the motivation for including such covariates in an IV analysis is similar to, but broader than, the case for including them in the analysis of data from a random-assignment experiment. As usual, you always hope that adding a carefully selected set of controls to the analysis will reduce residual variation, make standard errors smaller, and increase your statistical power. However, you must exercise caution. You must be convinced that any control variables that you add to an IVE—at either stage—are themselves exogenous; otherwise, you will be simply introducing additional biases into your analyses.

To illustrate the process of adding covariates into an IVE, we extend our 2SLS analysis of the civic-engagement data. Following Dee (2004), we continue to treat *DISTANCE* as the critical instrumental variable, but now we also include a vector of covariates that describe the participants' race/ethnicity in both the first- and second-stage regression models. For this purpose, we have used a vector of three dichotomous predictors to distinguish whether a respondent was *BLACK*, *HISPANIC*, or *OTHERRACE*. In each case, the relevant predictor takes on a value of 1 if the respondent is of that particular race/ethnicity, and 0 otherwise. We have omitted the dichotomous predictor, *WHITE*, to provide the reference category.

In Table 10.5, we present estimates of the critical regression parameters, obtained with the new covariates incorporated into the analysis. They can be compared with the estimates that we obtained in the absence of the covariates in Table 10.3. As you might expect, the inclusion of the covariates has increased the explanatory power of the models at both stages. The associated R^2 statistic has almost doubled, at each stage. This improvement in prediction is reflected in a reduction of standard errors associated with the second-stage parameter estimates. For instance, the standard error associated with question predictor *COLLEGE* in the second-stage model has declined by about 8%, from 0.0873 to 0.0806.

Of course, as in any statistical analysis, you need to exercise caution when adding covariates. You must weigh the potential improvement in predicted outcome sums-of-squares against the forfeiture of degrees of freedom. Here, in the second-stage model, for instance, we have paid for the improved prediction of *REGISTER* by our sacrifice of three degrees of freedom, one for each of the new slope parameters introduced in the model by our inclusion of the three race/ethnicity covariates. When sample size is large, as in this case, this is not a problem. But, if sample size were small, the number of additional covariates was large, and there was little improvement in fit, then the standard error associated with the question predictor could very well become larger and statistical power lower upon the addition of more covariates. These, however, are the same trade-offs that we are accustomed to making in all of our statistical analyses.

Given that fitting the first- and second-stage models without covariates resulted in a reasonably strong, statistically significant positive impact of college enrollment on subsequent civic engagement (see Table 10.3), it makes sense to ask why Dee included so many additional covariates in

Table 10.5 Civic engagement (in 1992) and educational attainment (in 1984) for 9,227 participants in the sophomore cohort of the HS&B survey. IV estimation of the *REGISTER* on *COLLEGE* relationship using 2SLS, with *DISTANCE* as the instrument and including participant race as covariates, at both the first and second stages

(a) 1st Stage: Outcome = COLLEGE

	Parameter	Estimate	St. Error
INTERCEPT	α_0	0.6431***	0.0091
DISTANCE	α_1	−0.0069***	0.0006
BLACK	α_2	−0.0577***	0.0160
HISPANIC	α_3	−0.1162***	0.0133
OTHERRACE	α_4	0.0337	0.0240
R^2		0.0217	

(b) 2nd Stage: Outcome = REGISTER

	Parameter	Estimate	Corrected St. Error
INTERCEPT	β_0	0.5266***	0.0463
$\widehat{COLLEGE}$	β_1	**0.2489***,†	0.0806
BLACK	β_2	0.0617***	0.0152
HISPANIC	β_3	0.0283~	0.0148
OTHERRACE	β_4	−0.1067***	0.0228
R^2		0.0345	

~$p < 0.10$; * $p < 0.05$; ** $p < 0.01$; *** $p < 0.001$
†One-sided test.

his models. He addresses this question explicitly in his paper, and his answer is linked to his defense of the credibility of his instruments. For instance, one potential threat to the credibility of Dee's instruments is that states might choose to locate two-year colleges near communities in which parents were well educated and the public high schools were thought to be of especially high quality. Students in these communities might not only have short commutes to the nearest community college, but also be especially likely to vote as adults because their families valued civic participation and because they attended high schools that emphasized its importance. As a result, students with short commutes to community colleges might have higher probabilities of registering to vote as adults, even if college enrollment had no causal impact on their interest in civic participation. If this were the case, then *DISTANCE* (and other measures of community college accessibility) would fail our "no third path" test for a credible instrument, and the results of our IVE would be flawed.

Dee's response to this threat to the validity of his instrument was to include several classes of covariate in his first- and second-stage models, arguing that once these characteristics had been controlled, the critical no third-path assumption on the proximity instrument would be satisfied. Not only did he include the participant demographics that we have incorporated here, he also included prior student achievement scores, measures of each family's prior socioeconomic status, characteristics of the high school that each student attended, and county-level variables that described the civic attitudes of the community in which each student lived when he or she was in high school.[22] This allowed Dee to make the case that, among students from families with the same observed socioeconomic status, living in communities with the same observed civic attitudes, and attending an observationally similar high school, there was no "third path" that connected the instruments representing the accessibility of the nearest two-year college directly to the probability that the students would register to vote as adults. This is clearly a stronger case than simply arguing that the length of the commute to the nearest community college (with no covariates in the first-stage model) had no direct influence on the probability of subsequent voter registration.

Notice that we—and Dee—have taken care to include the *same set of exogenous covariates* at both the first and second stages of the IVE. This decision is also motivated by a desire to preserve the credibility of the "no third path" assumption for the first-stage predictor that is being treated as an instrument. Of course, *all* of the predictors that anyone chooses to include in the first-stage model—both the instruments and the controls—must be exogenous. None of them can be correlated with their respective first-stage residuals, or the first-stage estimation will then be biased, and we will be lost from the start. However, in the first-stage model, instruments and covariates are only distinguished from each other by their suspected

---

22. Notice that several of Dee's chosen covariates—student tenth-grade test scores, for instance—might be easily considered endogenous if they had been measured concurrently with the student's decision to enroll in college (*COLLEGE*). However, the values of these covariates were "predetermined"—their values were measured prior to the period in which the value of the question predictor was determined (Kennedy, 1992, p. 370). In contrast, it would not have been appropriate for Dee to include adult labor-market earnings as a control variable in his second-stage equation, even though this variable may predict the probability of civic engagement. The reason is that this covariate is indeed endogenous in the second-stage model as its value was determined after the college-enrollment decision had been made. Not only may this covariate be correlated with unobserved determinants of civic engagement, such as motivation, it may also have been associated with the decision of whether to go to college. Adding a predictor that is potentially endogenous—at either stage—would compound your analytic problems rather than resolve them.

adherence, or lack of it, to the "no third path" assumption. If they are truly instruments, then they must *only* be related to the ultimate outcome *REGISTER*, through their impact on the potentially endogenous question predictor *COLLEGE*. This is the case, by assumption, for Dee's instrument *DISTANCE*. Dee did not need to impose this same restriction on the other exogenous covariates he included in the first-stage model; he intended these other predictors to serve simply as covariates, not instruments. Although they are also required to be exogenous, they are not restricted to act only indirectly on ultimate outcome *REGISTER* through the potentially endogenous question predictor. (And if they did meet the "no third path" assumption, they would be instruments too!) The exogenous covariates in the first-stage model may therefore act on the ultimate outcome both indirectly (through question predictor *COLLEGE*), and also directly—that is, by having a direct third path to the outcome of the second-stage equation. Of course, if covariates in the first-stage model are able to predict the ultimate outcome of the analyses directly, then you must include these covariates necessarily in the second-stage model so that they can display that path. Their inclusion accounts for their potential direct impact on the outcome of the second-stage model, *REGISTER*. Thus, to summarize, any exogenous covariate that you choose to include in the first-stage model and that you do not want to defend as an instrument must also be included in the second-stage model. Perhaps to prevent the inadvertent violation of this recommendation, statistical software packages such as Stata force you to include in the second-stage model all the covariates that you have listed for inclusion in the first-stage model (except any instruments, of course).

There is a parallel and conceptually convergent argument, based on the practice of 2SLS estimation that supports this principle that "all covariates in the first-stage model must also be included in the second-stage model." It goes like this: both instrument and covariates are present in the first-stage model, then the predicted values of the potentially endogenous question predictor obtained during the completed first stage of the 2SLS estimation will contain all the variation in the endogenous question predictor that was predicted by both the instrument and covariates. Then, when these predicted values replace the observed values of the potentially endogenous question predictor in the second-stage estimation, the estimated value of their associated regression coefficient will depend on both the earlier instrumental and covariate variation unless we control explicitly for covariate variation in the second-stage model too! To be unbiased, the estimated value of the regression coefficient associated with the question predictor must be derived only from the variation that originates in the instrument itself. Therefore, we must include the first-stage covariates as controls in the second-stage model in order to hold constant that extraneous variation.

Notice that, by implementing this data-analytic principle, the only predictor that is included in the first-stage model and excluded from the second-stage model is the instrument itself. Sometimes methodologists refer to this as the *exclusion principle* or *exclusion restriction*. If you have conducted an IV analysis, and someone asks you for your exclusion restriction, you are being asked to name your instrument and make a case for its credibility. In responding, you need to be ready for the comments of skeptics who want to argue that there may be a third path that relates your instrument directly to the outcome of the second-stage model. One of your arguments, like Dee's, can refer to the careful choice of covariates that you have included in both the first- and second-stage models to control for other processes that might have otherwise linked the instrument directly to the ultimate outcome.

Finally, although all first-stage predictors—other than instruments—must also be included in the second-stage model, the reverse is not necessarily true. You can choose to include selected additional covariates in the second-stage model—perhaps based on theory—and you are not *required* to include them in the first-stage model. They are simply additional covariates that you may argue are necessary theoretically or that are present to further reduce residual variance and improve power at the second stage. However, as Angrist and Pischke (2009, p. 189) point out, if these additional second-stage covariates are indeed exogenous (as they must be!), then you have nothing to lose by including them in the first-stage model too.

Incorporating Multiple Instruments into the First-Stage Model

If you are fortunate enough to have more than one viable instrument available, you can incorporate them all simultaneously in your first-stage model, and continue with your IVE, using either 2SLS or SEM (Angrist & Pischke, 2009). Provided the new instruments each satisfy the conditions that we have described earlier, including them in your first-stage model will only enhance your analysis and help ensure that your instruments, as a group, are strong. Their inclusion will mean that more of the exogenous variation present in the potentially endogenous predictor will be carved out during first-stage estimation, leading to improved precision for the asymptotically unbiased estimation of the critical causal relationship at the second stage and to an enhanced avoidance of the problems of weak instruments that we have described earlier.

In addition to the instrument *DISTANCE* that we included in our pedagogical presentation, Dee (2004) also used a second instrument, *NUMBER*, which counted the number of two-year colleges within each participant's county when the student was in tenth grade. Dee's rationale for regarding both these variables as viable instruments was that both were exogenous indicators of an implicit "offer" of higher education. He argued that neither of them was likely to predict subsequent voter registration directly. In other words, Dee argued that there was unlikely to be any credible direct third path between either of his instruments and his ultimate outcome variable, voter registration, especially once he had controlled for all his additional covariates. In Table 10.6, we present a 2SLS analysis of our subset of the civic-engagement data, with both of these instruments included in the first-stage model. We also retain the race/ethnicity covariates described earlier. Notice that the inclusion of the second instrument, *NUMBER*, has clearly led to improvements in our estimation.

Table 10.6 Civic engagement (in 1992) and educational attainment (in 1984) for 9,227 participants in the sophomore cohort of the HS&B survey. IV estimation of the *REGISTER* on *COLLEGE* relationship, using 2SLS, with *DISTANCE* and *NUMBER* as instruments and participant race as covariates, at both the first and second stages

(a) 1st Stage: Outcome = COLLEGE

	Parameter	Estimate	St. Error
INTERCEPT	α_0	0.5995***	0.0110
DISTANCE	α_1	−0.0057***	0.0006
NUMBER	α_2	0.0217***	0.0031
BLACK	α_3	−0.0568***	0.0159
HISPANIC	α_4	−0.1160***	0.0132
OTHERRACE	α_5	0.0304	0.0240
R^2		0.0269	

(b) 2ndStage: Outcome = REGISTER

	Parameter	Estimate	Corrected St. Error
INTERCEPT	β_0	0.5102***	0.0399
$\widehat{COLLEGE}$	β_1	**0.2776***,†**	0.0693
BLACK	β_2	0.0628***	0.0151
HISPANIC	β_3	0.0312*	0.0143
OTHERRACE	β_4	−0.1080***	0.0228
R^2		0.0291	

‾p <0.10; * p <0.05; ** p <0.01; *** p <0.001
†One-sided test.

For instance, we now do a better job of predicting potentially endogenous question predictor *COLLEGE* at the first stage—our first-stage R^2 statistic has risen by almost 25%, from 0.0217 in Table 10.3 to 0.0269 in the new analysis. This has resulted in a decline of 14% (from 0.0806 to 0.0693) in the standard error of the critical *COLLEGE* regression slope at the second-stage fitted model. The parameter estimate on the *COLLEGE* question predictor itself has also risen slightly, from 0.249 to 0.278. All in all, our statistical inference has benefitted from the inclusion of the second instrument.

The notion that you are not limited to working with a single instrument suggests two other obvious analytic opportunities. The first is that, if there are two predictors in the first-stage model that have legitimate status as instruments, then their interaction can also be a legitimate instrument. This leads us to form the cross-product of *DISTANCE* and *NUMBER*, and to introduce it as an instrument in the first-stage model. Similarly, we note that the statistical interactions of instruments and exogenous covariates—such as the interaction between *DISTANCE* and the covariates that represent participant race/ethnicity—may provide other effective instruments for inclusion in the first-stage model. In Table 10.7, we have implemented these two ideas, the first in analyses that result in *Model A* and the second in analyses that result in *Model B*. In Model A, we have included the original main effects of instruments *DISTANCE* and *NUMBER*, and their two-way interaction in the first-stage model, along with the participant race/ethnicity covariates that were introduced for the first time in the section "Incorporating Exogenous Covariates into Instrumental-Variable Estimation." Although there is no problem including these terms together as first-stage predictors, unfortunately the newly introduced two-way *DISTANCE* by *NUMBER* interaction has no statistically significant impact on the first-stage outcome. Thus, there is no subsequent change—and no improvement—in the estimated causal impact of *COLLEGE* on *REGISTER*, at the second stage. Comparing parallel estimates in Tables 10.6 and 10.7, for instance, we see that the comparable first- and second-stage R^2 statistics are almost identical (0.0269 vs. 0.0270 and 0.0291 vs. 0.0295, respectively). Also, there has been little or no change in the second-stage model in the estimated impact of *COLLEGE* (0.2776 vs. 0.2757) or in the associated standard error (0.0693 vs. 0.0691).

Under Model B of Table 10.7, we present the results of including the main effects of the original instruments, *COLLEGE* and *NUMBER*, in the first-stage model, along with all possible two-way interactions between the instruments and the three exogenous race/ethnicity covariates: *BLACK*, *HISPANIC*, and *OTHERRACE*. Again, the inclusion of the entire set of new "interaction instruments" brings about no substantial improvement in first-stage fit, as indicated by the minimal improvement of the R^2 statistic

Table 10.7 Civic engagement (in 1992) and educational attainment (in 1984) for 9,227 participants in the sophomore cohort of the HS&B survey. IV estimation of the *REGIS-TER* on *COLLEGE* regression slope, using 2SLS, with *DISTANCE* and *NUMBER* and their interactions with each other and with race as instruments, and with the main effects of race included at both stages as covariates

(a) 1st Stage: Outcome = COLLEGE

	Parameter	Model A		Model B	
		Estimate	St. Error	Estimate	St. Error
INTERCEPT	α_0	0.6028***	0.0114	0.5941***	0.0129
DISTANCE	α_1	−0.0061***	0.0007	−0.0056***	0.0008
NUMBER	α_2	0.0180***	0.0047	0.0250***	0.0040
BLACK	α_3	−0.0563***	0.0159	−0.0663*	0.0302
HISPANIC	α_4	−0.1160***	0.0132	−0.0964***	0.0247
OTHERRACE	α_5	0.0297	0.0240	0.0687	0.0429
DISTANCE×NUMBER	α_6	0.0006	0.0005		
DISTANCE×BLACK	α_7			0.0010	0.0021
NUMBER×BLACK	α_8			0.0012	0.099
DISTANCE×HISPANIC	α_9			0.0003	0.0016
NUMBER×HISPANIC	α_{10}			−0.0147~	0.0078
DISTANCE×OTHERRACE	α_{11}			−0.0037	0.0030
NUMBER×OTHERRACE	α_{12}			−0.0045	0.0123
R^2		0.0270		0.0276	

(b) 2nd Stage: Outcome = REGISTER

	Parameter	Model A		Model B	
		Estimate	Corrected St. Error	Estimate	Corrected St. Error
INTERCEPT	β_0	0.5113***	0.0398	0.5058***	0.0393
COLLEGE	β_1	**0.2757***,†**	0.0691	**0.2854***,†**	0.0682
BLACK	β_2	0.0627***	0.0151	0.0631***	0.0151
HISPANIC	β_3	0.0310*	0.0142	0.0320*	0.0142
OTHERRACE	β_4	−0.1080***	0.0228	−0.1084***	0.0228
R^2		0.0295		0.0274	

~$p < 0.10$; * $p < 0.05$; ** $p < 0.01$; *** $p < 0.001$
†One-sided test.

from 0.0269 in Table 10.6, to 0.0276 in Table 10.7. Thus, as you might expect, the estimated impact of *COLLEGE* on *REGISTER* at the second stage also appears largely unaffected by the addition of the new interaction instruments (the impact of *COLLEGE* rises only from 0.2776 to 0.2854) and the associated standard error declines only minimally.

The principle, however, remains intact and potentially useful, for applying IVE in other data: it is always a good idea to look beyond a simple main-effects specification of the first-stage model by considering interactions among your instruments, and between your instruments and your exogenous covariates. All these could function potentially as instruments and you could benefit if they did.[23]

Examining the Impact of Interactions Between the Endogenous Question Predictor and Exogenous Covariates in the Second-Stage Model

In many situations, a question of interest may be whether the impact of the endogenous question predictor on the outcome in the second-stage model differs among important subgroups. For example, in the case of Dee's 2004 study, a plausible hypothesis might be that enrollment in college has a greater impact on the probability that white students will register to vote as adults than it has on the probability that black or Hispanic students or students of other races will register to vote subsequently. A possible rationale underlying this hypothesis could be that when the HS&B data were collected during the 1980s, almost all candidates for public office were white; consequently, citizens from minority groups may have seen less value in registering to vote than did white citizens.

We could test the hypothesis that the effect of college enrollment on subsequent voter registration differs by race/ethnicity by including in the second-stage model not only the main effect of the endogenous predictor *COLLEGE*, but also its two-way interactions with each of *BLACK*, *HISPANIC*, and *OTHERRACE*. However, it is critical to understand that the statistical interaction between a potentially endogenous predictor like *COLLEGE* and an exogenous covariate like *BLACK* is itself potentially endogenous.

In cases in which the second-stage model includes multiple endogenous predictors, it is important to verify that you have satisfied what is known as the *rank condition* (Wooldridge, 2002). This condition says that *for every endogenous predictor included in the second stage, there must be at least one instrument included in the first stage*. This means that if we include one potentially endogenous main effect and three potentially endogenous interactions in the second-stage model, then we must include at least four instruments in the first-stage model. Given that it is usually incredibly

---

23. To keep the exposition as simple as possible, we do not make use of the second instrumental variable, *NUMBER*, in subsequent sections of this chapter.

hard to find—and justify—even a single instrument in most research projects, you might wonder if this is an insurmountable task. Fortunately, the required instruments are readily at hand. They are the corresponding interactions between the original instrument for the main effect of *COLLEGE*—that is, *DISTANCE*—and its interactions with the same exogenous covariates. Thus, just as *DISTANCE* is an arguably viable instrument for *COLLEGE*, the two-way interaction of *DISTANCE* and *BLACK* is a viable instrument for the potentially endogenous interaction of *COLLEGE* and *BLACK*.

We have introduced these new sets of interactions into the IVE analysis in Table 10.8. At the first stage, we have included the main effect of *DISTANCE* and its interactions with the race/ethnicity covariates as instruments. At the second stage, we have introduced the main effect of *COLLEGE* and its interactions with the same covariates; these latter interactions are then themselves potentially endogenous question predictors. Because there are now four potentially endogenous predictors at the second stage, we require four first-stage statistical models, one relating each endogenous predictor to the instruments available. Consequently, you will see that there are four discrete sections to the first-stage output in Table 10.8, one for each potentially endogenous second-stage predictor: *COLLEGE*, *COLLEGE×BLACK*, *COLLEGE×HISPANIC*, and *COLLEGE× OTHERRACE*. In each case, we have regressed each endogenous predictor on the full complement of instruments and covariates: *DISTANCE*, *DISTANCE×BLACK*, *DISTANCE×HISPANIC*, and *DISTANCE×OTHER-RACE*.[24] To save space in the table, we have listed parameter estimates and their associated statistics for only those first-stage predictors that actually play a role in predicting the respective first-stage outcome. Thus, you will see that all of the instruments and covariates can potentially play a role in predicting the main effect of *COLLEGE*, and so the impact of all of them and the remaining exogenous covariates are listed. In contrast, only the instruments *BLACK* and *DISTANCE×BLACK* are needed to predict the potentially endogenous interaction of *COLLEGE* and *BLACK*, as indicated in the second discrete section of the first-stage output in Table 10.8. Even if the full complement of predictors—main effects of instrument and covariates, and their interactions—are included in each of the first-stage models for each of the potentially endogenous question

---

24. This is a practice that is enforced by the programming structure of statistical software such as Stata.

Table 10.8 Civic engagement (in 1992) and educational attainment (in 1984) for 9,227 participants in the sophomore cohort of the HS&B survey. IV estimation of the *REGISTER* on *COLLEGE* relationship using 2SLS, including participant race as covariates at both the first and second stages. Second-stage model contains interactions between the endogenous question predictor *COLLEGE* and participant race, and first-stage model includes *DISTANCE* and its interactions with race as instruments

(a) 1st Stage:

	Parameter	Estimate	St. Error
Outcome = COLLEGE			
INTERCEPT	α_0	0.6452***	0.0101
DISTANCE	α_1	−0.0071***	0.0007
BLACK	α_2	−0.0651***	0.0228
HISPANIC	α_3	−0.1276***	0.0194
OTHERRACE	α_4	0.0590⁻	0.0351
DIST × BLACK	α_5	0.0009	0.0020
DIST × HISPANIC	α_6	0.0013	0.0016
DIST × OTHERRACE	α_7	−0.0030	0.0030
R^2		0.022	
Outcome = COLLEGE × BLACK			
BLACK	α_8	0.5801***	0.0081
DIST × BLACK	α_9	−0.0062***	0.0007
R^2		0.504	
Outcome = COLLEGE × HISPANIC			
HISPANIC	α_{10}	0.5176***	0.0087
DIST × HISPANIC	α_{11}	−0.0058***	0.0007
R^2		0.419	
Outcome = COLLEGE × OTHERRACE			
OTHERRACE	α_{12}	0.7041***	0.0076
DIST × OTHERRACE	α_{13}	−0.0101***	0.0006
R^2		0.617	

(b) 2nd Stage: Outcome = REGISTER

	Parameter	Estimate	Corrected St. Error
INTERCEPT	β_0	0.4640***	0.0553
$\widehat{COLLEGE}$	β_1	**0.3587***,†**	0.0965
BLACK	β_2	0.2780⁻	0.1627
HISPANIC	β_3	0.1765	0.1208
OTHERRACE	β_4	−0.1742	0.1756
$\widehat{COLLEGE}$ × BLACK	β_5	−0.3986	0.3021
$\widehat{COLLEGE}$ × HISPANIC	β_6	−0.2929	0.2478
$\widehat{COLLEGE}$ × OTHERRACE	β_7	−0.4634	0.2844
R^2		0.0125	

⁻p <0.10; * p <0.05; ** p <0.01; *** p <0.001
†One-sided test.

predictors, the un-needed predictors take on coefficients that have zero magnitude during the estimation process.[25,26]

Notice that the new "interaction instruments" are particularly effective in predicting their corresponding second-stage endogenous interactions. Thus, the interaction of *DISTANCE* and *BLACK* is an effective predictor of the potentially endogenous interaction of *COLLEGE* and *BLACK*, and consequently acquires an R^2 statistic of 0.504 at the first stage. The same is true for the other first-stage models. However, at the end of the day, not much differs at the second stage. Although the potentially endogenous main effect of *COLLEGE* continues to have a statistically significant impact on voter registration ($p < 0.001$), its companion interactions—although of large magnitude—do not have statistically significant impacts on the outcome. Thus, we can ultimately reject the notion that the effect of *COLLEGE* on *REGISTER* differs by race/ethnicity. This leads us to fall back on the results of the earlier analyses in Table 10.7.[27]

---

25. This statement is easy to confirm analytically, by fitting the requisite models by simultaneous-equations estimation. Then, both the "full" and "reduced" models can be fit and will provide identical answers, with un-needed coefficients taking on a value of zero during analysis if they are not set to zero in advance.

26. Another approach that can be used to test for the presence of interactions between the endogenous predictor and covariates in the second-stage model is 2SLS, conducted piecewise "by hand" using OLS regression analysis. Under the two-step approach, you fit a single first-stage model by regressing the endogenous question predictor (*COLLEGE*) on the main effect of the single instrument (*DISTANCE*) and covariates. Fitted values of *COLLEGE* are then output from the fitted first-stage model into a new variable, call it *PREDCOLL*. This latter variable is then introduced into the second-stage model, in place of *COLLEGE*, in the usual way. *PREDCOLL* can be interacted with exogenous predictors in the second-stage model, by forming cross-products and entering them as predictors also. The estimates obtained are identical to those obtained using the simultaneous methods described in the text, but you must adjust the standard errors by hand, which can be tedious.

27. Notice that the coefficients on *COLLEGE*BLACK*, *COLLEGE*HISPANIC*, and *COLLEGE*OTHERRACE* are all negative and of approximately the same size (in absolute value) as the positive coefficient on the main effect of *COLLEGE*. Recall that the estimate of the impact of college enrollment on the probability of voter registration for blacks, for example, is the sum of the coefficient on the main effect plus the coefficient on the interaction term. Thus, the pattern of coefficients suggests that Dee's finding that college enrollment results in an increase in the probability of voter registration may be driven by the behavior of white students. However, it would take analyses based on a much larger sample than that available in HS&B to reject the null hypothesis that the impact of college is the same for all racial/ethnic groups.

Choosing Appropriate Functional Forms for
Outcome/Predictor Relationships in
First- and Second-Stage Models

In presenting this conceptual introduction to IVE, we have not emphasized the importance of the functional form of our statistical models.
In fact, up to this point in the chapter, we have used a simple linear probability specification for both our first- and second-stage models. We did
this both for pedagogic reasons, and because the linear probability model
has a long history in statistical analysis. In fact, methodologists argue that
results obtained from IV analyses of dichotomous outcomes with first-
and second-stage linear probability models are *consistent*—are *asymptotically
unbiased*—in large datasets like the one we have analyzed here (Angrist &
Pischke, 2009). Our principal objective in using the linear probability
specification was to ensure that we provided a straightforward introduction to IVE that was focused on the concepts rather than the details.
In particular, we wanted to emphasize the central idea that, provided that
you possess viable instruments (like *DISTANCE* and *NUMBER*), you can
carve out exogenous variation in a potentially endogenous question predictor, *COLLEGE*, for use in the subsequent stage of estimation.

Of course, now that we have established the fundamental ideas behind
the basic IVE approach, we can stress some details. Clearly, for all the
usual reasons, it makes sense to select specifications for your first- and
second-stage models that best describe the functional forms of the relationships being modeled. This is no different from the process of model
specification in regular regression analysis, except that you must consider
the specifications of two linked statistical models that will be fitted, either
sequentially or simultaneously, during the IVE process. Consequently,
you must bring to bear all of your usual skills in conducting responsible
regression analysis. For instance, it makes sense to capitalize on appropriate transformations of outcome and/or predictors, guided by *Tukey's
ladder* (Tukey, 1977) or to adopt a sensible polynomial or nonlinear model
specification as the need arises in your data. We do not discuss the details
of this process further here, other than to note that it is an application of
standard statistical methods. In our own case, with dichotomous outcomes at both the first and second stages, it makes sense to adopt a probit
model at both stages, as Dee (2004) did. In Table 10.9, we present first-
and second-stage parameter estimates from an IV analysis that uses a
probit specification at both stages and simultaneous-equations estimation
in our subset of Dee's data. Notice that the coefficient on *COLLEGE* in
the second-stage model (0.7799) remains positive and statistically significant ($p < 0.001$). Subsequent analyses of marginal effects, evaluated at the

Table 10.9 Civic engagement (in 1992) and educational attainment (in 1984) for 9,227 participants in the sophomore cohort of the HS&B survey. IV estimation of the *REGISTER* on *COLLEGE* regression slope, using *bivariate* probit analysis, with *DISTANCE* and *NUMBER* as instruments and including covariates representing participant race, at the first and second stages

	Parameter	Estimate	St. Error
1st Stage: Outcome = COLLEGE			
INTERCEPT	α_0	0.2494***	0.0283
DISTANCE	α_1	−0.0144***	0.0016
NUMBER	α_2	0.0575***	0.0081
BLACK	α_3	−0.1451***	0.0409
HISPANIC	α_4	−0.2967***	0.0340
OTHERRACE	α_5	0.0833	0.0627
2nd Stage: Outcome = REGISTER			
INTERCEPT	β_0	0.0005	0.1125
COLLEGE	β_1	**0.7799***,†**	0.1855
BLACK	β_2	0.1810***	0.0434
HISPANIC	β_3	0.0876	0.0396
OTHERRACE	β_4	−0.2952***	0.0620
Model $\chi^2(df = 33)$		312.6***	

¬$p < 0.10$; * $p < 0.05$; ** $p < 0.01$; *** $p < 0.001$
†One-sided test.

sample mean of *COLLEGE*, indicate that enrollment in college results in a 16.13 percentage point increase in the probability that a student will register to vote as an adult.[28]

Finding and Defending Instruments

The primary challenge in using the IVE approach to answer an educational policy question is finding and defending an appropriate instrumental variable.[29] Two types of knowledge are especially important in the hunt for

---

28. The estimated coefficient on *COLLEGE* in the second-stage fitted probit model must be transformed into a more meaningful metric before it can be interpreted easily. This is usually achieved by estimating the instantaneous slope of the outcome/predictor relationship at the average values, or some other sensible specified values, of the covariates. Here, we have estimated its value when *COLLEGE* is set to its sample average of 0.55, controlling for the presence of other predictors in the model.

29. Many of the ideas in this section derive from the presentation of Angrist and Krueger (2001).

good instruments. The first is a thorough understanding of the relevant substantive theory relevant to the problem. For example, economic theory posits that students and their families compare the benefits and costs of available alternatives in deciding whether to enroll in an educational program. Consequently, any variable that affects either costs or benefits—for example, the length of the home-to-school commute—may affect the investment decision, and therefore be a potential instrument.

The second type of important knowledge concerns the setting in which the data for the study were, or are being, obtained. The better your understanding of the institutions and policies in the settings from which your data come, the stronger the position you will be in to find and defend an appropriate instrumental variable. For example, understanding the rationale that government agencies used in deciding how many schools or colleges to build during a particular time period, and where to place them, can be important in defending measures of the proximity of educational institutions as legitimate instruments for predicting the amount of education young people acquire. Also, knowledge of institutional rules, such as the minimum school-starting age and the minimum school-leaving age in particular settings, may suggest that the timing of a child's birth will provide a useful instrument for predicting educational attainment. We explain these kinds of arguments below.

In the next subsections, we describe three types of instruments that have been used effectively by social scientists to address questions of educational policy. We illustrate each type of instrument using evidence from a high-quality research study. For each study, we list the principal research question, the population that was studied, the variable chosen as the outcome, the potentially endogenous question predictor, the instrument(s), and the findings from the study. We then comment on the threats to internal validity that are common with each type of instrument—that is, the challenges to the assumption that the instrument satisfies the "no third path" assumption, and to the requirement that it predicts the outcome in the first-stage equation strongly.

Proximity of Educational Institutions

Variables that describe participants' proximity to relevant educational institutions are often used as instruments in the hope of carving out exogenous variation in educational attainment. As we noted earlier, the logic underlying their use is that, holding other things constant, the shorter a potential student's commute to the nearest appropriate educational institution, the lower the cost of enrollment and the higher the ensuing attainment. The variation in educational attainment predicted by using distance as an instrument can then be argued to be exogenous, providing that participants' geographic placement around the institutions are themselves distributed exogenously. Janet Currie and Enrico Moretti's (2003) study of the impact of college enrollment on women's subsequent parenting skills provides a compelling example of the use of this type of instrument.

There are three major threats to the internal validity of instruments that utilize research subjects' geographical access to educational institutions. The first is that educational institutions are often placed in communities populated by families with a high demand for education and, potentially, with unmeasured attributes, such as motivation, that would result in above-average life outcomes, such as labor-market earnings. The second is that colleges are placed in communities with high-quality public services, such as hospitals, that affect residents' life outcomes. The third is that families with high demand for educational services (and potentially with unmeasured attributes that contribute to subsequent above-average life outcomes) choose to live near appropriate educational institutions. Any of these scenarios could lead to a "third path" that permits the measure of proximity to impact a participant's subsequent life outcomes directly and therefore invalidates the use of the potential instrument.

Currie and Moretti (2003) demonstrate how the creative use of rich datasets allows researchers to respond to such threats to validity. The research question that they address is whether increasing the attainment of post-secondary education for women has a causal impact on the health of the children they bear. The authors concluded that this was indeed the case. In particular, they found that increasing maternal education reduced the probability that a woman's first child would be born prematurely or with very low birth weight (both of which are indicators of subsequent health problems for the child). They also found that increasing maternal education led to greater use of prenatal care (a positive predictor of infants' health) and reduced the probability that women smoked during pregnancy (a negative predictor of infants' health).

The data that Currie and Moretti used in their research came from the birth certificates of virtually all children born in the United States in the years from 1970 to 1999. These records contain information about a variety of birth outcomes, including birth weight and gestational age. They also contain information on the number of years of schooling that each mother had completed at the time of the birth of her child, when she began prenatal care during her pregnancy, whether she smoked during the pregnancy, and the county in which the child was born. The number of years of schooling that the mother had completed, as of the date of the birth of her first child, constituted the endogenous question predictor in Currie and Moretti's second-stage model. To be reasonably sure that the women had completed their formal education by the time of their first child's birth, Currie and Moretti restricted their sample to women who were between the ages of 24 and 45 when their first child was born.

Currie and Moretti knew that using OLS regression methods to fit a statistical model that specified the health of the first child as a function of the mother's educational attainment would not provide unbiased causal evidence that a mother's education affected her child's birth outcomes. The reason is that women who have relatively high educational attainments are likely to differ from those with relatively low educational attainments along many unmeasured dimensions, such as motivation, that may also affect their children's birth outcomes. The unmeasured differences among women with different educational attainments could then result in a spurious relationship between a mother's educational attainment and the health of her first child. Thus, Currie and Moretti recognized the need to find a credible instrument that they could use to carve out an exogenous portion of the potentially endogenous variation in a mother's educational attainment. To do this, they collected information on the number of four-year colleges and the number of two-year colleges per 1,000 residents, aged 18–22, that were present in each county in the United States in each year from 1940 through 1996. They then made the critical assumption that all women in the sample lived in the same county when they were 17 years of age that they lived in when their first child was born. This assumption allowed Currie and Moretti to merge the data on the availability of two- and four-year colleges in each woman's home county in the year in which she was 17 years old with the data on the birth records of the woman's first child. They then used these measures of college proximity as instruments for women's subsequent educational attainments. The instruments were strong. Currie and Moretti found that, for each additional four-year college per 1,000 college-aged residents in the county, the probability that a woman obtained a four-year degree before the birth of her first child was 19 percentage points higher. For each two-year college per 1,000 college-aged residents in the county, the probability that a woman obtained some college credits before the birth of her first child was 3.2 percentage points higher.

As mentioned earlier, Currie and Moretti faced three threats to the validity of these instruments. The first was that perhaps colleges had been placed in counties in which demand for college was high. The second was that counties with good college availability also had good health facilities that contributed to good health outcomes for infants. Both of these possibilities posed threats to the validity of college proximity as a suitable instrumental variable because they provided a plausible third path through which college availability may have had a direct impact on the health of newborns. Consequently, the authors used a variety of strategies to respond to this threat. Of particular importance, they included—in both their first- and second-stage models—the fixed effects of the two-way interaction between county and the child's year of birth. These fixed effects absorbed all of the variation in mothers' educational attainment and infants' health outcomes that could be accounted for by the observed and unobserved attributes of the county (including the quality of the health facilities) the year in which the child was born. In other words, Currie and Moretti's causal estimates of the impact of a mother's educational attainment on her first child's birth outcomes stemmed solely from differences in the availability of educational services among different cohorts of women bearing their first child in the same county the same year.

Although the inclusion of this rich set of county-by-birth-year fixed effects was important in refining the effect of, and defending, Currie and Moretti's choice of instruments, the authors pointed out that it might still be the case that differences over time in the availability of colleges in a county could be a response to a growing demand for college enrollment. This too would threaten the validity of Currie and Moretti's instruments because an increase in the availability of colleges in a particular county could reflect the in-migration of young women particularly motivated to obtain post-secondary education and also bear healthy children. In response to this potential threat, Currie and Moretti showed that although the availability of colleges when a woman was 17 years of age predicted her educational attainment as of the date of her first child's birth, this was not the case for another variable that measured the availability of colleges when the woman was 25 years of age. This evidence is important in refuting the possibility that colleges were placed in counties where demand for college enrollment was growing.

The second major threat to the validity of instruments based on the proximity of educational institutions is that families with a strong demand for education may choose to live near schools or colleges. This was a particularly important threat to the validity of Currie and Moretti's choice of instruments because, as mentioned earlier, they only knew the county in which the first child had been born (from the birth record), not the county in which the woman had lived when she was 17 years of age, and they had assumed that the former was the same as the latter. On the other hand, it is possible that some women moved to a county with good college availability in order to enroll in post-secondary education and then remained in that county. If the same unmeasured attributes that led some women to move to counties with abundant post-secondary educational facilities also led them to engage in the behaviors that resulted in their giving birth to healthy children (such as obtaining good prenatal care and not smoking during pregnancy), measures of the availability of post-secondary institutions would not be legitimate instruments. The reason is that such mobility would create a direct "third path" that linked availability of post-secondary educational institutions to children's health outcomes.

Currie and Moretti conceded that "endogenous mobility" was the primary threat to the validity of their instruments. To assess the severity of this threat, they also fitted their first-stage model using information on women from the National Longitudinal Survey of Youth (NLSY) dataset who had borne a child by 1996. The advantage of this dataset is that it provides information on the county in which each woman lived when she was 14 years of age. This allowed Currie and Moretti to fit a version of their first-stage model in which they predicted a woman's educational attainment in 1996 (when the youngest women in the NLSY dataset were 32 years of age) as a function of the availability of colleges in the county the year in which the woman was 14 years of age. Fitting the first-stage model with data from this sample of NLSY women produced estimates of the impact of the instruments on women's educational attainment that were very similar to those that the authors obtained in their primary dataset. Thus, this pattern supported Currie and Moretti's argument that endogenous mobility was not a major threat to the validity of their research strategy.

In summary, by using rich data from a variety of sources, Currie and Moretti were able to muster a compelling defense of the suitability of their measures of college proximity as credible instruments for women's subsequent educational attainments. Particularly important was the construction of a dataset that contained information on the first births of children to women aged 24–45 in particular counties in the United States over an extended time period.

Institutional Rules and Personal Characteristics

A second type of instrumental variable that has been used to carve out exogenous variation in endogenous question predictors derives from the institutional rules embedded in educational systems. Angrist and Krueger's (1991) study of the impact of educational attainment on the subsequent weekly earnings of males in the United States provides an example of the use of this type of instrument. The authors point out that most states in the United States require that children begin school the calendar year in which they turn six years old. This means that, if December 31 is the birth date cut-off, children who are born early in the calendar year enter school almost a year older than children who are born later. Most states also have compulsory schooling laws, and usually require students to remain in school until their 16th birthday. Thus, children whose birthdays fall early in the calendar year typically reach the age of 16 one grade lower than children whose birthdays fall later in the school year. This pattern led Angrist and Krueger to hypothesize that "quarter of birth"—that is, whether the child was born in Spring, Summer, Fall, or Winter—provided a set of credible instruments for identifying exogenous variation in educational attainment. At any subsequent age, children who had been born in a later quarter in the calendar year would tend to have higher completed educational attainment. Furthermore, these differences would be arguably exogenous because they were simply a consequence of the haphazard and idiosyncratic nature of birth timing. The authors applied their instruments in statistical models fitted to data from the 1960, 1970, and 1980 censuses of the population. They included in their analytic samples males who were 30–39 years of age, and those who were 40–49 years of age, at the time they completed the relevant census questionnaire.

The outcome variable in Angrist and Krueger's first-stage model was the number of years of schooling that each male had completed as of the date of the relevant census. And, as you might expect, the predictor variables at this stage were of two types: (a) exogenous variables that also served as covariates in the second-stage model, and (b) instruments. The first group included a vector of nine dichotomous variables to distinguish year of birth, and a vector of eight dichotomous variables that described region of residence. The instruments included three dichotomous variables that identified the quarter of birth, and the interactions of these quarter-of-birth predictors with the year-of-birth predictors.[30] To confirm their claim that the quarter of birth did indeed predict completed years of schooling, Angrist and Krueger demonstrated that, on average, men born in the first quarter of a calendar year had completed about one-tenth of a year less schooling by age-30 than men born in the last quarter of the calendar year. In their second-stage model, Angrist and Krueger used the exogenous variation in educational attainment that had been identified at the first stage to predict the logarithm of the men's weekly labor-market earnings. They found that, on average, each additional year of education had caused a 10% increase in average weekly earnings.

---

30. To demonstrate the robustness of their results, Angrist and Krueger present coefficients estimated from fitting first- and second-stage models with a variety of specifications.

Of course, the authors were careful to point out that their estimate was a local average treatment effect (LATE) that pertained only to males who wanted to leave school as soon as they were old enough to do so.

Angrist and Krueger faced two threats to the validity of their instruments. The first is that there may have been intrinsic differences in the unobserved abilities of males who were born in different quarters of the calendar year. If this were the case, then there could be a "third path" that connected quarter of birth directly to subsequent labor-market earnings, invalidating the use of quarter-of-birth indicators as instruments. The authors responded to this potential threat in the following way. First, they argued that quarter of birth should not affect the completed years of schooling of males who had college degrees because the ultimate educational decisions of this group would not have been constrained by compulsory schooling laws. Thus, for college graduates, there should not even be any "second path" that related quarter of birth to labor-market earnings *through* the impact on educational attainment. Consequently, evidence that quarter of birth predicted the labor-market earnings of college graduates would suggest the presence of a third path, directly relating quarter of birth to the ultimate earnings outcome. The presence of such a third path would invalidate the quarter-of-birth instruments.

Angrist and Krueger used their data on 40 to 49-year-old male college graduates in the 1980 Census data to test for the presence of the direct "third path." They achieved this by fitting a single OLS regression model in which they treated the ultimate outcome, logarithm of weekly earnings, as the outcome variable and all the first-stage covariates and instruments as predictors. In the annals of IVE, this is called the *reduced-form model*, and it corresponds to the statistical model that is obtained by collapsing the first-stage model into the second-stage model algebraically.[31] After fitting their reduced-form model, Angrist and Krueger conducted a test of the null hypothesis that the coefficients on the three quarter-of-birth dichotomous predictors were jointly equal to zero. They failed to reject this null hypothesis. They found the same result when they repeated the exercise using data on 40 to 49-year-old college graduates taken from the 1970 Census. This evidence led them to conclude that there was no direct path relating quarter of birth to the weekly earnings

---

31. Recall that the endogenous predictor both appears in the second-stage model (as the question predictor) and is the outcome of the first-stage model. Thus, you can take the right-hand side of the first-stage model and substitute it for the endogenous predictor in the second-stage model, and simplify the resulting combination algebraically to leave a "reduced-form" model in which the ultimate outcome is regressed directly on the instruments and covariates.

of *college graduates*. By analogy, they argued that this pattern would also hold true for males with lower completed years of schooling. This evidence and logic were central to Angrist and Krueger's argument that quarter-of-birth predictors satisfied the "no third path" requirement that was needed for an instrument to be legitimate.[32]

The second threat to the validity of Angrist and Krueger's instrumental-variables strategy is that their instruments predicted only a very small part of the total variation in the endogenous question predictor, years of completed schooling. As a result, their analyses could have been subject to the weak-instrument problem. As explained earlier, one problem with the implementation of IVE using weak instruments is that the results of fitting the second-stage model can be very sensitive to the presence in the point-cloud of even relatively few aberrant data points. Thus, IVE with weak instruments can produce substantially biased results, even when the analytic samples are very large (Bound, Jaeger, & Baker, 1995; Murray, 2006).

Angrist and Krueger's response to the weak-instrument threat was to check whether they did indeed have a problem. They conducted tests of the null hypothesis that the coefficients on the three quarter-of-birth dummy variables in their fitted first-stage model were jointly equal to zero. (Recall that this is the model in which the men's years of completed schooling is the outcome variable.) As reported in Table 1 of their 1991 paper, they were able to reject this null hypothesis when they fit the first-stage model to data on a sample of 30 to 39-year-old males ($F = 24.9$; $p <0.0001$) and to data from a sample of 40 to 49-year-old males ($F = 18.6$; $p <0.0001$), both samples taken from the 1980 Census. They presented these test results as evidence that their IV estimations did not suffer from a weak-instrument problem.[33]

---

32. Several studies published after the appearance of the Angrist and Krueger (1991) paper provide evidence that season of birth affects adult life outcomes through mechanisms other than via the effect of compulsory-schooling laws. See, for example, Bound and Jaeger (2000), and Buckles and Hungerman (2008).

33. Bound, Jaeger, and Baker (1995) argued that Angrist and Krueger's defense of their instruments was inadequate for two reasons. First, they did not find convincing Angrist and Krueger's defense of the "weak instrument" threat, pointing out that the values of the R^2 statistic from Angrist and Krueger's first-stage regressions were extraordinarily low. Second, Bound and his colleagues questioned whether the quarter-of-birth instruments that Angrist and Krueger used in their 1991 paper satisfy the "no third path" assumption.

Deviations from Cohort Trends

A third type of instrument that a number of scholars have used in educational policy research consists of estimates of deviations from smooth population trends. Caroline Hoxby's (2000) study of the causal impact of class size on student achievement in Connecticut schools provides a good example of the use of this type of instrument. Hoxby collected data on enrollment and class size, by grade level, for all elementary schools in Connecticut each year from 1974 through 1997. She also collected data on average student achievement, by grade, at the school level for the years 1992 to 1997 and by grade aggregated to the school district level from 1986 to 1997. She explained that it was not appropriate to use variation in class size across classrooms or schools at a single point in time to estimate the causal impact of class size on student achievement. The reason is that class sizes are influenced by the decisions of parents about the school attendance zone in which they choose to live and by the decisions of school administrators about the assignment of students to classes. One result of such decisions is that students in classes of different sizes may differ in unobserved ways that affect student achievement.

However, Hoxby argued that the availability of panel data on grade-level enrollments in individual schools over a 24-year period provided a solution to the endogenous class-size problem. She began by explaining that class size in any grade of a particular school depended on two things. The first were long-term and potentially endogenous school enrollment trends. The second were natural idiosyncrasies in birth timing that resulted in some school- and grade-specific enrollment cohorts being randomly larger or smaller than would be anticipated from the underlying smooth long-term trends. In other words, Hoxby argued that *deviations from the long-term trends* represented exogenous shocks in school-specific grade-level enrollments that could be used as a legitimate instrument for grade-level class size.

This line of reasoning led Hoxby to a three-phase estimation strategy. First, she fitted models that predicted the logarithm of grade-level enrollment in each school as a fourth-order polynomial function of year. These then were her models of the smooth long-term trends, by school. Second, she collected the residuals from each model, arguing that they represented the exogenous variation in the logarithm of enrollment for that school. Third, implementing her IVE, she used these residuals as instruments for the logarithm of class size in her first-stage model. The outcome in her second-stage model was a measure of average student achievement in each school and year. She found that the obtained residuals did indeed predict the logarithm of class size quite well at the first stage.[34] However, the exogenous portion of class size that was thereby carved out ended up having no causal impact on student achievement. She concluded that there was no causal relationship between class size and student achievement in her data. Hoxby defended her null finding by arguing that it was most likely that this idiosyncratic year-to-year variation in class size would be unlikely to lead teachers to change their instructional patterns in a manner that would affect student achievement.

The primary threat to the validity of Hoxby's choice of instrument is the possibility that her residual deviations from the smooth underlying enrollment trends were not simply a consequence of idiosyncrasies in the timing of births, but rather stemmed from purposeful actions by families that could also result in a "third path" that connected the values of the instrument to the ultimate levels of student achievement directly. For example, perhaps entrepreneurial parents who learned that their child was about to be placed in a large class could have transferred their child to another school in the same school district, moved to another school district, or sent their child to a private school. If the parents who responded in this way were those who also devoted a particularly large amount of time and resources at home to improving their child's achievement, these responses would create a direct third path that linked the enrollment deviations to children's achievement.

Hoxby presented four arguments in defense of her choice of instrument. First, she pointed out that the coefficients on the time predictors in her fourth-order polynomial enrollment model captured virtually all the smooth time trends, even the quite subtle ones. Consequently, it is highly likely that the residuals from these fitted curves (which served as her instrument) were indeed the results of idiosyncratic events. Second, she argued that even if the idiosyncratic variation did reflect the purposeful actions of a few families choosing one school over another, it is likely that the families would be choosing *among* public schools *in a particular district*. She then showed that the results of fitting her first- and second-stage models remained essentially the same when she refitted them on data that had been aggregated to the district level. Third, Hoxby refit the models from which she had derived her instrumental residuals, this time using data on the number of children in each district who were aged five on the school-entry date as her outcome variable, instead of the complete grade-level enrollment in the district. Replicate analyses using these

---

34. As reported in Table III (p. 1270) of Hoxby's (2000) paper, the *t*-statistics on the instrument in her first-stage regressions ranged in value from roughly 4 to 80, depending on the grade level and model specification.

new residuals as instruments produced the same results—no causal impact of class size on student achievement. The logic underlying this sensitivity analysis is that it removes any bias resulting from the actions of those parents who might have responded to large class sizes by moving to another school district (after the child was aged five) or by choosing a private school for their child. Fourth, Hoxby estimated the impact of class size on student achievement in her Connecticut sample using a second estimation strategy that was totally independent of her "residuals as instruments" strategy. This second strategy was similar to that used by Angrist and Lavy in the Maimonides' rule paper, which we described in Chapter 9. Hoxby found that this second set of estimates of the class-size effects on student achievement was virtually identical to the results that she had obtained using her first strategy. She argued that this supported her case that the threats to the validity of her first strategy were not compelling.

The Search Continues

The three types of instrumental variables that we have described in this section are among the most commonly used in the investigation of the causal impact of educational policies on academic outcomes. One reason is that they are relatively easy to understand and, through extensive use, they have acquired a considerable amount of face validity. The second reason is that, as we saw above, talented researchers have been able to present a variety of credible arguments to support the appropriateness of these types of instruments in particular settings. Indeed, defending the credibility of the instruments is usually the most difficult challenge in implementing an IVE strategy. The authors of each of the papers described in the previous sections went to great lengths to defend their instruments.

It is important to understand that the types of instruments described throughout this chapter are not the only ones that researchers have found useful. Indeed, creative researchers suggest new potential instrumental variables frequently, a few of which skeptical critics find compelling, and many not so compelling. And so, the search continues.

We have purposefully omitted from the discussion in this chapter two types of instruments that have been used very convincingly in many of the most important educational-policy studies of causal effects. These are instruments that describe the original assignment to experimental condition among participants in both random-assignment and natural experiments. In both cases, participants so assigned may contravene their assignments subsequently, thereby rendering their treatment status endogenous. However, because the original random assignment of participants to experimental conditions is known, it can be used as an instrument for carving out the exogenous variation in treatment take-up, despite the interference of the endogenous participant choices. This is a very powerful idea, because it is easy to argue persuasively that such instruments uphold the "no third path" assumption that has rendered other applications of IVE less than credible. We describe this use of *original random assignment as instrument* in the following chapter.

What to Read Next

The literature on instrumental-variables estimation is large and continues to grow. Angrist and Krueger's 2001 paper "Instrumental Variables and the Search for Identification: From Supply and Demand to Natural Experiments," provides a brief yet illuminating history of the development of the IVE approach, from its inception in research on agriculture to its growing use in research that capitalizes on the occurrence of natural experiments. Chapter 4 of Angrist and Pischke's *Mostly Harmless Econometrics* (2009) and Chapter 7 of Morgan and Winship's *Counterfactuals and Causal Inference* (2007) provide insightful descriptions of the strategy and cautions about its pitfalls.

11

Using IVE to Recover the Treatment Effect in a Quasi-Experiment

An important educational-policy issue in many developing countries is how to increase children's educational attainments efficiently. The conventional strategy has been to build and staff more public schools that either charge no fees or set fees well below those charged by private schools. However, concerns about costs and about the low quality of the public schools that typically serve children from low-income families have led some countries to try an alternative—namely, to provide families with financial aid to send their children to private schools. Colombia, for example, has pursued this policy option.

In 1991, the Colombian government introduced a program known by its acronym, PACES, which offered scholarships to students living in low-income neighborhoods to help pay for education at private secondary schools.[1] The goal of the PACES program, which ended in 1999, was to increase the educational attainments and skills of low-income students. The description of the program that we provide pertains to 1998, the date when data for an evaluation of the program were collected. In that year, the scholarships were worth about $200 annually, an amount that covered approximately 60% of the average annual tuition at participating private schools. About half of the nation's private secondary schools accepted the government-provided scholarships, and those that did not tended to be schools that charged relatively high tuitions and served primarily students from high-income families. Secondary school in Colombia begins

---

1. PACES is the acronym for Programa de Ampliación de Cobertura de la Educación Secundaria, which means Program to Increase Coverage of Secondary Education.

in the sixth grade and ends in the eleventh. Recipients of the PACES scholarships could renew them through eleventh grade so long as their academic progress was sufficient to merit promotion each year to the next grade.

The PACES program was administered by local governments, which covered 20% of the cost. The other 80% was covered by the central government. In many locales, including the capital city of Bogotá, demand for the secondary-school scholarships exceeded supply. This led local governments, including Bogotá's, to use lotteries to determine which children were offered scholarships. To be eligible for the government scholarship lottery in Bogotá, a child had to live in a designated low-income neighborhood, have attended a public primary school, and have been accepted at a private secondary school that participated in the PACES program.

The evaluators of the Colombia secondary-school voucher program, a group that included Joshua Angrist, Eric Bettinger, Erik Bloom, Elizabeth King, and Michael Kremer (2002), started out by addressing the following question: Did the *offer* of a PACES scholarship increase students' educational attainments? The evaluators hypothesized that there were several mechanisms through which this might be the case. First, some low-income families that wanted to send their child to a private secondary school could not have afforded to do so (at least for very long) in the absence of a scholarship. A second is that availability of a scholarship would allow some parents who might have sent their child to a private secondary school in any case to upgrade to a better (and more expensive) private school. A third is that the condition that renewal of the scholarship was contingent on promotion would induce some students to devote more attention to their studies than they otherwise would have.[2]

You, the careful reader, will recognize from Chapter 4 that you already know how to make use of information from a fair lottery to answer a research question about the impact of an offer of a scholarship from the PACES program. The lottery created two exogenously assigned groups: (a) a treatment group of participants who were offered a scholarship, and (b) a control group of participants who were not offered a scholarship. Using standard ordinary least-squares (OLS)-based regression methods on the sample of students who participated in the 1995 Bogotá lottery, the investigators found that the offer of a government-provided scholarship increased the probability that a student from a low-income family

---

2. The Angrist et al. (2002) paper explains how the authors used their hypotheses about the mechanisms underlying the program effects to inform their empirical work.

completed eighth grade within three years of starting secondary school by slightly more than 11 percentage points.[3] Obtaining this unbiased estimate of the causal impact of the offer was important to educational policymakers, who needed to decide whether the PACES scholarship program was a good use of scarce public resources.

The Notion of a "Quasi-Experiment"

Angrist and his colleagues also wanted to address a second research question: Does the *use* of financial aid to pay for secondary school increase the educational attainments of low-income students? There are two reasons why this second question differs from the first. One reason is that not all of the low-income families that won the lottery and were offered a government scholarship chose to use it. The second is that some families that lost out in the lottery were successful in finding financial aid from other sources. The challenge is to find a way to obtain an unbiased estimate of the answer to this second research question.

It is important to keep in mind that Angrist and his colleagues' second research question concerns the consequences of obtaining *and* making use of financial aid, not the consequences of attending a private school. The distinction is important because almost all students who participated in the PACES lottery, even those who were not awarded a PACES scholarship, enrolled in a private secondary school for grade 6. This is not surprising, given that a condition for eligibility for the PACES lottery was that students had to have been accepted by a private secondary school that participated in the PACES program. As mentioned earlier, some of the families that lost out in the PACES lottery were able to obtain financial aid from another source to help pay their child's private-school fees. Some families that lost out in the PACES lottery paid the private-school fees out of their own resources. However, many of these families were unable to pay the private-school fees in subsequent years and consequently their children left private school.

---

3. The estimates reported in the Angrist et al. (2002) paper range between 9 and 11 percentage points, depending on the covariates included in the statistical model. The figure that we report here comes from an OLS-fitted regression model in which the outcome was a dichotomous variable indicating whether a student had completed eighth grade by 1998, and the single predictor was a dichotomous variable that took on a value of 1 for students who were offered a government scholarship in the 1995 Bogotá lottery.

The challenge that Angrist and his colleagues faced was to find a way to obtain an asymptotically unbiased estimate of the causal impact of the use of financial aid on children's subsequent educational attainment when the *offer*—but not the *use*—of financial aid had been assigned randomly. In what follows, we reorient our account of the evaluation of the PACES scholarship program in Colombia to show how to answer this second research question. Rather than regard the PACES lottery in Bogotá as a randomized experiment designed to assess the causal impact of the offer of a government scholarship on subsequent educational attainment, we will regard it as a "flawed" (i.e., nonrandomized) experiment to assess the impact of the *use* of scholarship aid from any source. In other words, in our subsequent descriptions, the treatment of interest will be the use of scholarship aid from any source. Seen from this perspective, the assignment of participants to experimental conditions—that is, to a treatment group that made use of financial aid or to a control group that did not make use of financial aid—was tainted by self-selection. Thus, using the term we defined in Chapter 3, we will refer to the evaluation of the Colombia PACES program as a *quasi-experiment* to investigate the impact of the use of financial aid on educational attainment, rather than as a randomized experiment examining the impact of the offer of a PACES scholarship.

As we explained in Chapter 3, it was not so long ago that researchers tried to eliminate potential biases in their analyses of such quasi-experimental data by incorporating large numbers of covariates into their OLS regression analyses in the hope of "controlling away" the differences due to selection into the treatment and control groups. However, as we hope is now clear, this strategy is unlikely to be successful because students whose families took advantage of financial aid may have differed from those that did not in many unobserved ways. For instance, parents who made use of financial aid may have placed an especially high value on education, regardless of whether they were assigned a government-provided scholarship or not. Such a family value system may then have led to enhanced family support for the child's education and eventually to greater educational attainment, irrespective of any impact of the use of financial aid. Then, in naïve OLS analyses of the quasi-experimental data, investigators would have attributed these achievement differences spuriously to the effect of the use of financial aid unless all differences in relevant family values were controlled completely. Since many of the differences between the families that found and used financial aid and those that did not were unobserved, it is unlikely that the use of OLS methods, even including a rich set of covariates, would provide an unbiased estimate of the answer to the research question.

Using IVE to Estimate the Causal Impact of a Treatment
in a Quasi-Experiment

As we intimated in the previous chapter, instrumental-variables estimation (IVE) provides a powerful way to analyze such quasi-experimental data. The approach is simple: treat the original exogenous *offer* of a PACES scholarship as an instrument for the potentially endogenous question predictor, *use* of financial aid, and apply IVE to obtain an asymptotically unbiased estimate of the causal impact of use of financial aid on the ultimate outcome, educational attainment. The logic is also straightforward. First, the offer of a government-provided scholarship by fair lottery was clearly random and exogenous. It undoubtedly had an impact on the decision of at least some families to make use of financial aid to pay for a child's secondary-school education at a private school. In fact, we can confirm this relationship from the data themselves. Ninety-two percent of the students who were winners in the lottery made use of financial aid to pay the tuition at private secondary schools, compared to 24% of the losers in the lottery. So, the instrument and potentially endogenous question predictor are clearly related, providing the "first path" that is the initial important condition required for successful IVE. Second, the random receipt of a PACES scholarship is likely to affect a student's subsequent educational attainment only through its effect on the probability that a family made use of financial aid to pay for a child's tuition at a private secondary school. So, there is "no third path"—no *direct* impact of the random receipt of a PACES scholarship on subsequent educational attainment—as credible IVE also requires.

In what follows, we illustrate this new analytic strategy, using a subset of the data that Angrist and his colleagues used in their study of the PACES program. These data pertain to low-income students from the capital city, Bogotá, who were in fifth grade in 1995. For our outcome, we have chosen a measure of educational attainment, the dichotomous variable *FINISH8TH*, which takes on a value of 1 for students who had completed grade 8 by 1998, and a value of zero for those who had not. We present descriptive statistics on this outcome in Table 11.1. Notice that almost 70% of all children in our sample finished grade 8 on time. In the table, we also present descriptive statistics on our other two important variables. The first is *USE_FIN_AID*, a dichotomous variable that takes on a value of 1 for a child whose family used financial aid from any source to help pay for tuition at a private secondary school at any time during the years 1995–1998; 0, otherwise. We treat this variable as the potentially endogenous question predictor in our analyses of the quasi-experiment to evaluate the impact of financial-aid use on educational attainment.

Table 11.1 Sample means (and standard deviations, where appropriate) on the outcome variable, question predictor, instrument, and covariates, for a sample of students from Bogotá, Colombia, who participated in the 1995 lottery to obtain a government-funded private-school tuition scholarship, overall and by whether the child was offered financial aid

Variable	Sample Mean	Sample Mean		p-value (testing equality of pop. means)
		WON_LOTTRY = 1	WON_LOTTRY = 0	
	(n = 1,171)	(n = 592)	n = 571	
Outcome:				
FINISH8TH	0.681	0.736	0.625	0.000
Endogenous Question Predictor:				
USE_FIN_AID	0.582	0.915	0.240	0.000
Instrument:				
WON_LOTTRY	0.506	–	–	–
Covariates:				
BASE_AGE	12.00	11.97	12.04	0.42
	(1.35)	(1.35)	(1.34)	
MALE	0.505	0.505	0.504	0.98

Notice that about 58% of the students in our subsample did make use of financial aid for at least one year during the three-year period under study. The second variable listed is also dichotomous, and we have named it *WON_LOTTRY*. Under our new quasi-experimental conception of the Bogotá evaluation, this randomized offer of a government PACES scholarship is now an expression of the investigators' *intent* to provide financial aid, and is exogenous by randomization. *WON_LOTTRY* therefore has a value of 1 for students who won the lottery and were offered a government scholarship, and a value of 0 for students who lost out in the lottery. In our subsample of children from Bogotá who participated in the 1995 lottery, almost 51% of participants were assigned randomly to receive an offer of a government scholarship. Finally, in Table 11.1, we present parallel descriptive statistics on two other variables measured at baseline: (a) *BASE_AGE*, which measures the child's age (in years) on the date of the lottery, and (b) *MALE*, a dichotomous indicator that takes on a value of 1 for a male child, 0 for a female. We treat *BASE_AGE* and *MALE* as covariates in our instrumental-variables analysis, using the strategies described in the previous chapter to improve the precision of our estimates.

In the remaining columns of Table 11.1, we provide descriptive statistics on outcome *FINISH8TH*, potentially endogenous question predictor, *USE_FIN_AID*, and covariates *BASE_AGE* and *MALE* for the subsample of children who were offered a PACES scholarship (*WON_LOTTRY* = 1), and for the subsample of children who were not ($WON\_LOTTRY = 0$). We have also added a final column that contains the p-value from a t-test of the null hypothesis that the population means of each variable do not differ between those children who received the offer of a PACES scholarship and those who did not. Notice the interesting similarities and differences between the two groups, which ultimately drive the success of our instrumental-variables estimation. For instance, on average, age on the lottery date is the same in the two groups at baseline, as is the percentage of male students, as you would expect because the groups were formed by the random assignment of a tuition offer. After three years, however, there is about an 11 percentage point difference favoring the group that was offered PACES scholarships in the percentage of students who had completed grade 8. Notice that there are also statistically significant differences in the average value of the potentially endogenous question predictor, USE_FIN_AID, between the two groups. As mentioned earlier, almost 92% of the students who were offered a government scholarship used financial aid to pay private-school fees, whereas only 24% of students who lost out in the lottery did so. This confirms, as we suspected, that there is a strong relationship between our potential instrument, WON_LOTTRY, and our suspect and potentially endogenous question predictor, USE_FIN_AID. Therefore, we have met the first condition for a credible instrument.

Under our new quasi-experimental framework for investigating the impact of use of financial aid on students' educational attainment, variation in our question predictor, USE_FIN_AID, is potentially endogenous. Clearly, the choice of whether to use financial aid (from any source) depends not only on the lottery outcome but also on the many unseen resources, needs, and objectives of the family, each of which may also impact the child's subsequent educational attainment. Consequently, if we were to use OLS regression analysis to investigate the relationship between outcome $FINISH8TH$ and question predictor USE_FIN_AID (controlling for $BASE\_AGE$ and $MALE$), we would undoubtedly end up with a biased estimate of any causal effect. Instead, we have used the two-stage least-squares (2SLS) approach to obtain an IV estimate of the relationship, using the exogenous assignment of *intent to treat*, represented by WON_LOTTRY, as our instrument. Our first- and second-stage statistical models follow the pattern that we established in the previous chapter, as follows:

$$1^{st} : USE\_FIN\_AID_i = \alpha_0 + \alpha_1 WON\_LOTTRY_i + \alpha_2 BASE\_AGE_i$$
$$+ \alpha_3 MALE_i + \delta_i$$
$$2^{nd} : FINISH8TH_i = \beta_0 + \beta_1 USE\_\widehat{FIN}\_AID_i + \beta_2 BASE\_AGE_i$$
$$+ \beta_3 MALE_i + \varepsilon_i$$

$$(11.1)$$

with the usual notation and assumptions. We have written these models to reflect that, under 2SLS, the predicted values of potentially endogenous question predictor *USE_FIN_AID* are obtained at the first stage and used in place of the corresponding observed values at the second stage (with appropriate corrections to the standard errors).[4] We have also followed our own earlier advice and included covariates, *BASE_AGE* and *MALE*, in both the first- and second-stage models. Finally, for pedagogical clarity, we have again adopted the simple linear-probability specification for the first- and second-stage models.

We provide estimates, corrected standard errors, and approximate *p*-values for the model parameters, at both stages, in the upper and lower panels of Table 11.2. In addition, in the two right-hand columns of the lower panel, we have included estimates of corresponding parameters from a naïve OLS regression analysis of *FINISH8TH* on the potentially endogenous question predictor *USE_FIN_AID*, again controlling for *BASE_AGE* and *MALE*, for comparison.[5] Much of the table confirms what we already suspected from examining the descriptive statistics in Table 11.2.

---

4. As we noted in the previous chapter, if we had adopted a simultaneous-equations modeling (SEM) approach to conducting this IVE, we would have specified the models slightly differently, retaining *USE_FIN_AID* as the question predictor at the second stage, but permitting the first- and second-stage residuals, δ and ε, to covary in the population.

5. In our quasi-experimental example, the endogenous question predictor and instrument are both dichotomous. Under this condition, our original method-of-moments IV estimator reduces to a conceptually interesting form. Ignoring the effects of additional covariates, Equation 10.10 states that the population slope of the regression of outcome Y on potentially endogenous predictor X is a ratio of population covariances with instrument, I:

$$\beta_{YX} = \frac{\sigma_{YI}}{\sigma_{XI}}$$

Because instrument I is a dichotomy—with values of 1 and 0, say—this ratio of covariances reduces to a ratio of *differences in means*, conditional on the values of I:

$$\beta_{YX} = \frac{\mu_{Y|I=1} - \mu_{Y|I=0}}{\mu_{X|I=1} - \mu_{X|I=0}}$$

Because endogenous predictor X is a dichotomy, its averages are *proportions*, and so the denominator can be further simplified:

$$\beta_{YX} = \frac{\mu_{Y|I=1} - \mu_{Y|I=0}}{p(X=1|I=1) - p(X=1|I=0)}$$

This result has an interesting interpretation. First, the numerator is the difference in outcome means between subpopulations defined by the values of the instrument, 1 and 0. In our Colombia tuition-voucher example, for instance, it is the difference in outcome means between the subpopulation that received an offer of a scholarship and the subpopulation that did not. It is the population effect of *intent to treat* (ITT). Second, the denominator is the difference between subpopulations for whom $I = 1$ and $I = 0$,

Table 11.2 Instrumental-variables (2SLS) and naïve OLS estimates of the impact of use of financial aid on on-time graduation from grade 8, among low-income students from Bogotá, controlling for student gender and baseline age

First Stage: Outcome = USE_FIN_AID

	Parameter Estimate	Standard Error
INTERCEPT	0.433***	0.095
Instrument:		
WON_LOTTRY	**0.675*****	0.021
Covariates:		
BASE_AGE	−0.015⁻	0.008
MALE	−0.020	0.021
R^2 Statistic	0.471	

Second Stage: Outcome = FINISH8TH

	IV Estimates		Naïve OLS Estimates	
	Parameter Estimate	Standard Error	Parameter Estimate	Standard Error
INTERCEPT	1.378***	0.123	1.410**	0.121
Endogenous Question Predictor:				
$\overline{USE\_FIN\_AID}$	**0.159*****,†	0.039	0.121***	0.027
Covariates:				
BASE_AGE	−0.062***	0.010	−0.063***,†	0.010
MALE	−0.085**	0.027	−0.085**	0.026
R^2 Statistic	0.062		0.064	

~p <0.10; *p <0.05; **p <0.01; ***p <0.001
†One-sided test.

in the *proportions of participants* for whom the endogenous predictor takes on a value of 1. In our Colombia tuition-voucher example, this is the difference between the "offer" and "no-offer" groups in the *proportion* of children who made use of financial aid from any source. Combining these interpretations, we conclude that an asymptotically unbiased estimate of the effect of using financial aid on educational attainment can be obtained by rescaling the ITT estimate, using the difference in the sample proportion of children who made use of financial aid, in each of the original randomized offer and no-offer groups. (This is called a *Wald estimator*, after the eminent statistician, Abraham Wald.) This conclusion continues to hold when additional exogenous covariates are included, except that the effects of the new covariates must be partialed from the conditional averages being divided above. Including the additional covariates in the first and second stages of the 2SLS procedure achieves the conditioning automatically.

From the upper panel, at the first stage, we can examine the all-important first path that links instrument *WON_LOTTRY* to the potentially endogenous question predictor, *USE_FIN_AID*. Their relationship is strong and statistically significant (p <0.001), and the fitted probability that a child will use a scholarship is almost 68 percentage points higher among those who received the offer of a PACES government scholarship than among those who did not. Thus, *WON_LOTTRY* is confirmed as a strong instrument.[6] Notice, also, that covariate *BASE_AGE* has a negative relationship (p <0.10) with the outcome variable, indicating that older children were somewhat less likely to make use of financial aid than were those who were relatively young on the date of the lottery.

At the second stage (lower panel), we can examine the second path linking the predicted values of the potentially endogenous question predictor, *USE_FIN_AID*, to children's subsequent educational attainment. The results of the (biased) naïve OLS regression analysis suggest that the children whose families made use of financial aid were 12 percentage points more likely to have graduated from secondary school by 1998 than those who did not make use of a scholarship. In contrast, our IV estimate is almost 16 percentage points, almost one-third larger than the biased OLS estimate. Notice that both covariates, *BASE_AGE* and *MALE*, play a statistically significant role at the second stage, reducing residual variance and increasing statistical power.

Further Insight into the IVE (LATE) Estimate, in the Context of Quasi-Experimental Data

In the Venn diagrams of our previous chapter, we pointed out that although IVE does indeed provide an asymptotically unbiased estimate of the impact of a question predictor on an outcome, it does so only within the "overlap"—that is, the covariation—of the instrument and question predictor. Consequently, IV estimates capitalize only on variation in the question predictor that "falls within" or is "sensitive to" variation in the instrument. Thus, we argued that an estimate of a treatment effect obtained by IV methods should be regarded as an estimated *local average treatment effect*, or LATE. From a graphical perspective, this is not difficult to comprehend, as we can imagine ratios of covariances between corresponding variables being obtained within ellipses of covariation carved

---

6. The *F*-statistic associated with instrument, *WON_LOTTRY*, in the first-stage equation is very large indeed, with a value of 1,033.

out by the instrument. However, it is a little more difficult to understand what it means to say that the interpretation is credible within a corner of the real world in which participants' values of the question predictor are sensitive to or covary with their values of the instrument. The empirical situation that is the focus of this chapter, in which we use randomly assigned intent to treat as an instrument for potentially endogenous entry into an actual treatment, leads to new insight into the practical interpretation of the LATE estimate.

In a quasi-experiment like the one we have described here, when the investigator's original and randomly assigned intent-to-treat is revealed to the members of a population, there are several ways that each may respond. Some families will comply with the investigator's intent and end up in the designated treatment or control group. Others may go their own way, insisting on choosing the experimental condition they prefer, irrespective of the group to which they were assigned by the lottery. It serves us well at this point to define, label, and clarify these possible responses. Angrist, Imbens, and Rubin (1996) provide a carefully crafted framework for thinking about possible *compliance styles* that such participants in an experiment may exhibit.[7] In Figure 11.1, we present a simplified version of this framework. In so doing, we abstract from some of the details of the way the PACES scholarship program actually worked.

Consider a situation in which researchers actually knew the population of students in Colombia who were eligible for PACES scholarships in 1995 and who applied for these scholarships. Members of this population would have been students who lived in designated low-income neighborhoods, who were attending the fifth grade in a public elementary school, who had been accepted at a private secondary school that participated in the PACES scholarship program, and who applied for a PACES scholarship. We will call this the population of eligible volunteers. Now assume that all of the students in this population were assigned randomly either to a group that was offered PACES scholarships or to a group that was not. Next, assume that a random sample of students was chosen from the population of eligible volunteers. In Figure 11.1, we display the set of responses that members of the research sample might have elicited. Notice that in setting up and discussing this framework, we have stated that the members of the *population* of eligible volunteers *could have been* first designated as either potential "PACES scholarship" recipients or as potential "non-PACES scholarship" students before a random sample of

---

7. Our description of the use of IVE to identify causal effects within the context of Rubin's causal model draws heavily on the lucid description provided by Gennetian and her colleagues in Chapter 3 of the 2005 book edited by Howard Bloom.

Population Member Assigned to:

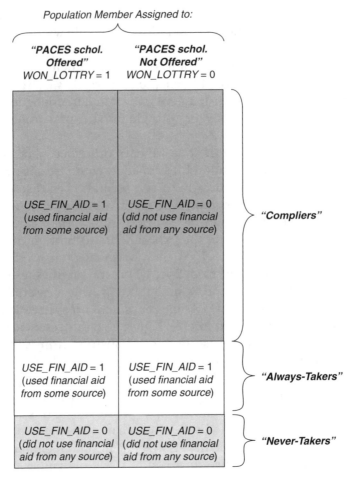

Figure 11.1 Compliance styles in the population of students from Bogotá, by offer of a government private-school tuition voucher, *WON_LOTTRY* (1 = scholarship voucher offered; 0 = no scholarship voucher offered), and ultimate use of financial aid, *USE_FIN_AID* (1 = used; 0 = did not use).

children was actually drawn from the population of eligible volunteers. The reason we did this is because, in what follows, we make an argument about this population, not about the sample.[8]

---

8. The reason we abstract from the details of the administration of the 1995 PACES lottery in Bogotá in presenting this framework is that we want to distinguish the population from the research sample. This distinction is not present in the Bogotá case because all members of the population of eligible volunteers in Bogotá participated in that PACES lottery.

At the top of the figure, labeling its columns, we designate population members' actual (random) assignment to the intent-to-treat conditions: The first column represents the subpopulation of students who were randomly offered a PACES scholarship (*WON_LOTTRY* = 1), the second column represents the sub population who were not (*WON_LOTTRY* = 0). In our quasi-experiment, members of each of these two subpopulations could then make an individual decision either to accept the status to which he or she was assigned or not. For the subpopulation of children who were offered PACES scholarships, accepting their status meant that they chose to use financial aid (so, *USE_FIN_AID* = 1). For the subpopulation of children who were not offered PACES scholarships, accepting their status means that they did not make use of financial aid from any source (so, *USE_FIN_AID* = 0). It is this decision about whether to make use of financial aid or not that we regard as the treatment in our quasi-experiment. Bearing these choices in mind, we can classify each subpopulation member as one of three mutually exclusive groups, distinguished by their compliance or their lack of compliance with the intent of the lottery. We label members of these three compliance styles as (a) *compliers*, (b) *always-takers*, and (c) *never-takers*. Any population of experimental subjects may contain members of each of these classes, although in potentially different (and unknown) proportions. Their presence in the two offered-scholarship and not-offered-scholarship subpopulations is represented by the three cells in each of the two columns we have displayed.

In constructing the figure, we have established the heights of the respective cells to reflect hypothetical proportions of each kind of participant that might be anticipated reasonably to occur in the population, and, of course, these proportions are the same in both the *WON_LOTTRY* = 1 and *WON_LOTTRY* = 0 subpopulations because, in our thought experiment, participants in the population were assigned randomly to these two conditions. We have chosen to make the largest proportion of participants into compliers, but there are also small proportions of always-takers and never-takers. In a practical quasi-experiment, of course, these exact population proportions are hidden from the investigator's view, and are determined by unknown characteristics of the population members themselves. Nonetheless, the act of thinking through these alternatives in the framework provided by Angrist, Imbens, and Rubin (1996) helps us understand exactly how the hidden choices made by participants can impact potential estimates of treatment impact. This, in turn, helps us to understand more deeply the consequences of IVE and the nature of the LATE estimator.

Now, let's examine the three kinds of compliance style that participants may possess in any experimental design. First, there are the compliers.

In designing the research, we hope that there are a lot of these. Compliers are willing to have their behavior determined by the outcomes of the lottery, regardless of the particular experimental condition to which they were assigned. Complying families who were assigned a PACES scholarship use financial aid to help pay their children's school fees at a private secondary school; complying families who were not assigned a PACES scholarship do not make use of financial aid from any source. The last two compliance styles in the Angrist, Imbens, and Rubin framework, labeled always-takers and never-takers, are also present potentially in empirical research. Always-takers are families who will find and make use of financial aid to pay private-school fees regardless of whether they had been assigned a PACES government scholarship. Never-takers are their mirror image—they will not make use of financial aid to pay children's fees at a private secondary school under any circumstances.[9]

What do these three categories of potential compliance style teach us about the interpretation of the instrumental-variables estimation of a LATE? They have no consequence if you are only interested in estimating and interpreting the causal effect of intent to treat (that is, the impact of the offer of a PACES scholarship). However, they are relevant if you want to know the impact on educational attainment of actually making use of financial aid to pay private-school fees. The first thing to keep firmly in mind is that, in any quasi-experiment, membership in these compliance classes is hidden from view. All we know for sure is what we can observe. In the case of the Bogotá study, this is whether the participant was offered a PACES scholarship, and whether that participant then made use of financial aid from any source. Notice that this information is not sufficient to enable us to distinguish the compliance style of the family. Among families that were assigned to the offer of a PACES scholarship, both those that were compliers and those that were always-takers actually make

---

9. Gennetian et al. (2005) also describe a fourth potential group of population members, whom they call *defiers*. These are participants whose experimental assignment induces them to do *exactly the opposite* of what the investigator intends—they are contrarians. Assigning them a PACES scholarship induces them *not* to use any scholarship; denying them a government scholarship induces them to find a scholarship from another source for their child. Such behavior is usually not anticipated in most experiments because it implies that these participants are *consistently* contrary—that they will always do the opposite of what the investigator asks them to do. To classify families as defiers, we must be convinced that they simply choose to do the opposite of their intent-to-treat assignment. Although logic demands the existence of this fourth class, in practice we believe that it is often an empty set, and so we have eliminated it from our argument here. This makes our presentation consistent with the framework presented by Angrist, Imbens, and Rubin (1996). These authors describe the "no defiers" assumption as the "monotonicity" assumption.

use of financial aid to pay fees at a private secondary school. So, we cannot distinguish between these two groups by observing their actions. Yet, the two groups may differ in unobserved ways—the latter group being prepared to use whatever effort is necessary to find financial aid from an alternative source if they lose out in the lottery for the government scholarships. Similarly, among families that were not assigned a government scholarship, neither the compliers nor the never-takers make use of financial aid to pay private secondary-school fees, and these groups cannot be distinguished on the basis of their overt actions. Yet again, these two groups may differ. The first are families that would like to make use of financial aid, but, after losing out in the PACES lottery, are unable to find aid from another source. The second are families that have decided not to make use of financial aid to pay private secondary-school fees under any circumstances.

You can imagine how problematic such differences in compliance style can be, if you are interested in the unbiased estimation of the causal impact of use of financial aid on students' educational attainment. If you were to form two contrasting groups naïvely, those children whose parents made use of financial aid and those children whose parents did not use financial aid, and compare the children's subsequent average educational attainment, you would be on shaky ground in claiming that any difference detected was due solely to the causal impact of financial aid. Why? Because both the group that made use of financial aid, and the group that did not, contain a self-selected and unknown mixture of participants of different compliance styles, each differing in unobserved ways. Among members of the group that made use of financial aid, some families (the compliers) would have done so because they were complying with their favorable outcome in the lottery. Others (the always-takers) would have done so because they searched for and found financial aid from another source after losing out in the lottery. Similarly, some members of the group that did not make use of financial aid (the compliers) let the unfavorable outcome of the lottery dictate their behavior. Others (the never-takers) would not have made use of financial aid under any circumstances, even if they had been offered it. Consequently, comparisons of average educational attainments of the group that made use of financial aid and the group that did not would be polluted potentially by the unseen personal choices of families with different motivations (and perhaps differences in their ability to support their children's efforts to succeed in secondary school).

In this context, it is interesting to ask: Exactly what comparison is being estimated by the execution of the IVE using the PACES data that we described earlier in this chapter? Or, more to the point perhaps, is the behavior of only some—and not all—of the compliance groups captured in an IV estimate of the LATE? The answer is straightforward, and is rooted in our initial conceptualization of the IV estimator as capitalizing only on variation in the question predictor that is sensitive to variation in the instrument. In fact, in our quasi-experimental evaluation of the effect of financial aid on subsequent educational attainment among children in Bogotá, our IV estimate summarizes only the behavior of the compliers— the families for which the outcome of the lottery affected their decision regarding their use of financial aid to pay private secondary-school fees. In other words, among the compliers, those families that were awarded a PACES scholarship in the lottery used the offered financial aid, and those that lost out in the lottery did not make use of financial aid from any source. The values of the outcome and the question predictor for any always-takers and never-takers present in the population do not affect the value of the LATE estimate that has been obtained by IVE.[10] Our conclusion is that, in a quasi-experiment, when self-selection into experimental conditions has intervened between the random assignment of intent to treat and the actual experience of experimental treatment (in our example, using or not using financial aid to pay private secondary-school fees), it is the responses of the unseen class of compliers that determine the magnitude and direction of the IV estimate.

Using IVE to Resolve "Fuzziness" in a Regression-Discontinuity Design

What strategies are effective in increasing the skills of students who lag behind their classmates? One policy that many schools have tried is to provide extra instruction to those who need it, either after the regular school day is finished or during the school vacation period. Another common, and quite controversial, policy is to mandate that students who do not meet achievement benchmarks be retained in the same grade for another school year. Recall from Chapter 8 that the Chicago Public Schools (CPS) introduced a policy, in 1996, that included elements of both of these remediation strategies. First, the district examined the results of the standardized reading and mathematics tests that students in

---

10. Angrist, Imbens, and Rubin (1996) prove this statement. A critical assumption underlying the interpretation of the IV estimator as the treatment effect for compliers is that the treatment effect for always-takers must not be influenced by the outcome of the random assignment—that is, by whether always-takers were assigned to the treatment or to the control group. The same applies to never-takers.

grade 3 took at the end of the school year.[11] It then mandated that all third-grade students whose scores fell below a cut-off score of 2.8 grade equivalents on the reading or mathematics test had to attend a six-week summer school that focused on building skills in these subjects. The summer school attendees then retook the achievement tests at the end of the summer instructional period. The policy specified that those students who then met the 2.8 grade equivalents benchmarks were promoted to fourth grade, and those who did not meet these benchmarks were retained in the third grade for another year. All students were tested in reading a year later.

The CPS policy was based on a sensible theory of action. The notion was that the policy would provide a significant amount of extra instruction in core subjects for lagging students. Summer school classes were small, typically with fewer than 15 students. For the summer session, principals hand-picked teachers whom they thought would be effective in teaching those students in need of remediation. All teachers were told to follow a highly structured curriculum designed to emphasize mastery of basic skills. The students had incentives to pay attention because their promotion to the following grade was contingent on their achieving scores of at least 2.8 grade equivalents on the end-of-summer reading and mathematics achievement tests.

One of the first steps that researchers Brian Jacob and Lars Lefgren (2004) undertook to evaluate whether it would be possible to conduct a strong evaluation of the consequences of the CPS policy was to examine whether the assignment rules specified in the policy had actually been followed. They did this by estimating—on the end-of-school-year reading examination that was used to determine which children would be assigned to attend summer school—the percentage of students obtaining each possible grade equivalent score who actually *attended* summer school. They then plotted this percentage versus the grade-equivalent reading score (centered to have a value of zero at the cut-off score of 2.8 grade equivalents).[12] In Figure 11.2, which is a reproduction of Figure 2 from Jacob and Lefgren's paper, we present the resulting graph. It shows that the rules for assigning participants were obeyed fairly well, but not perfectly. About 90% of the students who scored below the exogenously determined cut-off score of 2.8 grade equivalents attended the mandatory

---

11. As we discuss in Chapter 13, the policy pertained to students in grade 6 as well as to those in grade 3. To simplify the description of the policy, we focus here on the students in grade 3.
12. Students were much more likely to fail the reading than the mathematics achievement test. This led the investigators to focus their analysis on the former.

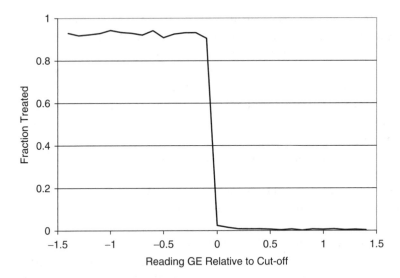

Figure 11.2 The relationship between the June reading scores (centered at the cut-off) for Chicago Public-School (CPS) students in grades 3 and 6 and the sample probability of attending summer school. Reproduced with permission from Figure 2, Jacob and Lefgren, 2004, p. 230.

summer school as the policy specified they should, and only a very small percentage of students scoring above the cut-off score did so. This good, but less than perfect, take-up of the summer program by participants meant that the cut-off score of 2.8 grade equivalents provided what methodologists refer to as a *fuzzy discontinuity*, dividing students into treatment and control groups well, but not perfectly, as a *sharp discontinuity* would have done.

If compliance with the policy mandate had been perfect, Jacob and Lefgren could have obtained an unbiased estimate of the impact of summer school attendance on reading scores one year later by fitting the *regression discontinuity* (RD) regression model specified in Equation 11.2 using OLS:[13]

$$READ_{i,t+1} = \beta_0 + \beta_1(READ_{i,t} - 2.8) + \beta_2(SUMMER_i) + \gamma'X + \varepsilon_i \quad (11.2)$$

where $SUMMER_i$ is a dichotomous variable that takes on a value of 1 if the ith child attended summer school (0, otherwise); predictor $READ_{i,t}$ represents the ith student's score on the standardized reading test that was taken

---

13. We have simplified the author's model specification for pedagogic purposes.

at the end of third grade and used as the forcing variable in the *RD* design; outcome $READ_{i,t+1}$ is the student's score on the standardized reading test taken one year later; X is a vector of exogenous time-invariant student characteristics; and residual ε_i is the error term.[14] The key point to understand is that if compliance with the assignment policy had been perfect, the dichotomous variable $SUMMER_i$ would have had the same value for every student as the exogenous variable $BELOW_i$, which we define as taking on a value of 1 for every student whose score on the end-of-third-grade reading examination $READ_{i,t}$ was less than 2.8 (0, otherwise). Had compliance with the CPS remediation policy been perfect, the estimate of β_2 would have provided an unbiased estimate of the impact of summer school attendance on the subsequent reading scores of children whose initial reading score $READ_{i,t}$ was very close to the cut-off score of 2.8 grade equivalents.

Since compliance with the policy mandate was not perfect, Jacob and Lefgren realized that simply fitting Equation 11.2 by OLS methods would result in a biased estimate of the causal impact of summer school attendance. The values of question predictor *SUMMER* were not assigned entirely exogenously. Although most students had complied with their assignment, not all had. Some students with reading scores above the cut-off actually participated in summer school, and some students with scores below the cut-off did not. It is likely that students who did not comply with their assignment had unobserved abilities and motivation that not only resulted in their crossing over, but also influenced their reading-achievement scores a year later. Thus, the endogeneity of the actual assignment of students to the treatment group (*SUMMER* = 1) meant that fitting Equation 11.2 by OLS regression methods would result in a biased estimate of the program effect.

Fortunately, we know that the solution to this problem is simple now that we understand an original exogenous assignment to an experimental condition can serve as a credible instrument for the potentially endogenous take-up of that treatment. We simply combine our interest in fitting the statistical model in Equation 11.2 with what we have learned about the application of IVE earlier in this chapter. We see from Figure 11.2 that exogenous assignment to experimental condition was indeed a strong predictor of the actual take-up of program—most of the students did what

---

14. In formal analyses, we would need to specify an error covariance structure that accounted for the clustering of students within schools.

they were told.[15] Thus, the potential instrument predicts the endogenous predictor strongly, as required. Second, it was unlikely that exogenous assignment to the program would affect reading achievement a year later for those immediately on either side of the cut-off, except through the provision of the summer program. Thus, there was no "third path." So, Jacob and Lefgren treated Equation 11.2 as the second stage of a two-stage model in which the first-stage model predicted enrollment in the *SUMMER* program by the exogenous RD assignment, as follows:

$$SUMMER_i = \alpha_0 + \alpha_1(READ_{i,t} - 2.8) + \alpha_2 BELOW_i + \boldsymbol{\varphi}'\boldsymbol{X} + \delta_i \quad (11.3)$$

where, as stated earlier, *BELOW* is a dichotomous instrument that describes whether the student was assigned exogenously to summer school (= 1), or not (= 0), and δ is a first-stage residual.[16]

Jacob and Lefgren used the 2SLS strategy to estimate the parameters of these two models and obtained IV estimates of the unbiased effect of the remediation policy on reading achievement one year later. They found that the combination of summer school and retention-in-grade for students whose end-of-school-year scores did not meet benchmarks had a positive impact on students' subsequent achievement. The magnitude of the impact was approximately equal to 15% of third-graders' average annual learning gain.

As Jacob and Lefgren emphasize, because this evaluation has an RD design, their result pertains only to students whose scores on the end-of-third-grade reading test fell just above or just below the cut-off, as these are the only students who were arguably equal in expectation prior to treatment. In other words, unless one is willing to make the heroic assumption that the policy would have the same effect for all students at every point on the reading scale, it is not appropriate to conclude from Jacob and Lefgren's research how the policy would have affected students whose end-of-third-grade scores were way below the 2.8 grade equivalents cut-off, or the consequence of extending the policy to higher-achieving students. Despite this limitation, the results are important because a key focus of the CPS policy was indeed to improve the skills of students whose scores fell close to the cut-off.

---

15. Jacob and Lefgren (2004) explain that Figure 2 in their paper (which is reproduced as Figure 11.2 here) is based on data pertaining to CPS students in grade 6 as well as those in grade 3. In a private communication, Brian Jacob told us that the relationship displayed in Figure 11.2 is virtually identical for students in the two grades.
16. Again, in formal analyses, we would specify an error covariance structure that accounted for the clustering of students within schools.

What to Read Next

To follow up on this topic, we recommend that you read Chapter 3 of *Learning More from Social Experiments*, a book edited by Howard Bloom (2005). In this chapter, Lisa Gennetian and her colleagues provide many of the technical details that support the arguments we have made in this chapter. They also provide references to many other relevant technical papers.

12

Dealing with Bias in Treatment Effects Estimated from Nonexperimental Data

In 1982, the sociologist James Coleman and two colleagues published an influential book, *High School Achievement: Public, Catholic, and Private Schools Compared*, the theme of which was that Catholic high schools in the United States were more effective than public high schools in educating students. This finding received massive media attention and was used to support the Reagan administration's proposal to provide tuition tax credits to families that wanted to send their children to non-public schools.

Critics were quick to challenge the research methodology that Coleman and his colleagues had employed to reach their conclusions.[1] They pointed out that the so-called Catholic-school advantage might easily stem, not from the relative effectiveness of Catholic schools, but from unobserved differences between the students whose parents chose to send them to Catholic schools and those whose parents chose to send them to public schools. The logic of this argument was that parents who cared deeply about the quality of their children's education may have been especially likely to pay the tuition required to send their children to Catholic schools. These same parents may also have been especially likely to try to enhance their children's skills at home, for example, by emphasizing the importance of reading, by monitoring their television watching, and by checking that their homework was completed. As a result, the average academic achievement of children attending Catholic schools could be greater than that of children attending public high schools even if the two types of

---

1. See, for example, Goldberger and Cain (1982).

schools were equally effective. In other words, the *choices* that families made in selecting Catholic school for their children may have deceived the researchers into overestimating the impact of the Catholic school "treatment." Methodologists refer to this as the *selection-bias* problem. As we have noted throughout our book, you face this problem when you evaluate any program in which participants or their advocates can choose the treatment conditions they will experience.

Coleman and his colleagues recognized that they faced the selection-bias problem, and responded by using a fix-up strategy that was conventional at that time. In their work, they had used multiple regression analysis to model the relationship between students' ultimate academic achievement and a dichotomous question predictor that distinguished between the Catholic- and public-school treatments. To this basic model, they added carefully selected covariates—representing the parents' socioeconomic status and other background characteristics—in an attempt to control away important pre existing differences between the Catholic and public high-school students and their families. Critics argued that this strategy was inadequate because one could never be sure that the full spectrum of underlying unobserved differences has been taken into account fully by the particular control predictors included, no matter how well chosen.

Of course, if Coleman and his colleagues had possessed a suitable instrument—an exogenous variable that predicted entry into Catholic school, and through it student achievement, all without the presence of an offending "third path"—they would have been able to solve their selection-bias problem. As explained in Chapters 10 and 11, they could have used instrumental-variables estimation (IVE) to obtain an asymptotically unbiased estimate of the size of the "Catholic-school advantage."[2] Our point is that, if you have a viable instrument, you simply do not need the methods that we are about to describe in this chapter. Without a viable instrument, though, all you can do is include covariates in your analysis in order to try to control for any extant differences among children who attended public or Catholic school, as Coleman attempted. But, no matter which covariates you decide to include, it will always be dangerous to draw causal conclusions from analyses of observational data. The reason is that you can only eliminate the bias due to the observables you

---

2. Some analysts have suggested that a family's religious affiliation (Evans & Schwab, 1995) and the distance between a family's residence and the nearest Catholic school (Neal, 1997) could serve as instrumental variables. However, Altonji and his colleagues (2005b) present evidence that these variables are not legitimate instruments in existing datasets.

include (which were primarily measures of family socioeconomic status, in Coleman's case).[3]

In recent years, approaches for incorporating sensible covariates into statistical models in order to remove *observed bias* from estimates of treatment effects, using observational data, have expanded dramatically. They now include new applications of *stratification* and *propensity score estimation*, in addition to the method of *direct control for covariates by regression analysis* that Coleman and his colleagues implemented. In this chapter, we describe these three approaches, point out the links among them, and explain how they differ in implementation and assumption.

We stress throughout the chapter that the credibility of all three strategies rests on the critical assumption of *unconfoundedness*. This is the assumption, laid out with clarity by Donald Rubin (1990), that once we have controlled for an explicit set of observed covariates, we can regard treatment assignment as exogenous. This may sound as though we are defining the problem away, but it is a point that Rubin has repeatedly emphasized, even in his earliest work (Rubin, 1974), and it serves as a stern warning. The methods that we describe in this chapter—despite their sophistication—are not magic. They are no better than the particular covariates they incorporate. If your theory is good, your knowledge of the selection process strong, and your covariates capture the selection process well, then you can certainly improve your estimation of causal effects with these methods. On the other hand, if any of these conditions does not hold, you are building a house on sand and it will not remain standing no matter how sophisticated its construction.

---

3. You might argue that you could keep piling additional covariates into the model in order to "whittle down" any bias present in the estimated Catholic-school advantage. However, there is a problem with this strategy—apart from the fact that adding each covariate costs an additional degree of freedom and leads to an accumulation of Type I error. As you add each new covariate, it can only predict that part of the variation in the outcome *that has not yet already been predicted by all the other covariates*. This means that the outcome variation available nominally for subsequent prediction by new covariates declines as the process continues. If covariates are intercorrelated (as they usually are!), and if they also correlated with the endogenous question predictor, *CATHOLIC* in our example, then you may face a burgeoning problem of *multicollinearity* as you proceed. In this case, your estimation may become increasingly sensitive to the presence of aberrant data points in the point cloud, leading your estimates to become increasingly erratic.

Reducing Observed Bias by the Method of Stratification

Stratifying on a Single Covariate

To illustrate the removal of observed bias from estimates of treatment effects, we draw on data from the National Educational Longitudinal Study–1988 (NELS-88), a longitudinal survey of students conducted by the National Center for Education Statistics. In the base year, 1988, students in grade 8 of U.S. schools were surveyed, one year before they entered secondary school. They were resurveyed in 1990 (when they should have been in tenth grade), and in 1992 (when they should have been in twelfth grade).[4] Data were collected on many topics, including on the following variables: (a) *MATH8* and *MATH12*, continuous measures of student mathematics achievement in eighth and twelfth grade on standardized tests, respectively; (b) *CATHOLIC*, a dichotomous indicator of whether the student attended a Catholic (= 1) or a public (= 0) high school; and (c) many prior characteristics measured in the base year, which we describe later. In our analyses throughout the chapter, we investigate the impact on a student's twelfth-grade mathematics achievement of attending a Catholic (versus a public) high school, while attempting to remove bias due to observed differences in base-year family income, parental educational attainment and expectations, and base-year student academic achievement and behavior. We were guided in our choice of covariates by the excellent paper written by Joseph Altonji, Todd Elder, and Christopher Taber (2005a).

Our analytic sample contains the 5,671 students from the NELS-88 dataset who were living in families with annual income of less than $75,000 (in 1988 dollars) in the base year of the survey.[5] Our rationale for limiting our sample to the children of these non–high-income families was motivated by our pedagogic needs, rather than by substance. By limiting the sample, we feel safe in working under the simplifying assumption that the Catholic-school advantage was *homogeneous* across all children, rather than having to consider a *heterogeneous* treatment effect that differed by

---

4. Although we do not make use of data beyond the 1992 survey, follow-up surveys of NELS-88 participants were also conducted in 1994 and 2000.
5. For pedagogic reasons, we have also limited our sample to students with no missing data on any variable included in our analyses. Thus, our sample size is smaller than that of the original NELS-88 sample and has not maintained its population generalizability. Consequently, we do not account for the complex survey sampling design in our analyses. However, our results do not differ dramatically from full-sample analyses that do take the design into account.

family income. Although there is evidence within the complete NELS-88 dataset that the Catholic-school advantage is smaller for high-income families than for families with lower incomes, within our restricted sub-sample, we are willing to assume homogeneity of the Catholic-school advantage across children. This allows us to simplify our presentation and focus more narrowly on the methods of bias correction. However, the same methods could easily be applied within the expanded sample and used to remove observed bias even when the Catholic-school advantage differed by values of covariates such as annual family income.

Do children do better academically if they attend Catholic rather than public high schools? If we were willing to ignore any self-selection into Catholic and public high schools, we could use standard ordinary least-squares (OLS) methods to regress outcome MATH12 on the main effect of question predictor CATHOLIC. In our example, if we do this, we find (as you might expect, given Coleman's findings) that children who attended Catholic high schools had higher mathematics achievement, on average, than those who attended public high schools ($\hat{\beta}_{CATHOLIC} = 3.895$; $p < 0.001$, one-sided).[6] This naïve estimated regression slope tells us that the twelfth-grade students at Catholic high schools have an average mathematics score that is about 4 points higher—that's around 40% of the outcome standard deviation[7]—than that of their public-school peers. Notice that the magnitude and direction of this slope estimate are just equal to the difference between the sample outcome means of Catholic and public high-school students ($54.540 - 50.645 = 3.895$). With a dichotomous predictor (like CATHOLIC, coded with values of 0 and 1), this is always the case. The trend line that joins the subsample outcome means in the "0" and "1" groups is always identical to the fitted trend line obtained in the corresponding OLS regression analyses of the same outcome on that predictor. We mention this equivalence here, because we rely on it later in the chapter, using both the terms "mean difference between subgroups" and the "fitted slope of the corresponding OLS trend-line," as suits our purpose.

Does this difference of almost half a standard deviation in the average mathematics score for students attending the two types of schools reflect the superior quality of Catholic schools? Or, is there an alternative explanation? Descriptive analyses, for instance, show that there are dramatic

---

6. Throughout this chapter, we have used one-sided tests in examining the hypothesis that Catholic schools are more effective than public schools in enhancing the mathematics achievement of students. We recognize that one could make the case for two-sided hypothesis tests.

7. The standard deviation of MATH12 is 9.502 in our subsample.

differences in the sample distributions of background characteristics, such as base-year average annual family income between students who attended Catholic high schools and those who attended public high schools. Unfortunately, in the NELS-88 survey, this latter covariate—which we have named *FAMINC8*—was measured only coarsely on an ordinal scale, with 15 income bands.[8] In our sample of children from non–high-income families, we are working with those participants whose values of *FAMINC8* ranged from 1 through 12. In our sample, the median base-year annual income of the families of eighth-graders who subsequently attended a Catholic high school was in the $35,000 to $49,999 range (in 1988 dollars), one full scale-point higher than the median annual income of families who sent their children subsequently to a public high school, which ranged from $25,000 to $34,999 ($p$ <0.001).[9] So, on average, families that sent their children to a Catholic high school had greater financial resources to pay for educational enrichment for their children than did families whose children attended a public high school. This pattern raises the question of the extent to which our naïve estimate of the Catholic-school advantage is biased by the unaccounted for impact of this observed covariate, *FAMINC8*.

One simple and robust method for eliminating from the estimate of the Catholic-school advantage any potential bias due to differences across students in base-year annual family income makes use of *sample stratification*. If we suspect that heterogeneity in family income across children—and its implicit relationship to twelfth-grade mathematics achievement—are biasing our estimate of the Catholic-school advantage, then all we need to do is find some way to eliminate the offending heterogeneity when estimating the advantage. We can do this most easily by subdividing the sample into "strata" according to base-year annual family income. Then, within each of these strata, we estimate the Catholic-school advantage. This, of course, leads to multiple estimates (one per stratum) of the principal relationship that we care about—the average mean difference in twelfth-grade mathematics achievement between Catholic and public high-school students. To obtain a single "final" estimate, we then simply average across strata.

---

8. Annual family income was coded as follows (in 1988 dollars): (1) no income, (2) less than $1,000, (3) $1,000–$2,999, (4) $3,000–$4,999, (5) $5,000–$7,499, (6) $7,500–$9,999, (7) $10,000–$14,999, (8) $15,000–$19,999, (9) $20,000–$24,999, (10) $25,000–$34,999, (11) $35,000–$49,999, (12) $50,000–$74,999, (13) $75,000–$99,999, (14) $100,000–$199,999, (15) more than $200,000.
9. Test for equality of medians, between groups: continuity-corrected $\chi^2(df = 1) = 104.7$ (p <0.001).

This three-step process of stratification, effect estimation, and averaging is simple and robust, but the choice of the particular strata is subtle and important. To succeed, sufficient numbers of both Catholic- and public-school children must be present within each stratum to allow the computation of average mathematics scores with reasonable precision for each group. Because of this sufficient numbers requirement, there is a tension involved in the design of the stratification. Creating more and narrower strata ensures less heterogeneity in base-year family income within each stratum. This is good because we need to diminish the heterogeneity in family income within a stratum in order to mitigate the bias in our corresponding estimate of the *MATH12/CATHOLIC* relationship. But it will also mean that there are fewer children providing scores within each stratum. This is bad because each subgroup analysis will then lack statistical power and will be more sensitive to the influence of aberrant cases. A consequence is that the multiple estimates of the Catholic-school advantage obtained *within* strata will be more scattered in value *across* strata. In the worst-case scenario, with many narrow strata, we may end up lacking participants in one or another of the treatment conditions entirely and be unable to estimate the very mean difference in which we are interested. These tensions must be balanced with care, and we have much more to say about them later, especially when we introduce the method of propensity score estimation.

In the NELS-88 example that we describe here, we made our stratification decisions iteratively, by inspecting the distribution of our sample of students by base-year annual family income. We grouped and regrouped the children, each time examining the distribution of base-year annual family income, by *CATHOLIC*, within each stratum. We sought a solution that had a small number of strata, within each of which future Catholic and public high-school students were "balanced" on their respective base-year family incomes. Our rationale is straightforward. If we can stratify so that, within each stratum, the sample distributions of base-year annual family income are essentially identical for the future Catholic and public high-school students, then we would be secure. Why? Because, within each stratum, we would then be estimating the Catholic-school advantage by comparing the average twelfth-grade mathematics achievement of groups of Catholic and public high-school students who were identical on their base-year annual family income. Consequently, within each stratum, our estimates of the Catholic-school advantage would not be affected by bias due to spurious differences in annual family income between the schooling groups. This lack of bias would then be preserved in our overall estimate when we averaged the within-stratum estimates across strata. This is the principle behind bias reduction by stratification.

Table 12.1 Descriptive statistics on annual family income, by stratum, overall and by type of high school attended, and average twelfth-grade mathematics achievement by income stratum and by high-school type ($n = 5,671$)

Stratum		Average Base-Year Annual Family Income (1988 dollars, 15-point ordinal scale)			Cell Frequencies		Average Mathematics Achievement (12th grade)		
Label	Income Range	Sample Variance	Sample Mean		Public	Catholic (% of stratum total)	Public	Catholic	Diff.
			Public	Catholic					
Hi_Inc	$35,000 to $74,999	0.24	11.38	11.42	1,969	344 (14.87%)	53.60	55.72	2.12***,†
Med_Inc	$20,000 to $34,999	0.22	9.65	9.73	1,745	177 (9.21%)	50.34	53.86	3.52***,†
Lo_Inc	≤$19,999	3.06	6.33	6.77	1,365	71 (4.94%)	46.77	50.54	3.76***,†
							Weighted Average ATE		**3.01**
							Weighted Average ATT		**2.74**

¯p <0.10; *p <0.05; **p <0.01; ***p <0.001
†One-sided test.

To clarify this process, we provide an example using our subset of NELS-88 data. For this part of our analysis, we have grouped all the students in our sample into three strata, which we have labeled the *Lo_Inc*, *Med_Inc*, and *Hi_Inc* family income groups.[10] In Table 12.1, we summarize the stratum membership (labeled by the corresponding range of base-year annual family income), and we list within-stratum statistics on base-year annual family income, the frequencies of students within stratum, and average twelfth-grade mathematics achievement by the type of high school attended. *Lo_Inc* families had base-year annual incomes of less than $20,000 (in 1988 dollars), *Hi_Inc* families had greater than $35,000, and the annual incomes of *Med_Inc* families fell between these limits.

First, notice that our partition has indeed led to reassuring reductions in the variability of annual family income within strata, when compared

---

10. There is no imperative to choose three groups. In fact, there is technical evidence, which we present later, that it is most effective to create at least five strata.

to the original variability in base-year annual family income in the full sample. The original full-sample variance of *FAMINC8* was almost 6 units (on NELS-88's 15-point ordinal scale). After stratification, there is little variability left in base-year annual family income within either the *Hi_Inc* or *Med_Inc* stratum (the sample variance in each is less than 0.25). We do not do quite so well with *Lo_Inc* families, though, where the within-stratum variance in *FAMINC8* is about 3 units, still about half of the original full-sample variance. However, we were reticent to split this stratum further in order to create additional strata with less heterogeneity in family income because only 77 children from the *Lo_Inc* families stratum entered a Catholic high school (seventh column, third row). We were worried about the precision of the estimated Catholic-school advantage within this cell. Also, we knew that we intended to stratify by other covariates later and would need to "spread" these 71 Catholic high-school students across additional dimensions. Thus, although we have concerns about the *Lo_Inc* group's contribution to our overall bias-correction process, due to its small size and larger heterogeneity in annual family income, we proceed with our presentation while asking you to bear in mind that we are least confident about its contribution. Notice that, among *Hi_Inc* families, a total of 2,313 students are compared, by type of high school, with 344 in Catholic high schools. Among *Med_Inc* families, there are 1,922 children in total, with 177 Catholic high-school students. Thus, in each of our three strata, we do indeed possess groups of Catholic and public high-school students whose twelfth-grade mathematics achievement can be compared.

Of particular importance, the average values of the base-year annual family income for Catholic and public high-school students within each stratum are now almost identical (Table 12.1, Columns 4 and 5). In the *Hi_Inc* stratum, the average values of annual family income are 11.42 and 11.38, respectively. They are separated by less than a few hundredths of a point! Similarly, the average base-year annual family incomes of the two groups are very close to each other in the other two strata, being separated by only 0.08 in the *Med_Inc* stratum and by 0.44 in the *Lo_Inc* stratum. Using *t*-tests, by *CATHOLIC*, we fail to reject the null hypotheses that the average base-year annual family incomes of public and Catholic high-school students are identical within each stratum in the population.[11]

---

11. When you iterate to a final set of strata, you may conduct many such hypothesis tests, leading to an accumulation of Type I error. To avoid this, you can invoke a *Bonferroni* correction to the α-level, in each test. In our work, for instance, we conducted each of our balancing tests at the 0.01 level.

Formally, we describe this condition by stating that participants in each of the three strata are "balanced" on base-year annual family income.[12]

However, to obtain credible bias-corrected estimates of the Catholic-school advantage, we would like the entire sample distributions of base-year annual family income to be identical for the Catholic and public high-school subgroups within each stratum. Such comparisons of entire distributions are difficult to make. But, if the sample distributions are identical, so should be their *moments*. In an ideal world, we would compare the subgroups not only on their means (*first moment*), but also on their variances (*second moment*), skewnesses (*third moment*), and so on. Such a process can be exhausting, and leads to a rapid accumulation of Type I error. So, typically, when we are striving for an optimal stratification, we focus only on achieving balance on the means.

Once a balanced stratification has been obtained on the covariate, family income, as in Table 12.1, you can estimate differences in average twelfth-grade mathematics achievement between the Catholic and public high-school students within stratum. In our table, these differences are listed in the last column. Compare them to the overall estimated Catholic-school advantage of 3.89 points that we obtained in our earlier naïve OLS regression analysis. All within-stratum estimates of the Catholic high-school advantage are positive, but they are smaller than the biased overall estimate. In fact, in strata where we have been the most successful in diminishing heterogeneity in annual family income and balancing the subgroup means (the *Hi_Inc* and *Med_Inc* strata), the new bias-corrected estimates range from around 0.25 point to almost 2 points lower than the initial biased estimate. In fact, in the *Hi_Inc* stratum—which contains the most children, and in which the Catholic and public subgroups means of base-year annual family income are almost indistinguishable—we observe the greatest bias reduction (of almost 2 points). This halves our previous naïve full-sample estimate of the Catholic-school advantage.

To provide an overall single-number estimate of the Catholic-school advantage, corrected for bias due to differences in base-year annual family income, we can form a weighted average of the three within-stratum estimates. In doing so, we have some choices about the weights. If we weight by the total number of high-school students present in each stratum, both

---

12. Our adoption of three strata in Table 12.1 results from an iterative "divisive" approach. We started by pooling all students into a single income stratum. When a within-stratum *t*-test suggested that we had not achieved balance on the sample means, by *CATHOLIC*, we split the stratum into successively narrower strata, until balance on the means was achieved in all strata. This process led to the three strata we present here. Software designed to help you stratify typically uses this approach.

public and Catholic, we obtain the estimated *average effect of the Catholic treatment*, or *ATE*. Its value is 3.01 (lower right corner, Table 12.1), almost a full point lower than the earlier biased estimate.[13] A reason that this estimate is so much lower than the naïve biased estimate is that the *Hi_Inc* stratum—which contributes the smallest within-stratum estimate—contains the greatest number of children, and so contributes most heavily to the final estimate. An alternative is to weight within-stratum estimates of the Catholic-school advantage by the number of treated (Catholic) students in each cell. Doing so provides an estimate of 2.74 (lower-right corner of Table 12.1).[14] This is called an estimate of the *average impact of the Catholic treatment on the treated*, or *ATT*. It is our best estimate of the difference in average twelfth-grade mathematics achievement between students who experienced the Catholic treatment and what their average would have been if they had not been treated.

To provide additional insight into how stratification functions to eliminate observed bias, we have used these stratum means and mean differences to simulate the OLS-fitted relationships between outcome *MATH12* and question predictor *CATHOLIC* within each of our three family income strata, in Figure 12.1. The fitted within-stratum trends are presented as three solid lines, labeled on the right. The dashed line represents the original naive OLS-fitted trend line, corresponding to our initial biased estimate of the Catholic-school advantage, obtained in the full sample. Notice, first, that the between-stratum differences we have commented on—which are evident in the last column of the table—are also clear in the plot. All three of the fitted within-stratum trends have slopes that are less steep than the naïve and biased full-sample slope estimate, with the slope of the fitted trend line obtained in the *Hi_Inc* stratum the least steep.[15]

---

13. The weighted average is $\{(2,313 \times 2.12) + (1,922 \times 3.52) + (1,436 \times 3.76)\}/5,671$. Its associated standard error can be obtained by pooling within-stratum standard deviations, or by applying a resampling method such as bootstrapping. Similar computations can be made for each of the overall bias-corrected estimates of the Catholic-school advantage that we have estimated in this chapter.

14. The weighted average is $\{(344 \times 2.12) + (177 \times 3.52) + (71 \times 3.76)\}/592$.

15. Unfortunately, there is some evidence in this plot of a potential interaction between *CATHOLIC* and *FAMINC8*, in that the slopes of the three line segments appear to diminish systematically at higher baseline annual family income. It was this heterogeneity in the impact of the Catholic schools that we were seeking to avoid by limiting our sample to children in "non-wealthy" families. Although we have not succeeded completely in this mission, we ignore the potential interaction in what follows and retain our focus on the main effect of Catholic versus public high school, in order to keep the exposition as simple as possible. This means, in essence, that we have averaged the heterogeneous treatment effects across family-income groups.

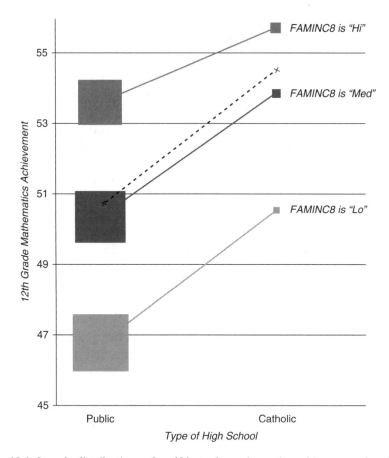

Figure 12.1 Sample distributions of twelfth-grade mathematics achievement, by whether students attended a public or a Catholic high school, within strata defined on *FAMINC8* (*n* = 5,671).

These plots, along with the entries in Table 12.1, provide insight into why the intrusion of base-year family income into the *MATH12/ CATHOLIC* relationship led the original naïve estimate to have a positive—"upward"—bias. In building your intuition, begin from the perspective of the three separate within-stratum relationships displayed in Figure 12.1 and try to resurrect mentally the full-sample relationship by combining the associated (and undisplayed) point clouds.[16] First, notice that the three within-stratum trend lines are ordered by the base-year

---

16. The point clouds surrounding these trend lines are not the familiar ellipses, because the principal predictor, *CATHOLIC*, is dichotomous.

family income stratum in which they originated. The fitted relationship from the Lo_Inc stratum, for instance, occupies the lowest elevation on the plot, and that of the Hi_Inc stratum, the highest. This, of course, is consistent with our substantive theory. The observed differences in elevation confirm that, regardless of whether students choose to go to a Catholic or public high school, children from higher-income homes tend to do better on tests of mathematics achievement in twelfth grade.

Second, recall the hypothesis that a positive relationship exists between annual base-year family income and whether the family chose to send their child to a Catholic or public high school. In the full sample, the estimated bivariate correlation between FAMINC8 and CATHOLIC is small—of magnitude 0.129—but it is convincingly positive (p <0.001). You can see evidence of this positive relationship in the sample percentages presented in the parentheses below the entries in the seventh column of Table 12.1. In the Lo_Inc stratum, only 71 out of 1,436 children—less than 5%—attend Catholic school. In the Med_Inc stratum, the corresponding figure is about 9%, whereas in the Hi_Inc stratum it is approximately 15%. (The percentages of children within each income stratum who attended each of the types of high school, respectively, are represented in Figure 12.1 by the relative sizes of the rectangles at either end of each trend line.)

Imagine the contributions of these joint trends to the full point cloud—that is, for the combination of the three stratum-specific point clouds. As we ascend through the full point cloud, traversing the stratum-specific point clouds from bottom to top, two effects occur simultaneously. First, mathematics achievement is elevated as we transition from lower-income to higher-income families. Second, a greater proportion of the children within each stratum appear on the right-hand (Catholic) side of the cloud than on the left-hand (public) side. Given these concurrent effects, the full point cloud will be more "top-right" and "bottom-left" heavy than any of the separate within-stratum point clouds. Thus, a MATH12 versus CATHOLIC trend line fitted in the full point cloud (illustrated by the dashed line in Figure 12.1) must be steeper than the trend lines fitted in any of the separate point clouds. The difference between the overall slope and the average of the within-stratum slopes is a summary of the bias that was introduced into the estimate by ignoring the impact of family income on both the choice of Catholic versus public high school and ultimate student achievement.

Essentially, then, when we examine the relationship between MATH12 and CATHOLIC naïvely in the full sample and do not adjust for the impact of annual family income, we observe a composite of the "true" relationship between mathematics achievement and attendance at Catholic versus public high school plus the biasing impact of family income, as it pushes children of higher-income families both to higher mathematics achievement and into Catholic high school. Of course, we put "true" in quotes here to emphasize that we are referring only to the biasing effect of a single observed covariate—base-year annual family income. We do not know whether other components of bias, which derive from influences of other characteristics of the children, remain unresolved. It is to this question that we turn next.

Stratifying on Covariates

Now, suppose our theory suggests that, in addition to the impact of differences in base-year annual family income, parents of children who display above-average prior academic skills are especially likely to enroll their child in a Catholic high school. If this is the case, then the children who enter Catholic high schools would not be equivalent in terms of prior academic ability to those children who enroll in public high schools. This too would create bias in the estimate of the Catholic-school advantage. In fact, there is evidence in the NELS-88 dataset that this is the case: Children who entered Catholic high schools had a base-year average mathematics achievement (53.66) that was about 2 points higher, on average, than that of children who entered public high schools (51.24), and the difference is statistically significant ($t = 5.78$; $p < 0.001$).

Thus, it makes sense to now remove observed bias that is attributable to both base-year annual family income and prior mathematics achievement simultaneously from our naïve estimate of the Catholic-school advantage. We can generalize the stratification approach easily to accommodate this, but it stretches the capabilities of the technique. For instance, in the NELS-88 dataset, student base-year mathematics achievement was measured by a standardized test, and information on this score is coded in our covariate, MATH8. In our sample, MATH8 ranges from about 34 to 77, with a mean of 51.5. Following our earlier strategy of creating strata within which children were relatively homogeneous on the new covariate, we have created four prior achievement strata:

- Hi_Ach: High achievement stratum—scores of 51 or more.
- MHi_Ach: Medium-high achievement stratum—scores from 44 to 51.
- MLo_Ach: Medium-low achievement stratum—scores from 38 to 44.
- Lo_Ach: Low achievement stratum—scores below 38.

Imposing this stratification again limits heterogeneity in prior mathematics achievement within each stratum, and we can again attain balance on the means of base-year mathematics achievement, by CATHOLIC, within each of the new strata.

Now, we have the option to go through the same exercise within these four base-year mathematics achievement strata as we did with our three original family-income strata, inspecting the distribution of children's grade 12 mathematics scores and providing respective estimates of the Catholic-school advantage. In fact, we have performed these analyses, and their consequences are as expected. However, our purpose here is greater than this. First, we want to illustrate how to use stratification to correct for bias due to both observed covariates—*FAMINC8* and *MATH8*—simultaneously. Second, we want to point out the problems that surface when multiple covariates are incorporated into the stratification process. Consequently, rather than stratifying by the child's base-year mathematics achievement alone, we have "crossed" the three base-year annual family-income strata with the four prior mathematics-ability strata to produce a cross-tabulation that contains 12 cells. Then, within each of these cells, we have estimated the average twelfth-grade mathematics achievement of children in the public schools and those in Catholic high schools and subtracted one from the other to obtain 12 estimates of the Catholic-school advantage. We list these estimates, along with their corresponding cell frequencies, in Table 12.2.

Notice that there has been a dramatic decline in the frequencies of students who participated in each of the separate Catholic/public comparisons, a result of spreading the original sample across many more cells. This problem of data sparseness has become particularly acute for children who attended Catholic high schools, a modest-sized group to begin with. For example, in strata where the *Med_Inc* and *Lo_Inc* base-year annual family-income groups are crossed with the *Lo_Ach* prior mathematics-achievement group (the eighth and twelfth strata from the top, in Table 12.2), only a total of three students are in Catholic high schools. The numbers of public high-school children in these cells are also smaller (96 and 142, respectively) than in other cells in the stratification. Comparisons in these sparse cells lack statistical power and precision.

This problem of *sparseness* is a standard concern in the application of stratification methods, even in large datasets. As we try to correct for bias along more and more dimensions, we find ourselves with cells that contain fewer and fewer observations. This results in erratic within-stratum estimates of the size of the treatment effect. This is illustrated by the estimates of the size of the Catholic-school advantage listed in the final column of Table 12.2. Some are very small, such as the estimate of 0.47 in the ninth (*Med_Inc* × *Hi_Ach*) stratum. Others are very large, such as the estimate of 5.76 in the twelfth (*Lo_Inc* × *Lo_Ach*) stratum. Notice that the outlying estimates tend to occur in cells containing very few Catholic high-school students. This is a generic problem with the method

Table 12.2 Sample frequencies and average twelfth-grade mathematics achievement, by high-school type, within 12 strata defined by the crossing of stratified versions of base-year annual family income and mathematics achievement (n = 5,671)

Stratum		Cell Frequencies		Average Mathematics Achievement (12th Grade)		
Base-Year Family Income	Base-Year Mathematics Achievement	Public	Catholic	Public	Catholic	Diff.
Hi_Inc	Hi_Ach	1,159	227	58.93	59.66	0.72
	MHi_Ach	432	73	49.18	50.71	1.53*,†
	MLo_Ach	321	38	42.75	44.23	1.48
	Lo_Ach	57	6	39.79	40.40	0.62
Med_Inc	Hi_Ach	790	93	57.42	59.42	2.00**,†
	MHi_Ach	469	49	47.95	50.14	2.19**,†
	MLo_Ach	390	33	41.92	44.56	2.64*,†
	Lo_Ach	96	2	37.94	39.77	1.83
Lo_Inc	Hi_Ach	405	36	56.12	56.59	0.47
	MHi_Ach	385	13	47.12	48.65	1.53
	MLo_Ach	433	21	40.99	41.70	0.71
	Lo_Ach	142	1	36.81	42.57	5.76
				Weighted Average ATE		*1.50*
				Weighted Average ATT		*1.31*

¯p <0.10; *p <0.05; **p <0.01; ***p <0.001
†One-sided test.

of stratification. With increased stratification, the magnitudes of the estimated treatment effects become increasingly erratic across cells (another example of the general principle that estimates obtained from samples of diminishing size become increasingly sensitive to the idiosyncrasies of sampling). The aberrant estimates that have been obtained in one or two of the cells of the stratification may even be due to the presence of just a few idiosyncratic cases within the offending cells. The influence of such cases on the estimated effects rises as cell sample sizes fall.

Rather than dwelling on these oddities, however, let's examine the big picture. Although there may be increased scatter among the 12 within-stratum biased-corrected estimates, perhaps the multiple estimates are still scattered around some reasonable "central" bias-corrected estimate of the Catholic-school advantage. Again, we can compute weighted averages of the 12 estimates to summarize the bias-corrected difference between Catholic and public high-school students in twelfth-grade mathematics achievement. For instance, the estimated ATE—in which the within-cell estimates have been weighted by the *total* cell sample size within cell—is 1.50 (listed in the lower right corner of Table 12.2).[17] Clearly, we have again reduced the observed bias in our naïve estimate of the Catholic-school advantage (3.89) dramatically from the intermediate estimate that we obtained by stratifying on base-year annual family income alone (3.01).

This progress toward successively smaller estimates of the Catholic-school advantage as we bias-correct for additional covariates prompts us to wonder whether, by incorporating further well-chosen covariates, we could reduce the apparent Catholic-school advantage to zero. Of course, it would be difficult to continue to add covariates into our stratification without exacerbating the technical problems that we just described. As we add covariates into the stratification design, the number of cells in the cross-tabulation increases multiplicatively and cell frequencies plummet. We have to deal with increasing data sparseness, diminishing statistical power, and poor precision for estimates of the Catholic-school advantage within the cells of the stratification, and the increasing scatter of the within-cell estimates. Clearly, there are practical limits to the application of the stratification approach in bias correction!

The most serious consequence of increasing the complexity of the stratification design by adding further covariates is that it leads eventually to an extreme form of data sparseness in which there may be either no Catholic high-school students or no public high-school students present in particular cells of the cross-tabulation. Then, we can no longer estimate the critical bias-corrected Catholic-school advantage in these cells. Methodologists use the expression a *lack of common support* to describe such regions in the space spanned by the covariates. In these regions, estimates of treatment effects cannot be made because the regions do not contain members of both the treatment and control groups that share the same values of the covariates.

We could, of course, proceed by eliminating the offending cells from contention. In some sense, this is not a problem because the public-school students who would be eliminated from the sample had no Catholic-school counterparts whom they matched on the values of the key covariates. We would be left comparing only those Catholic and public high-school students who are matched on the covariates. Perhaps this enhances the legitimacy of the obtained comparisons, despite the

---

17. Weighting by the within-cell frequencies of Catholic high-school students, the average effect of the treatment on the treated is 1.31 (lower right-hand cell in Table 12.2).

reduction in sample size. Nevertheless, in resolving selection bias by complex simultaneous stratification on observed covariates, it pays to remain alert to who is excluded from either of the two treatment conditions because they have no "neighbors" that match them on the other side.

Lack of common support can be particularly problematic in quasi-experimental studies in which rampant self-selection into the treatment and control conditions has occurred.[18] For example, in observational studies of the Catholic/public high-school difference in achievement, it could be that very few low-income families with relatively low-achieving children send their children to Catholic schools. If this were the case, then fine-grained stratification on family income and eighth-grade mathematics achievement could reveal an extreme lack of common support, leaving relatively few, viable bias-corrected comparisons to be estimated and pooled into an overall estimate.[19]

Estimates of treatment effects obtained by the strategy for observed-bias correction that we discuss next—the direct control for observed covariates in a regression framework—are also affected by problems of extreme sparseness and lack of common support in observational data. However, the impact of this lack of common support is usually concealed inadvertently in the analysis. By relying on strong assumptions of functional form and homoscedasticity, direct control for covariates through regression analysis can continue to incorporate data from the unmatched cases. The original sample size is preserved, and no cases are lost. However, the unmatched cases have only been retained by reliance on strong assumptions.

Finally, it is important to remember that sparseness and lack of common support are not the most difficult issues, as they can be surfaced, examined, explained, or worked around. The key problem—and one that underlies all methods for bias correction on the observables—remains substantive. For bias correction to be credible, by any method, you must

---

18. In experimental data, with decent sample sizes, there tends to be no equivalent problem because random assignment to experimental conditions ensures that the distribution of participants over all levels of every covariate is similar in both the treatment and control groups.

19. In fact, Catholic high schools serve a substantial number of children from relatively low-income families who exhibit quite modest academic skills as eighth-graders. Consequently, the problem of lack of common support is not an especially serious problem in comparing the achievement of Catholic high-school students and public high-school students using quite large datasets such as NELS-88. However, lack of common support is a much greater problem in comparing the achievement of students who attend non-Catholic private high schools and the achievement of students who attend public schools, using data from NELS-88 and other similar datasets.

have identified—and incorporated—the correct "observables." Only when you truly understand what has driven the selection process, can you defend your choice of the covariates for which to correct. Thus, it is the substantive issues that always remain the most critical in selection-bias correction, regardless of the sophistication of the method chosen to account for the influences of covariates.

We now move on to consider our second strategy for removing bias due to observables—the method of direct control for covariates, via regression modeling. This is the strategy that Coleman and his colleagues employed, and the one with which you are already the most familiar. It is interesting to contrast its consequences with those of the stratification method, especially from the perspective of the technical problems we have surfaced. It responds to these difficulties in different ways, with different kinds of costs.

Reducing Observed Bias by Direct Control for Covariates Using Regression Analysis

Given our theoretical position that family income and prior achievement are both elements of a selection process that drove better-prepared children from relatively high-income families disproportionately into Catholic high schools, it is natural to ask why we need to employ stratification to correct for the bias due to these observed covariates. Indeed, including measures of these two constructs directly as covariates in a multiple regression model that will address our research question seems a sensible way to proceed, although the approach is laden with assumptions that are often overlooked.

In most respects, the incorporation of base-year annual family income and prior achievement as covariates in the regression of *MATH12* on *CATHOLIC* is conceptually identical—as an approach to bias correction on observables—to the earlier stratification approach. Even though it may not appear so on the surface, direct control for covariates by regression analysis implicitly forces the Catholic-school advantage to be estimated simultaneously in "slices" of the dataset that are defined by the values of the covariates. In addition, by including only the main effect of question predictor *CATHOLIC* in the model, we force the estimated Catholic-school advantage to be identical across all these slices; that is, we force the *MATH12* versus *CATHOLIC* trend lines to be parallel within each cell defined by the covariates. Thus, in a very real sense, the overall covariate-adjusted regression estimate is an implicit average of all of the "slice-by-slice" estimates.[20] However, the regression approach draws deeply on functional-form assumptions—the requirement of parallel linear trends within each covariate-constrained cell. As a consequence, bias correction by direct control of covariates via regression analysis has the appearance of being less challenged by the technical problems of sparseness, power/precision, and scatter revealed under the stratification approach. However, its apparent effectiveness and ease of use come at the cost of a greater reliance on the built-in assumptions.

As an illustration of the technique, we display in Table 12.3 the results from the use of standard OLS methods to regress outcome *MATH12* on our question predictor, *CATHOLIC*, while controlling for the two critical covariates—*FAMINC8* and *MATH8*—that we have argued motivate a selection process that delivers children into their particular high-school choices. We present two fitted models in the table (*Model A* and *Model B*) that differ only in the way that the effects of the two selection predictors have been specified. Inspecting the results of both specifications, and considering their relative strengths can be informative, as we now show.

Conceptually, the first specification—Model A—emulates our earlier stratification-based correction for observed bias. In this model, we have retained the earlier "three-by-four" stratification on the *FAMINC8* and *MATH8* variables, by introducing a vector of 12 dichotomous predictors into the model to distinguish the main effects of each of the 12 cells in the cross-stratification. This is a fully crossed *fixed effects of cell* model, without an intercept parameter, which allows us to retain all 12 fixed effects of cell in the model, rather than removing one as a reference category. This model—although its specification seems unusual—is equivalent algebraically to the more common specification that contains the main effects of the stratified versions of *FAMINC8* and *MATH8*, and their two-way interaction. However, by adopting Model A, we have defined a model that is conceptually and pedagogically appealing. Essentially, it possesses 12 intercepts—one per cell—each of which is an estimate of the average

---

20. Technical details of the averaging process differ implicitly between the stratification and regression approaches. In our example, under stratification, we averaged the multiple within-cell estimates of the Catholic-school advantage by hand, weighting by some version of the cell frequencies. If we weight by the *total frequency* of students in each cell, we obtain an estimate of the overall ATE. If we weight by the *frequency of treated* (Catholic-school) participants in each cell, we obtain an estimate of the overall *average effect of the treatment on the treated*. In the regression approach, however, this choice is taken out of our hands by an averaging process built implicitly into the OLS estimation of the main effect of *CATHOLIC*. This latter averaging incorporates built-in weights that depend essentially on the precisions of the within-cell estimates. Thus, an OLS estimate of the Catholic-school advantage is a special kind of weighted ATE.

Table 12.3 Parameter estimates and approximate p-values from the OLS regression of twelfth-grade mathematics achievement on attendance at a Catholic versus public high school, controlling for base-year annual family-income (Model A: *FAMINC8*; Model B: *INC8*) and mathematics achievement (n = 5,671)

Predictor	OLS-Fitted Regression Model	
	A: *FAMINC8* and *MATH8* Stratified, Fully Crossed	B: *INC8* and *MATH8* Linear Main Effects, Two-Way Interaction
Hi_Inc × *Hi_Ach*	58.83***	
Hi_Inc × *MHi_Ach*	49.21***	
Hi_Inc × *MLo_Ach*	42.76***	
Hi_Inc × *Lo_Ach*	39.72***	
Med_Inc × *Hi_Ach*	57.49***	
Med_Inc × *MHi_Ach*	48.03***	
Med_Inc × *MLo_Ach*	42.03***	
Med_Inc × *Lo_Ach*	37.95***	
Lo_Inc × *MHi_Ach*	56.05***	
Lo_Inc × *MLo_Ach*	47.13***	
Lo_Inc × *MLo_Ach*	40.96***	
Lo_Inc × *Lo_Ach*	36.84***	
INTERCEPT		4.827***
INC8		0.164***
MATH8		0.872***
INC8 × *MATH8*		−0.002***
CATHOLIC	**1.33***,†**	**1.66***,†**
R² Statistic	0.601	0.697
Residual Variance	6.009	5.232

~p <0.10; *p <0.05; **p <0.01; ***p <0.001
†One-sided test.

twelfth-grade mathematics achievement of the *public* high-school students *in that cell*. Thus, directly from the parameter estimates in the fitted model, we know that the average mathematics achievement is 36.84 for students in public high schools whose families were in the lowest stratum of base-year annual income and whose base-year mathematics achievement was the lowest.[21] The only other effect that is included in Model A is the

---

21. These intercept estimates are not exactly identical to the sample estimates of cell means obtained in the stratification analyses. For instance, in the lowest stratum of both income and prior mathematics achievement, the cell average twelfth-grade mathematics achievement was 36.81 in the stratification analysis (Table 12.2, Row 12), not 36.84, as in the regression analysis. The reason that these estimates are not identical,

parameter of central interest to our research question—the main effect of question predictor *CATHOLIC*. The slope coefficient on this predictor summarizes the average effect of the adjusted Catholic treatment that we seek, and has a value of 1.33 (p <0.001), with its bias attributable to the observed covariates, base-year annual family income, and mathematics achievement, removed.[22] This new *direct control of covariates by regression analysis* estimate is somewhat smaller than, but of the same order of magnitude as, the bias-corrected estimate of the Catholic-school advantage that we obtained earlier by stratification (1.50, see Table 12.2), and both estimates are much lower than the naïve and uncorrected OLS estimate of 3.89.[23]

The advantage of this regression approach to observed bias correction is that we can pool all of the sampled children simultaneously into the same analysis, borrowing strength across cells to improve statistical power and smooth the relative influence of aberrant data points. However, we have bought these advantages by making additional assumptions—by imposing additional constraints on the model. We have assumed that the Catholic-school advantage is identical in each cell, in the population, and we have enforced that, in the model, via the analysis.[24] In addition, rather than simply letting the scatter of the data (and sample size) within each cell determine the standard error of the mean in that cell, we have assumed that the scatter is homoscedastic across cells, in the population, and have consequently pooled all that variation to obtain a common estimate of the standard error of the *CATHOLIC* slope.

---

and neither are other respective pairs, is because we estimated cell means *separately* during the stratification analyses, and each cell was free to take on its own mean and standard deviation, determined only by its own data, independent of data in all other cells. This is not the case under the regression specification, where we have analyzed all data simultaneously across 12 cells, under the assumption that the population Catholic- versus public-school difference is identical in each cell and that population residual variance is homoscedastic. These constraints, while tenable, have wrought minor changes in the estimated high-school means in each cell. So, the new quantities remain estimates of the average mathematics score in twelfth grade of the public high-school students in each cell, but assume that the Catholic-school advantage is identical in each cell and that residual variance is homoscedastic in the population. We benefit by this pooling of data across cells—in terms of power and precision—at the cost of relying on additional assumptions.

22. The regression approach estimates the ATE, not the ATT.

23. Again, the two estimates differ because of constraints imposed by the additional assumption on Model A's functional form.

24. We could test this assumption by including interactions between question predictor *CATHOLIC* and the fixed effects of the 12-cell *FAMINC8* by *MATH8* stratification. Follow-up analyses showed that none of the additional interactions made a statistically significant contribution to model fit, beyond Model A.

By making these new assumptions, we appear to have somewhat mitigated the impact of data sparseness. For instance, even if there were only one case in one or more of the cells in the stratification, either a public or a Catholic high-school student, we would still be able to fit the regression model using all of the data. But is this a sensible thing to do? It means that participants who do not have common support across all covariates have been included in the estimate. In other words, we may have estimated the Catholic-school advantage by comparing students who should not be compared, at least based on the observed values of our two critical covariates. The evident lack of common support, something about which we learned while correcting for observed bias by stratification, is not evident immediately under the regression approach. Of course, a thoughtful data analyst could enjoy the best of both worlds. He or she could determine the boundaries of the region of common support in exploratory data analyses and trim the sample appropriately, retaining only participants who enjoy common support across viable values of the covariates. Only then would he or she fit Model A in the new subsample.

Despite these warnings, you may now prefer to use the regression approach to fit Model A—after all, it did work well. So, why then did we fit a second regression model, Model B, the results of which are displayed in the last column of Table 12.3? We did this to emphasize that once you begin adding covariates to a regression model like this, you do more than assume that the Catholic-school advantage itself is homogeneous and the stochastic scatter homoscedastic across cells. You also—explicitly or implicitly—make assumptions about the functional form of all outcome: covariate relationships in each cell. In Model B, for instance, we have bias-corrected using the same baseline covariates and their two-way interaction, but we have used different specifications of their effects. First, we have replaced our measure of base-year annual family income, *FAMINC8*, by a new variable named *INC8*. This new predictor has values that represent the actual incomes of the families as closely as possible. For instance, students whose value of *FAMINC8* was 12 on the original ordinal scale— and whose income fell between $50,000 and $74,999—have been assigned a value of *INC8* midway between these bounds, at $62,500, and so on for other families, all amounts being expressed in thousands of 1988 dollars.[25] We have also assumed that the main effects of covariates *INC8* and *MATH8* on the outcome are linear. Recall that *FAMINC8*, in particular, was measured originally on an arbitrary ordinal 15-point scale—with

---

25. The converted values are: (1) $0K, (2) $0.5K, (3) $2K, (4) $4K, (5) $6.25K, (6) $8.75K, (7) $12.5K, (8) $17.5K, (9) $22.5K, (10) $30K, (11) $42.5K, (12) $62.5K, in 1988 dollars, where K = 1,000.

values in our sample ranging from 1 through 12. The steps between these original scale points were not equally spaced in monetary terms and, when we created our three original strata to limit observed variability in this covariate, we collapsed together many of the original categories. So, for instance, our *Lo_Inc* category included families with incomes that ranged from $0 through $19,999. The median family incomes in each of our three strata were not equally spaced, either. On the other hand, we made no assumption that the effect of annual family income was linear over its entire range. Thus, for children with a medium-low level of mathematics preparation (those in the *MLo_Ach* strata), the estimated difference in elevation between the *Med_Inc* and *Lo_Inc* intercepts was (42.03 − 40.96) or 1.07 (Table 12.3, Model A, rows 7 and 11). In contrast, the difference in estimated elevation between the *Hi_Inc* and *Med_Inc* intercepts is (42.76 − 42.03) or 0.73. The situation is different in Model B. Not only have we replaced *FAMINC8* by a variable that is measured in actual dollar amounts, we have included only its linear effect in the model. So, now, the effects of equal increments in *INC8* on the outcome are held implicitly to be equal by the linearity assumption. The same goes for *MATH8*, now modeled in its original test metric, with the impact of equal increments of test score on the outcome also held to be equal. Finally, the same goes for the two-way interaction. It is now the interaction of the linear effects of *INC8* and *MATH8*. In the Model A specification, we may have crudely collapsed categories of family income and test score, but we did not mandate linearity!

Notice that Model B actually fits better than Model A—its R^2 statistic is almost 10 percentage points higher, and its residual variance about 13% smaller. In addition, the estimated Catholic-school advantage is now 1.66, larger than the estimate obtained under Model A, but consistent with the estimate obtained under the stratification approach (1.50). The reason this improvement in fit has occurred is that: (a) the linearity assumptions may make sense, given the data coding; (b) we have managed to pick up on some of the additional variation in the covariates that was sacrificed when we stratified them; and (c) Model B is dramatically more parsimonious—we have estimated five parameters rather than 13.

Rather than designate one of these estimates of the Catholic-school advantage as "correct," our point is that differences in functional form between Models A and B make a difference. So, when you decide to adopt a direct control for covariates by regression modeling approach, you may no longer need to make arbitrary decisions about how to collapse the covariates and stratify, but you do have other, equally critical decisions to make. This point will resurface when we describe the use of *propensity scores* for bias correction, in the following section. Finally, it is worth mentioning that this is not the end of the process of selection-bias correction for observed covariates. If Model B had not fitted so well, we would have sought transformations of the covariates, perhaps polynomials, and included multiple interactions among the differently transformed variables, hoping for a successful and parsimonious specification. Perhaps we would not have found such a specification and, in the end, had to accept the coarsening of the covariates in the stratification process and fallen back on non-parsimonious Model A, with its 13 parameters, or even on the stratification method itself.

On the other hand, our choice of linear effects has served us well in this particular example. So, we could continue the process of bias adjustment by including other carefully selected covariates into the regression model. However, there is a better approach to controlling bias due to observed covariates in the estimation of treatment effects from non experimental data, and we turn now to this approach.

Reducing Observed Bias Using a Propensity-Score Approach

It is useful to consider our covariate-controlled regression analyses from a conceptually different point of view. In Model B, we needed three terms to incorporate our hypotheses about the selection process into the principal regression model: the main effect of *INC8*, the main effect of *MATH8*, and their interaction. Inspecting Model B, in Table 12.3, we see that our analyses have provided an estimate of the Catholic-school advantage while controlling statistically for a *particular linear composite of the covariates*. In fact, you can regard Model B as though it is telling you to regress *MATH12* on *CATHOLIC*, while controlling for an "optimal" composite of the covariates, given by (or proportional to):

$$\left\{ \begin{array}{c} Composite \\ Covariate \end{array} \right\} = 0.164 INC8 + 0.872 MATH8 - 0.002(INC8 \times MATH8)$$

By virtue of our acceptance of the OLS fit as "optimal" in some sense, we learn that this particular composite best captures the effects of selection on the outcome, given our choice of covariates. Of course, in reading the fitted model in this way, we have not learned much that is of practical use because we only discovered the respective "weights" that feature in the composite—that is 0.164, 0.872, and −0.002—via the regression analysis itself. Hypothetically, though, if we had known these weights in advance, we would not have needed to include the main effects and their interaction separately as controls. Instead, we could have obtained the same estimate of the magnitude of the Catholic-school advantage by forming a linear composite of the covariates in a prior step, using these weights or weights proportional to them, and including it as the sole covariate in our regression model.

We mention this hypothetical process because it communicates an important pedagogic message on which we can now capitalize. Suppose that, in our example, we possessed literally dozens, perhaps even hundreds, of covariates that were potential contributors to our observed bias correction. For example, in Table 1 of the original paper on this same topic by Altonji and his colleagues (2005a), the authors list five possible demographic covariates, six family background covariates, four geographic covariates, five covariates that describe prior parent and student expectations, and ten covariates that capture the student's eighth-grade achievement and behavior. This is a total of 26 potential main effects for which we could adjust. In addition to these, there are literally thousands of two-, three-, four-, and multi-way interactions that could be formed from these same covariates and also included as controls. If we were to add all of these covariates into our principal regression equation to try to whittle down the observed bias, we may even eventually run out of degrees of freedom, ramp up our Type I error, and reduce our statistical power dramatically, even in very large samples. More importantly, our analyses might lose their important theoretical orientation and simply become a fishing expedition in an enormous ocean of potential covariates, and their products and transformations.

From our introductory discussion earlier, you will guess that what we seek is a single "optimal" composite of all the observed covariates that we hope will describe the selection process effectively and for which we can control. This suggests that, as a first step in any correction for observed bias, it makes sense to focus first on the selection process itself in order to seek out explicitly some optimal composite of the hypothesized selection predictors—in advance of our principal regression analyses. Specifically, we might use logistic regression analysis to investigate the relationship between dichotomous variable *CATHOLIC*, which we now treat as an outcome in a new first-stage analysis, and the covariates that we think best describe that selection. From these results, we can then reconstruct a composite variable that best describes the selection of each child into Catholic or public high schools—specifically, for this purpose, we can use the fitted values of *CATHOLIC* for each child. Once we have fitted the first-stage selection model, these fitted values then estimate the probabilities—we will refer to them as *propensities*—that children in the sample will attend a Catholic high school. In what follows, we describe how these propensities are used in what has become known as *propensity-score analysis*.

With this new perspective in mind, we present a pair of fitted *selection models* for our NELS-88 example in Table 12.4. In both models, we have used logistic regression analysis to regress our dichotomous treatment variable, *CATHOLIC*, on the covariates that we have already hypothesized best describe children's selection into either a Catholic or a public high school: annual family income and student prior mathematics achievement, along with their two-way interaction. In Model A, we include only the linear (main) effects of both selection predictors and their corresponding two-way interaction. We do this with the recoded version of base-year family income, *INC8*.

Notice that by first fitting such selection models, we are able to test explicitly our hypotheses about the joint impact of base-year annual family income and prior mathematics achievement on children's selection into Catholic and public high schools. In Model A, for instance, we learn that our original hypotheses are strongly supported (χ^2 statistic = 120.13,

Table 12.4 Parameter estimates and approximate *p*-values for a pair of fitted logistic regression models in which attendance at a public or a Catholic high school (*CATHOLIC*) has been regressed on hypothesized selection predictors (*INC8* and *MATH8*) that describe the base-year annual family income and student mathematics achievement ($n = 5,671$)

Model A: Initial specification, with linear main effect of INC8

Predictor	Parameter Estimates
INTERCEPT	−5.209***
INC8	0.062***
MATH8	0.043***
INC8 × *MATH8*	−0.0007**
−2LL	3,675.2
Model LR χ^2 Statistic (3 df)	120.13***

Model B: Final specification, with quadratic main effect of INC8

Predictor	Parameter Estimates
INTERCEPT	−5.362***
INC8	0.087***
INC8²	−0.0004**
MATH8	0.036**
INC8 × *MATH8*	−0.0006*
−2LL	3,667.1
Model LR χ^2 Statistic (4 df)	128.2***

^-p <0.10; $^*p$ <0.05; $^{**}p$ <0.01; $^{***}p$ <0.001

p <0.001). Both the main effects of the covariates (p <0.001) and their two-way interaction (p <0.01) have statistically significant effects on the type of high school attended. We learn that it is more probable that children from higher-income homes and with greater eighth-grade mathematics achievement will attend a Catholic high school, although the effect of each predictor is moderated by the presence of the other. At higher levels of base-year annual family income, the impact of prior academic preparation is lessened, and vice versa.

In Model B (the lower panel of Table 12.4), we have refined our selection model by including a quadratic transformation of base-year annual family income. This leads to a statistically significant improvement in fit, as indicated by the decline in the $-2LL$ statistic of 8.1 points with the loss of one degree of freedom (p <0.01). As a selection model, we favor fitted Model B over Model A for reasons that we reveal below and that hark back to the issues of sparseness and common support that we described at the beginning of the chapter.

Notice that the parameter estimates listed in both panels were obtained by *maximum likelihood* estimation. In that sense, they are then "best" estimates of the population parameters, chosen to maximize the joint probability of observing all the outcome data—that is, the entire collection of 0's and 1's that represent the public- or Catholic-school choices of the sampled children, given the statistical model. Thus, in a real sense, these estimates provide us with a mathematical vision of how the covariate values can best be combined to discriminate between children who attend the two types of high school.[26] Their contributions, in this regard, can then be consolidated into a single number, for each child, by estimating his or her fitted value of the outcome. Because our outcome—*CATHOLIC*—is dichotomous, and its "upper" category represents the Catholic high-school choice, the fitted values are simply the estimated probabilities that each child will attend a Catholic high school. As noted earlier, in this application, we refer to these fitted probabilities as estimated *propensities*.[27] Providing that we have chosen the covariates well and

---

26. Here, we draw a conceptual link between logistic regression analysis and discriminant analysis, with the former being parametrically less stringent in that its covariates need not be drawn from a multivariate normal distribution (as the case with discriminant analysis).

27. Because we have specified a logistic function for the selection model, the estimated propensities are a nonlinear composite of covariate values and are optimal for discriminating between children who choose the Catholic- versus public-school options, *given the adequacy of the logistic model*. We could also have used a *probit* or a *linear-probability* function. In the former, the propensities would again be a nonlinear composite of covariate values; in the latter, a linear composite. However, the issue is

have specified the selection model correctly, the estimated propensities will summarize appropriately all that we know about the systematic nature of selection into Catholic and public high schools. They are that particular scalar function of the covariates that contains all of the information necessary to correct the estimated Catholic-school advantage for selection due to base-year annual family income and mathematics achievement (Rosenbaum & Rubin, 1984).[28]

We display in the histogram in panel A of Figure 12.2 the distribution of the estimated propensities obtained by fitting Model B across all sampled children.[29] In our NELS-88 example, these propensities are not large. They range from 0.016 to 0.173, with a median value of 0.106. The propensity scores provide an index—or scalar, in Rubin's terms—that optimally summarizes the information the covariates contain.

In the bottom panel of Figure 12.2, we re-present the sample distributions of the estimated propensities from Model B, divided into two panels by whether the child attended a Catholic or a public high school. Notice that the two sample distributions overlap completely, having almost identical ranges. But, as you might expect, the shapes of the two histograms differ somewhat, with the distribution of the propensities for the public high-school students having a much thicker lower tail. These differences, of course, embody the success with which we were able to predict the first-stage CATHOLIC outcome by our selection predictors, base-year annual family income and mathematics achievement.

The overlap of the sample distributions of the estimated propensities, by the values of CATHOLIC, is important because it suggests that students who enroll in Catholic high schools and those who enroll in public

---

not whether the composite is linear or nonlinear, but that the estimated propensities best discriminate among those who choose to go to Catholic versus public schools, given the particular covariates *and the model*. Thus, which of the three possible sets of propensities is optimal—the logit-based, probit-based, or linear-probability–based—depends on which of the three functions is appropriate. In practice, the choice between probit and logit functions makes little difference. But, the linear-probability function may lead to fitted values that fall outside the permissible range [0,1]. Traditionally, in propensity score estimation, the logit function has been preferred (Rosenbaum & Rubin, 1984).

28. Rosenbaum and Rubin (1984) show that this statement is true under the assumption of *unconfoundedness*. As explained earlier in the chapter, this critical assumption is that the treatment assignment is independent of the outcomes, *conditional on the covariates*. Or, in simpler terms, this means that we are assuming that, within each cell of a cross-tabulation formed by the values of the covariates, assignment to treatment and control conditions is random.

29. Notice that we have superimposed a *kernel density plot* in Panel A, to describe the smoothed envelope of the histogram. We provide similar smooth envelopes on all subsequent histograms displayed in figures in this chapter.

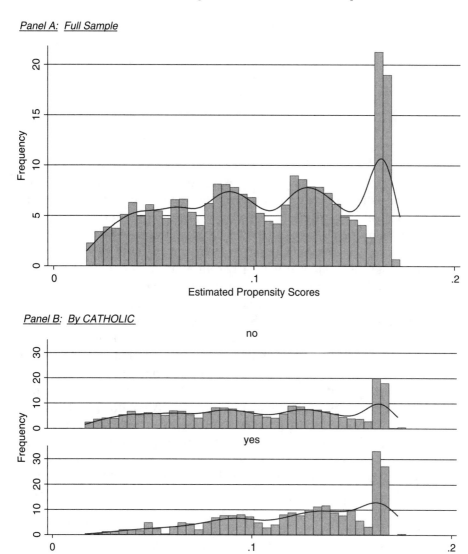

Figure 12.2 Histograms (and smoothed kernel-density estimates) of the propensities of selection into Catholic high school, from fitted Model B of Table 12.4, overall (Panel A) and by whether the child attended a Catholic or a public high school (Panel B).

high schools share a large region of common support on the covariates. It also suggests that if we were to now stratify the sample carefully, not by base-year annual family income and prior mathematics achievement, as before, but using our new scalar index, the *propensity score*, we could successfully anticipate finding both Catholic and public high-school children within each stratum. This, in turn, would imply that we could estimate the difference in average twelfth-grade mathematics achievement between Catholic and public high-school children within each stratum and pool the average differences across strata to obtain an overall estimate of the Catholic-school advantage. This is exactly what we do.

Estimation of the Treatment Effect by Stratifying on Propensity Scores

Once we have estimated these new propensity scores, we can correct for observed bias due to base-year annual family income and prior mathematics preparation by stratifying *on the propensities*, rather than on the covariates themselves. With our NELS-88 example, we began this process with propensities estimated from fitted Model A in Table 12.4, which contains only the linear main effect of baseline family income. Initially, we stipulated five initial strata or *blocks*, as they are known in the vernacular of propensity-score analysis. We made this choice based on technical recommendations that, with at least five blocks, you can eliminate more than nine-tenths of the observed bias that is present (Rosenbaum & Rubin, 1984). From that point, we iterated, as we described in our application of stratification earlier in the chapter. We first checked whether there was common support and whether balance had been attained within each of the blocks. In other words, we checked that there were both Catholic and public high-school students present in each propensity block, and that their average values on the covariates were no different within block. In fact, when you stratify on the propensities, it makes sense to check first that the average values of the propensities, within each block, are equal for Catholic and public high-school students. If this test is met in your proposed block structure, you can then delve more deeply and compare the average values of each of the covariates themselves, by *CATHOLIC*, within blocks. If these balancing checks fail, you can then split or recombine blocks iteratively. Only when the groups of Catholic and public high-school students in each block are balanced on *both* their mean propensities and on the means of all the covariates, can you conclude that you have an acceptable stratification and consequently move ahead to the second stage of the process in which you obtain bias-corrected estimates of the treatment effect.

In fact, it was just such an iterative process of balance checking and reblocking that led us to reject the initial Model A specification of the selection model in favor of Model B (Table 12.4). Under a variety of block structures, from three through 13 blocks, and even when within-block groups of Catholic and public high-school students were balanced on the propensity scores themselves, we found that the means of base-year annual family income were consistently out of balance in one or two of the upper blocks. When this kind of problem occurs, our advice is to question your specification of the selection model and seek out alternative specifications while remaining true to your theoretical decisions about which covariates to include. Typically, you can be guided in your respecification by being alert to where—that is, on which covariates—the failure to balance is occurring, and then seek an alternative specification for that particular covariate. Try sensible transformations of the offending covariate, based on the skewness of its sample distribution, or include polynomial versions of the covariate (as we did) to provide for a nonlinear relationship. Another useful strategy that can be effective is checking whether it makes sense to include interactions among the covariates as predictors in the selection model. We have not documented the additional data analyses that led from Model A to Model B here. However, the process is rendered data-analytically transparent by the new focus on finding a reasonable selection model as an initial step before correcting for observed selection bias. In our example, we were able to resolve the lack of balance in our initial blocking by adding a quadratic main effect of *INC8* to the selection equation.

Once our selection model was modified and refitted, we again used the obtained propensity scores to create a stratification that now contained six blocks, within which all necessary balancing conditions were met. We present this stratification in Table 12.5. Notice, first, as anticipated from Figure 12.2, we now enjoy common support across the six blocks—there are both Catholic and public high-school students present in each block. The first block, for instance, contains the 841 children whose propensities fell below 0.05, 810 of whom attended a public high school, and 31 of whom attended a Catholic high school. In addition, we confirmed balance in each block—the average values of the propensity scores, annual family income, and prior mathematics achievement for the two groups of students in each block were close in value. We cannot reject the null hypothesis of no mean difference by high school type, in the population, for either the propensities or any of the covariates in any block.[30]

Finally, we obtain within-stratum estimates of the Catholic high-school advantage by subtracting the corresponding within-block means (final column of the table). Again, although the subgroup estimates are scattered (from 0.36 through 3.07), weighting by the total within-stratum frequencies, we obtain an overall estimate of the average treatment effect—the

---

30. At a Bonferroni-adjusted α-level of 0.01, in each case.

Table 12.5 Six propensity-score strata, based on predicted values from Model B of Table 12.4. Within-block sample statistics include: (a) frequencies, (b) average propensity scores, (c) average base-year annual family income, (d) average base-year mathematics achievement, and (e) average twelfth-grade mathematics achievement by type of high school, and their difference ($n = 5,671$)

Propensity Blocks and Scores		Block Frequencies		Average Estimated Propensity Score		Average Base-Year Annual Family Income		Average Base-Year Mathematics Achievement (8th Grade)		Average Mathematics Achievement (12th Grade)		
Block	Range	Publ.	Cath.	Publ.	Cath.	Publ.	Cath.	Publ.	Cath.	Publ.	Cath.	Diff.
1	$\hat{p} <0.05$	810	31	0.036	0.040	8.47	9.81	43.16	44.68	42.74	45.35	2.61*,†
2	$0.05 \leq \hat{p} <0.075$	741	45	0.062	0.064	18.14	17.53	47.45	49.46	47.16	50.22	3.07**,†
3	$0.075 \leq \hat{p} <0.1$	928	100	0.088	0.089	26.64	26.57	48.80	49.63	48.79	49.63	0.84**,†
4	$0.1 \leq \hat{p} <0.125$	786	87	0.114	0.114	33.35	33.36	52.62	52.91	52.02	54.26	2.24*,†
5	$0.125 \leq \hat{p} <0.15$	810	145	0.136	0.137	40.73	41.47	55.15	54.79	54.72	56.54	1.82**,†
6	$0.15 \leq \hat{p} <0.2$	1,004	184	0.163	0.163	57.34	58.37	58.55	57.86	56.95	57.32	0.36

Weighted Average ATE 1.69
Weighted Average ATT 1.40

†$p <0.10$; *$p <0.05$; **$p <0.01$; ***$p <0.001$
†One-sided test.

Catholic-school advantage—of 1.69. This estimate is similar to the corresponding estimate that we obtained under the earlier direct control for covariates approach with the same covariates.[31] This time, though, notice that we have delved more deeply into the selection problem itself. We have modeled the selection process. We have checked for common (covariate) support and verified that there are Catholic and public high-school students in every block. We have checked the balancing property for the propensities and the covariates and found that it was met.

To conclude this subsection, we illustrate briefly how simple it is—given the propensity-score framework—to incorporate more covariates into the observed bias correction. For instance, as we have noted earlier, Altonji and his colleagues (2005a) argued that it made sense to include additional selection predictors such as base-year family background and prior parent and student expectations. Thus, we refitted our selection model in the lower panel of Table 12.4, Model B, adding covariates for the mother's and father's expectations for the student's education attainment, and measures of student misbehavior (including whether they got into fights at school, whether they failed to do homework, whether they were disruptive in class, and the risk of their dropping out), all measured in the base year. We refer to this supplemented model as *Model C*. Although we do not list its parameter estimates and goodness-of-fit statistics here, the model fitted well, and the additional covariates made a statistically significant improvement to its fit ($\Delta\chi^2 = 58.83$, $\Delta df = 6$, $p < 0.001$).

Based on propensity scores estimated from the more complex Model C, we repeated the blocking on propensity score process, this time ending up with five blocks. We list them in Table 12.6, along with statistics on the number of students within each block, average propensity score, and average twelfth-grade mathematics achievement, by the type of high school attended. There was again complete overlap of the sample distributions of the propensity scores, by type of high school, and so there are both Catholic and public high-school students within each block. Comparisons within block, by *CATHOLIC*, indicate that balance was achieved on the mean propensity scores and also on the means of all of the selection predictors in the model. Estimates of the Catholic-school advantage, within block, are scattered from 0.48 through 2.51, with an overall weighted-average estimated treatment effect of 1.78 (with the average effect of the treatment on the treated being 1.56). These estimates are similar in magnitude to our earlier bias-corrected estimates, and do not

---

31. The corresponding estimated effect of the Catholic-school treatment *on the treated* was 1.40, obtained by weighting within-block estimates by the number of Catholic high-school students within block.

Table 12.6 Five propensity-score blocks, based on predicted values from final Model C (which contains selected covariates in addition to those included in Model B). Within-block sample statistics include: (a) frequencies, (b) average propensity scores, and (c) average twelfth-grade mathematics achievement by type of high school, and their difference ($n = 5,671$)

Propensity Blocks and Scores		Block Frequencies		Average Estimated Propensity Score		Average Mathematics Achievement (12th Grade)		
Block	Range	Publ.	Cath.	Publ.	Cath.	Publ.	Cath.	Diff.
1	$\hat{p} <0.05$	1,089	34	0.030	0.035	43.66	46.01	2.35¬†
2	$0.05 \leq \hat{p} <0.1$	1,431	110	0.075	0.078	48.85	51.00	2.15*†
3	$0.1 \leq \hat{p} <0.15$	1,599	253	0.127	0.129	53.62	55.38	1.76**†
4	$0.15 \leq \hat{p} <0.2$	829	160	0.172	0.173	56.87	57.35	0.48
5	$0.2 \leq \hat{p} <0.3$	131	35	0.213	0.212	52.51	55.01	2.51¬†
						Weighted Average ATE		*1.78*
						Weighted Average ATT		*1.56*

¬$p <0.10$; *$p <0.05$; **$p <0.01$; ***$p <0.001$
†one-sided test.

represent much of a shift from the estimate we obtained by correcting for observed bias due only to base-year annual family income and the student's prior mathematics achievement.[32]

Estimation of the Treatment Effect by Matching on Propensity Scores

The fact that we can eliminate large amounts of observed selection bias by stratifying the sample into five or six blocks on the propensity scores tempts one to think that we may do better with seven blocks, or eight, and so on. As we create more blocks, we can anticipate removing more of the observed bias, provided that we remain within the region of common support and that the balancing property continues to be met. However, we know from Cochran and Rubin's work (1973) that you can do pretty well with as few as five blocks and so, beyond that, there may be diminishing returns.

Rather than continuing to search for blocking Nirvana, however, you can turn the search for an optimal number of blocks on its head. Rather than adopting a top-down approach in which you divide up well-populated blocks to form smaller and narrower blocks, and then check for overlap and balance in the new blocks, you can adopt a bottom-up approach. You can list all members of the treatment group (in this case, the Catholic high school students) and, for each of them, use the estimated propensity scores to find a "nearest neighbor" in the control group—that is, someone among the public high-school students whose propensity score matches theirs, as closely as is feasible.[33] For this pair, balance on the propensity scores will be present automatically, and usually on the covariates as well.[34] Once you have found viable neighbors for each treated participant, you can drop unused public high-school students from your analysis. They are not needed because either another control-group member is standing in their stead, or they fall outside the region of common support, as defined by their propensity score. This process is called *nearest-neighbor matching*.

---

32. Details of these analyses are available from the authors on request.
33. Because the estimated propensity scores depend on many continuous (and categorical) predictors, it is unlikely that two participants will share *exactly* the same propensity score.
34. This claim, of course, is not universally true, as two participants can have similar propensity scores but differ on their values of the covariates, the differences in the latter being offset by differences in the parameter estimates associated with the covariates in the selection model. However, when selection predictors have been chosen sensibly, it usually turns out to be a defensible claim.

There are two ways to conceptualize the process of matching nearest neighbors on propensity scores. First, you can regard nearest-neighbor matching as a kind of subsampling. It is a way of examining members of the control group, under the microscope of their propensities, to find that particular subgroup of control members that most closely resembles the members of the treatment group, one on one, based on the covariates that you believe matter most. Once the matched groups have been identified, their average outcomes can be compared using standard methods. Alternatively, you can think of nearest-neighbor matching as an extreme form of stratification, in which only two participants are present in each stratum, one Catholic high-school student and one public high-school student. These pairs have been chosen because their matched propensity scores suggest that their important characteristics—those that we believe are most closely linked to selection—are very similar. Unmatched public high-school students are eliminated because they are not needed, once viable neighbors have been found.[35]

Of course, our broad description of the nearest-neighbor matching algorithm disguises many technical complexities that must be faced in practical data analysis. We suggest that you consult the literature that we cite at the end of the chapter to learn more about their subtleties. However, just to alert you, here are a few of the questions you must answer. What should you do if there are multiple possible "control" matches for a particular member of the treatment group? Should you include all the matched neighbors in the control subsample? If you do include them, how do you deal with their multiple values on the final outcome in your estimation of the treatment effect? Should each of them count as a separate control participant? Should they be pooled into a single simulated "super-neighbor"? If you don't include all of the multiple possible matches, how should you pick the best one for the job—by a random drawing, or in a more systematic way? Should matching and resampling from the control group be conducted with, or without, replacement? If you do use a control-group member as a match for more than one treatment-group member, how do you estimate the standard errors associated with the difference in final outcome means? This is only a taste of the many questions relevant to nearest-neighbor matching that methodologists have tackled and resolved. Their solutions lie beyond our presentation here. However, in the next section, we describe a strategy that allows you to avoid these questions.

---

35. It is true that this process sacrifices statistical power as it eliminates members of the sample from the analysis. However, remember that we are using observational data, and that the sample members who have been eliminated were demonstrably non-equivalent to those who were retained.

By way of illustration, though, we have executed one particular form of nearest-neighbor matching in our NELS-88 example, using Stata's user-supported routine, *attnd* (Becker &Ichino, 2002). We implemented it using the propensity scores estimated in our final and most complex selection model, Model C. If more than one good match exists for any treated individual, the *attnd* algorithm picks one of the duplicates by a random draw to become the actual "neighbor" from the control group. It also picks out nearest neighbors with replacement, meaning that control-group members can serve as neighbors for more than one member of the treatment group. So, you can end up with a "matched" control group that is smaller than the treatment group.

In our example, after the matching process was over, each of our original Catholic high-school students had been matched with a public high-school neighbor who had an almost identical propensity score. For instance, among the Catholic high-school students, student #1485802 had a propensity score of 0.0099903 and was matched with public high-school student #709436, whose propensity score was 0.0100709. And, as you would expect with propensities that have been estimated in double precision, although their values on the selection predictors did not match exactly, these students had very similar values on the covariates. They both came from families with low incomes, they had low prior mathematics achievement, they never got into fights in school, and so on. In the end, we were left with a sample that contained the entire treated group of 592 Catholic high-school students and a comparison group of 553 matched public high-school "neighbors." Notice that the size of the matched control group was smaller than the size of the treatment group because some control-group members served as matches for more than one treatment-group member. The estimate of the ATE was 1.04, and the estimate of the average treatment effect on the treated (ATT) was 0.92. These estimates are smaller than our previous bias-corrected estimates of treatment effects. However, in both cases, we can reject the null hypothesis that the bias-corrected Catholic-school advantage is zero in the population.[36]

We conclude this discussion of the nearest-neighbor matching technique by describing another common application of the approach that capitalizes on access to a set of propensity scores. Let's suppose that you possess non experimental data on a sample of individuals who were

---

36. There is a lot of recent technical research on matching methods. For example, Abadie and Imbens (2008) show that the use of bootstrapping does not produce correct standard errors for matching estimators. We thank Juan Saavedra for pointing this out to us and for very helpful conversations about the topics discussed in this chapter.

all treated. For example, they may be low-income adult males who had participated in the National Supported Work (NSW) program, an initiative that provided participants with structured work experiences. Now, you want to learn whether the treatment improved labor-market outcomes for participants. However, you lack a control group. How can you best select a suitable control group from another dataset, such as the Current Population Survey (CPS), which the U.S. Bureau of the Census administers monthly to a sample of more than 50,000 U.S. households? Propensity-score analysis and nearest-neighbor matching provide one alternative. First, you merge all your data on the participants in the training program with the CPS data from an appropriate year. Second, you fit a sensible selection model that predicts whether an adult male participated in the training program, or not, in the combined dataset and estimate a propensity score for each person. Working with these propensities and nearest-neighbor matching, you then select a subsample of males from the CPS sample that can best serve as the control group for comparison of outcomes with your treatment group, in the usual way.

In recent years, a number of studies have examined whether this particular application of propensity scores and nearest-neighbor matching produces estimates of treatment effects that are similar to those obtained from random-assignment experiments. Not surprisingly, the results of these studies are mixed. For example, Rajeev Dehejia and Sadek Wahba (2002) find that the application of these techniques allowed them to replicate the results of the random-assignment evaluation of the NSW program using a comparison group drawn from the CPS. On the other hand, Diaz and Handa (2006) report that the use of these methods did not allow them to replicate consistently the experimental results from the analysis of Mexico's PROGRESA conditional cash-transfer program. The mixed nature of the results of studies that examine whether the application of matching methods can reproduce the results from random-assignment experiments should not surprise you. Much depends on the success of the researchers in understanding the selection process, in modeling it accurately, and in obtaining comparable measures of the critical covariates in all of the datasets used in the analysis.

Estimation of the Treatment Effect by Weighting by the Inverse of the Propensity Scores

In the previous subsection, we used nearest-neighbor matching to choose a control subset of 553 public high-school students, and we compared their twelfth-grade mathematics achievement with that of our treatment group of 592 Catholic high-school students. In the process, we eliminated from the estimate of the treatment effect thousands of public-school students who were legitimate members of the original survey sample, but didn't happen to become "nearest neighbors." This may seem wasteful. We now turn to a method of making use of propensity scores that allows us to utilize the information on all of the public-school students in the original sample.

Conceptually, you can regard our estimation of the Catholic-school advantage using the nearest-neighbor matching method as the creation of a *weighted* average of *all* the students' outcome values, whether they were selected as a nearest neighbor or not. This may seem like a strange statement to make, given that we dropped a large number of potential neighbors during the computation. In essence, we incorporated into our estimation of the treatment effect a set of weights that were dichotomous and could take on a value of either 1 or zero. It is as though we had assigned everyone in the Catholic high-school treatment group a weight of 1. There were 592 of these. Then, students in the public high-school control group were assigned a weight of 1 if they proved to be a suitable nearest neighbor (553 students) or a weight of zero if they were not a nearest neighbor to any Catholic-school student in the sample. Then, we estimated and compared the average twelfth-grade mathematics achievement outcome for Catholic and public high-school students, weighting each student's contribution by the respective dichotomous weight. All children with a weight of zero contributed nothing to the computation. We were left with the difference in outcome means between all the students in the Catholic-school treatment group and those in the public-school control group who had been assigned a weight of 1 by the matching process. And where did we obtain the values of these dichotomous weights? We got them indirectly by examining the values of each participant's propensity score! This raises the question of whether we might be able to use the propensities themselves—for every person—to create a more fine-grained set of weights, and then redo the computation while retaining everyone in the sample.

Begin by thinking about what the values of the propensities would have been if this had been an experiment in which children had been assigned randomly to the Catholic or public high school conditions. In this case, we would not have been able to predict *CATHOLIC* by any covariate, regardless of its theoretical support, because the random assignment would ensure that high-school assignment was uncorrelated with all potential covariates. So, all of the children's estimated propensities—regardless of their values on the covariates—would be identical, and we would learn nothing by fitting the first-stage selection model.[37] However, our data do not come from a random-assignment experiment, and we have indeed been able to predict whether a child went to a Catholic (or public) high school. In fact, the estimated propensities themselves describe the success of our prediction of selection. They summarize the extent to which a systematic selection process led each participant to attend the particular type of high school that he or she did, in fact, enter. In a sense, the propensities summarize how nonrandom the children's choices of high-school type were in our data. Then, throughout this entire section we have been trying essentially to correct estimates of the Catholic-school advantage for differences in the propensities across children.

To obtain an unbiased estimate of the impact of the Catholic-school treatment, we need to purge our estimate of the treatment effect of the impact of this selection. In carrying out this purging process, we can be guided by the magnitudes of the propensities themselves. Consider two Catholic high-school students, for instance—let's call them Andy and Bob—and let's suppose that we know that Andy's estimated propensity score $\hat{p}_{Andy}$ was much higher than Bob's, $\hat{p}_{Bob}$. We can then conclude that selection on the observable variables played a stronger and more predictable role in Andy's school choice than in Bob's. To bias-correct an estimate of the Catholic-school advantage that incorporated information from both of these students, we would want to downplay the contribution of Andy, whose choice was more predictable, in comparison to the contribution of Bob, whose choice was less so. Thus, we would want to down-weight the contribution made by Catholic high-school student Andy, relative to the contribution of Catholic high-school student Bob. We can achieve this by incorporating weights that are the *inverse* of their propensity scores,

$1/\hat{p}_{Andy}$ and $1/\hat{p}_{Bob}$, into our estimation of the average treatment effect. That way, Andy would have a lower weight than Bob, among Catholic high-school students.

How should the contributions of the public high-school students be weighted? The argument is similar. Consider two public high-school students, Yves and Zack. Recall that the propensities that we have estimated describe the fitted probability of entering Catholic high school for each student in the sample. For Yves and Zack, however, who went to public school, we want to weight by the inverse of their probabilities of entering their own kind of school, a public high school. These probabilities are

---

37. They would be equal to the overall proportion of Catholic high-school students in the full sample, 0.104.

therefore the complement of their propensities—that is, $(1 - \hat{p}_{Yves})$ and $(1 - \hat{p}_{Zack})$.[38] So, we would weight their contributions to the average treatment effect by their respective inverses, $1/(1 - \hat{p}_{Yves})$ and $1/(1 - \hat{p}_{Zack})$.

Technical work based on Rubin's potential outcomes framework has shown that such *inverse probability weights*—$1/\hat{p}$ for treatment participants, and $1/(1 - \hat{p})$ for control participants—are exactly the weights needed to counteract the effect of selection on an estimate of the average treatment effect (Imbens & Wooldridge, 2009), provided that you have estimated the propensity scores correctly. They are straightforward to compute from the obtained propensities, as shown, and can be incorporated readily into the estimation of the average mean difference in outcome between treatment and control groups. Although several explicit weighted estimators have been proposed, based on this principle, each incorporating inverse probability weights in a slightly different way, we recommend Imbens and Wooldridge's inverse-probability weighting (IPW) estimator (2009, Equation 18, p. 35),[39] the value of which can easily be estimated directly in a weighted least-squares (WLS) regression analysis. For instance, in our NELS-88 example, we used WLS regression analysis to regress *MATH12* on *CATHOLIC*, with IPW weights.[40] In this most sophisticated application of propensity scores, we find that the average Catholic-school advantage corrected for bias due to our final set of observed covariates is 1.47 ($p <0.001$), an effect that is consistent with our earlier estimates.

As a final comment on this method of using propensity scores, it is interesting to see how the application of the inverse-probability weights (that have proven effective in removing observed bias from our estimate

---

38. With only two choices, if the probability of choosing one of them is p, then the probability of choosing the other must be $(1 - p)$.

39. There is a typo in the extreme right-hand quotient in Imbens and Wooldridge's Equation (18). When corrected, it should read:

$$\hat{\tau}_{ipw} = \left(\sum_{i=1}^{N} \frac{W_i Y_i}{\hat{e}(X_i)} \bigg/ \sum_{i=1}^{N} \frac{W_i}{\hat{e}(X_i)} \right) - \left(\sum_{i=1}^{N} \frac{(1 - W_i)Y_i}{1 - \hat{e}(X_i)} \bigg/ \sum_{i=1}^{N} \frac{(1 - W_i)}{1 - \hat{e}(X_i)} \right)$$

(Imbens, private communication, 2009), where W_i is the value of the treatment indicator for the ith individual and takes on a value of 1, when the participant is a member of the treatment group (0, otherwise) and $\hat{e}(X_i)$ is the propensity score, predicted from covariates X.

40. Be cautious how you program and execute the WLS regression analysis, as the idiosyncrasies of your statistical software may affect how you need to communicate the IPW weights. To obtain the Imbens and Wooldridge IPW estimator by classical WLS regression analysis, the regression weights must be the square-roots of the IPW weights. However, some statistical routines require you to input WLS regression weights as squares—that is, as variance-based weights—in which case, the IPW weights themselves are the required form.

of the Catholic-school advantage) affects the sample distributions of the covariates from which they were derived. In Figure 12.3, we present kernel-smoothed density estimates of the sample distribution of our *MATH8* selection predictor, by levels of the question predictor *CATHOLIC*, before (*top panel*) and after weighting by the IPW weights (*bottom panel*). Notice that the application of the weights alters the sample densities so that the Catholic-school and public-school densities acquire similar shapes and overlap completely. In a sense, the inverse-probability weights have acted to restructure the Catholic-school and public-school densities for complete common support and balance. This same pattern holds for the distributions of all of the covariates.

A Return to the Substantive Question

As we mentioned at the beginning of this chapter, our choice of substantive question and the dataset that we used to illustrate these methods of reducing bias in treatment effects due to selection on observed variables was influenced by Altonji, Elder, and Taber's thoughtful paper (2005a). Their paper examined the question of whether Catholic high schools provide better education than public high schools, using a technique the authors had developed to assess the degree of omitted-variables bias from evidence on the extent to which the observed covariates are able to predict selection of students into the Catholic and public schools. We describe two related lessons from this paper that bear on efforts to address causal questions with non-experimental data, and that extend the presentation here.

One lesson concerns the importance of thinking carefully about the definition of the analytic sample. Altonji and his colleagues reported results based on two analytic samples. The first included all students in the NELS-88 database who attended either a Catholic or public high school. The second included only those students in NELS-88 who attended a Catholic school *in grade 8*. The authors presented two reasons why they believed that results based on the second, smaller sample were more credible. First, only 0.3% of students who attended a public school as an eighth-grader subsequently enrolled in a Catholic high school. Consequently, the authors argued that public-school eighth-graders were unlikely to be appropriate comparison group members for predicting what the educational outcomes of Catholic high-school students would have been, if they had attended a public high school. Second, the observed covariates chosen to model the selection process were much less successful in predicting

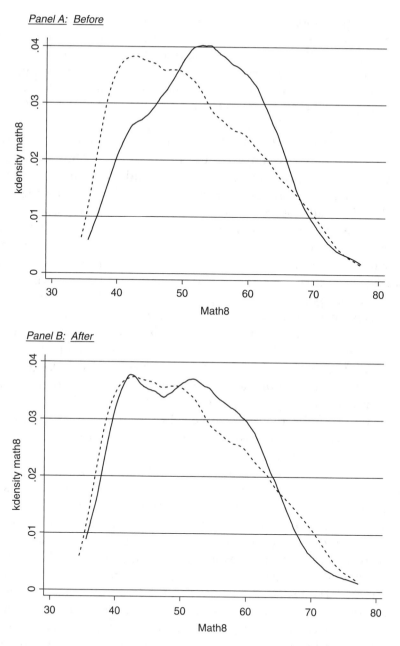

Figure 12.3 Kernel-density estimates of the sample distribution of selection predictor *MATH8*, by *CATHOLIC*, before and after application of the IPW weights.

choice of high-school type for students who attended a Catholic school as an eighth-grader than they were in predicting choice of high-school type in the larger NELS-88 sample. This pattern led the authors to conclude that bias in estimates of treatment effects stemming from the influences of unobserved differences between students who attended the two types of high schools was also likely to be smaller in the subsample of Catholic-school eighth-graders than in the larger sample.

The second lesson is that the direction of bias in estimates of treatment effects from non-experimental data is often not clear. Altonji and his colleagues focused, for instance, on whether a student graduated ultimately from high school. They found a substantial and statistically significant Catholic-school advantage. For example, their preferred estimate—based on the subsample of students who attended Catholic schools as eighth-graders—was between 5 and 8 percentage points (depending on the degree of bias that stemmed from the influences of unobserved variables). However, when they estimated this same parameter in the larger sample of all NELS-88 participants, using the same statistical models with the same sets of covariates, their estimates of the same treatment effect were less than half as large. Given the authors' compelling argument that omitted-variables bias was a bigger problem in the larger sample, this pattern suggests that controlling for a great many covariates in the larger sample resulted in an estimate of the Catholic school advantage that was *downwardly* biased. Thus, we conclude that not only do the influences of unobserved variables that determine selection into different treatments often create bias in estimates of treatment effects, but that often the direction of the bias is not clear.

The Altonji, Elder, and Taber paper (2005a) illustrates the progress that methodologists have made in devising creative and powerful strategies for using the rich information contained in many longitudinal surveys to address causal questions. In this respect, their paper contributes to the set of methods described in this chapter. In another respect, however, the paper provides a cautionary message to potential users of such techniques. The message is that selection into treatments is as likely to be based on unobserved variables as on observed variables, and this source of bias remains, even after the methods of selection described in this chapter have been applied. In other words, the assumption of unconfoundedness that underlies all of the techniques described in this chapter—that selection into treatment is solely a function of observed covariates—is an extremely stringent condition.

What to Read Next

A good place to start in learning more about the burgeoning literature on the topics described in this chapter is Imbens and Wooldridge's 2009 survey paper in the *Journal of Economic Literature*. The widely cited papers by Dehejia and Wahba (1999, 2002) and the ensuing interchange between Smith and Todd (2005a, 2005b) and Dehejia (2005) illustrate both the promise and pitfalls in using matching techniques to estimate causal impacts from non-experimental data.

13

Methodological Lessons from the Long Quest

Recall from Chapter 1 the statement that Paul Hanus made at the 1913 meeting of the National Education Association: "The only way to combat successfully mistaken common-sense as applied to educational affairs is to meet it with uncommon-sense in the same field—with technical information, the validity of which is indisputable" (Hanus, 1920). The quest for Hanus's "indisputable technical information" has been a long one, stretching out over the last century. However, advances made in recent decades have made it increasingly possible to conduct social science research that meets this standard. Some of these advances reflect improvements in our application and interpretation of powerful analytic approaches. For example, the efforts of Donald Rubin and other methodologists have clarified the assumptions under which random-assignment experiments can provide unbiased answers to educational policy questions. A body of work that began with contributions from psychologist Donald Campbell, and to which methodologists from several disciplines have contributed, has improved our understanding of the conditions under which the regression-discontinuity design can support causal inferences. Methodologists have also developed new insights into the application of instrumental-variables estimation and the practical utility of particular kinds of instruments.

Other notable advances have been in the use of computers and data warehouses for administrative record-keeping. For example, well-organized digitized records that provide extensive information on such important things as school enrollments, teacher assignments, student test scores, and the labor-market outcomes of adults have become available increasingly. This, in turn, has increased dramatically the feasibility of examining the causal consequences of a wide variety of educational-policy initiatives, and has also lowered the cost of doing so.

Still other important advances have been made in the sophistication of statistical software that makes it easy to analyze vast amounts of quantitative data using new and comprehensive analytic strategies. For example, as recently as the 1970s, researchers who wanted to correct the standard errors in regression analyses of data on students grouped within classrooms had to write their own computer programs to account for the clustering. Today, researchers can obtain the correct standard errors by choosing among options available in most software packages. Sophisticated statistical software and rapid computer processing even make it possible to estimate these standard errors using nonparametric resampling procedures—like the bootstrap—when conventional normal-theory assumptions are not appropriate.

These advances in research methodology, administrative record-keeping, and statistical software enhance our ability as researchers to investigate the causal consequences of educational-policy interventions. However, all this new potential will be realized only if researchers keep the lessons described in this book firmly in their minds. It is not enough to have access to bigger datasets, better methods, and more sophisticated software; you also have to make use of the data and tools in thoughtful ways. In this chapter, we review and comment further on some of the lessons from our book and illustrate them once again with examples drawn from a variety of well-designed and well-implemented quantitative studies, many of which we have already introduced in earlier chapters. While we do not discuss every strategic and analytic detail that has graced the pages of our book, we frame those we have selected here as a parting set of important "lessons learned."

Be Clear About Your Theory of Action

As explained in Chapter 2, basing an investigation on sound and relevant social science theory is critical to both the design of research for causal inference and to the interpretation of its findings. Social science theory informs the questions that must be addressed, the population of interest, the nature of the intervention, the outcomes that we expect a particular policy intervention to influence, the expected timing of those impacts, and the mechanisms through which the impacts are hypothesized to take place. Without sound theory, research becomes little more than an unguided fishing expedition and cannot be considered science. We illustrate the important roles that theory plays in social science research by again considering how a reduction in class size might result in higher student achievement. At its most basic level, a simple theory about why smaller class size would lead to higher student achievement seems straightforward: The smaller the class, the more time the teacher has to work with students, individually or in small groups. However, a little reflection leads one to the realization that this minimal theory must be refined if it is to address the many subtle questions that arise in designing a class-size-reduction policy and to evaluate the sensitivity of its consequences to design decisions. For example, what can theory tell us about whether it matters if all students are placed in smaller classes of the same size, or if students with particular characteristics are assigned to especially small classes? Does it matter how teachers are assigned to classes of different size? More refined theories that suggest answers to questions such as these shed light on the design of class-size reduction initiatives and on the interpretation of their results.

For example, in 2001, economist Edward Lazear published a theory of the links between class size and student achievement that addressed one of these questions. Lazear theorized that students differ in their propensity to disrupt the classroom learning-environment through their poor behavior. In his theory, the mechanism through which a smaller class size increases student achievement is that it reduces the amount of instructional time that is lost to student disruptions. One hypothesis stemming from Lazear's "disruptive-student" theory is that class-size reductions would then have a greater aggregate impact on student achievement if administrators grouped disruptive students strategically in especially small classes than if students are assigned randomly to smaller classes. The reason is that, in the larger classes now free of disruptions by unruly students, all students will achieve at higher levels. In testing this subtle hypothesis, it would be important to be able to identify disruptive children and obtain the permission of participants to place them in particularly small classes.

A quite different theory of why class size affects student achievement centers on teacher labor markets and working conditions. From this theoretical perspective, smaller classes offer more desirable working conditions for teachers. Consequently, schools that offer small classes will be more effective in attracting strong applicants for their teaching positions than will schools with larger classes (Murnane, 1981). In designing research to test this "working-conditions" hypothesis, it would be important to adopt a time-frame that is long enough to allow schools with reduced class sizes to recruit these stronger candidates for their teaching positions and to observe their impacts on subsequent student achievement.

These two theories about the mechanisms through which class size affects student achievement are relevant to the interpretation of the results from the Tennessee Student/Teacher Achievement Ratio (STAR) experiment. Recall from Chapter 3 that, in this experiment, teachers and students were assigned randomly either to small classes (of 13–17 students) or to regular- size classes (of 21–25 students). The results of the evaluation showed that, at the end of the first year of the experiment, students placed in small classes scored 4 percentage points higher, on average, on a standardized test of cognitive skills than did students placed in regular size classes (Krueger, 1999). Although advocates of class-size reduction applauded the positive impact of the intervention, critics argued that the impact was only modest in size, given the high financial cost of reducing the class sizes in the first place (Hanushek, 1998).

One thing missing from the debate about the results of the STAR experiment was recognition that the design of the experiment eliminated two mechanisms through which class-size reductions may affect student achievement. The assignment process in the STAR experiment meant that, on average, potentially disruptive children were distributed randomly among classes, rather than being clustered together in small classes. Recent ingenious research by Bryan Graham (2008) using data from the STAR experiment lends support for Lazear's "disruptive-student" hypothesis. The random assignment of teachers to classes of different size within the same school also meant that the STAR experiment did not provide an opportunity to test the "working-conditions" hypothesis.

The point of this example is to illustrate the importance of theory in designing and in interpreting the results of research to evaluate the impact of a policy intervention. The STAR experiment was a remarkable accomplishment that provided important new information about the consequences of class-size reductions. However, thinking about the theoretical mechanisms through which class size may influence student achievement leads to the realization that the experiment was not designed to test important hypotheses about two potential benefits of small classes: the ability to handle disruptive students well, and the ability to attract especially skilled teachers. It would take subsequent research, with different designs, to estimate the importance of these mechanisms.

Learn About Culture, Rules, and Institutions in the Research Setting

Developing a deep understanding of the culture of the setting in which your research takes place is critical to conducting research successfully.

The descriptions in Chapter 5 of the efforts of Abdul Latif Jameel Poverty Action Lab (J-PAL) researchers to build support for random-assignment evaluations of the Balsakhi program in Indian cities and a novel teacher-incentive program in rural India illustrate this lesson. Equally important is an understanding of the institutions and rules that affect the actions of the individuals and organizations participating in educational interventions. Brian Jacob and Lars Lefgren's (2004) evaluation of the mandatory summer-school and student-retention policy that the Chicago Public Schools (CPS) introduced in 1996 illustrates this point.

We explained in Chapters 8 and 11 that the CPS policy included mandatory summer school for third-grade students whose end-of-year mathematics or reading achievement fell below a prespecified level, and retention in grade for those students whose reading or mathematics achievement level after the completion of summer school was still below the minimum level for promotion. In fact, the policy also pertained to students in grade 6. Jacob and Lefgren assessed the consequences of the CPS policy by comparing the achievement of students in the treatment and control groups two years after the original promotion decisions had been made for the third- and sixth-graders. They found that retention in grade had a detrimental effect on the reading achievement of the former sixth-graders, but not on the reading achievement of the former third-graders.

Conversations with teachers and district officials about testing policies led Jacob and Lefgren to the following explanation for the difference in results across the original grade levels. Two years after retention and promotion decisions had been made for the former sixth-graders, the students who had been promoted were now in the eighth grade and faced a high-stakes test that they needed to pass in order to be promoted to ninth grade. The high stakes led these students to put their best efforts into doing well on the tests. In contrast, most of the students who had been retained in sixth grade originally were now only finishing the seventh grade, two years later. Facing no high stakes, these students had no incentive to work hard on the reading examination they took at the end of the school year. Thus, the differences in average reading scores detected two years later for students who had just met the standard for promotion out of sixth grade and for students who just fell short of the promotion standard may have stemmed from the difference in incentives to work hard on the reading examination they faced subsequently.

Among children who faced the promotion decision at the end of third grade, however, there were no differences in incentives when they took the corresponding reading tests two years later. The reason is that there were no high stakes attached to either the fourth- or fifth-grade test scores.

Putting this pattern together, Jacob and Lefgren concluded that their results were consistent with the conclusion that retention in grade had no long-term effect on the reading achievement of either third-grade students or sixth-grade students. The difference in the test patterns two years after promotion decisions were made could be accounted for by the pattern of stakes attached to the tests subsequently faced by the different groups.

This example illustrates the importance of developing a thorough understanding of the institutions and rules in the settings where an educational-policy intervention takes place. In the case of the Jacob and Lefgren study, knowledge of the details of Chicago's testing policy—including the stakes attached to tests administered at different grade levels—was important in shedding light on the likely explanation of an initially puzzling set of findings about the consequences of grade retention.

Understand the Counterfactual

The goal of causal research is to learn how a particular treatment affects outcomes for a well-defined population. The conceptual model underlying such research is a comparison of the distribution of the values of an outcome for the population subject to the treatment with the best educated guess of what the distribution of outcomes would have been for the same population in the absence of the policy. The chapters of our book describe a variety of strategies for estimating the distribution of outcomes under treatment and counterfactual conditions. In Chapter 5, we used the career-academies evaluation to illustrate the importance of being clear on the definition of the treatment. Here we use an example from an evaluation of a quite different initiative to illustrate the importance of being clear on the definition of the counterfactual.

In 2004, Mathematica Policy Research released the results of a random-assignment evaluation of how effective Teach for America (TFA) participants had been in increasing students' mathematics and reading achievement (Decker, Mayer, & Glazerman, 2004). The report attracted considerable media attention because TFA brings to public-school teaching academically talented graduates from highly competitive colleges and universities, many of whom would not have elected to go through lengthy conventional teacher-certification programs. The program is controversial because: (a) TFA participants' initial formal training is restricted to an intensive five-week summer program, (b) the majority of TFA participants leave their assigned classrooms after fulfilling a two-year commitment, and (c) TFA participants teach in schools that serve some of the nation's neediest children.

The Mathematica study found that elementary-school students taught by TFA participants achieved higher mathematics scores, on average, than students taught by other teachers in the same schools, and that there were no statistically significant differences between the average reading scores of students taught by the two groups of teachers. However, understanding the nature of the group to which TFA teachers were compared—the counterfactual—is important in interpreting the findings.

A close reading of the Mathematica evaluation reveals that a large percentage of the non-TFA teachers in the schools participating in the study—that is, the teachers in the comparison group—were remarkably ill-prepared to educate children at all. Less than 4% of them had graduated from a college or university that was classified as at least "very competitive"—compared to 22% of the national teaching force and 70% of TFA participants. In addition, almost 30% of the non-TFA teachers in these schools had no student-teaching experience at all.

The evaluation showed that TFA participants helped to alleviate the damage caused by state and local government policies and collectively bargained contracts that allowed many of the nation's most needy children to be taught by some of the nation's least well-prepared teachers. This is a praiseworthy accomplishment. However, understanding the counterfactual creates the realization that the Mathematica evaluation could only draw conclusions about the effectiveness of TFA participants compared to ill-prepared teachers, not to well-prepared, veteran teachers. This highlights the importance of designing public policies to attract well-prepared, experienced teachers to schools serving high concentrations of needy children.

Always Worry About Selection Bias

The creation of rich longitudinal datasets on children's educational experiences in recent decades has increased markedly the list of variables that researchers can use in attempting to control for selection bias in causal research based on observational data. The development of propensity-score matching methods has brought new tools to the efforts of researchers engaged in such efforts. Nonetheless, we want to emphasize that the assumption of *unconfoundedness*—that selection into different treatments is totally a function of observed variables—is typically very difficult to defend. We illustrate this by returning, once again, to the history of research on career academies.

Prior to the MDRC random-assignment study of career academies, a number of nonexperimental studies had found that participants in career academies had higher high-school graduation rates, better grades, and better end-of-school test scores than observationally similar students enrolled in other high-school programs (Stern, Raby, & Dayton, 1992). Of course, the implicit assumption underlying the interpretation of the results of these quasi-experimental studies was unconfoundedness—that, after controlling for observed covariates, students in the comparison groups did not differ from the students who were enrolled in a career academy. The MDRC random-assignment study of career academies showed that this assumption was not consistent with the evidence. Indeed, the MDRC study found no differences between the average values of these academic outcomes for students who won the lottery and received an offer of a place in a career academy and those students who lost in the lottery. The MDRC evaluation also showed that the control group in the random-assignment study had much higher high-school graduation rates and grades than observationally similar students who did not apply to the career-academy lottery. The explanation for both of these sets of results is that students who applied to participate in career academies had atypically high motivation levels. Consequently, the earlier studies, which lacked appropriate exogenous variation in the assignment of students to career academies, produced biased estimates of the causal impact of career academies on student outcomes.

The difference between the results of the MDRC random-assignment study and the results of the prior quasi-experimental and observational studies is not atypical. In fact, a number of researchers have demonstrated that applying even the most sophisticated statistical techniques to data that lack a source of exogenous treatment variation will not replicate credibly the results obtained in random-assignment experiments (Agodini & Dynarski, 2004; Glazerman, Levy, & Myers, 2003; LaLonde, 1986). This does not mean, however, that random-assignment evaluations are the only way to obtain unbiased estimates of the causal impacts of educational interventions. Natural experiments can also provide arguably exogenous variation in assignment to experimental condition that can sometimes be exploited to create treatment and control groups that are equal in expectation prior to the onset of the intervention. In fact, two groups of researchers have used a regression-discontinuity approach recently to re-analyze data from random-assignment experiments and concluded that the results are very similar (Buddelmeyer & Skoufias, 2004; Cook & Wong, forthcoming).

As we discussed in Chapter 12, researchers are often asked to evaluate the impact of an educational intervention in situations where no credible source of exogenous variation in assignment to experimental condition exists. In these cases, the investigator's ability to obtain an unbiased estimate of the causal impact of the intervention is often severely compromised. As Thomas Cook and his colleagues (2008) have demonstrated, this is especially true when researchers must turn to already collected nationally representative observational data to seek out a "comparison" group by matching participants on the basis of their demographic characteristics and those of their families. Cook and his colleagues argue, however, that the potential for limiting the bias of an estimate of the causal impact of an intervention, in the absence of actual exogenous variation in treatment, is improved if researchers can form a matched "comparison group" from participants at the same local sites where the intervention was implemented. This is especially true if it is possible to include strong correlates of the outcome, measured at baseline, as covariates in the matching process.

Use Multiple Outcome Measures

Even when policymakers are interested only in whether an educational intervention affects one particular outcome, there are two reasons why it is valuable to design evaluations that incorporate multiple measures of several outcomes. First, some educational interventions create incentives for educators to focus instruction on the skills needed to improve students' scores on a particular test. As Daniel Koretz (2008) has explained, often such "teaching to the test" leads to increased scores on the "high-stakes" test, but not to improved performances on other assessments of skills in the same domain. In such cases, the intervention is unlikely to benefit participants in the long run. On the other hand, some interventions aimed primarily at improving outcomes in one particular domain still have impacts in other domains. Examining potential theories of action drawn from different disciplines can often provide insights about types of outcomes to measure. In this section, we describe recent evaluations that illustrate these points.

Cecilia Rouse and Alan Krueger (2004) evaluated the effectiveness of software programs known as the Fast ForWard (FFW) Family of Programs in improving the reading skills of low-achieving elementary-school students in four schools in an urban school district in the United States. Low-achieving students were randomized to a treatment group that was asked to spend 90 minutes per day working with the FFW software. The control group did not have access to the software. The researchers used scores on four standardized tests of reading skills as outcomes, one of which was a test provided by the developer of the FFW software. Rouse and Krueger found that scores of the treatment group on the reading test provided by the software vendor were higher, on average, than the scores of the control group. However, this difference did not translate to a treatment–control group difference in scores on the other tests of reading. In particular, the students who were given access to the FFW software did not score better than the control group, on average, on the criterion-referenced state test that was aligned with the state's reading standards. This pattern led Rouse and Krueger to conclude that use of the Fast ForWard computer-aided instruction (CAI) programs did not result in improved reading skills for low-achieving urban students. Of course, their conclusion would have been different had they only examined scores on the test provided by the software developer.

The random-assignment evaluation of Moving to Opportunity (MTO) provides a compelling illustration of the second point. MTO is a ten-year experiment sponsored by the U.S. Department of Housing and Urban Development that provides a large random sample of low-income families with the opportunity to move from extremely disadvantaged urban neighborhoods to less distressed communities. Many social scientists hypothesized that the primary benefit of MTO would be improvement in labor-market outcomes for adults in treatment-group families. The logic was that the residential moves would place families closer to jobs. However, to date, the results of the evaluation have shown no improvements in labor-market outcomes. Had the evaluation focused solely on examining labor-market outcomes, the evidence regarding the effects of the MTO experiment would have been uniformly discouraging.

Fortunately, in planning the evaluation, the research team considered a variety of mechanisms through which moving to a better neighborhood could alter the lives of families. One of many hypotheses was that the opportunity to move out of high-crime neighborhoods would reduce stress levels for parents and improve their mental health. This hypothesis led the research team to collect data on a variety of measures of participants' mental health. One of the most striking finding to date from the MTO evaluation has been the marked improvement in the mental health of mothers (Kling, Liebman, & Katz, 2007). This finding has led the research team to plan for the next round of data collection and analysis, an assessment of whether improved health for mothers is a mechanism through which MTO leads to better cognitive and emotional development for young children. Results bearing on this hypothesis will be available by 2012.

Be on the Lookout for Longer-Term Effects

Most impact evaluations of educational interventions examine relatively short-term effects. For example, the Mathematica evaluation of TFA examined impacts on student test scores at the end of the school year in which each teacher worked with a particular group of students. This makes sense because the effects of particular teachers on students' skills are likely to become muted over subsequent years, as the students experience other teachers. At the same time, policymakers are interested especially in learning whether particular interventions have lasting effects, and evidence that they do or do not is especially important in evaluating whether to continue the interventions and whether to scale them up so that they serve more participants. For that reason, it is useful, when financially feasible, to design research in a manner that makes it possible to evaluate whether interventions have long-term impacts.

Recall that, on average, the MDRC evaluation team found no differences between the treatment group of students offered places in a career academy and the control group in terms of their high-school grades, test scores, graduation rates, or college-enrollment rates (Kemple, 2008). Thus, even though each participant contributed data on each of multiple outcome measures, the conclusion reached by the investigators by the end of the participants' high-school years was that the offer of a place in a career academy had not resulted in better academic outcomes. However, the evidence on outcomes that were measured subsequently—eight years after high-school graduation—was quite different. For instance, the original offer of a place in a career academy ultimately resulted in members of the treatment group enjoying labor-market earnings that were 11% higher than members of the control group, on average. Thus, the combination of a long-term evaluation and the use of multiple outcome measures resulted in an important—and surprising—set of results concerning the outcomes of career academies.

Develop a Plan for Examining Impacts on Subgroups

It is always possible that particular policies or interventions may have heterogeneous effects, meaning that the effects on particular outcomes for identifiable subgroups of participants may be different from the effects on other subgroups of participants. For example, girls in families that were part of the MTO treatment group experienced positive education and health impacts from moving to a better neighborhood, but boys did not (Kling, Liebman, & Katz, 2007). Such information about subgroup differences is often important in policy discussions about particular interventions. For that reason, it makes sense to design research in a manner that facilitates the exploration of heterogeneous effects. Often, however, this is less straightforward to do than it may seem initially.

We illustrate some of these challenges using evidence from the evaluation of the New York Scholarship Program (NYSP).

Recall from Chapter 4 Howell et al.'s (2002) finding that the offer of a scholarship to help pay tuition at a private elementary school resulted in an increase in the average academic achievement of African-American children. These researchers also reported that the scholarship offer did not result in an improvement in the average achievement of Hispanic children. Despite many attempts to explain these subgroup differences, they remain a puzzle. One challenge in solving the puzzle is achieving clarity on the definitions of the subgroups. In preparing the data for subgroup analysis, the Mathematica research team based their grouping of participants on the responses that mothers (or female guardians) provided to a question on the survey that asked about their own race/ethnicity. The question permitted mothers to select one, and only one, response from among the following choices: (a) black/African-American (non-Hispanic), (b) white (non-Hispanic), (c) Puerto Rican, Dominican, and other Hispanic. The evaluation team headed by William Howell and Paul Peterson then assigned a race of "black/African-American" to those participating children whose mothers chose this particular category to describe themselves.

In a subsequent reanalysis of the NYSP data, Princeton Professor Alan Krueger and doctoral student Pei Zhu pointed out that there were other, equally reasonable, ways to code students' race/ethnicity and to form subgroups (Krueger & Zhu, 2004). For example, you could code as "black/African-American" those children whose father *or* mother chose this category as a self-description. Krueger and Zhu reported that, when this broader definition was adopted, the number of students classified as "black/African-American" increased by approximately 10%. More importantly, they also reported that the impact of voucher receipt on the academic achievement for this larger group of students was smaller than the impact that Howell and Peterson had estimated and, in contrast to their finding, was not statistically significantly different from zero on a conventional test. The point that we wish to make here is that subgroup analyses can be treacherous, even in well-designed randomized experiments, because subgroup membership or classification itself may be a matter of personal choice among several plausible alternatives, and the evaluation results may depend on the choices made. You need to think carefully when defining the membership of these groups.

It is natural for researchers to want to examine whether a particular educational intervention had a larger or smaller impact on outcomes for some important subset of participants than for others. There is particular pressure to do so when researchers have found no statistically significant impact of the treatment on outcomes in the research sample as a whole. However, although investigating subgroup effects makes sense, there are two related dangers. The first concerns the subgroup definitions themselves. Often, as was the case in the NYSP, there are alternative plausible ways to define subgroups, and there is a natural tendency to explore the consequences of alternative definitions and to choose the one that provides the strongest results. Second, as more tests are conducted, Type I error accumulates, with a contingent increased risk of rejecting one or more null hypotheses incorrectly during the testing process. Although standard adjustments to testing procedures are available to compensate for the accumulation of Type I error, many researchers resist applying them because they (properly) reduce the probability of finding statistically significant effects for any one subgroup.

The key to investigating subgroup effects appropriately is to plan to do so as an integral part of the initial research design. This involves three steps. First, list all subgroups in which the treatment effect should be investigated and define each carefully as part of the research design. Second, conduct suitable statistical-power analyses to ensure that sample sizes are large enough to detect subgroup effects of a meaningful size, at predetermined levels of Type I error for each comparison. Third, adopt a sensible strategy for limiting the number of tests and comparisons conducted to those that are of critical substantive importance.

Interpret Your Research Results Correctly

Throughout this book, we have emphasized the importance of being clear about the interpretation of the results of causal research. Here, we review two aspects of this theme. The first is that the results of regression-discontinuity analyses and analyses in which instrumental variables are used to achieve identification are *local-average effects of a treatment*, or LATE estimates. They pertain only to a particular subgroup of participants in the research sample, and it is important to define the relevant subgroup. The second is that experiments typically provide estimates of the total effects of a policy intervention, not the effects of the intervention holding constant the levels of other inputs. We illustrate these two points using Angrist and colleagues' evaluation (2002, 2006) of the impact of a secondary private-school scholarship program (PACES) on the educational attainments of low-income students in Bogotá, Colombia.

Recall from Chapter 11 that the research team found that students who were offered a PACES scholarship had a higher rate of on-time graduation from eighth grade—by 11 percentage points—than eligible low-income students who had also applied for a PACES scholarship, but lost out in the lottery. Of course, this is an unbiased estimate of the causal impact of the *intent to treat*. Angrist and his colleagues then used instrumental-variables estimation to address their second question: Does making use of a scholarship to help pay private secondary-school fees increase the educational attainments of low-income students? One reason that the answer to this question differs from the answer to the first question is that 8% of the low-income students who won the lottery did not make use of the offer of a scholarship from the PACES program. A second is that almost one-quarter of those students who lost out in the lottery were successful eventually in obtaining a scholarship to help pay private secondary-school fees. Thus, the assignment of a scholarship take-up "treatment" was endogenous, a result in part of unobserved family motivations and skills.

Using the randomized assignment of the offer of a PACES scholarship as an instrument, the research team estimated that making use of a scholarship increased by 16 percentage points the probability that low-income students completed the eighth grade on time. Recall from our earlier discussion of instrumental-variables estimation that this is an estimate of the local-average treatment effect, or LATE estimate, and that it pertains to those students whose decision about whether to make use of a scholarship to pay secondary-school fees was sensitive to the PACES scholarship offer or the lack of this offer. It is the effect of the treatment for *compliers*, and not for those students in the population who would have always obtained a scholarship (the *always-takers*) or never have done so (the *never-takers*), regardless of their original assignment. Of course, we do not know which members of the student population fall into each of these classes, as they are unobserved features of individuals. If the impact of scholarship use is homogeneous across all population members, then the LATE estimate obtained by Angrist and his colleagues also applies universally to all students in the population. When only one instrument is available, it is not possible to explore whether this is the case or not.

It is also important to recognize that the LATE estimate does not provide an estimate of the impact of scholarship use on students' subsequent educational attainment, holding constant all other aspects of family dynamics. Instead, it provides an estimate of the total impact of financial aid on a student's subsequent educational attainment. The distinction may matter because the choice of whether to make use of a scholarship offer to help pay a child's secondary-school fees may not have been the only parental decision affected by the lottery outcome. For example, parents may have decided to reduce expenditures on books and other learning materials for the child who obtained and made use of a scholarship in order to free up money to help other children in their family who lacked this opportunity. The research team's estimate of the impact of financial aid on subsequent educational attainment is an estimate of the total impact, including the effects of any reallocation of financial resources and time that the parents made in response to the child using a scholarship.[1]

Pay Attention to Anomalous Results

As part of the struggle to have their work published in the best possible peer-reviewed journals, researchers often do not report evidence that particular interventions have no statistically significant effects on outcomes or effects that run counter to their theories. Instead, they focus their papers on describing the strongest results that support their theories. Unfortunately, this behavior hinders the accumulation of knowledge. Then, attempts to synthesize evidence about the efficacy of a particular intervention from published studies can only summarize positive evidence even in cases in which the vast majority of evaluations have found no effects of the intervention (but were either not published, or the contrary findings down played). This problem is often referred to as *publication bias*. Although there is no easy solution to the problem, the best defense against it may be the practices of conscientious referees who focus on the quality of the methodology used in a particular causal study, not on the consistency of the results. In this regard, it is important to keep in mind that unexpected results often occur in well-designed studies. We illustrate this with evidence from Angrist and Lavy's Maimonides' rule paper.

Recall from Chapter 9 that Angrist and Lavy (1999) made clever use of a natural experiment created by the exogenous application of Maimonides' rule to estimate the causal impact of differences in intended class sizes on student achievement. The substantive results that most readers of their classic paper remember are that class size had a substantial impact on the reading and mathematics achievement of students in fifth grade in the year 1991, and that the impact was especially large in schools that served high concentrations of economically disadvantaged students. In thinking about the substantive implications of this study—and for that matter, of all evaluations of the causal impacts of policy interventions—we believe it is

---

1. For more discussion of this point, see Todd and Wolpin (2003), and Duflo, Glennerster, and Kremer (2008).

important to pay attention to *all* of the results, including those that seem somewhat puzzling.

In their paper, Angrist and Lavy also reported results on the impact of class size on the reading and mathematics achievement of fourth-graders in 1991 and third-graders in 1992. The results for the fourth-graders were much weaker than those for the fifth-graders—the corresponding impact on reading achievement was less than half as large, and the impact on mathematics achievement was even smaller, and was not statistically significant. Angrist and Lavy suggest that this pattern could be due to the cumulative effect of class size: students who were taught in small fifth-grade classes were probably also in relatively small classes in their earlier grades, and each year brought additional benefits. Although this is a plausible explanation for why the impact of intended class size on student achievement should be somewhat smaller for fourth- than for fifth-graders, it does not explain why the fourth-grade impacts would be less than half as large as the corresponding fifth-grade impacts.

The results for third-graders are even more puzzling. Angrist and Lavy found no impact of differences in intended class size on the reading and mathematics achievement of third-graders in 1992 (the second and final year of the testing program that provided the student-achievement outcome). They speculated that this pattern stemmed from teachers' responses to the publication of the 1991 results. After reading the results, teachers may have devoted more time to test preparation in 1992, and thus weakened the relationship between students' test scores and their true skill levels. Angrist and Lavy's hypothesized explanation for their third-grade results raises questions about the quality of the information on students' skills that is generated by test-based accountability systems, an issue with which many countries grapple today.[2] The point that we want to emphasize, however, is the importance of paying attention to all of the results of well-designed research studies, not just the strongest. We see this as a necessary condition for research to have a beneficial impact on public policy debates concerning the consequences of particular educational initiatives. We applaud Angrist and Lavy for describing the puzzling results for the third- and fourth-grade students whose achievement they investigated.

---

2. To learn more about the difficulty of interpreting student test results under test-based accountability systems, see Koretz (2008).

Recognize That Good Research Always Raises
New Questions

Good research is expensive, especially random-assignment evaluations that follow participants over an extended period of time. For example, the MDRC random-assignment evaluation of career academies cost $12 million. For that reason, policymakers sometimes want assurances that a particular evaluation will provide definitive evidence about the consequences of a particular educational policy or program. In fact, however, even carefully designed studies typically raise as many questions as they answer. For that reason, it is important to design a sequence of studies to address important educational-policy questions, recognizing that each well-designed study will answer some questions and will also raise new questions that can inform the design of subsequent studies. We illustrate this point with evidence from the STAR class-size experiment.

Project STAR is one of the best-known evaluations of an educational intervention. Given its celebrity status and the transparency of its randomized-experimental design, you might think that experts' interpretations of its findings would be clear and unassailable. Yet, two internationally respected researchers disagreed on that interpretation. Frederick Mosteller, pioneering statistician and senior member of the Harvard University faculty, wrote in 1995: "After four years, it was clear that smaller classes did produce substantial improvement in early learning and cognitive studies. . ." (Mosteller, 1995, p. 113). In contrast, Eric Hanushek, one of the world's most creative and productive educational economists, wrote in 1998: "The most expansive conclusion that can be reached from Project STAR and the Lasting Benefits Study is that they might support an expectation of positive achievement effects from moving toward small kindergartens, and maybe small first grades. None of the STAR data support a wholesale reduction of class sizes across grades in schools" (Hanushek, 1998, p. 30).

A close reading of the Mosteller and Hanushek papers on Project STAR reveals that the two experts agreed on key findings. Both reported that, on average, students in small classes had higher achievement at the end of the first grade than did students in regular-size classes. They also agreed that the magnitude of the average achievement differential between students in small classes and those in regular-size classes was no larger at the end of the third grade than at the end of the first grade. Where they differed, however, is in their assumptions about what would have happened to the achievement of children in small classes had they been placed in regular-size classes in grades 2 and 3. Mosteller assumed that the achievement of the children in the treatment group would have fallen back to that of the children in the control group. This led him to conclude that the smaller class sizes for grades 2 and 3 were required for the treatment group to sustain its higher achievement. Hanushek assumed that the higher achievement for children in the treatment group would have been sustained if these children had been placed in regular-size classes in grades 2 and 3. Thus, he concluded that, since the achievement differences at the end of grade 3 were no larger than those detected at the end of grade 1, placement in small classes for grades 2 and 3 did not result in further achievement benefits. Unfortunately, Project STAR did not provide the evidence needed to determine whether Mosteller's or Hanushek's assumption was more accurate because the research design did not include the randomization of a subset of students into small classes for grades K and 1 and into regular-size classes in grades 2 and 3. This step needs to be taken in a new round of random-assignment studies of class-size reduction.

What to Read Next

Among the many books that provide thoughtful discussions of issues critical to the design of causal research are Shadish, Cook, and Campbell's *Experimental and Quasi-Experimental Designs* (2002), and Larry Orr's *Social Experiments* (1999).

14

Substantive Lessons and New Questions

At a meeting at United Nations Headquarters in New York City in September 2000, 189 world leaders committed their countries to pursue a set of eight Millennium Development Goals (MDGs). One of these goals was that, by the year 2015, "Children everywhere, boys and girls alike, will be able to complete a full course of primary schooling." Another was to "eliminate gender disparity in primary and secondary education, preferably by 2005, and in all levels of education no later than 2015."[1] The high priority that these world leaders gave to education in this remarkable set of commitments reflects compelling evidence that providing a high-quality education for all children is a powerful strategy for enhancing economic growth, promoting equality of opportunity, and reducing poverty.

Meeting the MDG education goals and realizing the social benefits of educational investments requires progress on two fronts: increasing the number of young people who attend school regularly, and improving the quality of the education that they receive. Of course, the details of the respective policy challenges differ among countries. For example, some countries, such as Liberia, are still struggling to achieve universal primary education. Middle-income countries, such as Colombia, are working to improve secondary-school graduation rates. Many high-income countries, such as the United States, seek to increase the number of young people, especially those from minority groups, who enroll in, and graduate from, post-secondary educational institutions.

---

1. See the description of the MDGs at: http://www.unmillenniumproject.org/goals/gti.htm#-goal2.

350

Despite these differences, a common element to the educational challenges that the countries of the world face is the interdependency of the access and quality challenges. Pursuing the access goal without investing in improvements in quality will typically be unsuccessful because parents will not send their children to schools where little learning takes place and teenagers will not attend school regularly if they see there is little value in doing so. In the last 20 years, a growing number of empirical studies have made effective use of the methodological advances described in this book to investigate the effects of particular policies on school enrollments or on students' educational outcomes. In this chapter, we close out our book by summarizing lessons from these high-quality studies. We also point out new questions arising from recent studies that will need attention in future research. In choosing the studies to mention in this final chapter, we only considered those with designs that we felt supported causal inference well. Within this set, we focused attention on studies that examined the consequences of providing more or better inputs to schools, of improving incentives for teachers or students, or of increasing the schooling choices of students.[2]

Of course, it will not surprise you that there are no sure-fire strategies for making progress toward the complementary goals of increasing school enrollment and improving educational quality. From reading our previous chapters, you know that it is the details of the intervention that matter. For example, two different initiatives to improve the pedagogy of incumbent teachers, often called *professional development*, may have the same name, but result in very different experiences for participating teachers. Also, sometimes a particular educational intervention will evoke quite different responses in different cultures. Michael Kremer and his colleagues (2009) found that to be the case in their evaluation of a merit-scholarship program for girls in two districts in Kenya. We provide more information later about the responses to this incentive program.

Keeping in mind the cautions just expressed, we present four guidelines for policy that emerge from the growing corpus of high-quality evaluations that have examined the causal impacts of educational interventions. First, school enrollment decisions are very sensitive to costs, especially for low-income families. Second, a necessary condition for improving school quality and student achievement is that the daily experiences of students must change. Third, providing explicit incentives for

---

2. The topics we explore do not exhaust the interventions aimed at improving student achievement that researchers have evaluated using high-quality causal research methods. For example, there are many studies examining the effectiveness of new curricula and of particular computer-based software programs.

teachers and students can be a powerful way of improving educational outcomes for students. Fourth, policies to increase the schooling options available to children from poor families have significant promise. We discuss each of these guidelines in turn, and in each case we point out puzzles in the available evidence and questions from recent studies that need to be examined in future research.

Policy Guideline 1: Lower the Cost of School Enrollment

The empirical evidence on how school enrollments can be increased is consistent and clear: it is lowering the cost of school enrollment that makes a big difference, especially to low-income families. There are at least three ways to lower these costs: reduce the time that students must spend commuting between home and school, reduce out-of-pocket costs that families must bear to send their children to school, and reduce the burden families experience from losing the labor of a child who attends school. Below, we summarize recent evidence from well-designed empirical studies of the impact of these three approaches on school enrollments and on longer-term outcomes.

Reduce Commuting Time

Between 1973 and 1979, Indonesia, the world's fourth most populous country, has engaged in a massive school construction project aimed at improving access to primary schools in regions where school enrollments had formerly been low. During this period, the government funded the construction of more than 61,000 primary schools. It also recruited teachers for these schools and paid their salaries. Esther Duflo (2001) studied the consequences of this remarkable natural experiment and found that it had a striking impact on both school enrollment and students' educational attainments. She estimated (p. 804) that the school-building program increased by 6 percentage points the probability that a child living in an area affected by the program would complete primary school.

The findings of Dana Burde and Leigh Linden's (2009) evaluation of the consequences of an intervention aimed at reducing home-to-school commuting distance for children in rural northwestern Afghanistan are consistent with Duflo's results. The intervention was to create and staff primary schools in a random sample of villages that had no primary schools previously. Children living in villages that served as controls in the experiment continued to travel to another village to attend school. The researchers found that the length of the home-to-school commute had a dramatic impact on school enrollment rates, with enrollment falling by 16 percentage points for every mile that children had to travel. The impact of distance to school on enrollment rates was especially large for girls. In fact, providing a community-based school virtually eliminated the gender gap in enrollment (which was 21 percentage points in control villages).

The study by Janet Currie and Enrico Moretti (2003), which we described in Chapter 10, has many similarities to Duflo's Indonesian study. These authors took advantage of a natural experiment that was created by the rapid growth in the number of two- and four-year colleges in the United States in the decades after World War II. They found that the construction of each new four-year college in a county (per 1,000 residents, aged 18–22) increased by 19 percentage points the probability that women aged 18–22 living in the county obtained a four-year college degree.

These three high-quality studies, conducted in very different contexts, demonstrate that providing new educational institutions close to the homes of potential students is one powerful way to increase enrollments.

Reduce Out-of-Pocket Educational Costs

One of the potential obstacles that face parents who want to increase the educational attainments of their children is the burden of out-of-pocket schooling costs that they bear, just to send their children to school. In some cases, these constitute school-tuition payments; in others, fees for books or school uniforms. A number of recent high-quality studies have shown that reducing such out-of-pocket costs results in a marked increase in school enrollments.

Since 2003, parents have not been required to pay school fees to enroll their children in public primary schools in Kenya. However, they do need to purchase school uniforms. To learn whether the cost of school uniforms posed an obstacle to school enrollment for Kenyan families, Esther Duflo and colleagues (2006) conducted a random-assignment experiment in which sixth-grade students in treatment-group schools were provided with free school uniforms. They found that the provision of free uniforms reduced the student dropout rate by more than 2 percentage points, which constitutes a 15% decline in that rate (p. 20).

As you learned in Chapter 8, Susan Dynarski (2003) exploited a natural experiment in the United States to study the impact of college costs on college enrollment and educational attainments. The natural experiment occurred in 1982, when the federal government eliminated a substantial subsidy of college costs that it had provided previously to children of deceased Social Security recipients. Dynarski found that an offer of $1,000 in scholarship aid increased the probability of attending college by almost 4 percentage points. Many other high-quality empirical studies have also confirmed that reducing out-of-pocket costs results in an increase in college enrollment.

Reduce Opportunity Costs

A third type of expense that families bear in sending their children to school is the loss of their children's labor. Economists use the term *opportunity cost* to refer to the value of the foregone time. As children become old enough to work, the opportunity costs associated with the loss of their time rise. In many countries, this is especially the case for girls, who are often called on to care for their younger siblings.

In 1997, the Mexican government introduced a conditional cash-transfer (CCT) program called PROGRESA, which was aimed at reducing poverty and providing incentives for low-income parents to invest in the human capital of their children. Families eligible for PROGRESA received monthly payments so long as their school-aged children remained enrolled in school and met their attendance targets, and so long as parents complied with requirements for health-care check-ups for family members. The payments could add as much as one-fifth to a family's total income, and depended on the number, ages, and gender mix of children in the family. Cash payments under PROGRESA were intentionally large for families with teenage girls. The reason was to stimulate school attendance in this group, which has had an especially low school-attendance rate historically. In effect, PROGRESA provided low-income families with a strong incentive to send their children to school (Fiszbein, Schady, & Ferreira, 2009).

PROGRESA was first implemented in a random sample of low-income rural communities, a design that made it possible to conduct a high-quality impact evaluation. The evaluation showed that PROGRESA increased the school-enrollment rate of sixth-graders by almost 9 percentage points (up from a baseline participation rate of 45%). This evidence was important in building support for the program—now called *Oportunidades*—which, by 2008, had become available to more than 20% of the Mexican population. The convincing nature of the empirical evidence for the causal impact of the PROGRESA intervention also contributed to the introduction of similar CCT programs in more than 25 other countries, including Bangladesh, Cambodia, Ecuador, and Turkey.

The major puzzle arising from causal research on initiatives to increase school-enrollment rates and the school attendance of children from low-income families concerns their impacts on the children's academic achievement and life outcomes. Some initiatives result in better long-term outcomes for children—for example, the school-building program in Indonesia. However, others, including PROGRESA, led to increased school attendance, but not to increased academic achievement, at least as measured by standardized test scores (Fiszbein, Schady, & Ferreira 2009). An important question to address in new research is why these discrepancies occurred.

Policy Guideline 2: Change Children's Daily Experiences in School

Until quite recently, the dominant strategy for improving school quality was to purchase more or better inputs—for example, provide more books; hire additional teachers so that class sizes could be reduced; or raise teacher salaries in order to attract more skilled teachers. The attraction of this approach is that teachers, students, and parents all enjoy having additional resources in classrooms and so the strategy is popular politically. Unfortunately, input-based improvement strategies do not result in improved student achievement consistently, and it is not difficult to understand why. The fundamental problem in a great many schools is that students do not receive consistently good instruction that is tailored to their needs. As a result, children are not engaged actively in learning while they are in school. A necessary condition for improving student achievement is increased student engagement, and this means changing the daily educational experiences of children in schools. Simply providing additional resources to the school or classroom, without changing how those resources are used, does not achieve the desired result.

Of course, the conclusion that resource levels do not affect student achievement is too strong. In some settings, the provision of additional resources does indeed make a difference to student outcomes because the new resources *do* result in a change in children's daily experiences in school. In fact, we argue that paying attention to whether a particular school-improvement strategy results in a change in children's daily experiences goes a long way toward predicting whether the intervention will succeed in improving student achievement. We illustrate this point with evidence from a number of high-quality studies that have investigated the impacts of input-based educational interventions.

More Books?

Paul Glewwe and his colleagues conducted a random-assignment evaluation of a program in rural Kenya that provided primary schools with additional textbooks written in English, the official language of instruction (Glewwe, Kremer, & Moulin, 2009). The intervention seemed promising because these schools possessed almost no textbooks. However, the evaluation showed that simply providing the additional textbooks did not result in greater academic achievement for the children in the treatment-group schools than for those in control-group schools, on average. The researchers' explanation was that English was the third language for most of the children, and they were not able to read the textbooks. Under these circumstances, it is not surprising that providing these books did not result in a change in children's daily experiences in school nor result in increases in their academic achievement. Of course, this finding raises the question of whether provision of books that were better tailored to the students' needs would have changed children's daily experiences enough to increase their reading skills. This is a question worth examining, especially in schools in which there are teachers trained to make use of books to stimulate children's interest in reading.

Smaller Classes?

In earlier chapters, we described two well-known studies of the impact of class size on student achievement. The Tennessee Student/Teacher Achievement Ratio (STAR) experiment provided strong evidence that spending the first year of school in a small class improved student achievement, especially for students from low-income families (Krueger, 1999). The likely explanation is that when children come to school for the first time, they have a lot to learn about how to behave in a structured classroom setting. In a relatively small class (13–17 students), children's initial experiences are different from those in a larger class because teachers are better able to help children acquire the appropriate behaviors.

Other relevant evidence for the impact of class size on student achievement comes from Angrist and Lavy's (1999) analyses of data from Israel, and from Miguel Urquiola's (2006) similar study of the impact of class size on the achievement of third-graders in schools in rural Bolivia. Both studies found that students in some middle-primary grades who were in small classes had higher reading and mathematics achievement, on average, than children schooled in larger classes. One possible explanation for these findings stems from the identification strategy they employed. Both studies used a regression-discontinuity design to exploit the consequences of natural experiments that had been inaugurated by the implementation of rules to govern maximum class size. The net effect of this identification strategy was that comparisons of achievement were between students in classes containing quite different numbers of students—for example, classes of 21 and 39 students on either side of a Maimonides-inspired class-size cut-off, in the Angrist and Lavy study. It seems plausible that the day-to-day school experiences of students in classes that differ in size by this amount could be quite different. This explanation is consistent with the findings of Caroline Hoxby's (2000) study of the impact of class size for students in Connecticut public elementary schools. Hoxby found no impact of differences in class sizes on students' average language and mathematics skills. However, the differences in class size in the Hoxby study were considerably smaller than the class-size differences in the Angrist and Lavy and Urquiola studies.[3] It seems sensible that the day-to-day school experiences of students in classes of 20 may not differ much from those in classes that contain 25 students.

As explained in Chapter 13, the impact of class size on student achievement in the Angrist and Lavy (1999) study in Israel differed by grade level, with the impacts of small classes in grade 4 being much smaller than the corresponding impacts in grade 5. Moreover, estimates from well-designed studies of the impacts of class size on student achievement in other countries also differ widely. An important question to address in future research is why class size has a substantial impact on student achievement at some grade levels but not in others, and in some settings but not others. We suggest that the design of studies to address this question should pay attention to the extent to which class size in particular settings affects children's daily experiences in the classroom. Our hypothesis is that class size will not make a difference to children's academic outcomes in settings in which it does not affect children's daily in-school experiences.

Better Teaching?

Studies conducted in a great many countries have documented that children have higher achievement, on average, in some classrooms than they do in others, and that differences in the quality of teaching are the likely explanation (Rivkin, Hanushek, & Kain, 2005). This unsurprising pattern suggests the potential value of devoting resources to either hiring teachers who are known to be more effective or to improving the skills of the incumbent teaching force. Many educational systems try to do both.

---

3. The standard deviation in class size in Hoxby (2000) ranged between 5.5 and 6.4 students, depending on the grade level (Appendix table, p. 1283). The standard deviation of class size in the discontinuity sample in the Angrist and Lavy (1999) study ranged between 7.2 and 7.4 (Table 1, p. 539). The standard deviation in class size in the Urquiola (2006) study was 9.9 (Table 1, p. 172).

For example, increasing the educational requirements that aspiring teachers must satisfy is a common strategy used to upgrade teacher quality. Some school systems have raised teachers' salaries in order to attract more talented applicants for teaching positions. Almost all school systems require that incumbent teachers participate in in-service training programs. Unfortunately, three obstacles hinder the effectiveness of these input-based approaches to improving teaching quality.

The first obstacle is that formal educational credentials are not good predictors of teaching effectiveness (Rivkin, Hanushek, & Kain, 2005). Consequently, improving the educational credentials that applicants for teaching positions must obtain is typically not an effective way to increase the quality of the teaching force. Nor are salary incentives effective consistently, because school directors have difficulty in identifying better teachers from pools of applicants. Consequently, salary increases often go to ineffective teachers as well as to those who are more successful in helping students learn.

The second obstacle to an input-based approach to improving teaching is that the types of professional-development programs that are easy to implement—for example, having teachers attend conferences or workshops in which they listen to the advice of "experts"—have little or no impact on the teachers' effectiveness in the classroom (Borko, 2004; Garet, Porter, & Desimone, 2001; Hill & Cohen, 2001). The third obstacle is that even when promising teachers are identified and assigned to schools that serve children with especially great learning needs, the teachers tend to move to schools where working conditions are better as soon as they acquire sufficient seniority to do so. In developing countries, this typically means moving from schools in rural areas to schools close to cities (Ezpeleta & Weiss, 1996; Reimers, 2006). In many developed countries, including the United States, it means moving out of inner-city schools to schools on the fringes of cities (Clotfelter, Ladd, & Vigdor, 2005). In both sets of circumstances, the net result is that children most in need of the best teachers are the least likely to be taught by them.

The evidence for the effectiveness of different strategies to improve the teaching that children receive on a daily basis raises many questions. Among the most policy-relevant are questions about the professional development (in-service training) available for incumbent teachers. Almost every public-school system invests resources in improving the skills of its teachers. Indeed, this is a major area of investment in many school systems. Yet, to our knowledge, there is no compelling evidence about whether particular professional-development strategies cause teachers to become more effective.

Policy Guideline 3: Improve Incentives

The evidence that input-based strategies, such as reducing class size and investing in the professional development of teachers, do not result consistently in improved education for children is sobering. This pattern has led to a growing interest in using different kinds of incentives to alter the behaviors of teachers or students, and thereby improve educational outcomes for children.

Improve Incentives for Teachers

The potential power of the incentive approach is illustrated by the evaluation of the teacher-incentive program in rural India that we described in Chapter 5. Recall that basing rural teachers' compensation on their school-attendance rate halved the percentage of days that teachers were absent from their positions, from 42% to 21%. Moreover, the increase in teacher attendance resulted in an increase of one-third in the amount of time that students received instruction. This, in turn, led to an increase of almost one-fifth of a standard deviation in students' scores on tests of their language and mathematical achievement. There is also evidence from the United States that financial incentives make a difference in attracting academically talented teachers to low-performing schools (Steele, Murnane, & Willett, 2010), and in inducing teachers to remain teaching in schools that serve high concentrations of poor children (Clotfelter et al., 2008). Thus, all of these studies support the hypothesis that financial incentives can play an important role in inducing teachers to take actions under their control—such as coming to school regularly, and teaching in schools where the need is particularly great.

The more difficult issue concerns the effectiveness of incentives for teachers to improve students' scores on standardized achievement tests. There is evidence that performance-based pay plans or merit pay, as such incentives are often called, did indeed result in improvements in student outcomes in some settings. However, there is also evidence that incentives for teachers to improve student test scores have led to dysfunctional responses in other settings.

On the positive side are the results of a random-assignment experiment in rural India that Karthik Muralidharan and Venkatesh Sundararaman (2009) evaluated. These researchers found that paying bonuses to primary-school teachers based on the average score improvement of their students on tests of language and mathematics skills led to improved student achievement in these subjects. Moreover, in this well-designed random-assignment experiment, the research team also found that students' average scores on science tests were higher in treatment-group schools than in control-group schools. This is important because it suggested that teachers had not simply reallocated instructional time to the particular subset of subjects (language and mathematics) on which their bonuses depended.

On the negative side, there is evidence from some settings that teachers' responses to incentives to improve their students' scores on standardized tests did not serve the students well. For example, the superintendent of the Chicago public schools introduced a new accountability policy in 1996. Under this policy, elementary schools in which less than 15% of students scored at, or above, national norms on a standardized test of reading skills would be placed on academic probation. Schools on probation that did not then make adequate progress in improving their students' reading scores would be reconstituted and their faculties dismissed or reassigned. Brian Jacob and Steven Levitt (2003) documented that, in at least 5% of Chicago's elementary schools, teachers or administrators responded to this incentive by editing their students' answers on the standardized reading test.

Although changing students' answers to test items is a troubling, and hopefully rare, response to an incentive program, many studies have documented other responses that similarly do not improve the quality of education provided to students. For example, David Figlio and Lawrence Getzler (2002) showed that a response to an incentive system designed to hold public-school educators in Florida accountable for improving students' skills was that schools then misclassified low-achieving students as disabled, so that their scores would not be counted in state-wide evaluations of school performance.

Our review of evidence from recent evaluations of incentive-based policies for teachers suggests two lessons, two questions, and a hypothesis. The first lesson is that incentives can play an important role in motivating teachers to engage in actions that are under their control – such as choosing to work in high-poverty schools. The second lesson is that incentives for teachers to improve student performance may play a constructive role in improving school performance in at least some settings. However, the challenge is to design the incentives so as to maximize the chance that responses will result in better education for children.

The first question concerns the extent to which responses to particular teacher-incentive plans depend on the characteristics of the setting and the skills and norms of the teaching force. For example, would the performance incentives for rural teachers in India that Muralidharan and Sundararaman (2009) studied elicit similar results in a setting in which teacher attendance was not a problem? The second question concerns long-term responses to incentives for teachers to improve student test scores. Would teachers' responses change over time as they learned more about the role that peer groups and particular instructional strategies played in influencing student test scores? If so, would teachers' long-term responses to performance incentives benefit children more or less than short-term responses? To learn the answers to these questions, it is important to conduct evaluations that examine long-run responses to particular incentive programs as well as short-run responses, and to do so in many different types of settings.

The hypothesis that we believe deserves testing stipulates that teachers' responses to incentives intended to improve student test scores are more likely to result in better education for children if they are combined with investments to provide teachers with the knowledge and tools to achieve this objective. In other words, the hypothesis is that incentives and capacity-building are complements, not substitutes.

Improve Incentives for Students

In most societies students have strong long-term incentives to do the hard work needed to excel in school and to increase both their skill levels and educational attainments. The cognitive skills that are taught in schools and the educational credentials that high-achieving students tend to obtain pay off handsomely in adult labor markets (Hanushek & Woessmann, 2008; Murnane, Willett, & Levy 1995). However, many students do not devote consistent effort to school work. One hypothesis to explain this latter phenomenon is that the behaviors of many students are dictated by more immediate concerns, and they do not pay much attention to longer-term outcomes. A second is that many students do not understand what they need to do in order to improve their academic performance. These hypotheses raise the question of whether providing more immediate incentives to do the hard work needed to acquire critical skills would have a positive impact on students' effort levels and on their academic performances. A related question concerns whether it is more effective to reward student skills as measured by grades or scores on standardized examinations or to reward behaviors such as reading books that may contribute to the development of those skills. The evidence bearing on the answers to these questions is both intriguing and puzzling.

Different Responses in Different Settings

Michael Kremer, Edward Miguel, and Rebecca Thornton (2009) examined the consequences of an experiment in Kenya in which samples of primary schools in two districts were randomized to treatment and control groups. The two districts, Busia and Teso, differed in several respects, including primary language and cultural traditions. Also, residents of Teso had less education, on average, than residents of Busia, and were more suspicious of outsiders. The experimental treatment consisted of providing academic scholarships to female students who scored well on district-wide academic examinations in five academic subjects. The experiment focused on girls because they had a higher dropout rate from primary schools than did boys. The scholarships paid school fees for the subsequent school year and also provided a small cash grant. All girls who attended treatment-group schools in the two districts were eligible to compete for the scholarships. Girls attending control-group schools were not eligible for the merit-based scholarships.

Kremer and his colleagues found that the experiment elicited very positive responses in Busia. Girls in that district who were eligible for the merit-based scholarships had higher test scores, on average, than girls in control-group schools. Moreover, average scores were even higher in treatment-group schools than in control-group schools among girls with low pre-test scores who were unlikely to win scholarships, and among boys, who were not eligible for the scholarships. The research team also found that teacher attendance was higher in treatment-group schools than in control-group schools in Busia, and attributed this to increased parental monitoring. Kremer and his colleagues concluded that the positive effects of the merit-based scholarships in Busia stemmed primarily from a combination of positive peer-group effects and greater teacher effort.

Responses to the merit-based scholarship program in Teso were quite different. Parents in Teso were less supportive of the program than those in Busia, and several schools in Teso dropped out of the experiment soon after its inception. Virtually none of the positive results that the research team found in Busia were present in the Teso sample. This pattern illustrates not only that the details of incentive plans matter, but also that the task of designing constructive incentives is often critically setting-specific. An incentive system that contributes to improved student achievement in one setting may not do so in another, and for reasons that may not be clear.

Heterogeneous Responses in the Same Setting

Another complexity in designing incentives is that they may elicit quite different responses from different groups in the same setting. For example, Angrist and Lavy (2009) found that an experimental program in Israel that provided financial rewards to secondary-school students in low-performing schools who achieved passing scores on the school-leaving

"Bagrut" examination had a large positive impact on the average performance of girls. Paradoxically, the incentives provided by the achievement awards had no impact on the performances of boys. Angrist, Lang, and Oreopoulos (2009) found a similar pattern in their evaluation of an experiment conducted in Canada in which first-year university students were assigned randomly to one of three treatment groups, or to a control group. One treatment group was offered academic support services, including mentoring by upper-class students and supplemental instruction. A second group was offered substantial cash awards, up to the equivalent of a full year's tuition, for meeting a target GPA (the GPA target for each student depended on the student's high-school GPA.) A third treatment group was offered a combination of the support services and incentives. The control group was eligible for standard university support services but nothing extra. The research team found that the *combination* of incentives and support was especially effective in improving the academic performance of women. In contrast, the academic achievement of males was unchanged by any of the interventions. The evidence from these experiments in Israel and Canada raise an intriguing question: Why did female students respond positively to financial incentives for good academic performance, but male students did not?

Student Responses Depend on What Is Rewarded

Recently, Roland Fryer (2010) completed a set of randomized experiments that shed light on the responses of poor minority children attending urban public schools in the United States to financial incentives for academic achievement and for activities that contribute to achievement. Fryer found that paying students to take actions that are conducive to learning, such as reading books, coming to school regularly, and behaving well in school resulted in improved scores on standardized tests. These results are consistent with the theme that changing children's daily experiences is a necessary condition for improving their academic achievement. In contrast to these encouraging findings, Fryer also found that paying students for achieving benchmarks on tests of reading and mathematics did not result in improved scores. His explanation for this pattern is that, when faced with incentives to score well on standardized tests of reading and mathematics, students in urban settings in the United States do not know what actions to take to improve their scores.

Summary of Evidence on Incentives for Students

Recent well-designed evaluations of experimental programs that provided financial rewards to students suggest two lessons and many new questions.

The first is that programs of this type have promise, as shown by the positive results of the student incentive program in Busia, Kenya. Second, incentives may be a way to increase students' use of the extra support services that a great many educational institutions offer to struggling students. Angrist, Lang, and Oreopoulos (2009) found this pattern in the responses of female college students in Canada to the combination of extra supports and financial rewards for academic achievement. Indeed, paying students to engage in behaviors known to contribute to skill development may be more effective in enhancing students' skills in some settings than rewarding their performances on standardized tests. Among the questions worthy of attention in new studies of these effects are why the same set of incentives elicits different responses in different settings, and why, in at least some settings, girls are more responsive to short-term incentives for improving academic performance than are boys.

Policy Guideline 4: Create More Schooling Options for Poor Children

In recent years, a growing number of countries have introduced programs that attempt to increase the schooling options for children from low-income families. Many programs do this by offering to families vouchers or scholarships that they can use to pay part or all of children's tuitions at private schools. Other programs provide public funds to private schools in return for serving students from low-income families. Still others, such as charter-school legislation in the United States, make it possible for entrepreneurs to start new public schools that are free from many of the restrictions that are thought to hamper efficient resource use in conventional public schools that are part of large school systems. One theory underlying these initiatives is that they will spur competition among schools, and this will result in performance improvements. A complementary theory is that providing parents with choices between public schools and private schools helps them to find schools that match their children's needs (Chubb & Moe, 1990).

There is enormous variation in the design of programs that seek to provide new schooling options for poor children. Eligibility for some programs, such as the New York Scholarship Program (NYSP) that we described in Chapter 4 and the Colombia secondary-school voucher initiative described in Chapter 11, was restricted to children from low-income families. Other initiatives, such as charter schools in the United States, are available to all children in a particular geographical area. Some programs incorporate explicit performance incentives for students or for schools.

For example, recipients of secondary-school tuition vouchers in Colombia must make satisfactory progress toward their diplomas each academic year in order to have their vouchers renewed (Angrist et al., 2002). A program in Pakistan makes per student payments to low-cost private schools contingent on successful student performance on periodic tests of academic skills (Barrera-Osorio & Raju, 2009). The program also provides substantial cash bonuses to the faculties of schools in which students do particularly well on the tests. Finally, some programs, such as the one in Pakistan and charter-school laws in the United States, prohibit participating schools from charging fees. Others, such as the NYSP and the Colombian program, allow private schools to charge fees in excess of the value of the voucher. In the next section, we describe recent evidence from initiatives to create new private-school options for poor children. We then turn to evidence bearing on charter schools in the United States, an attempt to create new public-school options.

New Private-School Options

As we described in Chapter 11, Joshua Angrist and his colleagues (2006) found that the Colombia secondary-school voucher program increased high-school graduation rates for students from low-income families. In an evaluation with a regression-discontinuity design, Felipe Barrera-Osorio and Dhushyanth Raju (2009) found that the private-school subsidy program in Pakistan increased markedly the number of students from low-income families who enrolled in school. A common thread connecting these programs is that both made continued funding contingent on improved student performance.

Private school-choice programs targeted at low-income students in particular cities in the United States also show some positive results, although the findings are not completely consistent. For example, in an evaluation with a random-assignment design, Cecilia Rouse (1998) found that a private-school tuition voucher program in Milwaukee led to improvements in the mathematics achievement of students from low-income families, but not in their reading achievement.

New Public-School Options

Several recent high-quality evaluations of urban charter schools in the United States show encouraging results. These include Dobbie and Fryer's (2009) study of the effectiveness of charter schools in the Harlem Children's Zone, Abdulkadiroglu and his colleagues' (2009) evaluation of charter schools in Boston, and Hoxby and Murarka's (2009) evaluation of charter schools in New York City. All of these evaluations found that children who won a lottery that provided the offer of a place in a charter school had higher test scores one or more years later than children who lost out in the lottery and typically then attended conventional public schools. In interpreting this evidence, it is important to keep in mind that these lottery-based evaluations only examine the effectiveness of charter schools that are heavily oversubscribed, and therefore have used lotteries to determine who is accepted. Many charter schools across the nation are not oversubscribed, and results from nation-wide evaluations of their effects on student test scores, which are necessarily conducted with less rigorous evaluation methods, are mixed.[4]

Although the evidence from many recent evaluations of charter schools is encouraging, many important questions remain. One is whether the charter schools that are more effective in increasing students' skills will flourish and those that are not will die. Given the complexity of the political processes that determine which schools are granted renewals of their charters, the answer is not obvious. Second, some charter schools require that parents sign pledges stating they will be responsible for ensuring their children adhere to a dress code and to rules regarding behavior and attendance. It is not clear the extent to which such requirements mean that "high commitment" charter schools will only ever serve a modest percentage of children from low-income families. Third, some charter schools make extraordinary demands on teachers, for example, requiring very long work days and that teachers respond to phone calls from students on evenings and weekends. It is not clear whether limits on the supply of skilled teachers who are willing to work under these conditions for sustained periods of time will limit the role of charter schools in educating poor students. Fourth, almost all of the evidence to date on the relative effectiveness of charter schools comes from analyses of student scores on standardized tests. Of course, the more important outcomes are success in post-secondary education, in labor markets, and in adult life. To date, there is little information on the extent to which charter schools are more effective than public schools in helping children from poor families achieve these outcomes.[5]

---

4. For example, see the Center for Research on Education Outcomes or CREDO (2009).
5. Many of the questions about charter schools described in this paragraph are taken from Curto, Fryer, and Howard (2010).

Summing Up

In recent decades, governments have introduced a large number of educational initiatives aimed at increasing the number of young people who attend school regularly and increasing the quality of education that they receive. A growing body of solid evidence provides insights into the effectiveness of alternative strategies for pursing these goals. We see four guidelines for policy stemming from recent high-quality evaluations of these initiatives.

One guideline is that educational enrollment rates, especially for children from low-income families, are extremely sensitive to costs. Consequently, policies that reduce the cost of school attendance—by lowering the commuting time of students, by reducing families' out-of-pocket costs, or by reducing the opportunity costs of children's school attendance—are effective in increasing the number of children from low-income families who enroll in, and attend, schools or colleges regularly.

A second guideline is that if a policy initiative is to improve students' skills, it must change their daily experiences in school. Although this may seem obvious, many initiatives—such as providing books that are not tailored to students' skill levels—fail this test. So do "one-shot" teacher training initiatives that lack follow-up.

A third guideline is that providing incentives for educators and students can play a constructive role in enhancing student achievement. However, great care is needed in designing such incentives because they are powerful tools that may elicit unanticipated dysfunctional responses.

The fourth guideline is that initiatives to increase schooling options for poor children have significant promise. However, there are important questions about scalability and the extent to which the new schooling options result in improved long-term outcomes for children.

We hope that these guidelines can serve a useful purpose by informing the design of policies aimed at improving educational quality. However, they are *guidelines*, not *recipes*. The important details of policy initiatives with common names like "educational vouchers," "class-size reduction," or "performance pay for teachers" will differ from place to place. Responses to their implementation will also differ, both because the details of program design differ, and because institutions and cultures matter and differ from place to place. For these reasons, the important work of providing causal evidence on the effects of a particular type of educational-policy initiative is not a matter of conducting one—or even a few—high-quality studies. Instead, it is a matter of conducting enough high-quality studies to reveal the ways that results depend on particular details of the empirical design, on the institutions in which interventions are embedded, and on the cultures that influence the priorities and behaviors of teachers, administrators, parents, children, and employers.

Final Words

At this point, we want to share the sentiment expressed by Winston Churchill when he reported the defeat of Rommel's Panzer divisions at the second battle of El Alamein, North Africa, a turning point in World War II. He said: "This is not the end. It is not even the beginning of the end. But it is, perhaps, the end of the beginning" (Knowles, 1999, p. 215). Likewise, although this is the end of our book, we hope that it is the beginning of your efforts to understand causal research, to use it, and to do it! You will need to continue to learn, because new research is providing improvements in methods for making causal inferences in educational and social science research constantly. Some of the new technical advances improve old research designs and old analytic methods. Some create new designs and methods. Other important work improves data quality. We anticipate rapid advances in all three of these domains in the future. We hope that our book will provide you with a strong foundation for understanding advances to come, and inspire you to continue to learn and apply these methods. Most of all, we hope that research informed by our book will lead us all to a better understanding of effective strategies for educating the world's children.

References

Aaron, H. J. (1978). *Politics and the professors: The great society in perspective.* Studies in social economics. Washington, DC: Brookings Institution.

Abadie, A. (January 2005). Semiparametric difference-in-differences estimators. *Review of Economic Studies, 72*(1), 1–19.

Abadie, A., Imbens, G.W. (November 2008). On the failure of the bootstrap for matching estimators. *Econometrica, 76*(6), 1537–57.

Abdulkadiroglu, A., Angrist, A., Dynarski, S., Kane, T. J., Pathak, P. (2009). *Accountability and flexibility in public schools: Evidence from Boston's charters and pilots.* Research Working Paper No. 15549. Cambridge, MA: National Bureau of Economic Research.

Agodini, R., Dynarski, M. (February 2004). Are experiments the only option? A look at dropout-prevention programs. *Review of Economics and Statistics, 86*(1), 180–94.

Almond, D., Edlund, L., Palme, M. (2007). *Chernobyl's subclinical legacy: Prenatal exposure to radioactive fallout and school outcomes in Sweden.* Research Working Paper No. 13347. Cambridge, MA: National Bureau of Economic Research.

Altonji, J. G., Elder, T. E., Taber, C. R. (February 2005a). Selection on observed and unobserved variables: Assessing the effectiveness of Catholic schools. *Journal of Political Economy, 113*(1), 151–84.

Altonji, J. G., Elder, T. E., Taber, C. R. (2005b). An evaluation of instrumental-variable strategies for estimating the effects of Catholic schooling. *Journal of Human Resources, 40*(4), 791–821.

Angrist, J., Bettinger, E., Bloom, E., King, E., Kremer, M. (December 2002). Vouchers for private schooling in Colombia: Evidence from a randomized natural experiment. *American Economic Review, 92*(5), 1535–58.

Angrist, J., Bettinger, E., Kremer, M. (June 2006). Long-term educational consequences of secondary-school vouchers: Evidence from administrative records in Colombia. *American Economic Review, 96*(3), 847–62.

Angrist, J. D., Dynarski, S. M., Kane, T. J., Pathak, P.A., Walters, C.R. (2010). *Who benefits from Kipp?* Research Working Paper No. 15740. Cambridge, MA: National Bureau of Economic Research.

Angrist, J., Lang, D., Oreopoulos, P. (January 2009). Incentives and services for college achievement: Evidence from a randomized trial. *American Economic Journal: Applied Economics, 1*(1), 136–63.

Angrist, J., Lavy, V. (September 2009). The effects of high stakes high-school achievement awards: Evidence from a randomized trial. *American Economic Review, 99*(4), 1384–414.

Angrist, J. D. (June 1990). Lifetime earnings and the Vietnam-era draft lottery: Evidence from Social Security administrative records. *American Economic Review, 80*(3), 313–36.

Angrist, J. D., Imbens, G.W., Rubin, D. B. (June 1996). Identification of causal effects using instrumental variables. *Journal of the American Statistical Association, 91*(434), 444–55.

Angrist, J. D., Krueger, A. B. (Fall 2001). Instrumental variables and the search for identification: From supply and demand to natural experiments. *Journal of Economic Perspectives, 15*(4), 69–85.

Angrist, J. D., Krueger, A. B. (November 1991). Does compulsory school attendance affect schooling and earnings? *Quarterly Journal of Economics, 106*(4), 979–1014.

Angrist, J. D., Lavy, V. (May 1999). Using Maimonides' rule to estimate the effect of class size on scholastic achievement. *Quarterly Journal of Economics, 114*(2), 533–75.

Angrist, J. D., Pischke, J. S. (2009). *Mostly harmless econometrics: An empiricist's companion*. Princeton, NJ: Princeton University Press.

Banerjee, A.V., Cole, S., Duflo, E., Linden, L. (August 2007). Remedying education: Evidence from two randomized experiments in India. *Quarterly Journal of Economics, 122*(3), 1235–64.

Barrera-Osorio, F., Raju, D. (2009). *Evaluating a test-based public subsidy program for low-cost private schools: Regression-discontinuity evidence from Pakistan*. Paper presented at the National Bureau of Economic Research Program on Education Meeting, April 30, 2009, Cambridge, MA.

Becker, G. S. (1964). *Human capital: A theoretical and empirical analysis, with special reference to education* (vol. 80). New York: National Bureau of Economic Research, distributed by Columbia University Press.

Becker, S. O., Ichino, A. (2002). Estimation of average treatment effects based on propensity scores. *Stata Journal, 2*(4), 358–77.

Black, S. (May 1999). Do better schools matter? Parental valuation of elementary education. *Quarterly Journal of Economics, 114*(2), 577–99.

Bloom, H. S. (Forthcoming). Modern regression-discontinuity analysis. In *Field experimentation: Methods for evaluating what works, for whom, under what circumstances, how, and why*. M. W. Lipsey, D. S. Cordray (Eds.). Newbury Park, CA: Sage.

Bloom, H. S., ed. (2005). *Learning more from social experiments: Evolving analytic approaches*. New York: Sage.

Bloom, H. S., Thompson, S. L., Unterman, R. (2010). *Transforming the High School Experience: How New York City's New Small Schools are Boosting Student Achievement and Graduation Rates*. New York: MDRC.

Boozer, M., Rouse, C. (July 2001). Intra-school variation in class size: Patterns and implications. *Journal of Urban Economics, 50*(1), 163–89.

Borko, H. (2004). Professional development and teacher learning: Mapping the terrain. *Educational Researcher, 33*(8), 3–15.

Borman, G. D. (2007). Final reading outcomes of the national randomized field trial of Success For All. *American Educational Research Journal, 44*(3), 701–31.

Borman, G. D., Slavin, R. E., Cheung, A. C. K. (Winter 2005b). The national randomized field trial of Success For All: Second-year outcomes. *American Educational Research Journal, 42*(4), 673–96.

Borman, G. D., Slavin, R. E., Cheung, A., Chamberlain, A. M., Madden, N. A., Chambers, B. (Spring 2005a). Success for all: First-year results from the national randomized field trial. *Educational Evaluation & Policy Analysis, 27*(1), 1–22.

Bound, J., Jaeger, D. A. (2000). Do compulsory school-attendance laws alone explain the association between quarter of birth and earnings? In Solomon W. Polachek (Ed.), *Worker well-being. Research in labor economics* (vol. 19, pp. 83–108). New York: Elsevier Science, JAI.

Bound, J., Jaeger, D. A., Baker, R. M. (June 1995). Problems with instrumental-variables estimation when the correlation between the instruments and the endogenous explanatory variable is weak. *Journal of the American Statistical Association, 90*(430), 443–50.

Browning, M., Heinesen, E. (2003). *Class size, teacher hours and educational attainment* (p. 15). Copenhagen, Denmark: Centre for Applied Microeconometrics, Institute of Economics, University of Copenhagen.

Buckles, K., Hungerman, D. M. (2008). *Season of birth and later outcomes: Old questions, new answers.* Research Working Paper, No. 14573. Cambridge, MA: National Bureau of Economic Research.

Buddelmeyer, H., Skoufias, E. (2004). *An evaluation of the performance of regression-discontinuity design on PROGRESA.* Policy Research Working Paper Series. Washington, DC: World Bank.

Burde, D., Linden, L. L. (2009). *The effect of proximity on school enrollment: Evidence from a randomized controlled trial in Afghanistan.* Working Paper. New York: Columbia University.

Callahan, R. E. (1962). *Education and the cult of efficiency: A study of the social forces that have shaped the administration of the public schools.* Chicago: University of Chicago Press.

Campbell, D. T. (1957). Factors relevant to the validity of experiments in social settings. *Psychological Bulletin, 54*(4), 297–312.

Case, A., Deaton, A. (August 1999). School inputs and educational outcomes in South Africa. *Quarterly Journal of Economics, 114*(3), 1047–84.

Chubb, J. E., Moe, T. M. (1990). *Politics, markets & America's schools.* Washington, DC: Brookings Institution.

Clotfelter, C. T., Glennie, E., Ladd, H. F., Vigdor, J. L. (2008). Would higher salaries keep teachers in high-poverty schools? Evidence from a policy intervention in North Carolina. *Journal of Public Economics*, (92), 1352–70.

Clotfelter, C. T., Ladd, H. F., Vigdor, J. (August 2005). Who teaches whom? Race and the distribution of novice teachers. *Economics of Education Review, 24*(4), 377–92.

Cochran, W., Rubin, D. B. (1973). Controlling bias in observational studies: A review. *Sankyha, 35*, 417–66.

Cohen, D. K., Raudenbush, S. W., Loewenberg-Ball, D. (Summer 2003). Resources, instruction, and research. *Educational Evaluation & Policy Analysis, 25*(2), 119–42.

Cohen, J. (1988). *Statistical power analysis for the behavioral sciences*, 2nd ed. Hillsdale, NJ: Lawrence. Erlbaum Associates.

Coleman, J. S., Campbell, E. Q., Hobson, C. J., McPartland, J., Mood, A. M., Weinfeld, F. D., York, R. L. (1966). *Equality of educational opportunity*. Washington, DC: U.S. Department of Health, Education, and Welfare, Office of Education.

Coleman, J. S., Hoffer, T., Kilgore, S. (1982). *High-school achievement: Public, Catholic, and private schools compared*. New York: Basic Books.

Cook, T. D. (February 2008). "Waiting for life to arrive": A history of the regression-discontinuity design in psychology, statistics and economics. *Journal of Econometrics, 142*(2), 636–54.

Cook, T. D., Shadish, W. R., Wong, V. C. (Autumn 2008). Three conditions under which experiments and observational studies produce comparable causal estimates: New findings from within-study comparisons. *Journal of Policy Analysis and Management, 27*(4), 724–50.

Cook, T. D., Wong, V. C. (forthcoming). Empirical tests of the validity of the regression-discontinuity design. *Annales d'Economie et de Statistique*.

Center for Research on Educational Outcomes (CREDO) (2009). *Multiple choice: Charter performance in 16 states*. Palo Alto, CA: Stanford University.

Currie, J., Moretti, E. (2003). Mother's education and the intergenerational transmission of human capital: Evidence from college openings. *Quarterly Journal of Economics, 118*(4), 495–532.

Davidoff, I., Leigh, A. (June 2008). How much do public schools really cost? Estimating the relationship between house prices and school quality. *Economic Record, 84*(265), 193–206.

Decker, P. T., Mayer, D. P., Glazerman, S. (2004). *The effects of Teach For America on students: Findings from a national evaluation*. Princeton, NJ: Mathematica Policy Research.

Dee, T. S. (August 2004). Are there civic returns to education? *Journal of Public Economics, 88*(9–10), 1697–720.

Dehejia, R. (March–April 2005). Practical propensity-score matching: A reply to Smith and Todd. *Journal of Econometrics, 125*(1–2), 355–64.

Dehejia, R. H., Wahba, S. (February 2002). Propensity-score-matching methods for nonexperimental causal studies. *Review of Economics and Statistics, 84*(1), 151–61.

Dehejia, R. H., Wahba, S. (December 1999). Causal effects in nonexperimental studies: Reevaluating the evaluation of training programs. *Journal of the American Statistical Association, 94*(448), 1053–62.

Deming, D. (2009). *Better schools, less crime?* Cambridge, MA: Harvard University. Unpublished Working Paper.

Deming, D., Hasting, J.S., Kane, T.J., Staiger, D.O. (2009). *School choice and college attendance: Evidence from randomized lotteries*. Cambridge, MA: Harvard University. Unpublished Working Paper.

Dewey, J. (1929). *The sources of a science of education*. New York: H. Liveright.

Diaz, J. J., Handa, S. (2006). An assessment of propensity score matching as a nonexperimental impact estimator: Evidence from Mexico's PROGRESA program. *Journal of Human Resources, 41*(2), 319–45.

Dobbelsteen, S., Levin, J., Oosterbeek, H. (February 2002). The causal effect of class size on scholastic achievement: Distinguishing the pure class-size effect from the effect of changes in class composition. *Oxford Bulletin of Economics and Statistics, 64*(1), 17–38.

Dobbie, W., Fryer, R. G., Jr. (2009). *Are high quality schools enough to close the achievement gap? Evidence from a social experiment in Harlem.* Research Working Paper, No. 15473. Cambridge, MA: National Bureau of Economic Research.

Duflo, E. (September 2001). Schooling- and labor-market consequences of school construction in Indonesia: Evidence from an unusual policy experiment. *American Economic Review, 91*(4), 795–813.

Duflo, E., Dupas, P., Kremer, M., Sinei, S. (2006). *Education and HIV/AIDS prevention: Evidence from a randomized evaluation in western Kenya.* Policy Research Working Paper Series WPS4024. Washington, DC: World Bank.

Duflo, E., Glennerster, R., Kremer, M. (2008). Using randomization in development-economics research: A toolkit. In T. Paul Schultz, John Strauss (Eds.), *Handbook of development economics* (pp. 3895–962). Amsterdam: Elsevier.

Duflo, E., Hanna, R., Ryan, S. (2008). *Monitoring works: Getting teachers to come to school.* CEPR Discussion Papers.

Duncombe, W., Yinger, J. (1999). Performance standards and educational-cost indices: You can't have one without the other. In Helen F. Ladd, R. A. Chalk and Janet S. Hansen (Eds.), *Equity and adequacy in education finance: Issues and perspectives.* Washington, DC: National Academy Press.

Dynarski, S. M. (March 2003). Does aid matter? Measuring the effect of student aid on college attendance and completion. *American Economic Review, 93*(1), 279–88.

Efron, B., Tibshirani, R. (1998). *An introduction to the bootstrap.* Monographs on statistics and applied probability (vol. 57) New York, NY/Boca Raton, FL: Chapman & Hall/CRC Press.

Epple, D., Romano, R. E. (1998). Competition between private and public schools: Vouchers, and peer-group effects. *American Economic Review, 88*(1), 33–62.

Erdfelder, E., Faul, F., Buchner, A. (1996). GPOWER: A general power analysis program. *Behavior Research Methods, Instruments, & Computers, 28*, 1–11.

Evans, W. N., Schwab, R. M. (November 1995). Finishing high school and starting college: Do Catholic schools make a difference? *Quarterly Journal of Economics, 110*(4), 941–74.

Ezpeleta, J., Weiss, E. (1996). Las escuelas rurales en zonas de pobreza y sus maestros: Tramas preexistentes y políticas innovadoras. *Revista Mexicana De Investigación Educativa, 1*(1), 53–69.

Fernandez, R., Rogerson, R. (2003). School vouchers as a redistributive device: An analysis of three alternative systems. In Caroline M. Hoxby (Ed.), *The economics of school choice* (pp. 195–226). Chicago: University of Chicago Press.

Figlio, D. N., Getzler, L. S. (2002). *Accountability, ability, and disability: Gaming the system.* Research Working Paper No. 9307. Cambridge, MA: National Bureau of Economic Research.

Fiske, E. B., Ladd, H. F. (2000). *When schools compete: A cautionary tail.* Washington, DC: Brookings Institution.

Fiszbein, A., Schady, N. R., Ferreira, F. H. G. (2009). *Conditional cash transfers: Reducing present and future poverty.* A World-Bank policy-research report. Washington, DC: World Bank.

Folger, J. (Fall 1989). Project STAR and class-size policy. *Peabody Journal of Education, 67*(1), 1–16.

Freeman, R. B. (1976). *The overeducated American*. New York: Academic Press.

Friedman, M. (1962). *Capitalism and freedom*. Chicago: University of Chicago Press.

Gamse, B. C., Jacob, R. T., Horst, M., Boulay, B., Unlu, F. (2008). *Reading First impact study: Final report*. NCEE 2009-4038. Washington, DC: National Center for Education Evaluation and Regional Assistance, Institute of Education Sciences, U.S. Department of Education.

Garet, M. S., Porter, A. C., Desimone, L. (Winter 2001). What makes professional development effective? Results from a national sample of teachers. *American Educational Research Journal, 38*(4), 915–45.

Gennetian, L. A., Morris, P. A., Bos, J. M., Bloom, H. S. (2005). Constructing instrumental variables from experimental data to explore how treatments produce effects. In Howard S. Bloom (Ed.), *Learning more from social experiments: Evolving analytic approaches* (pp. 75–114). New York: Sage.

Glazerman, S., Levy, D. M., Myers, D. (2003). Nonexperimental versus experimental estimates of earnings' impacts. *Annals of the American Academy, 589*, 63–93.

Glewwe, P., Kremer, M., Moulin, S. (January 2009). Many children left behind? Textbooks and test scores in Kenya. *American Economic Journal: Applied Economics, 1*(1), 112–35.

Goldberger, A. S., Cain, G. G. (1982). The causal analysis of cognitive outcomes in the Coleman, Hoffer and Kilgore report. *Sociology of Education, 55*(2), 103–22.

Goldin, C. D., Katz, L. F. (2008). *The race between education and technology*. Cambridge, MA: Belknap Press of Harvard University Press.

Graham, B. S. (May 2008). Identifying social interactions through conditional variance restrictions. *Econometrica, 76*(3), 643–60.

Greene, W. H. (1993). *Econometric analysis*, 2nd ed. New York: Macmillan.

Hanus, P. H. (1920). *School administration and school reports*. Boston: Houghton Mifflin.

Hanushek, E. (May 1971). Teacher characteristics and gains in student achievement: Estimation using micro data. *American Economic Review, 61*(2), 280–8.

Hanushek, E. A. (1998). *The evidence on class size*. Occasional Paper No. 98-1. Rochester, NY: W. Allen Wallis Institute of Political Economy, University of Rochester.

Hanushek, E. A., Woessmann, L. (September 2008). The role of cognitive skills in economic development. *Journal of Economic Literature, 46*(3), 607–68.

Hausman, J. A. (November 1978). Specification tests in econometrics. *Econometrica, 46*(6), 1251–71.

Hedges, L. V., et al. (April 1994). Does money matter? A meta-analysis of studies of the effects of differential school inputs on student outcomes. Part 1: An exchange. *Educational Researcher, 23*(3), 5–14.

Herbers, J. (1966). Negro education is found inferior. *New York Times*, July 1, 1966.

Hill, H. C., Cohen, D. K. (2001). *Learning policy: When state education reform works*. New Haven, CT: Yale University Press.

Holland, P. W. (December 1986). Statistics and causal inference. *Journal of the American Statistical Association, 81*(396), 945–60.

Howell, W. G., Peterson, P. E. (2006). *The education gap: Vouchers and urban schools*, Rev. ed. Washington, DC: Brookings Institution.

Howell, W. G., Wolf, P. J., Campbell, D. E., Peterson, P. E. (2002). School vouchers and academic performance: Results from three randomized field trials. *Journal of Policy Analysis and Management, 21*(2), 191–217.

Hoxby, C. (2000). *Peer effects in the classroom: Learning from gender and race variation.* Research Working Paper, No. 7867. Cambridge, MA: National Bureau of Economic Research.

Hoxby, C. M. (2003). Introduction. In Caroline M. Hoxby (Ed.), *The economics of school choice* (pp. 1–22). Chicago: University of Chicago Press.

Hoxby, C. M. (2001). *Ideal vouchers.* Cambridge MA: Harvard University. Unpublished manuscript.

Hoxby, C. M. (November 2000). The effects of class size on student achievement: New evidence from population variation. *Quarterly Journal of Economics, 115*(4), 1239–85.

Hoxby, C., Murarka, S. (2009). *Charter schools in New York City: Who enrolls and how they affect their students' achievement.* Research Working Paper, No.14852. Cambridge, MA: National Bureau of Economic Research.

Hsieh, C.-T., Urquiola, M. (September 2006). The effects of generalized school choice on achievement and stratification: Evidence from Chile's voucher program. *Journal of Public Economics, 90*(8–9), 1477–503.

Huang, G., Reiser, M., Parker, A., Muniec, J., Salvucci, S. (2003). *Institute of education sciences: Findings from interviews with education policymakers.* Washington, DC: U.S. Department of Education.

Imbens, G. W., Lemieux, T. (February 2008). Regression-discontinuity designs: A guide to practice. *Journal of Econometrics, 142*(2), 615–35.

Imbens, G. W., Wooldridge, J. M. (2009). Recent developments of the econometrics of program evaluation. *Journal of Economic Literature, 47*(1), 5–86.

Jacob, B. A., Lefgren, L. (February 2004). Remedial education and student achievement: A regression-discontinuity analysis. *Review of Economics and Statistics, 86*(1), 226–44.

Jacob, B. A., Levitt, S. D. (August 2003). Rotten apples: An investigation of the prevalence and predictors of teacher cheating. *Quarterly Journal of Economics, 118*(3), 843–77.

Jamison, D. T., Lau, L.J. (1982). *Farmer education and farm efficiency.* A World Bank research publication. Baltimore: Johns Hopkins University Press.

Kemple, J. J. (June 2008a). *Career academies: Long-term impacts on labor-market outcomes, educational attainment, and transitions to adulthood.* New York: MDRC.

Kemple, J. J., Willner, C. J. (2008b). *Technical resources for career academies: Long-term impacts on labor-market outcomes, educational attainment, and transitions to adulthood.* New York: MDRC.

Kennedy, P. (1992). *A guide to econometrics,* 3rd ed. Cambridge, MA: MIT Press.

Kling, J. R., Liebman, J. B., Katz, L. F. (January 2007). Experimental analysis of neighborhood effects. *Econometrica, 75*(1), 83–119.

Knowles, E. (1999). *The Oxford dictionary of quotations,* 5th ed. New York: Oxford University Press.

Koretz, D. M. (2008). *Measuring up: What educational testing really tells us.* Cambridge, MA: Harvard University Press.

Kremer, M., Miguel, E., Thornton, R. (2009). Incentives to learn. *Review of Economics and Statistics, 91*(3), 437–56.

Krueger, A., Whitmore, D. (2001). The effect of attending a small class in the early grades on college-test taking and middle-school test results: Evidence from project STAR. *Economic Journal, 111*, 1–28.

Krueger, A., Zhu, P. (2004). Another look at the New York City school-voucher experiment. *American Behavioral Scientist, 47*, 658–98.

Krueger, A. B. (May 1999). Experimental estimates of education production functions. *Quarterly Journal of Economics, 114*(2), 497–532.

LaLonde, R. J. (September 1986). Evaluating the econometric evaluations of training programs with experimental data. *American Economic Review, 76*(4), 604–20.

Lane, J. F. (2000). *Pierre Bourdieu: A critical introduction.* Modern European thinkers. Sterling, VA: Pluto Press.

Lavy, V. (2009). Performance pay and teachers' effort, productivity and grading ethics. *American Economic Review, 99*(5), 1979–2011.

Lazear, E. P. (August 2001). Educational production. *Quarterly Journal of Economics, 116*(3), 777–803.

Leuven, E., Oosterbeek, H., Ronning, M. (2008). *Quasi-experimental estimates of the effect of class size on achievement in Norway.* Discussion paper. Bonn, Germany: IZA.

Light, R. J., Singer, J. D., Willett, J. B. (1990). *By design: Planning research on higher education.* Cambridge, MA: Harvard University Press.

List, J. A., Wagner, M. (2010). *So you want to run an experiment, now what? Some simple rules of thumb for optimal experimental design.* Research Working Paper, No. 15701. Cambridge, MA: National Bureau of Economic Research.

Liu, X. F., Spybrook, J., Congdon, R., Raudenbush, S. (2005). *Optimal design for multi-level and longitudinal research, Version 0.35.* Ann Arbor, MI: Survey Research Center, Institute for Social Research, University of Michigan.

Ludwig, J., Miller, D. L. (February 2007). Does Head Start improve children's life chances? Evidence from a regression-discontinuity design. *Quarterly Journal of Economics, 122*(1), 159–208.

Ludwig, J., Miller, D. L. (2005). *Does head start improve children's life chances? Evidence from a regression-discontinuity design.* Research Working Paper, No. 11702. Cambridge, MA: National Bureau of Economic Research.

Mann, H. (1891). Report for 1846. In M. T. Peabody Mann, G. C. Mann, F. Pécant (Eds.), *Life and works of Horace Mann,* 5 vols. Boston/New York: Lee and Shepard/C. T. Dillingham.

McEwan, P. J., Urquiola, M., Vegas, E. (Spring 2008). School choice, stratification, and information on school performance: Lessons from Chile. *Economia: Journal of the Latin American and Caribbean Economic Association, 8*(2), 1, 27, 38–42.

McLaughlin, M. W. (1975). *Evaluation and reform: The elementary and Secondary Education Act of 1965, Title I.* A Rand educational policy study. Cambridge, MA: Ballinger.

Miller, R. G. (1974). The jackknife: A review. *Biometrika, 61*(1), 1–15.

Morgan, S. L., Winship, C. (2007). *Counterfactuals and causal inference: Methods and principles for social research.* New York: Cambridge University Press.

Mosteller, F. (1995). The Tennessee study of class size in the early school grades. *The Future of Children, 5*(2), 113–27.

Mosteller, F., Moynihan, D. P. (Eds.). (1972). *On equality of educational opportunity.* New York: Random House.

Muralidharan, K., Sundararaman, V. (2009). *Teacher performance pay: Experimental evidence from India.* Research Working Paper, No. 15323. Cambridge, MA: National Bureau of Economic Research.

Murnane, R. J. (1981). Interpreting the evidence on school effectiveness. *Teachers College Record, 83*(1), 19‒35.

Murnane, R. J., Levy, F. (1996). *Teaching the new basic skills.* New York: Free Press.

Murnane, R. J., Willett, J. B., Levy, F. (1995). The growing importance of cognitive skills in wage determination. *Review of Economics and Statistics, 77*(2), 251‒66.

Murray, M. P. (Fall 2006). Avoiding invalid instruments and coping with weak instruments. *Journal of Economic Perspectives, 20*(4), 111‒32.

National Board for Education Sciences. (2008). *National board for education sciences 5-year report, 2003 through 2008.* NBES 2009-6011. Washington, DC: National Bureau of Education Science.

Neal, D. (1997). The effects of Catholic secondary schooling on educational achievement. *Journal of Labor Economics, 15*(1), 98‒123.

Nechyba, T. J. (June 2003). What can be (and what has been) learned from general-equilibrium simulation models of school finance? *National Tax Journal, 56*(2), 387‒414.

Nelson, R. R., Phelps, E. S. (1966). Investment in humans, technological diffusion, and economic growth. *American Economic Review, 56*(2), 67‒75.

Orr, L. L. (1999). *Social experiments: Evaluating public programs with experimental methods.* Thousand Oaks, CA: Sage.

Oxford English Dictionary (1989). Weiner, E. S. C., Simpson, J. A. (Eds.). New York: Oxford University Press.

Papay, J. P., Murnane, R. J., Willett, J. B. (March 2010). The consequences of high-school exit examinations for low-income urban students: Evidence from Massachusetts. *Educational Evaluation and Policy Analysis, 32*(1), 5‒23.

Psacharopoulos, G. (Fall 2006). The value of investment in education: Theory, evidence, and policy. *Journal of Education Finance, 32*(2), 113‒36.

Rasbash, J., Steele, F., Browne, W. J., Goldstein, H. (2009). *A user's guide to MLwiN, 2.10.* Bristol, UK: Centre for Multilevel Modelling, University of Bristol.

Raudenbush, S. W., Bryk, A. S. (2002). *Hierarchical linear models: Applications and data-analysis methods,* 2nd ed. Thousand Oaks, CA.: Sage.

Raudenbush, S. W., Martinez, A., Spybrook, J. (March 2007). Strategies for improving precision in group-randomized experiments. *Educational Evaluation & Policy Analysis, 29*(1), 5‒29.

Reimers, F. (2006). Principally women. In L. Randall (Ed.), *Changing structure of Mexico: Political, social, and economic prospects,* 2nd ed. (pp. 278‒294). Armonk, NY: M.E. Sharpe.

Rivkin, S. G., Hanushek, E. A., Kain, J. F. (March 2005). Teachers, schools, and academic achievement. *Econometrica, 73*(2), 417‒58.

Rockoff, J. (2009). Field experiments in class size from the early twentieth century. *Journal of Economic Perspectives, 23*(4), 211‒30.

Rosenbaum, P. R., Rubin, D. B. (1984). Reducing bias in observational studies using subclassification on the propensity score. *Journal of the American Statistical Association, 79*(387), 516‒24.

Rosenzweig, M. R., Wolpin, K. I. (December 2000). Natural "natural experiments" in economics. *Journal of Economic Literature, 38*(4), 827‒74.

Rouse, C. E. (1998). Private-school vouchers and student achievement: An evaluation of the Milwaukee parental choice program. *Quarterly Journal of Economics, 113*(2), 553–602.

Rouse, C. E., Krueger, A. B. (August 2004). Putting computerized instruction to the test: A randomized evaluation of a "scientifically based" reading program. Special Issue. *Economics of Education Review, 23*(4), 323–38.

Rubin, D. B. (1990). Formal modes of statistical inference for causal effects. *Journal of Statistical Planning and Inference, 25*, 279–92.

Rubin, D. B. (1974). Estimating causal effects of treatments in randomized and nonrandomized studies. *Journal of Educational Psychology, 66*(5), 688–701.

Rutter, M. (1979). *Fifteen thousand hours: Secondary schools and their effects on children.* Cambridge, MA: Harvard University Press.

Sacerdote, B. (2008). *When the saints come marching in: Effects of Hurricanes Katrina and Rita on student evacuees.* Research Working Paper, No. 14385. Cambridge, MA: National Bureau of Economic Research.

Schiefelbein, E., Farrell, J. P. (1982). *Eight years of their lives: Through schooling to the labour market in Chile.* IDRC, 191e. Ottawa, Ontario, Canada: International Development Research Centre.

Shadish, W. R., Campbell, D. T., Cook, T. D. (2002). *Experimental and quasi-experimental designs for generalized causal inference.* Boston: Houghton Mifflin.

Shavelson, R. J., Towne, L. (Eds.). (2002). *Scientific research in education.* Washington, DC: National Academy Press.

Smith, J. A., Todd, P. E. (March April 2005a). Does matching overcome LaLonde's critique of non-experimental estimators? *Journal of Econometrics, 125*(1–2), 305–53.

Smith, J., Todd, P. (March April 2005b). Does matching overcome LaLonde's critique of non-experimental estimators? rejoinder. *Journal of Econometrics, 125*(1–2), 365–75.

Spence, A. M. (1974). *Market signaling: Informational transfer in hiring and related screening processes.* Harvard economic studies, vol. 143. Cambridge, MA: Harvard University Press.

Sproull, L., Wolf, D., Weiner, S. (1978). *Organizing an anarchy: Belief, bureaucracy, and politics in the national institute of education.* Chicago: University of Chicago Press.

Steele, J.L., Murnane, R.J., Willett, J.B. (2010). Do financial incentives help low-performing schools attract and keep academically talented teachers? Evidence from California. *Journal of Policy Analysis and Management, 29*(3).

Stern, D., Raby, M., Dayton, C. (1992). *Career academies: Partnerships for reconstructing American high schools.* San Francisco: Jossey-Bass.

Stock, J. H., Wright, J. H., Yogo, M. (October 2002). A survey of weak instruments and weak identification in generalized method of moments. *Journal of Business and Economic Statistics, 20*(4), 518–29.

Taylor, F. W. (1911). *The principles of scientific management.* New York: Harper and Brothers.

Todd, P. E., Wolpin, K. I. (February 2003). On the specification and estimation of the production function for cognitive achievement. *Economic Journal, 113*(485), F3–33.

Tukey, J. W. (1977). *Exploratory data analysis.* Reading, MA: Addison-Wesley.

Tyler, J. H., Murnane, R. J., Willett, J. B. (May 2000). Estimating the labor-market signaling value of the GED. *Quarterly Journal of Economics, 115*(2), 431–68.

Urquiola, M. (February 2006). Identifying class size effects in developing countries: Evidence from rural Bolivia. *Review of Economics and Statistics, 88*(1), 171–7.

Urquiola, M., Verhoogen, E. (March 2009). Class-size caps, sorting, and the regression-discontinuity design. *American Economic Review, 99*(1), 179–215.

Weiss, A. (Fall 1995). Human capital vs. signalling explanations of wages. *Journal of Economic Perspectives, 9*(4), 133–54.

Whitehurst, G. J. (2008a). *National board for education sciences: 5-year report, 2003 through 2008.* NBES 2009-6011. Washington, DC: National Board for Education Sciences.

Whitehurst, G. J. (2008b). *Rigor and relevance redux: Director's biennial report to congress.* IES 2009-6010. Washington, DC: Institute of Education Sciences, U.S. Department of Education.

Wooldridge, J. M. (2002). *Econometric analysis of cross-section and panel data.* Cambridge, MA: MIT Press.

Index